A TEXT-BOOK

ON

LABOR REFORM.

Engraved by Emily Sartain, Phil.

Yours As Ever

THE

LIFE, SPEECHES, LABORS

AND

ESSAYS

OF

WILLIAM H. SYLVIS,

LATE PRESIDENT OF THE IRON-MOULDERS' INTERNATIONAL UNION;
AND ALSO OF
THE NATIONAL LABOR UNION.

BY HIS BROTHER
JAMES C. SYLVIS,
OF SUNBURY, PA.

"We must show them that when a just monetary system has been established there will no longer exist a necessity for Trades Unions." — Wm. H. Sylvis.

PHILADELPHIA:
CLAXTON, REMSEN & HAFFELFINGER,
1872.

STEREOTYPED BY J. FAGAN & SON, PHILADELPHIA.

Dedication.

TO

HIS EXCELLENCY

JOHN W. GEARY,

GOVERNOR OF PENNSYLVANIA,

THE FEARLESS MAGISTRATE, THE PATRIOTIC STATESMAN, AND CHAMPION OF LABOR'S RIGHTS,

AND TO THE

WORKING PEOPLE OF THE UNITED STATES,

THIS BIOGRAPHY AND RECORD OF THEIR STAUNCH FRIEND AND FEAR-LESS ADVOCATE,

Is Respectfully and Affectionately Dedicated,

BY THE AUTHOR.

AUTHOR'S PREFACE.

IN presenting to the public a collection of a few of the speeches, essays, and writings of my departed and revered brother, with his biography, it seems but proper that I should say something in regard to the shape of the work, and my reasons for publishing the same. Immediately after his death, there was an earnest and unanimous desire expressed that his biography should be written and published, together with the choicest of his productions.

This work seems to have fallen to my lot, whether properly or not is for others, and not me, to decide. I knew him well and intimately, and loved him both as a brother and a laborer in the good cause of Labor Reform; and it was properly supposed that I knew more of him than any one else. My only regret is that I cannot afford to issue a larger book and a more complete record of what he has done. Indeed, its publication in its present shape has been a work of many and serious difficulties. When I undertook the task, I felt myself incompetent, and what I then needed most was a helping hand, which I finally found in the person of C. Ben Johnson, the able editor of the *Anthracite Monitor*, to whom I am greatly indebted for his assistance in the preparation of the biography. While engaged on the biography, Mr. Johnson also had the arduous task of editing the *Monitor;* hence I can recommend it to the people as a correct, well-written, instructive, and interesting biography. The next great difficulty was that I had not the funds necessary to put the work to press. Many were willing, but had not the means. In this dilemma, C. A. Reimensnyder, Esq., of this place, and others, came to my relief, by advancing money to go on with the work. For this assistance, all those who believe that this tribute is to the memory of a departed leader, as well as myself, are under lasting obligations; for, as I am like all other working-men — poor — had it not been for this aid, this work would not now have appeared.

Some may ask why so long a time has elapsed before the appearance of the work, as it was advertised to be out early in the summer of 1871; to this I reply that the delay has been owing mainly to the difficulty which I had to encounter in collecting material, date, etc., for the biography, which I had not in my possession at the time of my brother's death, most of which was to be found in newspapers and manuscripts in the possession of persons scattered all over the country; and much time was lost in such a large correspondence as was necessary for the collection of this information. In compiling the work, however, I had not so much trouble, as I had in my possession all of his published speeches, and nearly all of his other writings; which seemed almost providential, as he always made it a rule that when any of his speeches or writings were published to mail me a copy, and I always preserved them carefully. I have endeavored to make the work both interesting and instructive, and hope I have succeeded. No one knows the great amount of work and anxiety there is connected with such a task, but those who have tried it. And now, in concluding this preface, I would commend the work to the blessing of God and the acceptance of the people, hoping that the principles herein advocated may soon be a ruling power in the land; that we may become in fact — what we have long been in name — a free and happy people.

J. C. Sylvis.

Sunbury, March 29, 1872.

CONTENTS.

SPEECHES.

LETTERS.

ESSAYS.

BIOGRAPHY

OF

WILLIAM H. SYLVIS.

INTRODUCTORY.

WE shall offer no apology for presenting to the public the following record of the life and services of Wm. H. Sylvis. We believe it due to the memory of the ablest leader the workingmen of the country have yet had, that they should know of and appreciate his sacrifices and his labors in their behalf; besides, the deeds of less worthy men have many a time been commemorated in memoirs. The work of compiling this record has been one of more than ordinary difficulty, and we are by no means satisfied with it, now that it is finished, for the reason that it is far, very far, from being complete; nor could it have been made complete, without devoting to it more time and patient research than we have been able to give the subject.

The earlier years of the life of Mr. Sylvis were spent in comparative obscurity, devoted to humble, honest, and laborious pursuits. It was only during his later years that he worked himself into prominence, and he died, not at the zenith of his greatness, but just as he was about to achieve greatness. For these reasons we could not very closely follow the footsteps of his boyhood, nor accurately reproduce the scenes and incidents of his early manhood; nor did we think it necessary to the fulfilment of our object that we should do so. We have merely tried to give you, reader, a faint idea of the germ of great distinction that was lost to the world when Wm. H. Sylvis was carried away to "that bourne from whence no traveller returns."

In pursuance of this purpose, we have collected a few of the best of his addresses, and paid some attention to the records of his intimate connection with the rise and progress of the Iron-Moulders' International Union and the National Labor Union. We make bold to say here, that the achievements of the first-named organization, under the statesmanlike leadership of Mr. Sylvis, ought to be a strong incentive to workers in other branches of useful industry to avail themselves of the almost innumerable good results that must ever accrue from a wisely-directed combination among workingmen. From being one of the poorest paid branches of mechanical industry, iron-moulding has become one of the most profitable to the journeyman; and the most successful applications of the principle of co-operation to production ever made in this country have been made by the moulders.

We have incorporated with the work brief papers from the pens of a few of his most intimate friends and official associates in the labor movement, of which he was conceded by all to be "the bright particular star." These will give the reader some conception of the estimation in which he was held by those of his contemporaries who knew him best. But with all this, we are not satisfied. We might have told of the many times he denied himself comforts —such comforts, too, as were almost necessaries—and devoted the saving to the one great object of his life,—the promulgation of labor-reform doctrines; sacrifices, each small in itself, but in the aggregate attaining to greatness, and leaving him, at his death, without means sufficient to bury him; whereas, had he been more thoughtful of himself, and less liberal to the cause, he might have amassed quite a snug little competence. We might have told how he wore clothes until they became quite threadbare, and he could wear them no longer; how the shawl he wore to the day of his death,—which, during the year or two that he devoted to the resuscitation of the Iron-Moulders' Union, after, through his predecessor's unfaithfulness, it had well-nigh died out of existence,—was filled with little holes, burned there by the splashing of the molten iron from the ladles of moulders in strange cities, whom he was beseeching to organize; how he was more than once compelled to beg a ride from place to place on an engine, because he had not money sufficient to pay his fare; how, to give the National Labor movement a fair start, he had fully made up his mind to mortgage his furniture to prepay the expenses of the Philadelphia convention, though he died before it met; how suffering moulders "on the tramp" came to him for assistance, and, if deserving, were never sent away empty handed; how he was denied the privilege of working because he had the manhood to exact a decent respect of his rights from those who regarded him and his fellow-workingmen as mere wealth-making machines,—brutes with the forms of men but without the souls; how one, whose bitter enmity he had enlisted by his rigorous dealing with traitors, was so far malicious as to fire a pistol at him upon one occasion; how he had himself bolstered up in a sick-bed that he might dictate a scathing rebuke to men who had evinced a willingness to submit to tyranny when victory was almost within their grasp. All these things and many more we might have told. We might have filled a volume a dozen times the size of this one with words of wisdom coming from his lips and pen, bearing upon that most important question — the relative rights of labor and capital — that would be as apropos now as when written. It is because we might have done these things, that we are by no means fully satisfied with the work as it stands. Nevertheless, we are convinced that we have told sufficient to cause every reader who sincerely believes in labor reform, to keenly regret that William H. Sylvis is not still in the land of the living, still here to guide us in the difficult struggle we are making against organized capital power in the hands of bad men.

At the Philadelphia session of the National Labor Union, it fell to the writer to prepare a plan for the creation of a fund to be used in building a suitable monument to the memory of the great dead. The plan adopted called for small contributions from as many of the working-people as might be inclined to give. We would like to see a ten-cent subscription, by which, we think, sufficient money could be realized to enable the National Labor Union to erect a magnificent monument; and the subject deserves nothing less than a magnificent one. The matter is now in the hands of a committee; and though the fulfilment of the project should be delayed, it will be handed down from year to year until the working-people of the country, in their realization of the sublime principles of which Mr. Sylvis was the leading exponent, and out of gratitude for his services, will erect this deserved tribute to greatness.

We have been so busy with Mr. Sylvis's deeds as a trades-unionist and labor reformer, that we have totally overlooked his domestic virtues, and of these he possessed not a few. As a father, he was always kind and attentive, though ever a strict disciplinarian with his children; as a husband, he was more than affectionate, and some letters written to his wife during his absence from home, which have been shown us, teem with expressions of loving confidence in his mate, and are thoroughly permeated by that disposition so unusual in the husband,—and yet so beautiful,—to make his wife the sharer of his business secrets and adviser in the hour of perplexity; as a friend, we can from experience speak of his invariable willingness to assist the needy and condole with the afflicted. Nor was his time so wholly devoted to his work but that he found an odd moment now and again to give expression to beautiful heart-thoughts. Several rhythmical productions of his pen have come under our eye which display a keen perception of the poetic and a heartfelt imagery. He frequently wrote short sketches upon such topics as poets delight in; and some of these, written upon the fly-leaves of books and on scraps which have been found among his papers, are truly beautiful both in language and sentiment. We do not believe, however, that he ever gave anything of this nature publicity. Truly, Mr. Sylvis was a wonderful man—a man so much above the ordinary in all moral and mental particulars, so fearless, so incorruptible, so determined, and so constituted in every respect, that he seemed, to some, to have been especially created by nature for the position he adorned.

Our nation's working-people are learning, fast learning, their rights, and how to maintain them. But a little distance off rolls the thunder of a slowly but surely coming social revolution, under the influence of which our governmental structure will be subjected to such a cleansing, such a purifying process, as is not contemplated in the politician's philosophy. Class distinctions will be swept away; monopolies will crumble into dust; man will be measured by his manhood, not by his money, and rewarded according as he is honest and industrious, and not for his cunning in taking advantage of the necessities of the many. No agrarian theory of equal division is contemplated in, or is necessary to effect, this change; nothing but a simple and total abolition of those laws and customs which have given life and nourishment to the vast money and land monopolies by which this nation is to-day accursed; which tax the many poor and relieve the few rich; which donate the people's money and acres to, and confer exclusive and dangerous privileges upon, corporations upon the plea of national or sectional necessity. Wipe away these laws which encourage, and the ignorant inattention of the toiling citizen to his political rights which sanctions these wrongs, and you bring about the labor reformer's millennium, and bring it about just as he proposes to bring it about. And when it is here, then will the pioneers of our movement — those who conceived it, brought it into being, and cared tenderly and ardently and faithfully for it in its incipiency — secure that hold of the affections of the people which they have, by their devotion, so nobly earned. Then will this book be read with interest and regret that it is so incomplete — then, and not till then, will Wm. H. Sylvis, and those who fought the good fight with him, be honored as they deserve to be.

With these few words, we launch our book upon the sea of public opinion, hoping that it will be gently criticized; for the biographer does not claim for it that it is well written; and he has already confessed that his story is, to himself, incompletely and unsatisfactorily told.

CHAPTER I.

BOYHOOD.

THERE is a little village called Armagh, in Indiana County, Pennsylvania, situated about fifty-two miles east of the smoky city of Pittsburg. It is of most trifling size,—its houses giving shelter, at this date, to less than one hundred and fifty souls. Yet it is a place for which we shall always feel a deep reverence; for there it was that William H. Sylvis was ushered into this "troublous world." Armagh is named, they tell us, in honor of the city of Armagh, the archiepiscopal seat of the primate of all Ireland, said to have been founded by St. Patrick, in the year 450 A. D. In that village, on the 26th day of November, 1828, Maria Sylvis bore to her husband, Nicholas, a second son, whom they afterwards called William.

It has been stated in several public ways that the parents were of foreign birth. This is incorrect, as both were born in this country. The mother came from the Mott family, of New Jersey, several members of which have been in public life. Many will remember Hon. Henry S. Mott, who was elected canal commissioner of this State unanimously, he having received the nomination of both parties. General Mott, another relative, figured prominently in the late unfortunate rebellion. He commanded, if we recollect aright, a division in the Army of the Potomac. Mr. Sylvis, Sr. was a wagon-maker by trade, and at the time of William's birth was working as a journeyman. He was, of course, in poor circumstances, as all workingmen naturally are in this world, where capital demands such an inordinate recompense for its use that there is next to nothing of the fruits of labor left for those whose mission it is to toil. His family grew in accordance with the old proverb, " A fool for luck, and a poor man for children," which is not a very chastely-expressed, but a wondrously true, adage.

Finding it impossible to get along at Armagh, he removed to Mauch Chunk, Carbon County, where he became associated with Adam Sylvis, an uncle, in the boat-building business. At this time he was also, in some way, connected with the construction of the nine-mile gravity road leading to Summit Hill, or, what is called by many, "the old mines." This road is a thing of interest to tourists, as riding by gravity is a novelty to most people. Liliputian cars, about ten by five feet, are used; and, when loaded, the trip is sometimes made in twelve minutes. The fall averages ninety feet to the mile.

Two inclined planes are used in making the return trip— the first at Mount Pisgah, the second at Mount Jefferson, up which the cars are hoisted by stationary engines. At the Summit, Mount Pisgah plane is two thousand three hundred and twenty-two feet in length. The summit of the mount is six hundred and sixty-four feet above the base, eight hundred and fifty feet above the Lehigh, and fifteen hundred feet above tide. From here a fine view of the Lehigh Gap is to be had. To the second plane the fall is three hundred and two feet to the mile. The length of Mount Jefferson plane is two thousand and seventy feet, and its height four hundred and sixty feet. These notes may be of interest to some, and are inserted with that expectation.

At Mauch Chunk, the Sylvis family continued to grow, which probably had something to do with the fact that the father was unfortunate with his speculations, and found himself forced to retrace his steps to the western part of the State, where, after trying in various ways to obtain a livelihood, he settled in what was known as White Deer Valley, which is situated in Lycoming County. Here he opened a small wagon-shop, worked with the farmers in summer-time, and engaged in building houses. But his family was large, and he could no more than support it. The elder boys had by this time become old enough to be sent to school. But they were compelled to do chores in summer; and the winters being very severe in that section of the country, the attainments of the persons employed to teach being of the most ordinary kind, and the schools being located at a distance, the boys progressed very little. It may be said indeed they progressed not at all, for they did not ever succeed in mastering the rudiments of a common school education. William, who was a strong and healthy boy, did not share even these poor advantages — his services at home being too valuable to admit of their being dispensed with.

Mr. Sylvis was one of the many hundreds who fell victims to the panic of 1837; and when in after years his son was seeking out the causes which led to that and the other fearful panics which periodically followed it, his reasoning faculties were doubtless rendered more acute by the remembrance of his father's misfortune. His business was entirely broken up, and he was compelled to tramp about from place to place, working as a journeyman, leaving Mrs. Sylvis at home in charge of the children.

CHAPTER II.

MARRIAGE.

IT was at this time that young William first began to manifest that spirit of manly independence which so forcibly characterized the latter years of his life. He was young, yet old enough to appreciate the manifold difficulties his parents had to contend, and still were contending with. Knowing that his father had at some time previously favored a Mr. Pawling, a neighbor, in some way, he induced his mother — his father being at that time absent — to enter into negotiations with Pawling, which ended in his being taken into Pawling's family on an agreement under which that gentleman became responsible for William's support, in return for his time and services. William was at this time but eleven years old.

Shortly after this arrangement had been effected, Mr. Pawling became the candidate of the Whigs for a seat in the Legislature, to represent his (Lycoming) county. The campaign ended in Mr. Pawling's election; and during his necessary absence from home, William was left in sole charge of the family. The children of Mr. Pawling being all girls, William found plenty to do about the house and farm; and this work he did so faithfully as to earn the hearty commendation of his new master. The elder Mr. Sylvis was a Democrat of a pretty rabid stripe; but William, under the tuition of Pawling, even at that early age, soon became inoculated with Whig sentiments and prejudices, for he was a close observer and careful student of current history, and, though without education, a keen critic of every passing event.

Frequently he would, having first obtained Mr. Pawling's permission, spend Sunday with his father and the family; and upon such occasions he generally managed to get himself into a discussion with the old gentleman on the relative merits of Whigism and Democracy, and more than once Sylvis, Sr. was worsted in these arguments; though he had seen much more of life, and would naturally have been supposed to know much more of politics than his boy. The faith in the doctrines of the Whig party here obtained remained with him until its dissolution, and made him an ardent admirer of Henry Clay, the great Kentucky statesman, whose words and deeds William was ready to defend wherever occasion required or opportunity offered. And even to the day of his death, there was no more certain way of exciting Mr. Sylvis's ire than to question the greatness of his beau-ideal orator and statesman. William remained with Mr. Pawling until he was seventeen years of age, six years in all. A letter recently received from Mr. Pawling, who is now nearly fourscore years old, says:

"Before coming to me he had never been to school, and did not know his letters. I think we had no school the first winter. I taught him his letters and to spell a little. The next winter, and every winter during his stay with me, I sent him to school, — perhaps three months of each year. This was all the schooling he ever got. There were no branches then taught in our schools but reading, writing, and arithmetic. He had free access to my library, and in that way improved himself greatly; but he was, substantially, a self-made man. His morals were without reproach. I do not remember a single act or thing he did during the time he lived with us that did not meet my entire approbation. After the contract expired, I hired him for one year to work on the farm, at the usual rates of farm hands."

After serving his year on Mr. Pawling's farm, William returned to his father,—who had, in the interim, somewhat improved his fortunes,—and worked with him in a wagon-shop which the father had succeeded in establishing. From here he went to Union County, where he first worked as a helper, and then as a keeper, in the "Forest Iron-Works," after which he was taken into the foundry, where he began to learn the trade of iron-moulding. Before he had been at the place quite a year, the company failed, and William lost the greater part of the wages he had earned during his stay. Again compelled to go elsewhere for employment, he journeyed to Curwinsville, Clearfield County, at which place he finished his trade. Shortly after he became a journeyman, in company with a friend and fellow-workman, he rented the foundry at this place for a year, at the expiration of which time he went to Half Moon Valley, where he again worked as a journeyman moulder. During all of this time a liberal portion of his earnings was sent home, to lessen the burdens which were entailed upon his father. His stay at Half Moon Valley was short. Leaving there, he worked at different places in the vicinity; but not being satisfied with any of them, he did not remain in them, and finally settled himself at Hollidaysburg, where, still working as a journeyman, he boarded with a family by the name of Hunter. The youngest daughter of the Hunters,—then a little child,—named Florrie, was made an especial pet of by Mr. Sylvis, who taught her in Sunday-school, romped with her, and assumed an almost parental supervision of her training. That little child is now his widow. From Hollidaysburg Mr. Sylvis wended his way into what was then Union, now Snyder County, where he contracted an acquaintance with Miss Amelia A. Thomas, who was eight years his junior, and whom, after a short courtship, he married, April 11th, 1852.

After his marriage, Mr. Sylvis worked awhile at Beaver Furnace, at Half Moon Valley, at Philadelphia, — leaving his family at home at the Furnace, — and finally moved with his family to the city, where he went to housekeeping, working at the time as a journeyman in the foundry business.

We have but briefly sketched these incidents, for the reason that there is little in them of real interest that may not be told in a general way; and it is not our design to carry the reader through a tedious recital of the commonplace occurrences in his career. His history thus far may be thus condensed: He was the son of a poor father with a large family; thrown upon his own resources at a very early age, without educational qualifications to assist him in his battle of life, he learns a good trade, becomes a first-class mechanic, marries, and struggles along, just as millions of others in his situation are compelled to, — the provision of bread and meat for his wife and little ones being such a tax upon his powers as to preclude the possibility of his rising above the level of a manual laborer. But during all his troubles, he never forgot his parents, and when opportunity offered never failed to remit his mite to assist them.

About this time he became a great reader and student of politics, and especially of the elementary principles of political economy. This fact would not be at all surprising, had Mr. Sylvis had the advantages which nearly all boys in these days have; but it must be remembered that his education had been very defective; and his letters at this time display a lamentable deficiency even as regards common orthography and the primary principles of English grammar; yet throughout them runs a vein of strong common sense, that gave good promise of the future.

The next few years, spent in Philadelphia, were years of many and peculiar hardships. Much sickness in his family, his own sickness on two or three occasions, and an accident at the foundry, by which his foot was badly burned,—hot iron having been poured into his boot,—made it very difficult for him to even meet the demands of the butcher, the baker, and the landlord; yet even then he occasionally rendered his father pecuniary assistance.

On June 6th, 1855, the iron-moulders of Philadelphia organized themselves into a trades-union. Mr. Sylvis was at the time working at his trade; but, though already a believer in organized resistance to the impositions so frequently perpetrated by capitalists upon their employés, he did not at first become a member.

In October, 1857, a strike occurred in the shop at which he was working; its object being to resist a proposed reduction in wages of twelve per cent. A large number of the men signed a pledge not to accept these wages, some of whom were union men, and some had not yet joined. These met as a shop organization, Mr. Sylvis being their secretary, and also a member of what was called the "Committee on Corners," whose duty it was to picket the vicinity of the shop, in order that no strangers should be permitted to take the places of the strikers without first being warned of the reasons that had prompted them to cease work. In both of these positions he was a zealous worker. The strike continued for some weeks, when a number violated their pledge, and returned to work at the reduction. Some of the strikers, however, honorably fulfilled their promise, and Mr. Sylvis was among this number. On December 5th, the union passed a resolution admitting these to membership. At the meeting of the union, held on the second day of January following, Mr. Sylvis was elected recording secretary; and with his acceptance of that position, his career as an active trades-unionist may be said to have commenced. He had long believed in the union; but up to that time, for reasons best known to himself, he had not seen fit to become a member of it, though all who watched his subsequent course gave him credit for having been influenced against joining by honest considerations. Mr. Sylvis's excellent judgment, and his disposition to act the part of a zealot in everything he undertook, made him a valuable acquisition to Union No. 1, as is proven by the minutes of their proceedings, for upon every measure of importance proposed Mr. Sylvis "had his say," and that "say" was generally on the side of right and of the majority. All his actions seem to have been guided by a desire to confine altercations between the men and their employers to that natural difference in interest existing between buyer and seller. To avoid conflicts by avoiding unjust demands, and by making the organization so close and so powerful as to enforce submission to, before making even just demands, seemed to be his policy; and though the union, perhaps, did not always act upon this policy, as a rule, its moves were eminently equitable, and deserving of respect and success.

There was originality and humor in his style of keeping the minutes at this time, of which the following is a sample. "The president proceeded to appoint a committee on corners, but did not get far before a free blow was commenced. There appeared to be a superabundance of gas in the room, and it was found necessary to allow a portion of it to blow off before anything further could be done. Finally the breeze subsided, and the business was proceeded with." We have not preserved his orthography, which was so poor as to conclusively prove that his school-days had been few.

A local organization has its powers, but a trades organization, to be of real service, should have ramifications in every locality to which the trade extends. If unity in one city is good, unity in many places is better. So argued Mr. Sylvis, when, on April 10th, he submitted a proposition directing that correspondence with the St. Louis, and other unions of moulders already in operation, be opened with a view to the settlement of some basis of co-operation between them; and again, on December 14th, 1858, when he offered a resolution appointing a committee to urge the holding of a national convention of representatives of all the iron-moulders' unions in the country. Of the committee appointed under this resolution, Mr. Sylvis was secretary; a position, under the circumstances, of more real importance even than the chairmanship. The first meeting of the committee was held at Mr. Sylvis's house, on December 11th. After maturely deliberating the important proposition in hand, a circular was issued, urging upon the several unions then in existence the importance of a national organization. The circular set forth the fact that the Philadelphia Union had weathered the panic of 1857, and maintained prices, while in many other cities the men, for want of organization, had been compelled to submit to a reduction. It declared that "the interests of capital and labor are one and inseparable," and enumerated the benefits to accrue from having prices regulated all over the country by the one standard. Sundry questions as to the number of moulders, and other trade matters, were asked, with a view to the compilation of useful statistics. To this circular favorable responses were received, and valuable information upon several matters of interest to the trade at large. Three strikes were at the time in progress, one at Providence, one at Port Chester, and one at Albany, the latter being for 1857 prices, against an overplus of apprentices, and in resistance of the store-order system. The bosses of Albany had combined, and were in communication with those in other places, asking the formation of a "Founders' League," for the purpose of importing workmen from Europe to take the places of the employés, who, under the influence of the union agitation, then at its height, had already become restive, and were displaying a disposition to ask and enforce a decent respect for their rights as men. The Philadelphia founders, however, discouraged the scheme; some of them because of a conviction that they were sufficiently powerful to strangle the incipient organizations of the men without resorting to such an extreme. Generally, wherever local organizations of any kind of workingmen existed, an effort was being made to regain the prices paid prior to 1857, which the "panic" or "crisis" had materially reduced; and the moulders, being of course no exception to the rule, were greatly stimulated thereby in their effort to form a national organization. All the answers to the circulars that were received were favorable; and, influenced by this fact, the committee issued a call, dated June 15th, for a national convention to be held on July 5th, 1859. This call was signed, Isaac A. Sheppard, President; Wm. H. Sylvis, Recording Secretary. The meetings having been held in Mr. Sylvis's house, the expense incurred by the committee aggregated only $10.24, which sum was mainly expended for printing and postage. This brings us to the meeting of the first national convention of iron-moulders ever held on the continent, and to the end of the chapter.

CHAPTER III.

FIRST NATIONAL CONVENTION.

ON July 5th, 1859, thirty-five delegates, representing organizations of iron-moulders located at Philadelphia, St. Louis, Albany, Troy, Cincinnati, Providence, Jersey City, Peekskill, Utica, Port Chester, N. Y., Wilmington, and Baltimore, met in convention at Philadelphia. As indicating the fraternal spirit already felt, the Stamford Union, instead of sending a delegate, donated all the money in its treasury to their striking brothers of Port Chester. Of this convention, William C. Rea, of Missouri, was made president. The time of the convention was, of course, principally occupied with the work of organization. Mr. Sylvis was one of the committee of five appointed by the chair to prepare an address to the iron-moulders of the United States. The address reported was written by Mr. Sylvis. It was adopted and issued with the constitution, to which it, to this day, is attached, in the shape of a preamble, as evidencing Mr. Sylvis's abilities as a writer at that time, and his conception of the work of organization they were engaged in establishing. We quote it entire.

"PREAMBLE.

"'Labor has no protection—the weak are devoured by the strong. All wealth and all power centre in the hands of the few, and the many are their victims and their bondsmen.'

"So says an able writer in a treatise on association, and, in studying the history of the past, the impartial thinker must be impressed with the truth of the above quotation. In all countries and all times capital has been used by those possessing it to monopolize particular branches of business, until the vast and various industrial pursuits of the world have been brought under the immediate control of a comparatively small portion of mankind. Although an unequal distribution of the world's wealth, it is perhaps necessary that it should be so. To attain to the highest degree of success in any undertaking, it is necessary to have the most perfect and systematic arrangement possible; to acquire such a system, it requires the management of a business to be placed as nearly as practicable under the control of one mind; thus concentration of wealth and business tact conduces to the most perfect working of the vast business machinery of the world. And there is, perhaps, no other organization of society so well calculated to benefit the laborer and advance the moral and social condition of the mechanic of this country, if those possessed of wealth were *all* actuated by those pure and philanthropic principles so necessary to the happiness of all; but, alas! for the *poor* of humanity, such is not the case.

"'WEALTH IS POWER,' and practical experience teaches us that it is a power but too often used to oppress and degrade the daily laborer. Year after year the capital of the country becomes more and more concentrated in the hands of a few, and, in proportion as the wealth of the country becomes centralized, its power increases, and the laboring-classes are impoverished. It, therefore, becomes us, as men who have to battle with the stern realities of life, to look this matter fair in the face; there is no dodging the question; let every man give it a fair, full, and candid consideration, and then act according to his honest convictions. *What position are we, the mechanics of America, to hold in society?* Are we to receive an equivalent for our labor sufficient to maintain us in comparative independence and respectability, to procure the means with which to educate our children, and qualify them to play their part in the world's drama; or must we be forced to bow the suppliant knee to wealth, and earn by unprofitable toil a life too void of solace to confirm the very chains that bind us to our doom?

"'IN UNION THERE IS STRENGTH,' and in the formation of a national organization, embracing every moulder in the country, a union founded upon a basis broad as the land in which we live, lies our only hope. Single-handed, we can accomplish nothing; but united, there is no power of wrong we may not openly defy. Let the moulders of such places as have not already moved in this matter, organize as quickly as possible, and connect themselves with the national organization. Do not be humbugged into the idea that this thing cannot succeed.

"We are no theorists; this is no visionary plan, but one eminently practicable. Nor can injustice be done to any one; no undue advantage can be taken of any of our employers. There *is* not, *there cannot be,* any good reason why they should not pay us a fair price for our labor. If the profits of their business are not sufficient to remunerate them for the trouble of doing business, *let the consumer make up the balance.*

"The stereotyped argument of our employers, in every attempt to reduce wages, is, that their large expenses and small profits will not warrant the present prices for labor; therefore, those just able to live now must be content with less hereafter.

"In answer, we maintain that the expenses are not unreasonable, and the profits are large and, in the aggregate, great; there is no good reason why we should not receive a fair equivalent for our labor. A small reduction seriously diminishes the already scanty means of the operative, and puts a large sum in the employer's pocket. And yet some of the foundry proprietors would appear charitable before the world. We ask: Is it *charitable,* is it *humane,* is it *honest,* to take from the laborer, who is already fed, clothed, and lodged too poorly, a portion of his food and raiment, and deprive his family of the necessaries of life, by the common resort — a reduction of his wages? It must not be so. To rescue our trade from the condition into which it has fallen, and raise ourselves to that condition in society to which we, as mechanics, are justly entitled, and to place ourselves on a foundation sufficiently strong to secure us from further encroachment, and to elevate the moral, social, and intellectual condition of every moulder in the country, is the object of our international organization; and to the consummation of so desirable an object, we, the delegates in convention assembled, do pledge ourselves to unceasing efforts and untold sacrifices."

This little appeal may not be remarkable for its etymological purity; its construction may indeed be such as to chill the nerve of a theorizing grammarian; but its plainly and forcibly expressed truths mark it as having come from a pen freighted with the thoughts of a heart filled with sympathy for the cause in which it was employed. It is evidence that, even at that early day of his career as an advocate of labor's rights, its writer saw deeper into the subject than was common with his kind, and foresaw that a grand battle between labor and capital was imminent, in which he had already determined to take a leader's part.

After constituting the officers of the convention a provisional government to hold power during the interim, the convention adjourned to meet in the city of Albany, January 10th, 1860.

It is our intention to follow, as closely as is necessary to indicate his policy, a few of Mr. Sylvis's acts in connection with several annual sessions of the Iron-Moulders' National (and International) Union, because experience has proven that, in nearly every position he assumed, he saw clearly the way to success. This feature of the book, we hope, will be valuable to others under similar circumstances, as trades-unions have become so important, so necessary to the sustenance of the workingmen, and the acts and sayings of trades-union leaders are nowadays so closely scrutinized and criticized, that neither they nor the unions can lose by patterning after and considering the advice of one who was so uniformly successful.

Mr. Sylvis attended the Albany session as a delegate from Philadelphia Union, No. 1. On the second day of the session, by an informal ballot, he was made a nominee for president; but was beaten at the election subsequently held, by Isaac I. Neal, though he was afterwards elected treasurer. The first resolution considered at this session was one offered by Mr. Sylvis, which may be looked upon as formally recording the birth of the National Union. The resolution was in these words: Resolved, That this convention does now resolve itself into a national union, adopt the constitution as adopted by the Philadelphia convention, and that a committee of five be appointed by the chair to report such amendments to and revisions of the constitution as they may deem proper.

It will thus be seen that it was Mr. Sylvis's motion that gave rise to the agitation, and his motion that announced the culmination of the project to bind together in a common brotherhood all the moulders' unions in the country. At this session, Mr. Sylvis was made chairman of a committee to prepare the card system, now in use in the iron-moulder organizations, the most admirable system for the purpose yet conceived. Of course it has from time to time been altered and improved, yet it remains substantially as originally reported by Mr. Sylvis, and all of its improvements, or nearly all, are due to the thoughtful care for matters of detail which was one of the most remarkable characteristics of his administration.

Much of the time of the Albany convention was spent in debating the piece-work and helper, or Bucksheer, systems — both of which were denounced by resolutions; piece-work, it was contended, had a tendency to make men selfish, and to give to a few, who were content to work early and late, a chance to monopolize the trade, to the exclusion of better men who, while recognizing the necessity of industry, were yet unwilling to sacrifice their physical vigor by such abject slavishness to gain. Mr. Sylvis was at this time, and ever afterwards, a bitter opponent of piece-working, not because he did not admit it to be right that men should be paid in accordance with the quantity and quality of their product, but he believed in the objections above alluded to; and further, because he knew, what is daily becoming more apparent, that there is an unseen something controlling the products of skilled manual labor, which almost invariably keeps the supply of those products in excess of the demand, and therefore recognized the necessity of curtailment, by limiting or restricting the greedy. Piece-work, under regulations looking to a fair division of the amount of work to be done among all those willing and possessing the requisite skill and strength to do it, was not objectionable to him; but it was so nearly an impossibility to make even active trades-unionists see that they contribute in any degree to the troubles of which they complain, and so difficult to induce them to alter their plan of working in accordance with the dictates of an intelligent judgment in such cases, that the total abolition of piece-work, at least so far as the iron-moulding trade was concerned, seemed to him to be the best, and indeed the only available remedy under the circumstances. We cannot have things as we wish them, but must take them as we find them. If the current of trade was confined to natural channels, and not directed by artfully contrived fiscal and other means, designed for the emolument of a few cunning ones, at great cost to the many, we would not have such a number of or such serious difficulties to contend with; but, having them to contend with, we ought manfully to face them, even at the risk of placing ourselves in opposition to what, under other circumstances, would be eminently right and proper.

Mr. Sylvis performed the duties of the treasuryship with an uncommon zeal; but the treasurer of any organization is an officer whose actions are closely watched, and be he ever so honest, it is scarcely possible for him to escape calumny. Particularly is it impossible in the case of the treasurer of a trades organization. Workingmen are necessarily the most ignorant, and consequently the most bigoted and envious of all classes. The better feelings of our nature are not brought out by hard and illy remunerated toil. Toleration and its refined development — charity — cannot be expected to have an abiding place in the hearts of those who, because of their poverty, are compelled to devote their lives to work, work, everlasting work, with a recompense that barely enables them to satisfy the demands of the landlord, the victualler, and the clothier. Hence all such, or nearly all who are connected with trades-unions, look with suspicion upon the men to whom is allotted the handling of the funds of their organizations, let it be ever so little that they have contributed to those funds, or let the stake be what it may. Besides, comparatively few workingmen have been subjected to the refining influences of an education, and men without education are generally without confidence in their fellow-men, and inclined to look with a poignant jealousy upon those of their kind who have been so formed by nature, or by training, as to be above them in the scale of intelligence, and when such are made leaders of trades organizations, given positions of honor, trust, or emolument in them, they are sure to become targets for the malicious insinuations of the ignorant and suspicious. Mr. Sylvis was subjected to a most trying ordeal of this nature. Because he was determined, and had a way of giving blunt expression to his convictions, the jealousy aroused against him soon became absolute hate on the part of a number of men who should have known better. Some added fuel to the fire by giving utterance to mysteriously spoken sentences about ambition, dictatorship, etc. Nevertheless, Mr. Sylvis continued to work faithfully for the interests of his class, determined that no shadow of blame should rightfully attach to him while he continued in office, and, at the next session of the union, to sever his official connection therewith. Just prior to the meeting of the Cincinnati convention, under date of December 25th, he wrote a letter to the *Mechanics' Own*—a newspaper published in Philadelphia, and devoted to the interests of the working-classes—as treasurer, giving certain information and advice. In this letter he referred to the opposition to him that had developed itself, saying: "I have been assailed by a faction confined to no particular locality, but existing chiefly in my own city, and, I am sorry to say, in my own union, whose object appears to have been to crush me beneath their weight, and sink me into oblivion, which they flatter themselves they have succeeded in doing. To their accusation that I have been dishonest in the discharge of my duties as treasurer, that I was dragged into the union, and am only a good union man because I was compelled to be, that I had a desire to sell out the union, and various other charges about dictatorship, ambition, etc., I have no reply to make, for, by noticing them in any way, I would be letting myself down to their level; and I am willing to abide by the decision of time, the great arbiter of all things." In another part of this letter he says, "I am glad to shake off the restraints of the most disagreeable position I have ever held in my life."

And just here we desire all such of our readers as are connected with workingmen's organizations to stop and ask themselves these four questions. Has it never occurred to you that you are yourselves in a great measure responsible for the wrongs of many of the defaulting officers of your organizations? Has it never occurred to you that your disposition to accuse every man of ambition who evinces a willingness to assume the burdens of office in your organizations, has a tendency to keep good men from trying for or even accepting office when you would force them into it? When you have found yourself criticizing the actions of some union official, finding fault with him because of his failures, have you ever "put yourself in his place," and considered how hard it is to work for grumblers? how impossible it is to work with the necessary vim, and successfully, in such an up-hill business as is the managing of trades-unions, unless supported by the encouragement and hearty co-operation of all hands interested? We are assured that, if you answer these questions from your consciences, many things will appear clear to you that have heretofore seemed all chaos and confusion. What you have considered unavoidable misfortunes, or the logical results of ignorance, inattention, or treason on the part of your officers, will appear in their true light as the essential consequences of your own shortcomings.

Mr. Sylvis had been a faithful, hard-working officer, yet there were those who had accused him of all sorts of crimes; and so bitter and malignant were these, notwithstanding his uncompromising devotion to the union, his readiness to do all that in his power lay for its advancement, he was forced to confess himself glad to "shake off the restraints of the most disagreeable position he ever held in his life."

In the letter we have quoted, Mr. Sylvis intimates that his enemies had gained a victory over him. He had reference to his defeat as a candidate for delegate to the Cincinnati convention. He had tested his strength in the union, towards whose success he had contributed so much of his time and talents, but found that the "prophet had no honor in his own country," or, rather, that the majority of those for whom he had labored had gone over to the side of his enemies, and had succumbed to their rule.

But Mr. Sylvis was not a man to yield when he knew himself to be in the right. An ardent believer in the ultimate triumph of the right, he maintained a bold front, and, in the face of a persecution that would have driven most other men out of the movement, he fought the enemy, and in the end triumphed. He attended the Cincinnati convention, which met on January 8th, 1861, for the purpose of reporting his official actions as treasurer during the official year then terminating. Under the constitution, he was awarded a seat, with all the privileges of an ex-delegate, which included *all* the rights of delegates except the right to vote. The precise words of the constitution, as it then stood, are as follows:

> "Persons having once been received as representatives to this union shall be permanent members of the same so long as they remain in good standing in their respective unions, proof of which they shall present; and said unions shall retain their connection with this body. *They shall have all the rights of representative delegates except that of voting.*"

The following day Mr. Sylvis, in the meantime having been an active participant in the proceedings, was nominated as one of the candidates for the treasurership. Objection being entered that, as an ex-delegate, he was not eligible, he replied at length, citing the constitutional provision above quoted. That it was the intention of those who framed the constitution to make ex-delegates eligible to office, we do not know; but that the clause we have quoted gives them that right, is clear to all who can read and understand our language. The president, however, decided him ineligible. The decision was appealed from, but was sustained by a vote of thirty yeas to twenty nays. Among those who voted aye we notice the names of several who afterwards learned his real worth, and were, at the time of his death, among Mr. Sylvis's most ardent admirers and staunch supporters. Later in the session, a committee was appointed to revise the constitution. The committee consisted of one from each State represented, and one for each of the Canadas. When the president had announced his selections, a motion was made that Wm. H. Sylvis, of Pa., be added to the committee. This motion having been agreed to, a delegate rose, and excitedly asked "what rights former delegates had and *did not have* in the convention." The chair, of course, explained that the union, in sustaining his ruling, had decided them not entitled to hold office, and, by the vote just taken, that they have a right to serve on committees. Less than this would have sufficed to send most men off in a huff, goaded them to withdraw at once and forever from the organization; but, as we have before remarked, Mr. Sylvis was a man of determination as well as brains, and having made up his mind that to conquer he must fight, he remained, sat with the committee; and the revised constitution, reported and adopted later in the session, owed some of its most salient features to his forethought and keen appreciation of what trades-unions' jurisprudence ought to be.

According to the report which Mr. Sylvis, as treasurer, rendered to the convention, $6,125.06 had passed into his hands during the year, all of which had been paid in by twenty-eight unions. Of this sum, $5,511.30 had been expended to support strikes at Albany, Buffalo, and Spuyten Duyvil, New York. Desperate efforts were made by the enemies of Mr. Sylvis to prove his report faulty; all of which were, however, unsuccessful. One delegate went so far as to move a reconsideration of the vote by which his official expenses were ordered paid; but that motion failed; and the report proved to be in every respect accurate and explicit in detail. There is no possible room to doubt that more than one personal enemy of Mr. Sylvis was present at this convention, and it was obvious that they tried all in their power to harass him, and create a suspicion as to his rectitude. Had he not afterwards risen to prominence in the organization, and by his unswerving fealty proven, beyond cavil, how real was his love for it, there are many who, to this day, would have been convinced that he was other than an honest man. But he did rise, and gave the lie to every calumny hatched against him, and the aspersions of his enemies only added to the respect in which he was afterwards held by nearly all who knew him. The ruling of the president, above mentioned, left him the following year without an office. Yet, although he was officially declared ineligible, there was at least one man in the convention who had full faith in him, for in each of the four ballots taken for treasurer, there was one vote for William H. Sylvis. It must have been a satisfaction to the man who polled that vote, whoever he was, to know how effectually Mr. Sylvis eventually silenced his enemies, and forced them to yield tribute to his power, and how speedily and deservedly he increased his circle of friends until it included nearly all who knew him. Had it been us, we should have been proud of our foresight.

CHAPTER IV.

SERVICES IN THE ARMY.

MR. SYLVIS returned from the Cincinnati convention, according to his after confession, somewhat discouraged; but his unconquerable faith in the union soon again asserted its sway over him; and we find abundant evidence on the record of Philadelphia Union, No. 1, of the active interest he continued to take in its proceedings at this time. But the country was in a state of great agitation, and on the eve of the greatest civil war of which there is any record in history. Among the workingmen, a few choice spirits, North and South, knowing that all the burdens, and none of the honors, of war are entailed upon labor, were engaged in an effort to frustrate the plans of those who seemed to desire, and whose fanaticism was calculated to precipitate, hostilities. Mr. Sylvis was heart and soul with these men. They first held a meeting at Louisville, at which William Horan, Robert P. Gilchrist, and other moulders, friends of Mr. Sylvis, were among the leading spirits. At this meeting, resolutions were passed declaring that workingmen, without distinction of party, believe that our national prosperity and hopes of happiness depend upon the perpetuity of the Union; that, in the election of Abraham Lincoln, they see no reasonable pretext for the abandonment of the mighty fabric of government; that workingmen have no real or vital interest in the mere abstract questions used to divide the masses; calling upon the workingmen of every Congressional district through the land to hold meetings, and demand the resignation of those among their representatives at Washington, who, ultra and sectional men, are now above their actions, imperilling the safety of the Union; and, finally, declaring that Kentucky mechanics are Union men, but not submissionists; that they know their rights, and, knowing, dare maintain them in the Union or out of it."

This meeting, which was not a meeting of apologists for secession, but of honest workingmen desirous of doing what they could towards averting a war that just then seemed almost inevitable, was followed by similar meetings in other parts of the country, both North and South, which culminated in the holding of a convention at Philadelphia, on the twenty-second day of February, the former call emanating from Louisville.

This convention, though not so well attended as had been expected, contained representatives from quite a number of States. It was called to order by Mr. Sylvis, who took a most active part in its earnest, though fruitless deliberations.

South Carolina had seceded on December 20; five other States had "gone out" during January; the public mind was inflamed by these revolutionary acts and the inflammatory declarations of the most rampant of the Northern anti-slaveryites; hence the efforts of these workingmen, though prompted solely by a love of Republican institutions, and a desire that the already too actively burdened labor of the country should not be still further oppressed by the costs of a protracted war, were without the desired effect.

There are but few workingmen who will now refuse to admit that, had the advice of these men been listened to, the war might have been averted, and our statute-books would not now be filled with iniquitous and grievously oppressive measures, which, if not soon repealed, or in some degree modified, may yet result in another and equally disastrous conflict.

Mr. Sylvis was one of a committee of thirty-four appointed to provide for the comfort and convenience of the delegates to the convention, and to arrange for a workingmen's procession, and a grand mass meeting. The procession was a large and imposing one, several of the trades carrying emblematical representations of their callings. Among other features, the glass-blowers carried thirty-four glass globes, each having the name of a State painted upon it. In the evening, at the mass meeting, these globes were arranged on the stage in the rear of the speakers, and that one bearing the name of South Carolina burst.

Mr. Sylvis was among the speakers at the meeting. All of the addresses were spirited, and evinced a willingness on the part of the speakers to sacrifice their political differences to the one great object of preserving the Union.

Of this convention, Mr. Sylvis wrote, under date of February 12th, to the *Mechanics' Own*, saying, "We are going to have a workingmen's national convention in the city on the 22d. The call has been issued by the workingmen of Kentucky, and should be responded to by the workingmen of all sections of the country. Under the leadership of political demagogues and traitors scattered all over the land, North and South, East and West, the country is going to the devil as fast as it can. And unless the masses rise up in their might, and teach their representatives what to do, the good old ship will go to pieces. We hope to see every State represented in the coming convention, if only by one man; but let each State send as many as it can." The letter further urged the holding of meetings on the 22d of February, the reading of Washington's farewell address, and speeches for the Union, "in order," said Mr. Sylvis, "that we may learn once more to be governed by the good old principles of 1776," and concluded with a notice of a meeting to be held on that day, for a similar purpose, at Independence Square, "beneath the shadows of the old State House, to refresh our souls in the memories of the past, and make one more strong pull for the Union."

When the Whig party ceased to exist, Mr. Sylvis became a Democrat. In the election of 1860, he had been a supporter of Mr. Douglas, whom he looked upon as a happy medium between the two radical factions then contesting for the supremacy. With the defeat of Douglas, he did not cease to be a Democrat; but the above letter will show that he regarded the safety of the Union, and the avoidance of war, as matters of far greater moment than the success, at that time, of either Democracy or Republicanism. He was, as his letters attest, suspicious of the doctrines of both, as they were being interpreted by their recognized and trusted exponents, and chose between them only as between two evils.

The "committee of thirty-four" was continued after the adjournment of the convention, and had several meetings, Mr. Sylvis acting in the capacity of corresponding secretary. A letter written by him, dated March 23d, says, "The business of this committee is to perfect and perpetuate an organization among the industrial classes of the city and State, for the purpose of placing in positions of public trust men of known honesty and ability; men who know the real wants of the people, and who will represent us according to our wishes; men who have not made politics a trade; men who, for a consideration, will not become the mere tools of rotten corporations and aristocratic monopolies; men who will devote their time and energies to the making of good laws, and direct their administration in such a way as will best subserve the interests of the whole people."

The proposition was a most commendable one, but the popular mind was not in a proper condition to receive and consider it carefully, hence nothing came of the labors of the committee, though they were shared by some of Philadelphia's best citizens. On the 12th of April, less than three weeks after the publication of his last letter, the first gun was fired on Sumpter, and the youngest of us know what followed. The flag had been fired upon, and the whole North was in a blaze of excitement. The great rebellion had begun.

When hostilities actually commenced, Mr. Sylvis, with the assistance of Michael Weaver, an old Mexican soldier, recruited a company, of which he was offered the first lieutenancy. For some time previous to this, Mr. Sylvis had been, owing to the depressed condition of his trade, out of employment, and there was no immediate prospect of his being able to better his condition. Nevertheless, his wife earnestly protested against his accepting the commission; and for a long time he was undecided whether to accept or reject. The problem was ultimately solved without his assistance. The company, when organized, was tendered to Colonel (afterwards governor) Geary, whose regiment was called the Twenty-eighth Pennsylvania. But Colonel Geary had already mustered in his full complement of fifteen companies, and was compelled to decline the offer. The company was then tendered to Colonel Lujéane, an Italian, who had held a Professorship in the Philadelphia High-School, from which he had been expelled, and who was then organizing the Ninety-ninth Pennsylvania volunteers. But before the regiment could be mustered in, Lujéane, because of his tyranny and manifest incompetency, became so obnoxious to the men of the company of which Mr.

Sylvis was to be first lieutenant, that it disbanded, a majority of the members enlisting in other regiments which were preparing for the front.

Mr. Sylvis was not among this number. He went to Washington, where he worked as a teamster, at which employment he continued several months; after which he returned to Philadelphia, where he was given work at his trade by Messrs. Liebrandt and McDowell, with which firm he continued until the invasion of Pennsylvania by General Lee, previous to the battle of Antietam. The moulders in the employ of Liebrandt and McDowell had organized themselves into a militia company, and when the call for troops was made to repel the insurgents, this company was the first to offer its services to the mayor of the city. Of this company, Edward Sheible was elected captain, and Wm. H. Sylvis, orderly sergeant.

The company proceeded under orders to Harrisburg, where it was, with other companies, speedily formed into what was called the Twentieth Pennsylvania Militia, of which Wm. B. Thomas, of Philadelphia, was commissioned colonel. The regiment was taken to Hagerstown, Md., at which place they arrived just in time to hear of the retreat of Lee. A forward movement was immediately ordered, as everybody supposed, to pursue Lee. On this march a ludicrous incident occurred, which has gone into history, and is worthy of recital here.

The section of country the regiment was then in was totally strange to every member. At eight o'clock in the evening, the line moved to march over what the men thought the roughest piece of the road in this country,— and, as every one who was in the army can testify, there are some very bad roads south of Mason's and Dixon's line. The only information they possessed of their whereabouts had been gleaned of farmers and others encountered on the line of march. After many halts, ordered for the purpose of ascertaining, if possible, the locality in which they were, and after six hours' hard travelling, they were brought to a sudden stand-still by the appearance directly in advance of them of what seemed to be innumerable lights. A halt was of course immediately ordered, and a few pickets thrown out, of which few Sylvis was a volunteer — their duty being to ascertain what the lights were. These advanced cautiously, and soon learned that they were the camp-fires of a sister militia regiment. The adjutant, who had gone ahead on his horse, finding all right, returned at good speed, followed by the pickets, to communicate to the colonel the result of their reconnoissance. The colonel, not knowing that such a large number had been sent ahead, naturally supposed those approaching him to be enemies, and that an attack was to be made. Knowing the inefficiency of his force to meet a column such as he supposed was advancing upon him, he immediately cried out, "Don't fire; I surrender!" thus rendering up his regiment captive to his own adjutant. This circumstance created much merriment, and was the cause of much chaffing among the men. The regiment being encamped at Greencastle, Pa., this joke was bandied about to such an extent that Colonel Thomas felt called upon to make a public explanation; so, in a speech, he declared that, "If it had been a regiment of rebels, he would have felt justified in surrendering as preferable to fighting with a handful of green men, who did not know which end of a cartridge to tear off, and hardly which end of a gun to shoot out of."

One incident of the march spoken of is worthy of especial notice. The regiment consisted of eight hundred and forty men; the distance marched was nearly twenty miles, and was travelled in about six hours. Upon reaching their destination, the number had dwindled down to one hundred and twenty men, the balance having become wearied out and dropped off during the last half of the distance travelled. Of these one hundred and twenty, eighty-four were in the company of which Mr. Sylvis was sergeant, they having lost but one man. Mr. Sylvis's duties as orderly sergeant were performed well and faithfully. The position he held was one of comparatively trivial importance; yet a good orderly sergeant is much better than a bad general, and Mr. Sylvis was a good orderly sergeant. Though a strict disciplinarian during the short time they were associated together, he enlisted the respect and confidence of the men to a greater degree than did any of the other officers. His term of service was brief; but it is the belief of those who were in a position to know, that in the volunteer service he would have achieved distinction and commanded respect, had his family duties permitted him to follow the bent of his inclinations, which would, unquestionably, have attracted him into the army at the commencement of the rebellion. This points us to another of Mr. Sylvis's manly traits. We speak of his unswerving fealty to the interests of his family. Though they might have had many more comforts than he gave them, had he devoted his earnings, as others devote theirs, exclusively to themselves and families, yet, while he expended every cent of his surplus in the great cause of labor reform, he never permitted them to suffer. In a letter to his brother, dated May 5th, 1861, he says: "I have been elected first lieutenant of a company of infantry, but I have not yet made up my mind to accept the office. I would accept it, were it not for my family. My wife is almost crazy about it. She wants me to go to the country, and remain there until the war is over; but I cannot see how we can live in the country much better than here. We have no money, and it is very hard to live anywhere without money."

While his desire was to accept the position, in deference to the wishes of his wife he worked himself out of the absolute poverty in which he then was by going to the capital, and laboring as a teamster, — employment that nine out of ten, possessing one-half of his attainments, would not have deemed sufficiently respectable, and would have well-nigh starved before accepting.

CHAPTER V.

LABORS THROUGHOUT THE COUNTRY.

IN the last chapter, we carried Mr. Sylvis up to the fall of 1862. It will now be necessary to go back again to the spring of the year. There had been no convention of the moulders held. The war excitement had so demoralized the organization that very many of the leading men who were consulted deemed it best to hold over. Mr. Sylvis was among the number, and argued that the condition of the trade and the country would not warrant it. But as the year advanced trade got better, and as the prices of necessaries kept going up, there were stirring debates on the question of wages in such of the unions as yet held together. No. 1 appointed a committee, of which Sylvis was chairman, to communicate with the bosses in reference to an advance. He sent mildly-written letters to each firm, presenting the great disparity then existing between the prices paid to labor and those charged labor for provisions, rents, clothing, &c. But the "bosses," knowing that the union was not in good condition, and desiring to make as much hay as possible while the sun was shining so propitiously, with one excuse and another delayed the matter for several months. In the meantime Mr. Sylvis put himself into correspondence with the few organizations that had not totally disintegrated, with a view of holding a convention in January, 1863. Some of the officers of the preceding convention had neglected their duties, and few of them evinced a willingness to co-operate with Mr. Sylvis in his effort to resuscitate the national organization. Nevertheless his zeal was not in the least abated by these discouragements, and he continued his efforts, which were crowned with such marked success, that, on January 6th, twenty delegates, representing fourteen unions, met in Pittsburg. The following morning, before any business had been done, Mr. Sylvis was unanimously elected president.

At this session it was made apparent that the national organization had become so badly demoralized as to be almost useless, and that something must be done speedily to prevent its going totally to pieces. There was much debating as to what was needed to re-invest the organization with some of its lost vigor. Many propositions were offered and discarded. Finally, the delegates were, on motion, instructed to ascertain the sense of their respective unions as to the propriety of sending out an agent for that purpose, and to canvass for the proposed newspaper organ; the delegates to report as soon as possible to the president, and the president, provided he should have such assurance as would, in his judgment, warrant him in so doing, to proceed himself, or by deputy, immediately to perform those duties.

The published proceedings of the convention show that Mr. Sylvis was assigned almost a monopoly of the work necessary to be done to return to the organization its lost position of strength and usefulness. The duty of preparing forms of charter, cards, and other blanks, of regaining possession of the lost financial and other records of the union, and much other detail work, was given him to perform; and right nobly, as afterwards transpired, did he discharge his important trust.

About a month after the adjournment of the convention, six out of the eight Philadelphia founders condescended to send a letter to the union, agreeing to a scale of prices, which added nothing to the prices of most of the work, and only six or seven per cent. to those paid for the very poorest "jobs;" but they demanded an abandonment of the rule of the union limiting the number of apprentices.

In this connection, it is but just that we should go back a year or two to show the position which the union had always held on this important and vexed question. In February, 1860, immediately after the adjournment of the Albany convention, Mr. Sylvis offered, at a meeting of No. 1, a resolution providing for the appointment of a committee of two moulders from each shop, to meet two from each firm in convention, for the purpose of settling upon some fixed system of apprenticeship. The resolution was agreed to; and notes were sent, signed by Mr. Sylvis as chairman of the committee, to each firm, stating the position taken by the union, and concluding with these words:

> "We offer the above in good faith, and with a desire to put an end to some of the vexed questions that are continually breeding discord and contention, and hope you will respond in a like spirit."

In answer, all of the firms save one declared that they did not see any necessity for holding any such convention, and insisted upon the propriety of each firm dealing with its own employés. It is evident that these answers were written after consultation by the employers one with another. Then the union proposed that apprentices should be regularly indentured for four years; that none should be taken under sixteen years of age, or who were not morally, mentally, and physically qualified to become master workmen; agreeing, in return, to instruct such boys in every branch of the trade, and take them as partners during the last year of their apprenticeship. The firms refused to enter into this arrangement, and at a subsequent meeting the committee so reported, and was discharged.

We have alluded to these circumstances to show that the union had always manifested a desire to settle the apprenticeship question on a compromise basis, and was therefore justified in refusing to abandon altogether its position on the question at the simple dictation of the employers. There had been, up to this time, no advance in wages since the breaking out of the rebellion, but the prices of almost every article that entered into the domestic economy of the workingman had doubled, and of course the proposition of the employers was not agreed to. A long strike was the consequence. The employers evidently intended that it should be. Encouraged by the known weakness of the National Union, disclosed by the small attendance at Pittsburg, they hoped to break up No. 1, which was regarded as the back-bone of the organization. They called for the co-operation of the founders in other cities, requesting that no Philadelphia moulders be employed by them; but business was too good for those appealed to to manifest such a feeling of magnanimity, and only one case of refusal is recorded. In February there were one hundred and fifty on strike. Scarcely a union working under the jurisdiction of the national body but had Philadelphia moulders employed.

A few months later, out of three hundred and eighty-four union men, ninety-seven had enlisted, and were serving in the army, and thirty-seven only were out of employment, the rest having secured employment elsewhere. In August, there were only twenty-eight on strike, and of this number some were working as laborers. The shops were running; one with four "scabs" and fifty boys, another with five "scabs" and twenty-four boys, another with nine "scabs" and sixteen boys, and still another with nineteen "scabs" and an indefinite number of boys. In September, less than $100 per week was required to support those still out.

At one time a number of the boys were induced to quit work. They were arrested and taken before Judge Ludlow, who decided that their credentials were all "one-sided," and not legal. In October, according to a letter written by Mr. Sylvis, "two or three superannuated, two or three who could not be driven away, and two or three good men to engineer the movement, were all that remained." Some of these were eleven months on the union pay-roll. We have alluded to this strike because it was one of the most stubbornly contested and best conducted trade-contests that ever took place in this country. Asking pardon for this digression, we request the reader to now go back with us to the time immediately following the adjournment of the Pittsburg convention. Mr. Sylvis, as soon as he returned to Philadelphia, acquainted his union with what the International Union had done.

No. 1 gave him one hundred dollars to begin his work with. He then issued a circular, and, receiving a number of favorable responses, made preparations for starting upon his tour of experiment, of which he said, in his report the following year, "I had no very clear conception of the extent of the task before me, or the means by which it was to be accomplished."

It should be mentioned here that it had not been made incumbent upon the unions to pay a tax to support him on his journey, but had been left optional with them to give or not to give, as they should deem proper.

On the third of January he began his journey. During the year he visited every union working under the jurisdiction of the international organization at least once, some twice, and some even three times. He organized nineteen new unions, reorganized sixteen that had dissolved, and wherever he went infused new life into the organization. In doing these things he travelled over ten thousand miles, into and across nearly all the States east of the Rocky Mountains, excepting those in rebellion, and of these he visited Kentucky, Tennessee, and Missouri, and through both of the Canadas. He worked diligently and constantly through the entire year, and his report, as submitted to the convention, shows how economically. From that document it appears that the total amount expended was eight hundred and ninety-nine dollars and eighty-six cents, being an excess of seventeen cents over the amount received.

His family lived at St. Mary's during the time; and the following items of expenditure taken from his report will show how they were supported; will show that they, as well as Mr. Sylvis's self, were stinted to build up the moulders' organization:

School-books for children . . .	$ 3.10
Shoes for family	10.00
Clothes for family	18.75
House rent	25.00
Paid to wife at different times for household expenses	108.00

All of the balance was spent in travelling, excepting the following sums, which are among his reported items of expenditure:

Paid taxes	$ 2.00
Paid dues to societies of which I am a member	6.00
Clothes for myself during year . .	58.90
Mending boots different times . . .	3.00
One valise	4.00
Books purchased	10.50

In fact, Mr. Sylvis gave the entire year an amount of energy and perseverance that few possess, and his wonderful organizing powers to the moulders for the actual expenses incurred in purchasing necessities for himself and family.

The next convention, which met at Pittsburg on Wednesday, January 6th, 1864, was attended by forty-four delegates, representing thirty-three unions; seventeen other unions reported by letter. Mr. Sylvis's report to this body was a very able document. It begins with a concise record of his year's work, which is supplemented with such modest sentences as the following: "It is gratifying to me to witness the present prosperous condition of our organization. At the commencement of the year just closed, a feeling of despondency and many doubts as to the possibility of organizing order out of the chaos, produced by the unfortunate events now and for a long time past agitating the country, and an almost total neglect of duty by those intrusted with the management of our affairs, (the officers of the International Union for the year ending January 1st, 1863, and many of the officers of the local unions, are to blame in this respect), had settled down upon most, if not all, who gave the subject their attention. It was evident to all, at the last convention, that an unusual effort must be made, or all would be lost. That effort has been made, and the results are before the world, and need no further comment from me at this time. I have endeavored faithfully, and to the best of my ability, to carry out the instructions of the last convention. I neither claim nor deserve the credit of the great results that have followed these efforts; I have had the earnest co-operation of every good man, and to them belong the honors, if any there be."

Besides containing a carefully prepared record of the events of the year, the report makes many recommendations bearing upon the government of the organization. Among other things, it advised the issue of a monthly trade journal, and such measures as would secure the permanent establishment of the *Trades Review*, a labor organ then being published in Philadelphia; showing that Mr. Sylvis was a firm believer in the power of printers' ink. The questions of eight hours, co-operation, and others of importance to workingmen, were also ably dwelt upon.

The committee to whom was referred the subject of the president's compensation, reported that Mr. Sylvis had devoted his whole time to the organization, and "most earnestly" recommended that, as he had expended only $279.13 to support himself and family, the sum of $350 additional be donated to him. The report of the committee was adopted; and Mr. Sylvis, who was re-elected president,—receiving thirty-two out of thirty-eight ballots cast,—was voted a salary of $600 for the ensuing year—for which he was to devote his entire time to the duties of his office. Two recommendations contained in the report of Mr. Sylvis to this convention have since culminated in grand results. These were, first, the propriety of establishing international foundries on the co-operative principle; and, second, a resolution that had been adopted at a session of the Machinists' and Blacksmiths' International Union, urging the formation of a national trades assembly. The committee which was appointed upon the first of these recommendations, gave birth to the agitation which has since made the moulders so greatly successful in their application of the principle of co-operation to production, as is evidenced in the existence of several co-operative foundries in Troy, Albany, Cincinnati, and other places, which are now making a great deal of money by assuring to themselves, not only the wages made by ordinary workers, but the profits earned or secured by capitalists in foundries conducted on the wages system. The second recommendation was the cause of the enlistment of the moulders in the movement to establish a national organization of workingmen, which movement ultimately took shape, and to-day exists as the National Labor Union. The greater part of the time of the Buffalo convention was occupied in the discussion of questions of no real interest outside of the trade.

During the year following, Mr. Sylvis devoted himself principally to the building up of the organization in the Eastern States, where he succeeded in establishing thirty-eight new unions, besides eight others in the North-Western States. In addition, he reorganized seven old unions that had suspended, making a total gain for the year of fifty-three unions. In his report he says:

> "Out of all the charters issued since the commencement of my administration, two years ago, but one has been returned; showing a degree of prosperity and stability unequalled in the history of any similar organization on the continent."

In another part of the report, elated at the success which had attended his almost herculean efforts to build up the organization, after comparing its condition at that time with its depressed and disorganized state when he assumed control, he says:

> "In the contemplation of the above facts, and the cheering prospects for the future, can be found sufficient cause for rejoicing. The union, once shaken to its very centre, with column after column falling in ruins around us, has been relieved from surrounding dangers. Confidence, once shaken, has again taken the place of universal despondency, and all is now radiant with the sunshine of hope. Onward, onward, has been the march of progress—meeting with obstacles, but overcoming them; creating new demands, but supplying them. Thus difficulty after difficulty has disappeared before the onward march of determination and energy, until our noble union stands out in bold relief a proud monument, beneath whose gigantic column lies buried the errors and mistakes of the past. Let us all rejoice."

From this time forward the moulders' organization prospered. New unions were formed each succeeding year; trades grievances were obliterated, disputes settled; and the *morale* of the organization improved under the administration of Mr. Sylvis, who was annually re-elected president, and held the position at the time of his death. He made enemies — numbers of them. A fearless disposition such as his could not but prompt its possessor to a course calculated to make an enemy of every submissivist, whose submission meant self-degradation, and of every traitor or madcap who sought to prostitute the power of the union to base or foolish purposes. He made enemies outside of his organization, bitter enemies, who would have wrought his downfall had they possessed half his courage and persistence; for it is a truth, alas! that trades-unionists are generally more willing to listen to the accusers of their officers than to their defenders; more ready to hear their leaders called hard names, vilified and abused, than to afford them that opportunity which should be every accused man's — the opportunity of self-defence. Several of these enemies were men of whom better things might have been expected. These concentrated their efforts in a grand struggle to secure his displacement from the position he honored at the New York session held in January, 1866. But Mr. Sylvis and his friends proved themselves equal to the emergency; and it is a notable fact, that the leaders of the wanton crusade then and there made have never prospered since.

In October, 1865, Mr. Sylvis was visited with a severe affliction in the death of his wife, who had borne him four sons, — Henry Clay, born at Beaver Furnace, April 11th, 1852; Oliver Perry, born August 23d, 1855; Lewis Clark, born April 8th, 1857; and John Martin, born August 30th, 1859, — the three latter in Philadelphia. For nearly two years prior to her death, she had resided at St. Mary's, Pennsylvania; Mr. Sylvis thinking it better that she should be there than in a large city, while he was so much away from home. He brought her back to Philadelphia, and within two weeks of that time she contracted a malignant form of the typhoid fever, of which she died. She was ever a good wife to him, and he felt her loss most acutely.

About a year after this, Mr. Sylvis, wanting a guardian for his boys and a companion whose society should be a pleasant relief from his manifold cares, bethought him of the little girl he had nursed and petted at Hollidaysburg, and who had since grown to womanhood. He went to her home, laid siege to her affections, and in a short time brought her to Philadelphia as his wife. She bore him one other son, whom he named Casper Dent.

In addition to his labors as president of the moulders, Mr. Sylvis was an active and willing sharer of the labors of the Philadelphia Trades Assembly, to which he was long a delegate. During his connection with this body, he made many enemies, especially among strong partisans. He was not of those who shudder at the mere mention of politics in connection with workingmen's organizations. He believed that if it is right for workingmen to resist impositions by strikes, and other expedients peculiar to trades-union movements, it is equally right that they should defend themselves, when the occasion requires it, with the ballot. During the strike of the Philadelphia moulders, the *North American* had taken sides against the strikers, and had published, in support of its position, many misstatements. Some of these were indeed glaring. As an instance, that paper asserted in one of its issues that the moulders had been receiving $4.50 per day; that they had struck and obtained an increase of fifty per cent., thus making their wages $6.75; and that, not content with this outrage, they had again struck for absolute control of the shops. No intelligent reader needs to be told that these statements were false; and no one will wonder that they excited the ire of so zealous a trades-unionist as Mr. Sylvis, and made him an enemy of the publisher of that paper, Morton McMichael.

Mr. Sylvis looked upon an enemy of the labor movement as a personal enemy; and while he was ever inclined to moderation in dealing with those who had done him personal injury, he was slow to forgive those who gave their influence against the side of right and the workingmen. When Morton McMichael became a candidate for Mayor of Philadelphia, Mr. Sylvis remembered what had been done by the *North American* against the moulders, and exerted his influence among the workingmen to secure his defeat. He publicly accused Mr. McMichael of having bitterly opposed the workingmen. Mr. McMichael denied the charge, and protested against what he called "the perversion of organizations intended for wise and beneficial purposes to mischievous partisan agencies." Then a mass meeting of workingmen was called, of which Mr. Sylvis was chairman, and resolutions were passed declaring it the duty of every man who earns his bread by the sweat of his brow, to vote for every man of either party who is more favorable to the cause of labor than his opponent, "and to vote against any man of any party who IS NOW, OR EVER HAS BEEN, AN ENEMY TO WORKINGMEN." There is no doubt that Mr. Sylvis inspired, though he may not have written, these resolutions. This fight against Mr. McMichael was made the foundation of a charge that Mr. Sylvis was working in the interests of the Democrats. This charge he emphatically denied, declaring that his attack was not made against the Republican party; that "the party is distinct from Mr. McMichael, and is not involved in the censure which is directed against him, because he has been the enemy of the workingman; and even in his denial of the charge failed to take ground in their favor." Mr. Sylvis made several speeches at this time, charging Mr. McMichael with having supported what was known as the "Tioga Outrage" on the coal-miners of Pennsylvania, their wives and children, under the provision of the landlord and tenant act, designed to oppress those of the miners who had the manhood to resist tyranny, and taking the ground that if capital can use political power to imprison workingmen for resisting attempted reductions of wages, and can, by political action, make it illegal for workingmen to form unions, as was done, or rather attempted to be done, by the infamous Hastings Bell, the workingmen can and ought to use their political power to counteract such tyranny, and can counteract it in no other way. This fight against Mr. McMichael was a spirited one, and doubtless cost him many votes; but the power of his party was too strong at the time to permit his defeat. Certain it is that it made Mr. Sylvis many enemies, who never could or would be made to believe but that he had been influenced by his Democratic prejudices; and Mr. Sylvis was at that time more of a Democrat than a Republican, though he was little of either.

CHAPTER VI.

CLOSING LABORS, AND DEATH.

FROM Mr. Sylvis's earliest connection with the Iron-Moulders' Union, he had calculated upon the ultimate amalgamation of all workingmen's organizations into one grand body, which, if intelligently controlled, could be made sufficiently powerful to prevent or punish any trespass upon the rights of the toiling millions. At different times he had had many consultations and much correspondence with other prominent trade-unionists and reformers upon the subject. It was left, however, for the Machinists' and Blacksmiths' Union to be the first to make a formal proposition looking to the unification of all trades organizations. That body, at its session in 1863, appointed a committee "to request the appointment of similar committees from other national and international trades-unions, to meet them fully empowered to form a national trades assembly," to facilitate the advancement of the interests of labor, by organizing subordinate trades assemblies. Mr. Sylvis, as has already been mentioned in his report to the Buffalo convention in January, 1864, called attention to the subject as one "well worthy of consideration." The matter was referred to a committee of three, who reported in favor of appointing the committee as requested. The committee was appointed; but the other national trade-unions failing to act, the matter was dropped.

In February, 1866, William Harding, of Brooklyn, then president of the Coachmakers' International Union, being on a visit to Philadelphia, met Mr. Sylvis at his office, and the question of a national trade assembly, or labor union, was thoroughly discussed between them; the result of the consultation being a call for a preliminary meeting in New York City on March 26th, 1866. Mr. Sylvis was unable to be present, but deputized Isaac J. Neal, of Jersey City, to represent the iron-moulders in his stead. This meeting issued a call for a convention to be held in Baltimore, August 20th, 1866, which call was signed by William Harding, John Reid, and John H. Fay. At this time there appeared to be among the prime movers no clearly defined understanding as to the amount or nature of the power that it would be wise or safe to vest with the proposed organization. Upon one point only all agreed, and that was the necessity of some way consolidating the forces of labor in such a manner as to secure a harmonious unity of all the parts. The following extract from the call issued will serve to show that room was left for making it sufficiently broad to be comprehensive of much more than those matters ordinarily involved in trades-unionism:

"The agitation of the question of eight hours as a day's labor has assumed an importance requiring concerted and harmonious action *upon all matters appertaining to the inauguration of labor reforms;*" and "It is essential that a National Congress should be held, to form a basis upon which we may harmoniously and concertedly move in its prosecution."

The convention met according to call, but Mr. Sylvis, being at the time under the care of a physician, was unable to be present. Mr. William Cathers, then president of the Baltimore Trades Assembly, called the convention to order, and named John Hinchcliffe, of Illinois, as temporary chairman. The subjects of eight hours, trades-unions, co-operation, public lands, the national debt, etc., occupied the greater portion of the time of the convention, and committees were appointed to consider and report upon each of those mentioned.

The report of the committee appointed to consider the eight-hour question gave rise to an animated and, at times, excited debate, which consumed by far the "biggest half" of the session, and developed a disposition upon the part of many delegates in favor of a formal recommendation that "no workingman should vote for any aspirant to public office who fails to pledge himself to the eight-hour doctrine." Some went so far as to advocate the immediate establishment of a "National Labor Party;" but while it is evident that nearly all believed in the ultimate necessity for such a party, the majority considered that a start at the time would be premature and unwise. Some few there were who thought it would be best to trust wholly to agitation, and the moral influence of numbers, as an incentive to one or the other of the old parties to take up for advocacy the political questions affecting labor; apparently ignoring the necessity that would still exist for a majority of the workingmen to vote with whatever party might decide to be so liberal, so just, or so mindful of the power of labor; and ignoring, as well, another fact, that it is far easier to induce a man to vote for his own measures, unconnected with others against which he is prejudiced, than it is to make a Democrat out of a Republican, or *vice versa*, or even to induce a member of one party to vote the other ticket for the sake of any particular measure, however important it may be. These latter, however, were few in number, and powerless to stay the tide of popular opinion. Mr. Edward Schleger, of Illinois, who represented the German Workingmen's Association of Chicago, was particularly plain and eloquent in his demand for the immediate formation of a new party. During the debate, he said that he wanted "a specific plan of action. A new party of the people must be in the minority when it first comes into action. But what of that? Time and perseverance will give us victory; and if we are not willing to sacrifice time and employ perseverance, we are not deserving of victory. It is useless to hold conventions, if we fear so greatly to touch the prejudices of others. A new labor party *must* be formed, composed of the elements of American labor. We are shy of fighting the old political parties, but should not be. If we are right, let us go ahead. The Free Soil party originated with a few thousand voters; but if it had not been formed, Lincoln would never have been President of the United States. This great central committe must propose some definite plan of action. A political question is one that is decided at the ballot-box, and *here* must this question be met."

These are sentences picked here and there from his address, which serve to show its tenor. In attestation of their appreciation of his views and abilities, the delegates afterwards elected Mr. Schleger vice-president at large.

Many other delegates favored independent political action in equally eloquent addresses, and nearly all made open acknowledgment of their belief that the movement had necessarily to become a political one before it could hope to succeed in establishing the reforms demanded by the needs of the toiler.

The platform finally adopted declared, in a preamble, that "the alarming encroachments of capital upon the rights of the producing classes of the United States have rendered it imperative that they should calmly and deliberately devise the most effective means by which the same may be arrested." The first resolve was, "That the first and grand desideratum of the hour, in order to deliver the labor of the country from this thraldom, is the enactment of a law whereby eight hours shall be made to constitute a legal day's work in every state of the American Union."

The platform further advised the encouragement of co-operation, deprecated the contract system of prison labor, recommended the support of newspapers devoted exclusively to the interests of the industrial classes, asked for the speedy restoration of the agricultural interests of the Southern States, pledged support to "the sewing women and daughters of toil of the land," called attention to the subject of tenement-houses as "a system sadly in need of reform," and declared that "the whole public domain should be disposed of to settlers only."

The report of the committee on trades-unions and strikes, which was adopted, recommended the organization of all mechanics into trades-unions, and all other workingmen into general labor-unions; a more rigid enforcement of the apprenticeship system as a preventive against filling the country with "botches," and the establishment of workingmen's lyceums, institutes, and reading-rooms. With regard to the subject of strikes, this committee reported it as their "deliberate opinion that, as a rule, they are productive of great injury to the laboring-classes; that many have been injudicious and ill-advised, and the result of impulse rather than principle; that those who have been the fiercest in their advocacy have been the first to advocate submission;" and on these grounds recommended that they "be discountenanced, except as a *dernier ressort*, and after all means for an amicable adjustment have been exhausted;" and that each trades assembly appoint an arbitration committee for the settlement of all disputes between employer and employed, "by the earlier adoption of which means," the committee believed, "a majority of the ill-advised, so-called strikes that had occurred would have been prevented."

This mention of what was done will advise the reader,

in part, of the purposes of the founders of the National Labor Union. The task before them was one of much magnitude; and there is here exhibited a disposition to meet it fairly and squarely, but a doubt as to the means that should be employed. Strikes are discouraged, and arbitration recommended as a proper substitute; but measures are proposed that seem to require a resort to the ballot-box; and yet, while a large number of the delegates were apparently ready to resort to independent political action, and so declared themselves, no recommendation to that effect was made by the organization, though individual recommendations of that kind were numerous.

J. C. C. Whaley, of Washington, D. C., was chosen president. Mr. Whaley is a printer, a gentleman of ability and refinement, though he is but a mechanic, and has been an ardent labor reformer.

After the adjournment of the convention, a committee, headed by John Hinchcliffe, waited upon President Johnson, and informed him of the objects of the organization they had just formed. The President, in response, said he was in sympathy with them as regards convict labor, and the reservation of the public lands for actual settlers, and cited his record to prove his assertion. On the eight-hour question, he said: "As to the number of hours which should constitute a day's work, that is a matter of detail and experience which they could consider and settle as they went along; but he would say he was in favor of the shortest number of hours for a day's work that would accomplish its ends."

Mr. Sylvis was, at this time, publishing for the moulders a thirty-two page monthly, called *The Iron-Moulders' International Journal*, which was ably and creditably conducted; was a complete compendium of labor news from all parts of the world, and a fearless exponent of the principles sought to be established for the good of those who toil in workshops, on the farm, or in the mine. He took greater pride in, and was better satisfied with, this journal than in any other effort of his life; but, for some reason, the moulders ordered its discontinuance after the first year, and, much against Mr. Sylvis's inclination, the order was, of course, executed.

His opinion of what was done at the Baltimore convention is fully set down in an editorial which appeared in the *Journal* for the succeeding month, from which we make the following extract:

"The great event, since our last issue, was the meeting of the Labor Congress in Baltimore on the 20th ultimo. The convention was a great success. We always believed that it would be. It was not only a great success in point of numbers and mental calibre, but its legislation was such that every workingman can look to it with mingled feelings of pride and satisfaction. When we say that the convention was a great success, we do not wish to be understood as indorsing all that was done, or as believing that all was done that should have been; we, however, consider the sins of omission much more numerous than those of commission, and to these only shall we revert at present. It was confidently expected that measures would be adopted looking to the permanent organization of the trades under one head; and that a constitution and rules would be adopted, giving to the new organization a form patterned somewhat after the Congress of the United States, giving to it only recommendatory and specially delegated powers; said constitution to be submitted to the various labor organizations throughout the country for their adoption or rejection; and only such as indorsed them to be entitled to representation in the next convention. This would have given a character and importance to the movement which it does not now possess."

Alluding to the neglect of the convention to provide ways and means, the article adds:

"The fact is, the convention met, held a five days' session, built a splendid railroad track, placed upon it a locomotive complete in all its parts; provided an engineer and numerous assistants, placed them upon the foot-board, told them to go ahead, and then suddenly adjourned without providing wood and water to get up steam; and there the whole machine will stand until the third Monday in August, 1867, when, it is hoped, there will be such a coming together of workingmen as will astonish the oldest inhabitant, and that the work so nobly begun at Baltimore will be completed."

The article concludes:

"We again say the convention was a great success, notwithstanding the selfish and senseless croaking and opposition of some whose vision is so contracted that they cannot see beyond the narrow limits of the little village in which they live."

This article indorses, in a general way, the principles enunciated, and finds fault only because of defects in the plan of organization; on the subject of independent political action he had been for a long time undecided what stand to take. It will be remembered that, as a member of the "committee of thirty-four," just prior to the breaking out of the rebellion, he had favored political action by the workingman. In a card published during his fight against Mr. McMichael, he said, "I will vote and work against any man of any party who opposes the labor movement; and I consider it the duty of every workingman to do the same;" and on sundry other occasions he had spoken and written against certain individuals and cliques who were especially hostile to labor; but yet, as to the propriety of organizing a distinct labor party, his convictions were not strong until after the holding of the Baltimore convention, when he several times publicly declared for the new party. On one occasion he said:

"We have tried the balance-power or make-weight expedient of questioning candidates, and throwing our votes in favor of such as indorsed or were pledged to our interests. How vain and futile this expedient has proven is known to all. It is but a history of broken promises and violated pledges, and invariably ends in exposing our weakness; for, say what you will, men of opposite opinions to the candidate will not trust him in the face of such frequent deceptions. This and other considerations have convinced us that, if we resort to political action at all, we must keep clear of all entangling alliances. With a distinct workingman's party in the field, there can be no distrust, no want of confidence. When it becomes a fixed fact that workingmen can vote for men *of* them and *with* them, the incentive will be sufficient to unite the masses in one grand struggle for victory. We should then know *for whom* and *for what* we voted. Every toiler would feel that he held his destiny in his own hands; and the road to reform would be so direct and open, that none but the corrupt and false-hearted would desert the banner of labor; and the sooner the organization could be rid of such an element, the better for the good and true men of the cause."

Frequently, about this time, he expressed not only his belief in a labor party, but his conviction that the prevailing sentiment of workingmen was in favor of such a move.

With the features of the platform, each and all of them, Mr. Sylvis had frequently expressed his sympathy; and the decision of the convention with regard to strikes tallied exactly with views he had a long time previously pronounced. Knowing that men smarting under a real or imaginary grievance are apt to allow themselves to be led away and controlled by the impulses of the moment, and in many cases to give way to a spirit of retaliation, which is always wrong, from the very commencement of his career he did all he could to prevent unnecessary conflicts; though he always held — as does every properly spirited workingman —

that the right to strike, under sufficient provocation, is a sacred one, and can never be justly interfered with by the government. As president of the moulders, he never once permitted a strike to take place at the expense of the International Union until it was constitutionally sanctioned; not because he feared to take the responsibility, but because he deprecated strikes, — because, as he said in his report to the Boston convention, "he looked upon a strike as a very serious thing, only to be resorted to in extreme cases;" and he had faith in the willingness of the union to maintain strikers, whenever the circumstances justified them in so doing.

Mr. Sylvis believed in the principles enunciated at Baltimore; in fact, they were his principles before the Baltimore convention was held. He believed also in the propriety and feasibility of going farther than the convention had ventured to go; and he saw many points of weakness in the plan laid down for the perpetuation of the National Labor Union, by which name the Baltimore convention had decided to call the organization it had formed; and immediately upon his recovery from the sickness which had prevented his participating in its labors, entered with his usual energy and vim into the plans of those who devoted themselves during the year following to perfecting the work then scarcely laid out.

The following year the National Labor Union met in Chicago. It was well attended, and Mr. Sylvis took an active and prominent part in its proceedings. One who was present as a delegate afterwards said, in an article upon Mr. Sylvis:

"We first met him at Chicago in 1867, and recognized at once what we had felt the want of at Baltimore — the presence of the leader in a great movement. In a quiet, unassuming way, in a few brief sentences, he disposed of question after question, invariably carrying the congress with him almost unanimously, and silencing all opposition."

It was at this session that the financial feature was added to the platform. To this phase of the problem Mr. Sylvis had devoted considerable study, and his advocacy contributed no little towards securing its adoption. He was not a willing candidate for the presidency, but received a hearty support for the position from a number of the delegates. Several ballots had to be taken before a choice was effected; and at one time, despite his protestations that he was not a candidate, he barely escaped an election. The idea of a national labor bureau was broached at this convention, for the first time, by Mr. Sylvis. He argued, in its favor, that labor is the most important of all material interests; that upon it all others hinged; and that, if there is any virtue in giving to any interest a separate and distinct department of the government to protect and nourish it — and there certainly is, — labor is the interest, of all others, entitled to that consideration. The demand for a bureau was unanimously made a part of the platform. The Chicago convention attracted a much greater share of public attention than its predecessor. Many things left undone at Baltimore were done at Chicago; but after the adjournment, it was ascertained that the plan of organization was yet by no means perfect; so that but little was done during the year in the way of formally organizing labor unions.

Many individual efforts were, however, made to induce one or the other of the existing parties to indorse the principles of the National Labor Union. Leading Democrats were consulted, and quite a number seemed willing that their platform should be modified so as to include a portion at least of the demands of the National Labor Union; and at one time there seemed to be good reasons for believing that the party would, in return for the vote of the workingmen, agree to support their principles. Meanwhile, propositions to run an independent labor reform ticket were numerously made. The *Workingman's Advocate* urged Samuel F. Cary, of Ohio, as a fit candidate for the presidency. The *Welcome Workman*, then published in Philadelphia by Jonathan C. Fincher, while deprecating the putting of an independent ticket in the field, proposed to add to the strength of the ticket, which it was intended to head with Cary's name, by suggesting Wm. H. Sylvis for the vice-presidency. The *People's Weekly*, of Baltimore, which advocated the platform of the National Labor Union but supported the Democratic party, named for the consideration of that party, for president, George H. Pendleton; for vice-president, Wm. H. Sylvis. Other papers talked of Chase and Sylvis as a good ticket. The *People's Weekly* published a short sketch of Mr. Sylvis, and pushed his claims vigorously; but the subject of all this agitation worked quietly and determinedly on in the interest of the national labor movement and of his trade organization; and although it is probable that he would have accepted a nomination either from the Democrats or from the labor reformers as an independent party, he made no effort to secure either.

The third session or congress of the National Labor Union met in New York, in August, 1868. By this time the organization had obtained great notoriety, and not a little popularity. Its principles had spread and been studied until their converts from among men of all classes and conditions of life were numbered by thousands. It had commenced to exert some political influence, and politicians were beginning to court its power. Its principles were such as could not be established except through the connivance, and with the assistance, of one or the other of the old parties, or the establishment of a new labor party.

As you already know, the proposition to form such a party had been more than once publicly made; and papers published in the labor interest spoke confidently of the early approach of the day when the army of labor, reunited, should deposit its ballots for right, and against the money tyranny. The official documents of the national labor union, each and all of them, indicated an intention — which nearly all in the movement shared — of resorting to independent political action as soon as the proper time should arrive. Yet there were a number whose partisan prejudices were so strong that they could not abide the idea that labor should contaminate itself by touching politics; just as though the contamination would not be greater from contact with the old and corrupt parties than it would have been through the accomplishment of the project to form a new and pure party. Trades-unionists, who had been toadied and petted by politicians because of their power with the workingmen, saw that power waning. Willing slaves to party name were affrighted, and even good men were exercised and cautious lest the new party should follow in the footsteps of its predecessors, and become corrupt and an instrument of wrong in the hands of designing men, instead of, as intended, a power for justice to the toiler. The more bitter of the opponents of the new idea concentrated their efforts, and entered into an organized campaign against those features of the platform which seemed to require a resort to the ballot-box.

The following extract from a letter written by Mr. Sylvis to the New York State Workingmen's Assembly will serve to show the opinion entertained by Mr. Sylvis upon the propriety of workingmen taking to the ballot for relief, after he had had so much and such varied experience as a trades-unionist:

"I would ask of the assembly, if it can consistently indorse the platform of principles of the national labor movement, to recommend to the local unions in the State the necessity of connecting themselves with the National Labor Union. I would like very much if two or three short, positive, and pointed resolutions would be adopted, setting forth the views of the assembly on this important matter.

"The very greatest drawback to the labor reform movement is the fact that the trades-unions hold themselves aloof from the movement. This is not only a singular, but a very unfortunate fact. If it were possible to make all the trades-unions in the country see the importance of this movement, and appreciate the fact that if we can succeed in establishing our monetary system as the law of the land, it would so change the whole face of society as to do away with the necessity of trades-unions entirely; there would be no trouble to accomplish the whole labor reform movement in a very short time. I have long since come to the conclusion that no permanent reform can ever be established through the agency of trades-unions as they are now and have been conducted. They are purely defensive in their character, and experience has taught all of us, who have been for any considerable time connected with them, that to keep them alive at all requires a continued struggle and a vast expenditure of time and money. The organization I have the honor to represent has spent money enough within the past ten years to have effected an entire revolution in our monetary system, and secure whatever congressional legislation we may need.

"Within the past ten years we have spent a million and a half of dollars; and to-day we have the same struggles to maintain ourselves we ever had, and there will be no end to it until the workingmen of the country wake up to the necessity of seeking a remedy through the ballot-box. All the evils under which we groan are legislative, that is, they are the results of bad laws; and there is no way to reach the matter, and effect a cure, but by a repeal of those laws, and this can only be done through political action. You must excuse me for occupying so much of your time on this point; its very great importance must be my excuse."

The financial features fell in for an especial share of abuse and ridicule; the objects of the leaders were misinterpreted; and the leaders maligned and accused of being in the movement from motives of self-interest. During the session a strenuous effort was made to expunge from the platform the portions we have mentioned; but the true, tried, and fearless men, headed by Sylvis, fought the good fight of defence, and came off victors. The debates were lively, and the platform ably sustained.*

Mr. Sylvis was elected president at this session; and upon taking the chair was loudly called upon for a speech. Thinking that most too much time had already been devoted to speech-making, he took the gavel in his hand, and said, "I have made all the speech I am going to make this morning. The union will now proceed to business." The enemies of the platform having been utterly routed, the further proceedings of the convention were harmonious and profitable, inasmuch as little time was expended in useless palaver, and all devoted themselves with a will to the business incident to the occasion. The New York *Sun* made mention of several of the leading delegates to this session. We make the following extract from its article:

"A finer body of workingmen has never convened in this city, than the delegates to the labor congress now in session here. All of them represent labor organizations, but all do not labor themselves with hand and muscle. Many of them have achieved a wide reputation by their writings and speeches upon co-operative labor reform, and kindred topics. Foremost among them all stands Wm. H. Sylvis, president of the Iron-Moulders' International Union of North America, whose name is as familiar as household words to the workingmen of America, both by his writings and his speeches. He is a medium-sized

* The platform there adopted will be found in another part of the book, with some additions.

man, strongly built, of florid complexion, light beard and moustache, and a face and eyes beaming with intelligence. Perseverance and determination are as plainly written in his countenance as if the words were penned there with indelible ink. Mr. Sylvis has done more for labor organizations, and co-operation in America, than any other living man. By his individual efforts, the iron-moulders of the United States, and of the British provinces, have been organized into local unions, now numbering one hundred and ninety-eight, and these again into one grand international union, which now numbers over ten thousand members. Mr. Sylvis is self-made. He never went to school six days in his life, and when first elected secretary of his local union, was unable to write his name or keep the books of his society. But he is a man of brain and of indomitable perseverance, and such a man could not long remain in the bondage of ignorance. Since the organization of the Iron-Moulders' Union, in 1853, they have spent over one million five hundred thousand dollars on strikes and lock-outs,—a large sum in itself, but small compared with the advantage accruing to the trade therefrom. The union has now several co-operative foundries throughout the country, six of them being in this State; and they aim, by co-operation, to own and possess all the work of their trade on this continent some day. It is with them only a question of time. These foundries return as high as eighty-three per cent. upon the capital invested. In the debates of the labor congress, Mr. Sylvis does not say much, but when he speaks, he generally carries the majority of the house with him."

Mr. Sylvis's educational advantages are here somewhat under-estimated, but in the main the article is correct. The compliment paid him in the closing sentence was certainly a deserved one, as all who have had the pleasure of listening to his simple eloquence and unanswerable logic can testify.

Mr. Sylvis returned from New York prepared to do for the National Labor Union just what he had done for the

Iron-Moulders' International Union, when the helm of that organization was placed in his hands. On October 1st, he issued a circular, from which the following is an extract:

"The second annual session of the National Labor Union has just closed. I had the high honor to be called upon to act as president of the National Labor Union by the unanimous voice of the delegates.

"Having accepted the position, I now propose to go to work, and I shall expect every man and woman who desires to see the success of our movement will go to work. We have undertaken a gigantic task — a social and political revolution such as the world has never seen. To succeed, within a reasonable time, it will require the united energies and persistent efforts of every friend of the cause. While I promise you that I shall not be found wanting in energy, perseverance, and patience, you must not forget that I can do nothing without your co-operation.

"The convention resolved to proceed at once to the organization of a 'Labor Reform Party, having for its object the election of representative men to our State and national councils.'

"The organization of a new party,— a workingman's party,— for the purpose of getting control of Congress and the several State Legislatures, is a huge work; but it can and must be done. We have been the tools of professional politicians of all parties long enough; let us now cut loose from all party ties, and organize a workingman's party, founded upon honesty, economy, and equal rights and equal privileges to all men. The day of monster monopolies and class legislation must come to a close. Let our motto be, 'Our God, our country, our currency.' Money has ruled us long enough; let us see if we cannot rule money for a time. We want equal taxation upon all property according to its real value, no matter whether it be in the shape of houses or government bonds. Let our cry be REFORM — down with a moneyed aristocracy and up with the people.

"Now let every man and woman go to work. Do not wait. Remember that 'procrastination is the thief of time.' Let each one start out with a determination that we will make the

President in 1872, and that between now and then we will control Congress and the State Legislatures. If we will but set out in earnest to accomplish this great work, obnoxious laws will soon disappear from our statute-books; plain, practical laws for the protection and encouragement of the deserving will take their place, and the drones who fatten upon the earnings of the poor will be compelled to make an honest living or starve. Don't let us wait to be pushed into a corner. Stop acting on the defensive — take the aggressive; make war upon every opposing power; have faith in the right, and success will come. I ask every one who may have a suggestion to make or a question to ask, to put it on paper and send it to me. I shall proceed, with the aid of others, to adopt a system of operations as fast as possible."

The promulgation of this circular gave rise to considerable agitation, and elicited a large number of letters from all parts of the country. These encouraged Mr. Sylvis to issue another circular, dated November 16th, in which he alluded to the interest already awakened, and declared himself ready to issue charters.

This second circular concludes as follows:

" A number of applications for charters have already been received, and the organization is gradually assuming a definite shape. There are about three thousand trades-unions in the United States. The members of these unions are more generally acquainted with the principles of our platform, and the objects of the National Labor Union, than the rest of the people. Efforts should therefore be made to have them take hold of this matter with energy. These three thousand well-organized unions see and *feel* that, by the adoption of the principles embodied in our platform by the national government, more will be done to establish an equitable standard of wages, a fair division of profits, reasonable hours, and a universal emancipation from the power of capital, than can ever be accomplished by trades-unions as now organized. *We must show them that when a just monetary system has been established, there will no longer exist a necessity for trade-unions.* I therefore call upon every trades-union in the land to take hold of this matter in earnest. Let us adopt the motto of General Jackson: 'Put your shoulder to the wheel, trust in God, and push along the column.' There is rapidly building up in this country a privileged moneyed aristocracy, such as nowhere else exists. The whole productive powers of the nation have become subservient to and dependent upon this moneyed aristocracy. They control the whole currency of the country, and with the money control the government.

"Our people are being divided into two classes — the rich and the poor, the producers and the non-producers; the busy bees in the industrial hive, and the idle drones who fatten upon what they steal.

"The working-people of our nation, white and black, male and female, are sinking to a condition of serfdom. Even now a slavery exists in our land worse than ever existed under the old slave system. The centre of the slave-power no longer exists south of Mason's and Dixon's line. It has been transferred to Wall Street; its vitality is to be found in our huge national bank swindle, and a false monetary system. The war abolished the right of property in man, but it did not abolish slavery. This movement we are now engaged in is the great anti-slavery movement, and we must push on the work of emancipation until slavery is abolished in every corner of our country. Our objective point is a new monetary system, a system that will take from a few men the power to control the money, and give to the people a cheap, secure, and abundant currency. This done, and the people will be free. Then will come such a social revolution as the world has never witnessed; honest industry in every department will receive its just reward, and public thieves will be compelled to make an honest living or starve. LET US ALL GO TO WORK."

It was with such appeals as this one, that Mr. Sylvis soon succeeded in awakening the dormant energies of labor reformers everywhere, in increasing and organizing sentiment, and bringing application after application for charter to his office. His position on the subject of trades-unions was one that required considerable courage for a man in his circumstances to take; but he had the courage, and, knowing it to be right, took it, regardless of the possible consequences to himself. The sentence in the above circular which we have italicized, shows that, by this time, he had learned from experience to look upon trades-unions as mere preparatory institutions, without the power to do other than defensive battle, and frequently unequal to that task — but schools of training, in which workingmen might and ought to learn how, and acquire the discipline necessary, to enable them to accomplish their work of reform.

He wrote to everybody whom he thought would co-operate with him; in short, devoted a goodly portion of his time, and every penny he could spare (for the National Labor Union collected little or no revenue at this time), to the work of agitation and organization.

On the 6th of February, 1869, in company with Richard Trevellick, his successor as president of the National Labor Union, he started from Wilmington, Del., on a tour through the South, with the threefold object of resuscitating and reinvigorating some old moulders' unions that were languishing, organizing new ones, and spreading the principles of the National Labor Union. He was unusually short of funds at this time; and his trip was therefore not so profitable as it would otherwise have been. But his work for the moulders was well done; and he succeeded also in sowing the seeds of the National Labor Union in many places to such purpose that labor unions sprang up, and were represented at the conventions held the following August. During this trip, he conceived an affection for the Southern climate, and, upon his return, talked much of going there to live, should an opportunity occur. He conversed with leading Southern statesmen and business men, and in several instances secured their hearty co-operation in the course in which his whole soul and being were enlisted.

Mr. Sylvis worked from this time forward almost up to the day of his death as it seemed he only could work, taking advantage of every chance offered to force the principles of the National Labor Union before the people and before the public men. Scarcely a meeting of workingmen was held in any part of the country, but he was there, in person or by letter, advocating those principles, and asking indorsement and co-operation. He had become joint proprietor of *The Workingman's Advocate,* published simultaneously in Chicago and Philadelphia, which was the official organ of the National Labor Union; and found time, amid all his other labors, to contribute to its columns many articles upon the several phases of the movement; and his articles were always terse, and written with a view of reaching the common understanding, and not, as is too frequently the case with writers, for the purpose of exhibiting a mastery of language. His letters to the attorney-general, and others in official position, were evidence of his wonderful pertinacity, and that indomitable courage which made him fearless of any controversy, no matter with whom it might be, after he had once assured himself that right was upon his side. A letter, which gives evidence of this spirit, was written to President Johnson in the fall of 1869. The wages of the moulders and other mechanics in the navy-yard at Charlestown, Mass., were reduced below what was being paid outside.

Mr. Sylvis went to Washington, and called upon the President with a statement of the grievance, afterwards going to Secretary Welles, who promised to order an investigation. A commission was afterwards delegated with the duty of ascertaining the rate of wages paid by private parties. This commission reported, and upon that report the commandant insisted upon a reduction. Then the moulders themselves, under the direction of Mr. Sylvis, had a statement prepared, showing the difference between the wages paid in the yard and those paid outside, which was sworn to and sent to the secretary of the navy, by whom it was transmitted to the commandant. That officer answered that the matter had been investigated by the commission, which had reported adversely to any change.

Upon receipt of the information, Mr. Sylvis wrote the letter referred to. He said:

"Here is an injustice practised upon as hard working and poorly paid men as there are in the service of the government, and we cannot believe that you will permit it to continue. Our sworn statement is true, notwithstanding the report of the commission. We do not say that the commission has done an intentional wrong; but they did not go at their work in a manner to learn the truth. Who they went to, and how they obtained their information, is unknown to us; but *we do know* that we had no voice in the matter. None of our men were on the commission; none of our men were before it to give evidence; nor was any moulder consulted. If that is what the navy department calls an investigation, we wish to be delivered from any more of them. We have made a sworn statement that the wages paid in the yard are less than are paid outside.

"That statement is in the hands of the secretary of the navy, who has acted upon it as a false statement, because the commandant and his commission have said something else. I suppose he considers our sworn statement of no weight alongside of the naked assertion of the comman-

8

dant. The commandant is a government official, and we are *only* workingmen. We think it would be more to the credit of the government, if the salaries of a whole host of office-holders who receive from ten to fifty times as much as we do, and do much less work, were reduced, instead of endeavoring to reduce expenses by cutting down the wages of the laborer, who, at best, can hardly make both ends meet. We again assert the reduction of our wages to be an outrage, and against it we desire to offer an earnest protest. Believing that when the facts are made known to you, you will interpose your authority and instruct the secretary of the navy to countermand the order by which our wages have been reduced, I am, &c."

This letter he sent to Samuel F. Cary, then a member of Congress, to be by him delivered to the President.

In the letter of transmittal he said: "I desire you to read this letter before presenting it. You may think it very strong; but it is just what I wish to say, just what I would say, could I see Mr. Johnson. We have been grossly abused in this matter, and we intend to fight it to the bitter end."

Mr. Sylvis's efforts during the several months immediately preceding his death were directed to the securing of a large representation at the Philadelphia session.

Generals Cary and Butler had both made speeches in Congress in indorsement of the monetary system of the National Labor Union; and Senator Sprague, though he had not indorsed that system, had at least made a damaging *exposé* of the evils of the old system. These speeches, and a letter which had been written to President Grant by John Maguire, of St. Louis, at Mr. Sylvis's request, in which the plans and purposes of the National Labor Union were dwelt upon with ability and at length, were widely circulated from Mr. Sylvis's office, and letters were continually being sent to friends of the movement everywhere. These efforts, together with Mr. Sylvis's southern trip and his frequent appeals made through the newspapers and on the stump, added much to the wide-spread interest already felt, and assured a larger attendance than had been present at any previous convention.

But it was ordained that he should not live to witness the fulfilment of that assurance. For several years he had not enjoyed good health, though he was seldom so sick as to require him to cease work. He ate very rapidly, and without paying proper attention to the necessity for masticating his food, and thus, by forcing his stomach to do what his teeth were made for, impaired his digestion, and contracted the disease which ended in his death. This at least is the opinion of those who were intimately associated with him at the time.

On the morning of Thursday, July 22d, he came to the office as usual, and commenced the preparation of his address to the National Labor Union, which he intended should be a complete *résumé* of what had been accomplished since his accession to the presidency, but shortly after felt so unwell that he was compelled to leave for home. At five o'clock his family physician was summoned, who pronounced his ailing to be a severe attack of inflammation of the bowels, but expressed the belief that the disease would speedily succumb to the remedies prescribed. His hopes or predictions were unrealized, as a restless night was spent, the disease increasing hourly in intensity. On Friday he was cheered by the arrival of his friend, Richard Trevellick, who, up to the hour of his death, continued his constant attendant, and ministered to his necessities. On Saturday he seemed considerably revived; so much so, indeed, as to make buoyant the spirits of his anxious friends, and encourage the hope that the crisis had been passed.

These hopes were of short duration, for on Sunday morning it was deemed expedient to summon additional aid. Consequently a consultation was held, and the terrible truth was made known that his sickness was unto death, of which fact he already seemed to be aware.

On Monday morning at nine o'clock a great change for the worst had taken place, the disease having continued to baffle all the aid and skill of his physicians. At midnight his spiritual adviser, the Rev. Mr. Kemp, pastor of the Fitzwater Street Methodist Episcopal Mission Church, was summoned, and at his request engaged in prayer. In reply to the inquiry if he had any fears in view of his approaching dissolution, and if his mind was at peace, he calmly replied, "If it pleases God to take me, I have no fears of death; I believe I am grounded in the true faith; Christ has pardoned my sins." At two o'clock, when asked by his wife how he felt, he said, "Go to bed, birdie, you will make yourself sick by waiting so much." At twenty minutes past three, he again asked Mr. Kemp to supplicate the throne of grace, and while so engaged a heavenly light seemed to overspread his countenance. Fervently clasping his hands, he exclaimed, "Glory to God, glory to God; I am going home to Christ; I *know* my sins are all forgiven." These were his last words, though he was conscious to the moment of his departure. He continued growing fainter and weaker until twenty-five minutes to six o'clock, when his peaceful spirit burst its tenement of clay and took its flight to its eternal home. And so passed from earth to heaven one of the best, the purest, and the grandest men that the nineteenth century has produced.

For several years prior to his death, Mr. Sylvis was associated with the temperance movement, and in its ranks was a zealous advocate of the cold-water doctrine. He had also become a regular member of the Methodist Church, and an active Sunday-school worker.

The news of the death of the chieftain of the labor movement was soon telegraphed to all parts of the country, and words of condolence for the widow and friends soon came pouring in. All in the labor movement felt that they had lost their best man.

The funeral, which took place on Friday morning, July 30th, was largely attended by representatives of the movement from all parts of the country. The iron-moulders of Philadelphia participated *en masse*, and nearly all the unions in neighboring localities were represented by delegations. His temperance lodge, Minnehaha Circle, Temple of Honor, several workingmen's societies, and a large number of personal friends, were also in line; but among all the long line of mourners that followed his body to its burial-place, none seemed to be more deeply affected than his Sabbath-school class boys, who had learned to love their teacher for his invariable good-nature, and the skill with which he portrayed to their young minds the rewards in store for those who lead a righteous life. The Rev. Mr. Kemp's funeral sermon, which was preached from the text, "My ways are not as your ways, nor my thoughts as your thoughts; for as the heavens are high above the earth, so are my ways above your ways, my thoughts above your thoughts," left scarcely a dry eye in the homely little structure at which he worshipped, and where it was delivered. It was an eloquent and fitting tribute to the virtues and well-earned fame of the deceased.

The body was laid in Laurel Hill Cemetery, situated on the bank of the romantic Schuylkill, above the city, where now slumbers the mortal remains of a great and good man, a worthy citizen, a lovely husband, a never failing friend, and a kind and indulgent parent.

A most fitting conclusion to this work is the following beautiful tribute from affection's pencil to the virtues of a departed hero, a eulogy delivered by his business partner and bosom friend, A. C. Cameron, of Illinois, before the Philadelphia congress of the National Labor Union:

EULOGY BY MR. A. C. CAMERON.

THERE are times, Mr. President and gentlemen, alike in seasons of sorrow and joy, when language fails to convey the emotions of the human soul; times when the heart, knowing its own grief, would fain hide it in its inmost recesses and cherish the feelings it cannot express. Such, I am sure, are the feelings of all present who truly appreciate the character and loss of our dear departed friend, William H. Sylvis. The death of a good man is a calamity always to be deplored. The loss of such a man at such a time, and under such circumstances, is one of those inscrutable dispensations which must remain among the *arcana* of him

> "Who moves in a mysterious way,
> His wonders to perform;
> Who plants his footsteps in the sea,
> And rides upon the storm."

To a character of such a scope, to a mind so fertile, possessed of such resources and God-given powers, I feel myself unable to do justice. Fortunately, the life and memory of such a man require no eulogium at my hands. The shafts of malice and the tongue of praise can neither detract from nor add to a fame which was secured by a life-long devotion to the interests of oppressed humanity. His life is the best panegyric; his character his best epitaph, and a glorious legacy. Essentially a self-made man, born in poverty and raised in obscurity, thrown upon his own resources in early boyhood, friendless and alone, by his talents, indomitable energy, and force of character, he came to be recognized as one of the foremost men of the nation; and there are those here who deem it no flattery or flight of fancy to state that the prospects of his one day securing the highest office within the gift of the American people, was second to that of no living man. Under these circumstances I shall not attempt a delineation of his character, but shall simply and briefly refer to a few of the more prominent traits which commanded and received the admiration of all. Prominent among the most peculiar features of his character were his indomitable energy and perseverance; and it is doubtless owing, in a great measure, to the possession of these traits, that his remarkable success may be attributed. Failure was a word which had been stricken from his vocabulary. Attempt meant success. To dare was to do. The difficulties before which others would have quailed, disappeared before his magic influence and exhaustless resources, and were invariably accepted as incentives to more persistent effort. His action, however, resembled more the brilliancy of the fixed star than the flash of the meteor; was based more on the principle that it is the constant dripping which wears away the stone, than on that erratic, dazzling, Napoleonic genius which embellishes utopian and impracticable schemes; systematic, methodical, eminently practical in all his transactions, his faith was based on the weapons of truth and the intelligence and independence of the American people. His simplicity, force, and independence of character, and his ability to transfer his views and his courage to those with whom he was brought into contact, was marvellous in the extreme. William H. Sylvis was no sycophant; he courted neither the smiles nor the frowns of those in power. Conscious of his own integrity and the success of those principles to which his life was devoted, with a faith that never faltered and a hope that never died, he pursued the even tenor of his way, and pressed on to the goal of his ambition — the arrival of that time when

> "Man to man, the world o'er,
> Shall brothers be, and a' that;"

when tyranny and oppression of every kind and character shall be uprooted and destroyed, and when the freemen of our country shall occupy that proud position which God in his kind providence intended they should occupy. Inexorable in the right — as God gave him to see the right — neither threats nor favors could swerve him from his conscientious conviction. The beautiful lines of Cowper may here be appropriately quoted:

> "No meretricious graces to beguile," &c.

His enlarged views; his comprehensive judgment; his splendid executive ability; his catholic spirit, and thorough knowledge of human nature — each of which is worthy of a eulogy, all of which he possessed in an eminent degree — were qualifications which peculiarly adapted him for the responsible position to which he was called, which he filled with so much honor to himself and benefit to the country at large, and which is as well known to my hearers as to myself. As a writer, he was pointed and forcible, and possessed, in an eminent degree, the happy faculty of saying just what he meant, and enabling his readers to comprehend his meaning — features which any successful journalist can duly appreciate. He was no respecter of persons. The wrong was denounced, whether in high places or low; while many and many a wrong-doer has been exposed, and many a tyrant made to wince beneath his trenchant blows. In his social relations, as a bosom friend and confidant, I had the pleasure of knowing him intimately and well; and in all our associations I found him high-toned, noble, generous, and true; while in this connection, as in his public career, every personal aspiration was subordinate to a desire for the "success of the great cause." To the bereaved consort and afflicted family, let us tender our condolence. May He who tempers the wind to the shorn lamb, and who watches over even the sparrow's fall, give her strength to bear with Christian resignation the mysterious dispensation, and the assurance that she shall meet him beyond the swelling floods, where death and parting are never known. And now that he has gone from our midst; that his active, plodding brain has been stilled forever; that his words of counsel and encouragement will be heard no more, let it be our highest ambition to carry to successful completion the good work so gloriously begun. Let us re-pledge our devotion to the dissemination of those principles to which his life was devoted, and in the attainment of which the welfare of the human race is involved; and although we may not be able to emblazon our names in letters of such shining light, or engrave them high on the scroll of fame as he, yet we shall be emulating his virtues by following his example, by making the precepts which made him so truly great our precepts, leave behind us the fragrance of a well-spent life, and a memory to be honored and revered.

Then up and be doing. The night has ended.

THE FALLEN CHIEFTAIN.

BY JOHN JAMES.

A NOBLE spirit's fled;
  A gallant heart is torn;
A soul that knew no dread,
  To its native realm is borne.
The flock have lost their herd—
  His voice is silent now;
No more we'll hear his kindly word,
  Nor view his manly brow;
But here in sorrow must deplore
That such a *hero's* gone before.

Our star of hope is dimm'd,
  A cloud is o'er it cast;
The mind that ever trimm'd
  Our lamps, has thought its last.
The gem in all our crown,
  The purest, brightest, best,
Death ruthlessly has claimed his own,
  And pierced his noble breast;
While comfortless, whole thousands mourn
To think he never can return.

The oak, so strong, is fell'd,
  And withering now lies low;
How oft it has repell'd
  Storms that would o'er us blow.
But now, alas! no more,
  It towers into the sky,—
With branches spreading widely o'er,
  To shelter *all* thereby—
Fallen, mould'ring in the clay,
While we lament the fatal day.

Alas! to know he's gone—
  Such honesty and worth;

How strange 't is ever prone,
  To quit so soon this earth!
So we must still bewail,
  And see the virtuous die,
While villany may live and rail,
  And cheat, deceive, and *lie.*
Yet goodness, greatness, truth, and zeal,
Must sink beneath death's tyrant heel.

Thou must have felt a throe,
  Oh! death, to kill a heart,
Who but to *wrong* a foe —
  A *man* in every part.
He did not fear thy blow,
  Nor shrank he from thy dart;
He felt it was his time to go,
  And yielded to its smart.
The war's unequal thou dost make,
And sweetness still thou lovest to take.

Mourn, ye reformers, mourn,
  Your leader is no more;
From forth your midst is torn
  The greatest in the *core.*
Let every heart sincere,
  In memory let fall
A heartfelt, sympathetic tear
  Upon his humble pall:
Our simple tribute to the mind
That has no equal left behind.

But on some Joshua may
  The heavenly command
Devolve to lead the way
  Into the Promised Land.
Or, as on Elisha, may
  The inspired mantle fall
Upon some one, to-day,
  Designed to lead us all
Unto that great and happy goal
That SYLVIS meant was for the whole.

SPEECHES.

Address delivered at Buffalo, N. Y., January, 1864.

Mr. Chairman and Gentlemen of the Convention:—In rising in my place to address you upon this occasion, I am fully impressed with the magnitude of the undertaking, the importance of the occasion, and the expectations of yourselves and those assembled here to listen to what I may have to say. I am also oppressed with a sense of my own littleness and inability to cope with the great questions before me.

I, however, believe it to be the duty of every man occupying a public position as a leader in this labor movement, to place himself upon record, and give to the world his views, however humble they may be. This, sir, must be my apology for occupying a small portion of your valuable time.

We come to these conventions as the representatives of a great people—of a mechanical community, having an organization second to none on this continent. We hold a few sessions, and pass a few laws, in our opinion necessary, and then return to our constituents with a dry and condensed report of our proceedings, without a word of the discussions arising from a consideration of the various questions, leaving the people most interested in these laws in total darkness as to the great principles upon which we have founded this legislation. I believe that a due regard for the interests and welfare of our constituents demands at our hands an exposition of our views.

This labor question, Mr. Chairman, is one that has troubled the minds of men for centuries past. Men in all ages and sections of the civilized world have been found who have endeavored, by laborious and extended writings and researches, to solve the great problem of political and social science, and the origin and distribution of the wealth of nations. Thousands of volumes have been written by as many different men, upon the principles that underlie the present social structure. Unfortunately, these economists have universally belonged to that class which they are pleased to call the "higher orders," the "cream of society," the "privileged classes," etc. Men whose hands were never soiled by honest labor; men entirely destitute of all practical knowledge of the wants and condition of the masses; consequently, their ideas have ever sympathized with the interests of capital, while the rights of labor, and indeed labor itself, except so far as it may be made an element of wealth in the hands of these "privileged classes," have been entirely ignored. These men have, with but one or two exceptions, taken the ground and founded their arguments upon the assumed facts, that the soil is the source of all wealth. That there is an identity of interests between labor and capital, that labor and capital are copartners, that the two elements go hand-in-hand, and constitute one vast firm, who carry on and control the vast business of the world; that labor is an article of commerce, and that the price of labor is regulated by the laws of supply and demand.

Nothing, to my mind, can be more absurd than all these propositions. It may be considered presumption in so humble an individual as I to set myself up in opposition to these great authors, but, nevertheless, I claim the right to do so.

Assuming the position that labor is the real source of all wealth, and that its legitimate and proper distribution depends upon a proper and well-regulated political and social system, I shall proceed to discuss the several questions connected with the subject from that stand-point. The condition of the toiling millions forming, as I believe they do, the foundation of all wealth, and the substratum of political and social life, should engage the earnest attention of good men in every station of life; for it must be evident that, unless the condition of the laboring-classes be in strict harmony with the social well-being and commercial wealth of the nation, the people must live in constant dread of a thousand evils that must arise from a neglect of this great principle.

Adam Smith, in his "Wealth of Nations," lays it down as a great truth, that "unless the material comfort of the working-classes in a commonwealth progress in a parallel ratio with the increasing wealth of the community, there is really no progress of any extent or value made by that nation;" its ultimate fate will be retrogression and decay. No question of equal importance to this can be entertained. The amount of national wealth, the progress of manufacture, the cultivation of the soil, commercial credit, civil and religious liberty,— these are all questions of great moment, but not to be compared with the social and material condition of the laboring-classes — for they are the producers of all wealth; they uphold the entire political and social fabric, and without them capital would have no commercial existence, nor civilization the elements of expansion and progress.

Labor then being the foundation of all capital, and taking upon itself the divine mission to give birth and success to civilization and human progress, must have an eternal claim upon the value and profits of its own productions; this claim appears to be entirely forgotten by the wealthy, or, if not forgotten, entirely ignored. This view of this interesting subject, that labor has a claim upon its own productions—a right to the profits of its own investments, because it is the foundation, the corner-stone of the entire political and social structure, is one worthy the consideration of every man who toils, whether with his hands or his head. I shall give it a proper consideration when I pass to the subject of co-operation.

Ages upon ages have rolled away since "commerce set its mark of selfishness, the signet of its all-enslaving power, upon a shining ore, and called it gold;" and from then to now a gradual concentration or centralization of wealth has been going on until now, in many of the older countries, the entire wealth of the nation is centred in the hands of a few individuals, and the many are their victims and their bondsmen.

It has ever been the study and purpose of these men, who arrogate to themselves the right to the enjoyment of all the power and wealth of the world, to make labor entirely subservient to their will—to own it and use it as a part of their machinery, with no other expense than that required to furnish the fuel to keep the machine in motion—all the necessary repairs having to be made by the machine itself. And experience teaches us that in every country they have partly succeeded in their diabolical plan, and in those places where they have obtained control of the law-making power, they have succeeded entirely.

If these things be so, and who will contradict them, what becomes of this so much talked-of identity of interests? In denying the existence of an identity of interests between labor and capital, I do not wish to be understood as saying that there is no identity of interests between *labor* and *money*. I deny that there is an identity of interest between *labor* and *capitalists*. The fact that capital denies to labor the right to regulate its own affairs, would take from the workingman the right to place a valuation upon his own labor, destroys at once the theory of an identity of interests; if, as is held by them, the interests of the two are identical, and their positions and relations mutual, there would be no interference whatever one with another; the workingman would be left free to place his own price upon his labor, as capitalists are to say what interest or profits they shall have upon money invested. This identity of interests amounts to simply this and nothing more. Capitalists employ labor for the amount of profit realized, and workingmen labor for the amount of wages received. This is the only relation existing between them; they are two distinct elements, or rather two distinct classes, with interests as widely separated as the poles. We find capitalists ever watchful of their interests — ever ready to make everything bend to their desires. Then why should not laborers be equally watchful of their interests — equally ready to take advantage of every circumstance to secure good wages and social elevation? Were labor left free to control itself, as it should be and must be, instead of there being an identity of interests, a mutual relation between the two classes, there is an antagonism that ever did and ever will exist; a sort of an irrepressible conflict that commenced with the world, and will only end with it.

If workingmen and capitalists are equal co-partners, composing one vast firm by which the industry of the world is carried on and controlled, why do they not share equally in the profits? Why does capital take to itself the whole loaf, while labor is left to gather up the crumbs?

Why does capital roll in luxury and wealth, while labor is left to eke out a miserable existence in poverty and want? Are these the evidences of an identity of interests, of mutual relations, of equal partnership? No, sir. On the contrary, they are evidences of an antagonism. This antagonism is the general origin of all "strikes." Labor has always the same complaints to make, and capital always the same oppressive rules to make, and power to employ. Were it not for this antagonism, labor would often escape the penalty of much misery and moral degradation, and capital the disgrace and ruin consequent upon such dangerous collisions. There is not only a never-ending conflict between the two classes, but capital is, in all cases, the aggressor. Labor is always found on the defensive, because

1. Capitol enjoys individual power, and in the exercise of that is given to encroach upon the rights and privileges of labor.

2. Labor is individually weak, and only becomes powerful when banded together for self-defence.

3. Capital is jealous of control, or even of remonstrance, and will often object to the interference of labor, even when such an interference would be beneficial to its own interests.

4. Capital is selfish and regardless of the fate, feelings, or condition of labor. The physical condition, intellectual development, and moral training of labor are neglected for that inordinate power which accumulated wealth supplies.

5. Capital is haughty, proud, and insolent, and spurns with contempt the remonstrances of the oppressed, the respectful entreaties of the defrauded, and the cries of the poor and abject.

6. Capital seldom forgives; it loses the finer feelings of the human heart, and knows no other commercial principle than that embodied in the famous axiom of the "Free Trade" school, which says, "buy in the cheapest market

9*

and sell in the dearest," but which, if applied to labor means, "keep down the price of labor and starve the workingmen; so shall thy profits be many, and thy wealth increased." It must follow, from the admission of these premises, that the interests of employer and employee are not identical. That on the one side, employers are interested, because of profit, to keep down the price of labor; while on the other side, the employees are justified, on account of self-interest, to keep up wages. Thus labor and capital are antagonistic.

Again: The deplorable and disastrous struggles that have taken place between capital and labor within a few years, and those that are now going on or have just terminated, must be an evidence of a great evil, of the encroachments of capital, and the defensive position of labor. Surely where such things exist, there can be no identity of interests. If there is this mutuality of interests, this oneness of feeling, I ask, sir, what means this universal uprising of the workingmen of this continent, who are rushing together as with the power of the whirlwind towards one common centre? A "union of workingmen." Surely they must be impelled by some powerful stimulus, by the presence of some terrible evil; for bear in mind that these organizations are contrary to our deep-seated notions of individual independence, and therefore can only be effected by the existence of a stronger feeling and the presence of a greater evil.

Surely these things cannot be where there is an identity of interests. No, sir, they are the result of an antagonism that always has existed, and ever will. One more observation, Mr. Chairman, and I shall pass to the consideration of another branch of the subject. Why is it, if the interests of the two classes are identical, that the few monopolize all the wealth, power, and honors of the world —

that after a few years of little toil they accumulate vast wealth, they can live through their allotted years in luxury and ease, leaving behind them, at the close of life, a marble pile, a granite column, or, perchance, their names written upon the scroll of fame, it may be in letters of *gold*, but nevertheless there, while the toiling many, the authors of all their greatness and glory, after having been doomed to years of unremitting drudgery, care, and misery, go down to a premature grave "unwept, unhonored, and unsung." Is all this the result of this much-vaunted mutuality?

The theory that the laws of supply and demand govern the price of labor, and that therefore, when work is plenty and labor scarce, wages will be high, and when work is scarce and labor plenty, wages will be low, is, in my opinion, a fallacy as transparent as the other. The great mistake is in making of labor an article of commerce, to be bought and sold in the market the same as a pound of butter, or a bushel of wheat, and subject to and controlled by the same laws, and in the same manner as these articles.

The legitimate workings of the laws of supply and demand, in their influence upon an article of commerce, is as follows: If there be two bushels of wheat in the market, to-day, and but one purchaser, and he wanting but one bushel, the price, we will say, will be a dollar a bushel; and if to-morrow there be but one bushel, and two purchasers wanting a bushel each, the price will go up to two dollars; and the operation is just the same upon every other article of commerce. Take cotton, for an example. A short supply has run the price up to a point almost without a parallel, and does not a short supply of any other article, continued for the same length of time, produce the same results? And yet we find that for the past two years there has been a gradually increasing demand for labor, almost, if not altogether corresponding to the demand for cotton. Has the price of labor kept pace with that of cotton? If not, then there must be something wrong with the theory that labor is an article of commerce. I do not place my labor in the market alongside of a pound of butter. A pound of butter is a perishable article; my labor is not. A pound of butter has no control over itself; I have over my labor. A pound of butter cannot say that it will not be bought or sold for less or more than a given price. I can dispose of my labor as I please.

The tendency of the price of labor is ever downward. For the proof of this we need not go to the older countries, where labor is reduced to the lowest possible condition of wretchedness. The evidences are scattered around us in disagreeable abundance. Witness the terrible condition of the thirty thousand sewing-women of New York, who, by working literally day and night, only earn from $1 to $3 per week, many of them being the only support of aged and infirm parents, or families of helpless children. It requires no stretch of the imagination to conjure up the horrible condition of suffering to which these helpless creatures are reduced. Recent investigations develop the startling fact that in the lower sections of New York alone there are over *six thousand families living under the ground.* Placing the average at five souls to the family, we have an aggregate of over *thirty thousand human beings* literally buried alive, huddled together like cattle in a pen, hid away in dark and noisome dungeons, where no cheering streak of sunshine, or breath of pure air, so bountifully supplied by the Divine Creator, can ever come, steeped in a gulf of mental and moral darkness, such as make "angels weep." "Are these things the result of the laws of supply and demand operating upon labor?" Go with me to the *magnificent* cotton-mills of the Eastern States, and I will show you a picture such as you have never seen. A few years ago men received fair wages in these mills, and were able to live comfortably from their earnings, and to raise and educate their children well; but now, by this downward tendency of the price of labor, by this gradual reduction of wages, it requires the combined labor of the husband, wife, and every child old enough to walk to the factory, for from twelve to fifteen hours a day, to earn sufficient to keep body and soul together. There can be found thousands of human beings, men, women, and children, who are mental, moral, and physical deformities.

"Are these things the result of a harmony of interests?" There is ever going on a gradual reduction of the price of labor. On the recurrence of every political or financial revulsion, wages are reduced; but whoever heard of a corresponding advance on the return of good times? If labor is an article of commerce, and subject to the same laws that regulate other articles, it would be just like other articles. When left free to the operations of these laws, the rise and fall each day would exactly correspond with the demand for it; the price would be regulated from time to time with the same nicety that other articles are.

If this supply and demand doctrine be correct, why is it that during the past two years of unparalleled business prosperity, and an unusual and ever increasing demand for labor, we have had more "strikes," a more universal organizing of workingmen, for the purpose of forcing up wages, than ever before? If, Mr. Chairman, we find that the price of labor is not regulated by the demand for it, and supply of it, then the proposition that labor is an article of commerce, and subject to the laws that control such articles, must fall to the ground. I am well aware, sir, that this view of these important questions is unpopular; but I believe it to be so only because it is new, because it runs in direct opposition to the old and almost universally received opinions upon these questions. But, sir, I have the most unbounded confidence in the ultimate triumph of *right.* You may bury it beneath a mountain of wrong, but, like a cork in the water, it is sure to come to the surface sooner or later. I have no faith whatever in the stability or ultimate succcess of our organization, until we place it upon the eternal rock of justice and truth. My endeavors to search out our true position, and the true relations existing between labor and capital, has confirmed me in the views I hold upon these questions. Believing that I have sufficiently ventilated this portion of the subject to make it plain to every candid mind that this supply and demand doctrine, so much talked about and harped upon by capitalists, is another of those fallacies imposed upon the credulous masses, the more easily to impose upon them, I shall now proceed to the consideration of another branch of the great question.

The terrible condition of poverty and degradation to which the working-people of most European countries are reduced, and the awful fact written in dark and portentous characters upon the horizon of the dawning future, that we (the laboring-people of this great continent) must surely, and at no distant day, occupy the same low and miserable condition, has awakened in the mind of every workingman who values his own happiness, and who loves his God, his country, and his family, and who has a proper appreciation of the great blessings of civilization and human progress, from a religious and moral point of view as well as commercial, and wishes to hand down to posterity these inestimable blessings, a strong and earnest desire to adopt some measures whereby to turn back the tide of oppression and human bondage that is threatening to ingulf us in mental and moral darkness before it is ever too late. It has long been evident to all that by individual action nothing whatever could be accomplished. I am fully imbued with that great American idea of individual independence, and much as I admire it as a characteristic of our race, yet I cannot fail to see that, if adhered to in our dealings with capitalists, it must sooner or later bring us to one common ruin.

It having been demonstrated by experience that if here and there a spirit more bold than the rest would remonstrate against the wrongs and impositions practised upon all, he would be immediately sacrificed as an intimidation to the whole body, it became necessary to discover, if possible, some means by which this evil could be avoided. Combination was thought of. Men began to talk about harmony of action, unity of purpose, oneness of interests, which shortly took practical shape in the formation of trades-unions; and it is astonishing to see with what rapidity these fraternizing influences drew men together. To-day there is scarcely a branch of industry without its organization. In England they are much more powerful than here. It is true, they are older, and perhaps more highly prized. There some of them have entire control of their trades, having in some of the large towns central offices, to which the employers have to send up for hands when they want them. Capital may know when there is a scarcity of labor; but they never know when there is a superabundance, because men are not allowed to go to the shops and apply for work. In reference to the great central power of one of these organizations, Lord Campbell recently said, in the Court of the Queen's Bench: "I must confess I look with some alarm upon this general association sitting in London *dictating to masters* what they *shall* pay their men, and levying contributions for the support of such society all over the kingdom, that might raise a fund as large as the revenue of some of the sovereign States of Europe." Thus far the attempts at forming unions on this continent have been feeble compared to those there; but energy and perseverance, directed by caution, intelligence, and wisdom, will do for us what they have done for them. But upon the threshold of our efforts, we are met by the opposition of capitalists. They deny to us the right to combine; not that they have any legal objections to offer (for happily there is no law against it yet), but they raise a question of right and wrong. They tell us that we have no moral nor social right to form these combinations; that we are bringing together the various elements of the industrial world, and creating a power that we will not be able to control, and that the commercial manufacturing interests, as well as society generally, will ultimately suffer by it; that we are creating a monopoly dangerous to the best interests of the country; that we are intruding upon the sacred precincts of the favored few, and that our actions will one day recoil upon our own heads, and bring general and wide-spread ruin upon those whom we would benefit. All this is done for a purpose; their object is to divert the attention of the honest and unsuspecting from the course dictated by reason and common sense. Capitalists, and the professional robbers of the hard earnings of the toiling millions, political and professional demagogues, and other drones upon society, have been so long used to lording it over the poor man; so long used to moulding us to their own fashions, and making of us the stepping-stones to their wealth, ease, and elevation, that any effort by us to shake off this power that has been "grinding us to the dust of misery," threatening with mental and moral darkness, misery, and despair not only ourselves but our posterity for all time to come, is looked upon by them as dangerous to the best interests of society. They see in this great reformation the ultimate destruction of their power over the people; they see the transparent sophistry fabricated by them to deceive the masses penetrated, and that, unless the movement can be crushed in its infancy, their power will have departed. This explains the holy horror and the flow of pious rhetoric with which they of late cajole the "dear people," and cry out against the immoral tendencies of "trade-unions." I believe that all men are "endowed by their Creator with certain inalienable rights," among which is the divine right to labor, the right to an interest in the soil, the right to free homes, the right to limit the hours of toil to suit our physical capacities, the right to place a valuation upon our own labor proportionate to our social and corporeal wants, the right to the first social position in the land, the right to a voice in the councils of the nation, the right to control and direct legislation for the good of the majority, the right to compel the drones of society to seek useful employment (or become public instead of private paupers), and the right to adopt whatever means we please within the pale of reason and law to secure these rights. And why, may I ask, should we listen to the croakings of the opposition? Are we not full-grown men? Are we not capable of taking our destiny into our own hands, and of fashioning it after our own designs? They tell us we have no right to combine to protect all that we hold dear in the world; that these combinations are immoral, unnatural, and an interference with the individual rights of each other. In the face of these protestations we find them combining for every conceivable purpose; and these combinations, when formed for good purposes, have been the source of vast benefit to the world; but capitalists combine for evil as well as good purposes. We find combinations almost everywhere for the purpose of speculating in every article of commerce, and monopolizing and controlling every branch of industry and every source of wealth. Against many of these combinations, and especially those for the purpose of speculating in the necessaries of life, and making fortunes from the necessities of the poor, we might raise objections founded upon moral principles. But we will not stop to do so; we will not waste our time in useless controversy with these sanctimonious hypocrites, but pursue the even tenor of our way, and hew out our destiny in our own way.

"We have no right to combine." All nature frowns the liar into culprit silence. This magnificent globe and everything thereon is the result of combination. Man himself is the most beautiful and wonderful combination ever conceived by the mind or fashioned by the hand of Deity. Combination is one of nature's universal laws. What, sir, I would ask, has developed this mighty continent? What has converted this once vast and unbroken wilderness, where for ages the red man roamed in unmolested and undisturbed solitude, into teeming fields, whose broad bosom is dotted over with magnificent cities, and beautiful villages, and millions of happy homes; whose hill-tops are crowned with churches, and school-houses, and institutions of science and literature of every kind and character; whose rivers and lakes bear upon their broad waves the commerce of ten thousand towns, and tens of thousands of farms and mines; over whose mountain, field, and forest there is stretching, in their serpentine course, a thousand railroads, the inventive genius of whose sons has made the earth and the elements alike subservient to their will. Answering capitalists reply: "We did it. Gold, the power of wealth, produced these grand results." No, gentlemen, you did not; it was a combination of bone and muscle directed by mechanical and practical mind that presented to the world this glorious picture of human progress. It is true that, after labor had commenced the work, capitalists saw the opportunity and stepped in to rob the poor man of his prize. "But," says capital, "we are entitled to an equal share of the credit because we go hand-in-hand with labor." No, sir; labor always goes first, and capital follows after. We, however, have no objection to an equal division of the credit and honor, providing we get an equal share of the profits. But there is no equality about it. Capitalists not only appropriate to themselves all the profits, but all the honor and glory; while humble labor goes unrewarded but by the taunts and jeers of the usurper. We are perfectly willing the profits and honors should be equally divided between us. That is just what we want, and just what we intend to have; for that was this great reformation inaugurated; and for that will it be pushed forward until the two elements of capital, money and labor, are concentrated in the hands of and controlled by those who produce them. But, sir, let us not deceive ourselves. Let us not go searching after pearls in a pigsty, nor waste our time with attempts to accomplish impossibilities. I am not one of those who believe in a coming millennium. This world must be inhabited by a new species of human beings, or the present race very materially changed before such a day will dawn upon the world. Whether such an event will ever come is one of those mysteries hidden in the unexplored future, and known only to the Divine Creator.

I do not believe the time will ever come when the "lion will lie down with the lamb," when "nations will cease to war against nations," or when the rich man will take the poor man into his parlor and acknowledge him his equal, and treat him as such. All visionary schemes and theoretical abstractions must be discarded. We must know just where we are, what we want, and how to get it.

Is there any reason why we should not occupy a social position equal to other men? Labor is the foundation of the entire political, social, and commercial structure. Labor is the author of all wealth; it is labor that breathes into the nostrils of inert matter its commercial existence. And yet we are told by the aristocracy — by these sticklers for the divine right to rule the world — that we are only fitted to be the "hewers of wood and drawers of water;" and, therefore, should be kept in constant subjection.

Does a foreign or domestic enemy threaten us with war, the strong arm of labor must drive back the foe; and of this we find no fault, for who is so much interested in the preservation of a great and good government on this continent as the toiling millions. The present sad and humiliating condition of our once proud and happy country is a sad commentary upon the rottenness and corruption of those who set themselves up as the custodians of our most precious rights. A sad solution of the doctrine that the few should rule the many.

I have long been impressed with the opinion that God, in the amplitude of his omniscient wisdom, reserved this continent, and discovered it to the world in the fulness of time, as an asylum wherein the toil-worn sons of humanity could find an abiding place free from the curse of landless and homeless toil. In the early days, when the future of this great continent was but dimly seen, a poet sung:

"Has Heaven reserved, in pity for the poor,
No pathless waste, no undiscovered shore,
No secret island in the boundless main,
No peaceful desert yet unclaimed by Spain?
Quick let us rise, the happy seas explore,
And bear Oppression's insolence no more.
This mournful truth is everywhere confessed,
SLOW RISES WORTH BY POVERTY OPPRESSED."

Yes, here is that land which "Heaven reserved in pity for the poor;" and it depends upon ourselves whether or not we will enjoy the priceless blessing. It is an inheritance bequeathed to us by the great Giver of all good, and we must prepare ourselves for its possession, qualify ourselves for its enjoyment. Again, Mr. Chairman, why should we not occupy a high social and political position? There is no reason why we *should not,* but there are many reasons why we *do not.*

1. We are not sufficiently educated to properly understand the true principles of social and political science, and too apt to listen to the teachings of those whose interest it is to foster prejudices rather than cultivate intelligence.

2. Our labor occupies too large a portion of our time to enable us to read, study, and reflect. A high degree of intelligence is necessary to enable us to discharge all the duties of citizens. If we were sufficiently well paid for from six to eight hours work a day, to furnish ourselves with the means of cultivation, we would do better work and be more useful men.

3. There is not sufficient union and harmony among us to secure the blessings and conditions we so much need and desire. This can only be accomplished by an earnest, united, and properly directed effort by those who see and appreciate the condition and wants of labor, and understand the true way to ameliorate this condition, and supply these wants.

4. Low wages prevent us from exercising that moral influence over our fellow-men which enables men of wealth to control the social and political affairs of a nation. This can only be accomplished by a thorough combination and co-operation among all branches of industry.

5. The want of a well-regulated apprentice system has filled the land with a vast number of inferior workmen, who, not being masters of their trade, are more or less subject to the whims and caprices of capitalists.

To secure these blessings, two things are absolutely necessary. We want more time and more money; fewer hours of toil, and more wages for what we do. These wants we will supply, and these evils we will remedy through the instrumentality of our organizations. We must have a thorough combination of all branches of labor. And then by co-operation we must erect our own workshops, and establish our own stores, and till our own farms, and live in our own houses — in short, we must absolutely control within ourselves the two elements of capital — labor and money. Then we will not only secure a fair standard of wages, but all the profits of our labor. We must erect our own halls wherein we can establish our own libraries, reading- and lecture-rooms, under the control and management of our own men; and we must have time to use them. We must do our own thinking, and infuse into the minds of our people a high tone of morals. We must learn to respect ourselves, and be proud of our occupations and positions. We must hold up our heads, and not be ashamed nor afraid to walk upon the fashionable side of the street.

Mr. Chairman, I acknowledge no superiority except that of moral worth — the man who is morally better than I am is my superior, and none others. Every workingman should learn to think so. You may say there is such a thing as mental superiority. Brains are the gift of God, and because one man has more than another, is no reason why he should treat with contempt or disrespect the man who has less. You may say there is a superiority of wealth. It is true that one man is rich while another is poor; but the poor man may be much the more honest, and much the better Christian, though not so *respectable*. This question of wages is one of the most vital importance. These men, who arrogate to themselves the right to monopolize all the wealth of the nation, are the worst enemies of mankind. This desire to make labor entirely subject to capital, by establishing a low standard of wages as possible, leaving to labor only a bare subsistence, is a development of the most sordid, selfish, and pernicious propensities of the human heart.

An English writer, treating of this subject, says: "This advantage bids fair, in the course of time, to realize Mr. Cobden's Utopia, which is 'to make Great Britain into one vast workshop — the workshop of the world.' This view of the ultimate destiny of our beloved country may have peculiar charms in the eyes of capitalists, but I must confess it possesses little or no charms in mine, unless the condition of the working-classes, who are expected to toil in this vast workshop, shall be permitted to keep pace with our national wealth and prosperity. As it rests, however, at present, this condition is neither satisfactory nor hopeful. In Lancashire and Yorkshire, for instance, two counties which may be regarded as a sample of the working-classes in Mr. Cobden's utopian workshop, there are *five millions* of Englishmen, whose moral and intellectual poverty is quite in keeping with their physical prostration and social wretchedness. Life in these districts is one unceasing round of toil, without relief, eating and drinking and sleeping; there is little time for anything else. At five in the morning, 'the warner,' with a regularity as punctual as 'quarter-day,' summons the deep sleepers to the shuttle and the loom, while the restless wheels and the humming machinery cease not their vibrations until the sun is down; time to snatch a hasty meal being the only interval."

How much better off are the operatives in many of the manufacturing districts on this continent? Scarcely any. Any one who will take the trouble to investigate and study their condition, will find thousands sunk to a degree of mental, moral, social, and physical wretchedness horrible to contemplate, whose very souls are crushed within their living bodies. These capitalists are no respecters of persons, either. All upon whose heads rest the curse or crime of poverty are treated alike. Gentle woman, the loveliest of God's creation, and the tender infant, scarce able to lisp its mother's name, are alike the victims of their rapacity.

That country cannot be *free*, where men of wealth, regardless of their moral fitness or mental qualifications, can buy themselves into political and other positions, while the useful, industrious, and honest poor man is consigned to obscurity. That nation cannot be truly great, that people cannot be truly happy, where labor is poorly paid.

The history of the world praises nothing more certainly, nothing with clearer demonstrations, than that where wages are lowest there is the greatest poverty and suffering; there the condition of the laborer is most forlorn and wretched; there is the least moral and intellectual culture; and there our race is sunk into the depths of political and social degradation, incapable of raising itself to that lofty elevation attained by a free and enlightened people capable of governing their own affairs. It tends to the very opposite of everything dearest to us, for the descent carries with it not only wages, but all the high and noble qualities which fit us for self-government.

This view of this all-important question should not only bring to us the warm and earnest sympathy, but the active co-operation of every good man, no matter what station or position in life he may occupy.

We must have a sufficient compensation for our labor to bring around us not only all the necessaries, but all the comforts and, if we want them, all the luxuries of life.

I am asked, "How are we to secure these things?" By combination, by association, by co-operation. "Well, what do these terms mean?" Combination or association is so beautifully explained by a modern writer, that I can do no better than quote them here. He says: "You are *men*—that is to say, creatures capable of rational, social, and intellectual progress, solely through the medium of association — a progress to which none may assign a limit. The country is not an aggregate, but an *association*. Association centuples your strength; it makes the thoughts of others and the progress of others your own, while it elevates and sanctifies your natures, through the affections and the growing sentiment of the unity of the human family. In proportion as your association with your brother man is extended, in proportion as it is intimate and comprehensive, will you advance on the path of individual improvement.

" Humanity is as a man who lives and learns forever. Your task is to found the universal family — to build up the city of God — and unremittingly to labor towards the active, progressive fulfilment of his great work in humanity. The right of association is as sacred as religion itself, which is an association of souls. You are all the sons of God. You are, therefore, brothers. Who then may, without guilt, set limit to association, the communion among brothers? Consider association both your duty and your right. Association must be peaceful, association must be public. Bring your wages here; economize; abstain from every excess, whether of drink or otherwise. Emancipate yourselves from poverty by privation."

These are ponderous words. Lay them up in your mind and digest them well, and you will have a full knowledge of the meaning of the terms combination, association.

Again I am asked, "And what is co-operation?" Co-operation is the banding together, by mutual agreement, of a number of individuals for the accomplishment of a given object. If that object be to start a store, build houses, establish manufactories or other enterprises, they each pay into the common fund a certain amount of money in instalments of given amounts at given times; and when the aggregate amounts to a sufficient sum, the enterprise is started. An honest and trusty person is placed in charge, whose duty it is to make purchases and sales, to have a general supervision over the interests of the establishment, to keep correct accounts of all transactions, subject to inspection by a board of trustees or auditors, and at all times open to the inspection of the shareholders. A price sufficiently above the net cost to insure a fair profit is fixed upon each article, and the same price is charged to all purchasers, whether shareholders or not. These profits are divided equally among the shareholders, according to the amounts purchased by each, or placed to their credit and left in the concern for the purpose of increasing the business, or of making necessary repairs and improvements. The advantages arising from a system of this kind are so diversified, that to enter into a detail of each, and the minutiæ of its workings, would occupy too large a portion of your time, and more ability than I can bestow upon it. Co-operation is the great idea of the age: it is the only means by which we can fully control both labor and money, by which we can secure to ourselves the wealth we have been so long creating for the use of others; for by it we secure a fair standard of wages, and a fair share of the profits arising from our industry.

"What is co-operation?" "Co-operation is a united movement by workingmen to realize better times for themselves and their families. How? Through co-operation or union in getting and saving. Oh, the vast strength of unity! Remember the 'bundle of sticks,' brother workmen, and band yourselves together. Be of one mind in support of truth; have faith in the lovely principle of co-operation, and you may cast your mountain of woe into the sea of oblivion. Co-operation aims at elevating men morally, mentally, socially, physically, and politically. This it will do by freeing us from the carking cares of poverty and wretchedness, which chain millions to a merely animal existence, and blessing us with the plenty and happiness that come of sympathy and united action for a good end."

Our first object must be to obtain organized and united action, to promote and regulate the formation of co-operative societies, to collect and preserve balance-sheets, books of rules, reports, and all other information connected with and relating to the subject, as a guide for future action. The history of the co-operative associations of Europe presents a picture of success truly gratifying to every lover of human progress on the road to moral and Christian elevation.

"The problems which in ancient days
Have vexed the minds and hearts of men,
Are, to co-operation's praise,
Wrought out by hand, and tongue, and pen.
These virtues win my sympathies,
And tie me to co-operate;
And as our strength in union lies,
Let love increase and patience wait."

The subject of female labor is one that demands our attention and most earnest consideration. There are many reasons why females should not labor outside of the domestic circle. Being forced into the field, the factory, and the workshop, (and they do not go there from choice, but because necessity compels them,) they come in direct competition with men in the great field of labor; and being compelled of necessity, from their defenceless condition, to work for low wages, they exercise a vast influence over the price of labor in almost every department. If they received the same wages that men do for similar work, this objection would in a great measure disappear. But there is another reason, founded upon moral principle and common humanity, far above and beyond this, why they should not be thus employed. Woman was created and intended to be man's companion, not his slave. Endowed as she is with all her loveliness and powers to please, she exercises an almost unlimited influence over the more stern and unbending disposition of man's nature. If there are reasons why man should be educated, there are many more and stronger reasons why woman should receive the soundest and most practical mental and moral training. She was created to be the presiding deity of the home circle, the instructor of our children, to guide the tottering footsteps of tender infancy in the paths of rectitude and virtue, to smooth down the wrinkles of our perverse nature, to weep over our shortcomings, and make us glad in the days of adversity, to counsel, comfort, and console us in our declining years.

> "Woman's warm heart and gentle hand, in God's eternal plan,
> Were formed to soften, soothe, refine, exalt, and comfort man."

Who is there among us that does not know and has not felt the powerful influences of a good and noble woman? one in whom, after the busy toil and care of the day are past, we can confide our little secrets and consult upon the great issues of life. These, sir, are my views upon this question. This I believe to be the true and divine mission of woman, this her proper sphere; and those men who would and do turn her from it are the worst enemies of our race, the Shylocks of the age, the robbers of woman's virtue; they make commerce of the blood and tears of helpless women, and merchandise of souls. In the poverty, wretchedness, and utter ruin of their helpless victims, they see nothing but an accumulating pile of gold. In the weeping and wailing of the distressed, they hear nothing but a "metallic ring." To the abolition of this wrong imposed upon the tender sex should be devoted every attribute of our nature, every impulse of our heart, and every energy and ability with which we are endowed.

Mr. Chairman, I have heretofore so fully expressed myself upon the apprentice question, that I do not deem it necessary to give it more than a passing notice at this time. Of all others, this is the most difficult we have to deal with, as it is, perhaps, the most important, for from this flow many of the evils under which we labor; and I must confess that the way to regulate it and escape its baneful influences do not appear very clear to my mind. There are, however, two things, in my opinion, necessary to be done before we can hope to make much progress in this direction. First, we want legislation. We want a law by which each boy entering a shop to learn a trade shall be bound to serve a certain number of years, and at the end of his apprenticeship he shall receive from his master a certificate, setting forth that he has served the required time, and is, therefore, a lawful journeyman; and it shall be unlawful for any one to employ him to work at the trade he undertook to learn, without such certificate. Secondly, we want a sound public opinion regarding this matter. This we can have in a little while, if we pursue the proper course. It is poor men's sons who learn trades. These men must be talked to and reasoned with, and an occasional well written article upon the questions widely and universally spread among them, so that both men and boys can read and learn. They must be made to see that, in nine cases out of ten, boys entering shops to learn trades have little or no chance of getting a thorough knowledge of the business, because the master assumes no responsibilities, and that the boy has only to remain as long as he feels inclined; and whenever he feels that he has a slight insight of the trade, he can leave, and set himself up as a journeyman. It is by these means that a very large number of inferior workmen are thrown upon the community. I am satisfied, that if we can inculcate a sound public sentiment on this question, and secure the necessary legislation, we will have nearly, if not quite, eradicated this evil.

Another matter needing our serious attention is that of "prison labor." I do not wish to be understood as being opposed to convict labor, nor as having any sympathy for the felon beyond that which I feel for poor fallen humanity everywhere. It is against the present sytem of prison labor that I wish to raise my voice. The object of confining in prison those convicted of crime is to rid society of their presence, and to endeavor, during their confinement, to reform them, so that when again turned loose upon the world they may become good citizens. This is the intention of the law. The first object of the law is of course accomplished; and as an illustration of what is accomplished in a reformatory way, I will describe what I recently saw in a prison-house in Detroit, Michigan; and the same system is practised everywhere. There they carry on chair-making quite extensively. Most that I saw were making chairs, or rather parts of chairs. One makes backs, another bottoms, another legs, another rungs, and so on to the end. This they call learning a trade in prison. But a convict may make chair-backs for any length of time, and when his term expires he will know no more about making a bottom, or putting a chair together, than the man in the moon. One of the worst features of this chair-making is, that a portion of the work is done by females. Of course, the young lady who serves out a term of years, and learns the very desirable accomplishment of plaiting chair-bottoms, will be well able to go out and battle with the world for the rest of her life. A portion of the work is done by free labor, and that very poorly paid for. The net cost of making these chairs is far below the same articles outside. These chairs are sold to a contractor, who puts them into the market at a very low price. Thus the honest and industrious chair-maker outside is brought into direct competition with this cheap prison labor. I may be asked, "What will you do with them? Do you propose to keep them in idleness?" Not by any means. But you have no more right to impose upon a convict than upon "any other man." If their term be long enough, I would have them learn some useful occupation. I would have them work at whatever can be found for them to do, but pay them the same price that is paid for similar work outside. Do not bring the honest mechanic into unfair competition with the felon. But these sanctimonious hypocrites, who are always talking about reforming the world, hold up their hands in holy horror and exclaim, "What! would you give them money?" Yes, gentlemen, I would give them money. I would pay them for everything they do the highest price paid for the same kind of work outside, and deduct from their earnings the amount it costs to keep them there; and at the end of their term I would hand over to them the balances, or perchance they might have a needy and helpless family, who should have it each week. This course would be doing justice to the honest and innocent mechanic, who has not incurred the penalty of the law; and in thousands of cases the money thus raised would save the convict from the further commission of crime, and perhaps his innocent wife and children from beggary and want. The prison-labor system, as it stands at present, is a festering sore fastened upon society, that can never be healed over until a new order of things can be introduced.

The eight-hour question is one demanding our most earnest and enlightened consideration. It is a subject of such vast and momentous importance, that I cannot help expressing my inability to approach it in a manner anything like satisfactory even to myself. Many, indeed, if not all the wrongs under which the toiling millions groan, may be traced to the ignorance of the masses; and that ignorance is the direct and inevitable result of over-work. So large a portion of the working-classes is taken up by active, physical toil, that mental cultivation, however strong the desire for it may be, is rendered impossible. And yet we are scoffed at for the want of cultivation, and pointed to the various institutions of learning scattered in abundance around us. It is true that churches are erected, school-houses are built, mechanics' institutions are founded, and libraries, free and otherwise, are ready to receive us, to instruct our understanding and shape our judgment; but alas! we lack *the time to use them* — time, so precious to the wise man, so worthless to the fool, but which is the treasure of earth to the over-worked and under-paid sons of toil. Poor millions! they only want time.

Solomon, the wise king of Israel, declared there was a "time for every thing." I once thought so, too; but experience has dispelled the illusion. Time there is, indeed, precious and plentiful, but it is devoted to the god of this world, to the worship of Mammon, to the aggrandizement of the few, to the accumulation of wealth. Labor is denied a claim, a right, an ownership to it. The poor needle-woman, the overtasked workmen of every kind, only want time to improve their condition. "Time! time! time!" is the cry ere eternity approach, and then "time shall be no more." Man is permitted a little time of God to prepare himself for a higher, nobler, happier existence beyond the grave. But his *fellow-man* steps in, and, like a stealthy highwayman, robs him of his treasure. Still, I predict for this movement an ample and glorious result; it will carry in its train a thousand blessings. To diminish the hours of toil is to increase the value of labor, is to multiply the number of laborers, is to add to the moral dignity and religious spirit of the times, is to change for the better the social state and character of the people, and this will be to strengthen the patriotism, the commercial credit, and the political institutions of the country.

"Physiologically speaking, eight hours of physical toil, no matter in what department of industry, is a reasonable amount of physical exertion for the average individual strength of man in one day." The highest authorities who have spoken and written concerning physical man, testify the same thing. To combine, therefore, to agitate, to organize throughout the length and breadth of the land, is a step in the right direction. The object is not only legal and legitimate, but it has a moral sanction above and beyond all these. It is honorable in those who concede it as well as those who labor for it. The vast numbers of laboring-people who are confined in our large cities are justified, in every sense of the word, to bring the prolonged hours of toil within reasonable limits. Compelled of necessity to seek a dwelling-place for their families in the most remote suburbs of these vast collections of humanity, where they can most economically eke out the scanty earnings of the week, they are compelled to rise at the *first* hours of early morn, in order to reach the great gates of the capitalist, to enter upon the long hours of toil that stretch their weary length until the close of day. But the labor is not yet at an end. Again they have to exert their exhausted frames and weary limbs over many a weary mile before they can sit down to rest or enjoy the society of wife and children. In what physical state, in what mental condition, is this exhausted laborer to enter upon the duties of the social circle, or the cultivation of the mind? Alas! his toil-worn limbs refuse their office any longer. The eyes, wearied with con-

11 *

tinual vigilance, sink blinded within their aching and throbbing sockets, and the slumberer, half fed, half cleansed, half caressing and caressed, is prostrated in a sleep that hardly knows a waking. Again, and yet again, is this process of walking, toiling, eating, and sleeping repeated; nature engaged in fearful conflict with mind acted upon by the laws of necessity and social existence. All this time the capitalist is well cared for. A railroad car or cab, or it may be his own private carriage, conveys him at the sober hour of ten to his place of business, and the same reconveys him home again at the business hour of four. *He* has *time* to live, to converse, to attend the evening *soirée* or the club. Time is of little or no consequence to him. The pleasures of idleness fall heavy upon his taste, and labor even becomes an agreeable relaxation. Again, when the business of life is done, and the little toil of a few years has accumulated vast wealth, capital retires to its country mansion and rural enjoyment, while worn-out labor asks permission to enter an almshouse and die.

Such, sir, are some of our claims to a little more time. Time to breathe, to rest, to repose, to think, — a little time transferred from the busy workshop to the quiet family circle, to enjoy the child's caresses, the wife's smile, the friendly greeting of a neighbor, the grave counsel of a visiting pastor, the perusal of a newspaper, the chapter in the family Bible, — time to think of our Creator's bounty, to forget man's tyranny, to remember heaven's promises, and to refresh the weary soul with prayer.

Mr. Chairman, I am convinced this movement must succeed. "The onward progress of man's soul in humanity and justice on earth must bear him nearer to the courts of heaven."

Sir, although there remain many highly important and interesting points of this great subject yet untouched, but having, I fear, exhausted your patience and my own strength, I shall, after a very few more remarks, leave it.

How long, oh, how long, must the toiling millions, the authors of all the wealth and affluence that surround us on every side, be doomed to groan beneath the Juggernaut-wheels of oppression? Let us trust not long. We have made the beginning, and the end is visible.

Through that thick gloom, that for ages has hung like a pall over the poor man's home, enshrouding in total darkness mental, moral, social, political, and physical, can be seen the dawning of a better day. Away in the misty future is visible the glimmering rays of a rising sun which, if we are but true to ourselves, will soon break in all its splendor upon us.

Let us depart from this convention with new resolves, with enlarged and exalted ideas, with our faith in the glorious cause strengthened and refined, and a firmer determination, let what may come, to push on the great and good work

> "Of winning, fettering, moulding, welding, banding
> The hearts of millions, till they move as one."

ADDRESS DELIVERED AT CHICAGO, JANUARY 9, 1865.

Gentlemen of the Convention: — I wish again to make use of the opportunity of your meeting in annual session to address you upon the mighty events that are transpiring around us, and present for your consideration, and the consideration of my fellow-workmen everywhere, my humble views upon some of the great questions of the day.

Time, in its ceaseless rounds, has again brought us to the

close of another year: a year laden with events which have caused the nations of the earth to pause and gaze in wonder and astonishment. A political revolution, before which all others of which history speaks sinks into insignificance, has left its trail of blood upon the sky, which will remain to astonish and appall all future generations; the results of which will settle for ages, and, perhaps, forever, the great experiment of republican institutions; the great problem of man's capacity for self-government. While these events have been transpiring around us, others, no less important in their bearing upon the future destiny of the nation and the world, though partially obscured for the time by the brilliancy of these, have been taking place. The year that has just closed its doors behind us, has witnessed the rise and progress of a social revolution such as the world has never known. The hard test of reason and honest, practical thought has penetrated to the very bottom of social economy, and the vast upheaval of the social strata, bringing to the surface the diamond and the rotten-stone, the pure gold and the dross, is the result. So gigantic in its proportions, so potent in its influences, and so tremendous in its bearings upon the present and the future, has this reformation become, that were it not for the more brilliant and dazzling events by which we are surrounded, the civilized world would watch, with increasing interest, the development of every new movement. The true friends of human progress, throughout the world, would hail it as the dawning of that good time coming, when right and wrong shall wage their last fierce conflict; when all forms of tyranny over the mind and soul of man shall cease; when reason shall rule the nations of the earth; when the dark clouds of error and superstition shall roll away, and when loud echoing over the rolling flood shall come the anthems of the free—the promised words:

"Of liberty and reason,
Of righteousness and peace,
Foretelling that elysium
When hate and strife shall cease.

"Of 'land for all the landless,'
Ordained of God above;
Of 'free homes for the homeless,'
Of 'truth, and hope, and love.'"

But although these events have attracted less attention than others, they are none the less important on that account. What would it profit us, as a nation, were we to preserve our institutions and destroy the morals of the people; save our Constitution, and sink the masses into hopeless ignorance, poverty, and crime; all the forms of our republican institutions to remain on the statute-books, and the great body of the people sunk so low as to be incapable of comprehending their most simple and essential principles; with the wealth of the nation concentrated in the hands of the few, and the toiling many reduced to squalid poverty and utter dependence on the lords of the land, and with every position of profit and honor filled by the proud and opulent? Again, allow me to ask, what would it profit us if the forms of our institutions were preserved and all else lost? But, Mr. Chairman, I am told that I have mounted upon fancy's wing and gone rioting through the fields of imagination, and present a picture that is overdrawn; a state of affairs that can never come to pass; that our institutions are built upon a foundation as firm as the "eternal hills," against which the angry waves of foreign and domestic strife may surge in vain. But, fellow-workmen, be not deceived. Allow not yourselves to be rocked into a false security by these sweet lullabies. Remember that tyrants have ever sung of safety to the people while grinding the sword to stab their liberties. Remember, too, that all popular governments must depend for their stability and success upon the virtue and intelligence of the masses; that tyranny is founded upon ignorance, and liberty upon education; and that while long hours, low wages, and few privileges are the strength and support of the one, they are entirely incompatible with the other. Again, I am told that by "vulgar arguments" and "coarse language," I am appealing to the passions of the "ignorant masses," and sowing the seeds of discontent where once were happiness and "mutual confidence;" that my teachings are "destroying those relations which should always exist between employers and employés," and which, if persisted in, will eventually bring about a "collision between capital and labor." Mr. Chairman, to the charge of "vulgar arguments" and "coarse language," I have no reply to make; but, allow me to ask, in what consists that mutual confidence? In this, sir, and in this only. Employers were *confident* of their ability to impose upon us to whatever extent they pleased, and we were *confident* of our ability to resist their encroachments. That my teachings are destructive of those relations that *should* exist between the two, I deny; that they are destroying the relations that *do* exist between them, I freely admit. Those relations are, for the most part, that of master and slave, and are totally at variance with the spirit of the institutions of a free people, and the relations that should exist between equals; and, sir, if any effort I can make will contribute to the total downfall and destruction of such relations, I shall consider the work of my lifetime accomplished; and to accomplish this, my most earnest efforts shall be directed to the education, elevation, and emancipation of the "ignorant masses."

"A collision between capital and labor" already exists. At present, it is only a clashing of interests, a social revolution, a war of classes — with such weapons as fair argument, honesty of purpose, a true regard for the best interests of society, lofty, noble, and unselfish patriotism, a just regard for the individual rights of every man, a firm reliance upon the great Builder of the universe, and the ultimate destruction of the power of wrong and the triumph of right, on the one side, and selfishness, envy, sophistry, ignorance, falsehood, flattery, covetousness, intrigue, enmity, pride, robbery, ambition, &c., on the other. But if those who employ this language mean a collision of a sterner character, I have only to repeat the language of Judge Tilford, while denouncing a recent attempt at a reduction of wages: "It cannot and must not be. By the laws of ancient Rome, a convicted traitor was hurled from the Tarpean Rock. Let the man who, in this crisis, advocates the reduction of wages, 'or the subjugation of labor to the whims and caprices of the wealthy, by denying to labor the right to regulate its own affairs,' be girdled and encircled with burning fagots, and receive the fate of the Roman felon." If the doctrines and principles promulgated and taught by the advocates of union among workingmen, and the efforts of those engaged in this movement to secure to labor the fruits of its toil, and the full enjoyment of all the blessings of an enlightened civilization, will produce such a collision, let it come. Let me say to those who hold such language, and who are endeavoring by such means to frighten us into submission, that we are terribly in earnest, and that, sooner than turn back from the point we have reached, and the course we have marked out, we will accept the fearful issue. To us, this question is something more, something dearer, than constitutional ties or church relations or country itself, and the sooner those who are, by means the most dishonorable, attempting to destroy our organizations come to understand our true feelings, and what we mean, the better it will be for all concerned. An able writer on this subject says:

"Capitalists have deliberately attempted to destroy trades-unions. Fortunately, their strength was ludicrously inadequate to the task. They were like a drunkard sitting on a barrel of gunpowder, and trying to ignite it with a damp match. Society is held together, or, to speak in a tongue they understand better, property is preserved, not by policemen, but by ideas — by the faith which each man has in some principle other than brute force. Destroy that faith, rudely snatch from him that idea, by sharing which, with others, he has been bound to society, and you have anarchy." Destroy that faith, take away that idea, bring that anarchy, and scenes would follow before which the French revolution, or our own rebellion, would grow pale, and sink into insignificance.

Mr. Chairman, I have dwelt long upon this subject. I have done so because it is one of the most vital and momentous importance. It is impossible for us to foresee to what extremities we may be driven. I have considered it my duty to raise my voice at this time, and proclaim a warning to those who are to-day boasting of their power to destroy our organizations, that they may know our intentions; may know that we are in earnest; may know that we are ready to meet whatever issues may be forced upon us; and then, if, with this warning before them, they force a collision, upon them must rest the responsibility.

But a few days ago, Mr. Chairman, one of these men, more honest than the rest, solemnly declared to me that it was the fixed purpose of the capitalists of the country to destroy our organizations; and that the day was not far distant when the condition of the workingmen would be far worse than ever before; when men who are now active in the union movement would be forced upon their bended knees to beg for work; because, said he, "a spirit of retaliation has been aroused in the bosom of every employer, the fruits of which are being manifested in the wide-spread and universal organization of capitalists for the avowed and publicly proclaimed purpose of destroying your unions." A retrospective glance over the events of the past year, and a brief review of a few of the most important events such as bear directly upon the point on our anvil, will be both interesting and instructive, and will serve to show us, too, that we have been much nearer to scenes from which every honest man must shrink with horror than most men have dreamed. On the 29th day of April, 1864, the following order was issued:

GENERAL ORDER, NO. 65.

HEADQUARTERS DEPARTMENT OF THE MISSOURI,
ST. LOUIS, April 26, 1864.

It having come to the knowledge of the Commanding General that combinations exist in the city of St. Louis, having for their object to prevent journeymen-mechanics, apprentices, and laborers from working in manufacturing establishments, except on terms prescribed to the proprietors thereof by parties not interested therein, which terms have no relation to the matter of wages to be paid to employés, but to the internal management of such establishments; and it appearing that, in consequence of such combinations and the practices of those concerned in them, the operations of some establishments where articles are produced which are required for use in the navigation of the Western waters, and in the military, naval, and transport service of the United States, have been broken up, and the production of such articles stopped or suspended; the following order is promulgated, any violation thereof will be punished as a military offence:

I. No person shall, directly or indirectly, attempt to deter or prevent any other person from working on such terms as he may agree upon in any manufacturing establishment where any article is ordinarily made which may be required for use in the navigation of the Western waters, or in the military, naval, or transport service of the United States.

12

II. No person shall watch around or hang about any such establishment for the purpose of annoying the employés thereof, or learning who are employed therein.

III. No association or combination shall be formed or continue, or meeting be held, having for its object to prescribe to the proprietors of any such establishment whom they shall employ therein, or how they shall conduct the operations thereof.

IV. All employés in such establishments will be protected by military authority against all attempts by any person to interfere with or annoy them in their work, or in consequence of their being engaged in it.

V. The proprietors of every such establishment in the county of St. Louis will forthwith transmit to the office of the Provost-Marshal General the names of all persons who have, since the 15th day of March, 1864, left their employ to engage in any such combination or association as that above referred to; or have been induced to leave by the operations of any such combination or association, or by the individual efforts concerned therein. The places of residence of such persons, as far as known, will be stated, together with a list, by name, of all who have taken an active part in any combination or effort to control the conduct of any such establishment, or to prevent persons from working therein.

VI. The post commander, Colonel J. H. Baker, 10th Minnesota Volunteers, is charged, under the direction of the district commander, with the execution of this order. All persons applying for the aid of the military forces, in this connection, will report direct to Colonel Baker.

VII. In putting down this attack upon private rights and the military power of the nation by organizations led by bad men, the General confidently relies upon the support and aid of the city authorities, and of all right-minded men.

By command of Major-General Rosecrans.

O. D. Greene,
Assistant Adjutant-General.

Official. Frank Eno,
Assistant Adjutant-General.

At the time of the appearance of this order two strikes were in progress in the city of St. Louis — machinists and blacksmiths, and tailors. Several members of the two unions were arrested, and an intense excitement, silent, to be sure, but none the less intense on that account, was the result. A demonstration by the workingmen against this invasion of their rights could not be made, because that city was then ruled by martial law. A respectful petition, numerously signed, asking for a modification of the order, was presented to the General, but without effect. This order was brought about by a combined effort on the part of the employers of that city. I cannot suppose that a man occupying the proud position of major-general in the American army could be led, by mercenary motives, to commit such an outrage upon the workingmen of his department. But he was waited upon by, and made the dupe of, bad men, who represented those engaged in the strikes and in the union movement as "roughs," among whom were many disloyal men, and that, altogether, they were a dangerous class; and those whose shops were idle because of the strikes, and who were, in part, engaged on government work, plead their necessities, and convinced the General that the men were making unreasonable demands altogether beyond their power to comply with; and that it had become a military necessity that these men should be forced back into the shops at the point of the bayonet. The General supposed these men to be honest, because they were rich and held high positions in society; while he spurned, with contempt, the honest poor man who waited upon him, and the order went forth to the world, and there it will stand upon history's page, a lasting disgrace to its author and all who were connected with it. Again, on the 19th day of May, 1864, the following order was promulgated:

HEADQUARTERS DISTRICT OF KENTUCKY,
OFFICE PROVOST-MARSHAL GENERAL,
LOUISVILLE, May 19th, 1864.

[*Orders.*]

It having come to the knowledge of the General Government that combinations exist in this city, having for their object to prevent mechanics and laborers from working in manufacturing establishments, except on terms prescribed to the proprietors thereof by parties not interested therein, which terms have no relation to the wages paid, but to the internal management of such establishments; and it appearing that, in consequence of such combinations, and the practices of those connected with them, that the operations of some establishments where articles are manufactured for the naval and transport service of the United States, and for military railroads of the same, are in danger of being suspended, and the interests of the service injured thereby, it is ordered:

I. No person shall directly or indirectly attempt to prevent any other person from working on such terms as he may agree upon in any manufacturing establishment where articles are made which may be required in the military or naval service of the United States.

II. No combinations shall be formed or meetings held, having for their object to prescribe to the proprietors of any such establishment whom they shall employ therein, or how they shall conduct the operations thereof.

III. The proprietors of such establishments in the city of Louisville will forthwith transmit to the office of the Provost-Marshal of the city the names of all persons who have, since the 18th day of April, 1864, left their employ to engage in any such combination as that above referred to, or have been induced to leave by the efforts of any one concerned therein. The places of residence of persons who have taken an active part in any combination, or effort to control, the conduct of any such establishment, or to prevent persons from working therein, will be given.

IV. The post commander and the provost-marshal of the city

of Louisville are charged with the enforcement of this order. Any violation of it will be punished as a military offence.

V. In putting down this attack upon private rights and the interests of the service by organizations led by bad men, the General Commanding confidently relies upon the support and aid of the city authorities, and of all right-minded men.

By order of Brigadier-General Burbridge.

STEPHEN E. JONES,
Capt. and A. D. C., P. M. G. D., Ky.

This order was issued under about the same circumstances as Order No. 65, and for a like purpose, the only difference being that there are the strongest reasons for believing that General Burbridge was in the confidence of the employers, aware of all their plans and objects, and that he was actuated by the most selfish and dishonorable motives.

On the 10th day of March last, a strike took place among the laborers at Cold Springs, N. Y. These men were in the employ of R. P. Parrott, who was engaged in the manufacture of shot, shell, &c., for the Government, and who is the inventor of the "Parrott gun." The men were receiving from a dollar to a dollar and a quarter per day. Owing to the very large advance in the prices of all the necessaries of life, they made a very respectful request that their wages should be advanced to a dollar and a half per day. This request was refused, and a strike was the consequence. Two days after the strike took place, four of them were arrested and sent to Fort Lafayette, where they remained for seven weeks, when they were liberated without a trial, although a trial was demanded. Two companies of United States soldiers were ordered to the place, and martial law proclaimed, and the men forced to resume work at the old prices. Three of these poor men, who were robbed of seven weeks of their time, and confined in prison for no offence other than exercising their right to refuse to work at a less price than they were pleased to ask — a right belonging to every American citizen — were not permitted to return to their homes, were driven from their abiding places, exiled in a free land, their families forced from the town, forced to move beyond the limits of this tyrant's domains, whose rule is as absolute as is that of the Emperor of all the Russias.

The following bill was presented to the New York Legislature at its last session:

An Act to punish unlawful interference with employers and employés.

The people of the State of New York, represented in the Senate and Assembly, do enact as follows:

Section 1. Any person who shall himself, or in combination with any other person or persons, by force or threats of any kind, either

1. Prevent or deter, or attempt to prevent or deter, any other person or persons from engaging or continuing in any lawful employment, labor or undertaking, in such manner and upon such terms as he or they may choose or accept.

2. Prevent or deter, or attempt to prevent or deter, any other person or persons from employing such workmen, laborers, or employés that he or they desire to employ, and in such manner and on such terms as he or they may choose or accept, shall be guilty of a misdemeanor.

Section 2. Any person who shall himself, or in combination with any other person or persons, commit either of the offences described in the first section of this act, shall be guilty of a misdemeanor.

Section 3. This provides a punishment for persons convicted under the above sections by imprisonment in the county jail, not exceeding one year, or by fine not exceeding $250, or by both such fine and imprisonment.

Section 4. This Act shall take effect immediately.

This bill was introduced by Senator Hastings, the Representative of the Troy District — a district, the voting population of which is very largely, perhaps three-fourths, mechanics and laboring men. The primary object in the introduction of this bill was the breaking up of the Moulders', and Machinists' and Blacksmiths' Unions in that State; but its provisions are such that every trade organization in New York would have been crushed out of existence had it become a law; but, fortunately, the workingmen of the great Empire State were equal to the emergency. The introduction of this bill created among the working-people of New York one of those profound and intense excitements, such as sometimes seize a whole people when about to be overwhelmed by some terrible disaster. The great body of our fellow-workmen in that State saw, as it were by inspiration, the terrible dangers that were threatening their liberties with destruction, heard with awful distinctness the clanking of the chains that were being forged at Albany, with which to bind them to the chariot-wheels of opulence and oppression. And as one man, and with one voice, they rose up from one end of the State to the other to protest against its passage. And to this watchfulness and determination they and every workingman on this continent are indebted for the defeat of the boldest scheme yet attempted to accomplish the subjugation of labor. A similar bill was introduced into the Massachusetts Legislature by a Mr. Brown; this bill passed one branch of that body, but was sunk in committee of the other by a timely demonstration on the part of the workingmen of Boston. The names of Hastings and Brown will go down to posterity as the first American legislators, who, for a price, made themselves the willing instruments of a few pampered menials who sought to steal away the rights of the people. Their names should be hung up in every workingman's house, and their children taught to hate them.

Mr. Chairman, I have selected these cases from among many, such as the breaking up of the Miners' Association, in the Eastern coal fields, by government interference; the defeat of the Reading Railroad engineers by the same means; the confiscation of the back pay of the moulders in the Brooklyn Navy-Yard, who struck for higher wages; the introduction of the convict labor system into the Sing Sing prison, by which a large number of honest men were thrown out of employment, etc. I have presented the above cases, and gone into detail, because they best answered my purpose, and because they stand out as the most glaring assaults upon, and most infamous interference with, the rights of the laboring-people. I am aware, sir, that this is a delicate subject, and I do not wish to be understood as fixing any of the blame for these abuses upon the authorities at Washington. It is true that some of these petty tyrants, "clothed in a little brief authority," have been retained in the positions they have disgraced; but a reason for this may be found in the fact that the matter has never been fairly presented to the authorities. I presume it is hardly necessary for me to enter into any arguments to prove that the workingmen, the great body of the people, the bone and muscle of the nation, the very pillars of our temple of liberty, are loyal; that, I take it, would be sheer mockery, would be adding insult to injury: for the evidences of our loyalty we need only point to the history of the war; to the fact, that while armed treason and rebellion threatened our institutions with destruction, while the proud and opulent of the land were plotting the downfall of our government, the toiling millions stood like a wall of adamant between it and the destructive elements of revolution, between the country and all its foes. These outrages upon the rights of the people have created a profound sensation, have made impressions that can never be erased. It is true that the muttering thunders of the confined volcano were scarcely audible above the surface, but they were none the less deep because in secret.

History points us to a period in the life of one of the proudest nations of the earth, when, through foreign foes and domestic traitors, the liberties of the people were lost; and thus in the almost hopelessness of their condition, while the wealthy were fawning at the feet of the proud conqueror, or assisting in a division of the nation's wealth, the mechanics, the laborers, the "the ignorant masses," who had had, for a long time previous, trades-unions almost similar to our own, were holding secret councils in their lodge-rooms, and devising ways and means whereby to drive the invaders from the land and re-establish the government; and as the iron heel of the conqueror became more firmly fixed upon the necks of the people, and as taxes increased, and one privilege after another disappeared, the slowly gathering anger of the people became more audible, muttering at first to itself in secret, then bursting forth here and there in resistance to some act of more flagrant oppression and extortion, at length triumphing in a wild and irresistible explosion, in the massacre of Bruges and the bloody victory of Courtrai. Let those who would trample under foot the rights of the working-people of this nation, beware lest history repeats itself, and the names of St. Louis and New York be substituted for Bruges and Courtrai.

Mr. Chairman, my object has been accomplished. I have wished to show to the country, and especially to those in authority, how near we have been to scenes that would appall the stoutest heart. In ordinary times a collision would have been inevitable; nothing but the patient patriotism of the people, and their desire in no way to embarrass the government, prevented it. But "there is a point where forbearance ceases to be a virtue," — that point *may* be reached.

Mr. Chairman, after all that has been said and written in defence of trades-unions, and the necessity for their existence, it would seem almost superfluous to refer to the subject at all. But we seem to have just arrived at that point where it becomes necessary to arouse the dormant energies of the mind, and summon to our assistance every new and available argument, to convince our fellow-workmen that in combination and co-operation lies our only hope for the future. Taking it for granted that the question of *right* has been disposed of, I shall therefore proceed briefly to argue the question from the stand-point of necessity. That a *necessity* exists for some action on the part of the laboring masses, if they wish to counteract the influences and avoid the evils of a centralization of wealth and the downward tendency of the price of labor, I think all will admit. I think a brief survey of the field will prove interesting. I believe that one of the most powerful arguments that can be produced, and one which will make the most profound and lasting impression on the minds of my hearers—and I am talking to every workingman on the American continent—is a comprehensive and, as far as possible, statistical contrast between those branches of industry which are yet without their trade organizations, and those which have them so far perfected as to derive benefit therefrom. And, first, let us consider, for a moment, the condition of the laboring-classes in those countries where, for ages, the wealth of the land has been slowly, but surely, concentrating in the hands of the few; and where, through the operations of the downward tendency of the price of labor, the poor have been multiplied and reduced to the lowest possible condition of poverty and degradation.

In all these countries the sons of toil have been the serfs of the land, the slaves of a master, or the inheritors of those brands of bondage and badges of servility which held them in a state very little superior to that of our southern negroes. The tenure of their existence was eternal toil; the recompense of their labor a bare subsistence; the profits of their industry was the property of their masters. Thus were the wages of labor almost universally decided by power instead of justice; the smallest pittance compatible with life has been allotted to the children of industry. The origin of the wages of labor came from masters who arrogated to themselves absolute power. Beginning with Egypt, the laborers were slaves; it is the same with the Turks; it was the same with Greece and Rome. Then arose the feudal barons of Germany, of France, and of Britain, with their serfs, their clans, their retainers, varied epithets by which to designate *slaves.* And this pittance of ancient and feudal times to *slaves* is now the principal of the wages of labor under our equal rights and charters of liberty in this the middle of the nineteenth century. What but a principle of slavery could have made it a felony, as it was, and is now, the case in nearly every country in the Old World, for a workingman to demand the true and just wages of his labor? If mechanics combine to raise their wages, the laws punish them as conspirators against the good of society, and the dungeon awaits them as it does the robber. But the laws have made it a just and meritorious act that *capitalists shall combine* to strip the man of labor of his earnings, and reduce him to a dry crust and a gourd of water. Thus does power invert justice, and derange the order of nature.

I have stated, Mr. Chairman, that the wealth of the countries of the Old World was slowly, but surely, concentrating in the hands of a few individuals; this is a contradiction of the position taken by many political economists; without multiplying evidences, I simply propose to refer to a few examples. By a reference to well authenticated tables, we find that in the year 1786 the soil of England was owned by 250,000 corporators and proprietors; and, in 1822, the number had fallen to 30,000; thus, in thirty-six years, 220,000 persons ceased to be landholders, leaving the whole soil of England centred in the hands of 30,000 individuals. This vast domain is distributed something like this: the Marquis of Breadalbane rides out of his house a hundred miles in a straight line to the sea on his own property; the Duke of Sutherland owns the county of Sutherland stretching across Scotland from sea to sea; the Duke of Devonshire, besides his other estates, owns 96,000 acres in the county of Derby; the Duke of Richmond has 40,000 acres at Goodwood and 300,000 acres at Gordon Castle; the Duke of Norfolk's park in Sussex is fifteen miles in circuit. The large domains are growing larger, and the great estates are absorbing the small freeholds. What is true of landed property is equally true of every other species of wealth.

England presents to view a pyramid, but an inverted one, the apex of which rests upon a vast population, a portion of which is uninstructed to a degree almost incredible, while another large portion is instructed in a very small degree, and the whole are wanting activity. Piled on these is a vast poor-house establishment, with its hosts of officers. On this again stands Manchester, and on this rests a large mass of great merchants and bankers, trading largely on credit and but little capital. On the top of this rest numerous great corporations, making large dividends out of Irish rents, and taxes on the coal consumed by the artisans of London, or the salt eaten by the unfortunate people of India, or the proceeds of high interest charged to unhappy traders. On the top of this we see a great church collecting millions to be divided among archbishops, bishops, prebends and rectors, while curates do the work and starve on servants' wages. Next, we see a great aristocracy, with vast possessions cultivated by men who live in mud hovels, and earn nine shillings a week, ($2.10,) and mortgages so heavy that record officers are undesirable. Piled on this, Pelion upon Ossa, we have a fleet and army requiring a hundred millions of dollars annually for their support. Over all stands the ministers and great officers of state, surrounded by hosts of chancellors and ex-chancellors, pensioners, sinecurists, and recipients of the public moneys, of all grades and conditions of life, from the great duke to the tide-waiter and letter-sorter. The machine is top-heavy. It rests on the shoulders of the very poor; upon those of the little children and poor women of Manchester; upon the *five millions* of workingmen who toil in the vast workshops of Lancashire and Yorkshire, whose moral and intellectual poverty is quite in keeping with their physical prostration and social wretchedness; upon the eighteen thousand colliers and laborers of South Staffordshire, and the fifty or sixty thousand women and children dependent upon them for support. In short, it rests upon the shoulders of the toiling millions, who produce what the few monopolize. What is true of England is equally true of every other country in the Old World. "France, too, presents to view another great inverted pyramid resting on the shoulders of the miserable people of Paris, one-half of whom receive alms in the form of bread tickets when the crops are short, and the more miserable operatives of Lyons and Sedan. The part which stands high in the air, and which should be the bottom, is broad; and there we see the king busily employed in raising materials from below to widen the top, creating *appanages* and viceroyalties for his children, while all around are watching for the time when the whole machine will topple over, burying in its ruins king, princes, princesses, *appanages*, viceroyalites and all." Some idea may be formed of this stupendous pyramid, when we consider that the whole number of officials appointed and paid by that government liable to removal and promotion, and annuitants and pensioners, was, in 1850, about 940,000, and the amount of salaries and pensions was about $85,000,000, to this was not added the army, 400,000, and the navy, 60,000. What an army of non-producers. "Poverty and wretchedness, the necessary consequences of misgovernment, exist everywhere in that great country, and where they are found, the habit of union can have no place. Society is divided into two great classes, separated by an impassable gulf — those who labor to produce and may not enjoy, and those who enjoy without producing." Mr. Chairman, I will pursue the point no further. Argument might be piled upon argument, and examples from history mutiplied indefinitely, but I think enough has been said to establish the truth of the proposition that where all *power* is centred in the few, there also will all wealth accumulate.

Now let us for a moment glance at the other proposition, "that as the wealth of a nation becomes centred in the hands of the few, the power of that few increases, and the many sink lower and lower in the social scale." And to prove this position, I shall again summon statistical evidences as the best possible argument. The science of statistics is to political economy what steam is to the steam-engine. No theory, however plausible the argument in its favor may be, can stand before an array of accurate statistical information. Assuming this to be a fact, then it must follow that the writer who can produce the best authenticated statistical evidences in favor of his proposition, will be entitled to the larger amount of confidence. The downward tendency of the price of labor commenced with the spirit of monopoly, and together they have travelled through all the ages of the past. Where one extreme is found there will be the other also.

Vast accumulations of wealth in individual hands have

ever produced the extremest poverty among the many; thus, in those countries where we see all wealth and all power centred in the hands of the few, we find the masses of the people steeped in ignorance and vice, and all that train of evils which hangs like a withering blight over society.

I have, Mr. Chairman, by a few brief statistics, showed to what extent the wealth of European countries was monopolized. Now see what is the condition of the great masses of the people of these countries. By a reference to carefully prepared tables, we find that the wages of farm laborers in England and Ireland do not exceed, at the highest, over *thirty-seven cents* per day. In most parts of Ireland, the farm laborer gets but *twenty-five cents* per day, and boards and lodges himself; and at that rate he cannot find employment more than half the time. The day's work, moreover, is from daylight till dark. No ten-hour system there! In Ghent, Belgium, the average price is about *thirty cents* per day, the workmen finding themselves. In the neighborhood of Bonn, on the Rhine, it is about *twenty-five cents* per day. In Wiesbaden it is from *thirty* to *thirty-five cents* per day. At the farm of the Agricultural Institute of Geisberg, near Wiesbaden, the price paid is *twenty-four cents* per day; the men in all cases boarding themselves. In and about Heidelberg, in the Grand Duchy of Baden, it varies from *twenty-nine* to *thirty-one cents* per day. In and around Cassel the daily wages amount to *thirty-seven cents.* At the Agricultural College of Weihenstephan, the pay for female laborers in the field is about *eighteen cents* per day, finding themselves. This is in harvest-time, when the price is higher than at other seasons.

The price of potatoes in the neighborhood of Dublin is *sixty cents* a bushel. Parsnips *twenty dollars* a ton. The price of good butter throughout Ireland is, on an average, *twenty-three cents* a pound; so that a man must work a whole day, from twelve to fourteen hours, to earn a pound of butter. The Model Farm, at Glasneven, got *thirty-six cents* a pound in January, 1864. The price of flour is about as high on the continent as in America, and the same quality of meats as high. In many portions of France, wages are still lower than these figures. In every country in Europe, everywhere in the Old World, we find the same low standard. The history of the world praises nothing more certainly, nothing with clearer demonstration, than that, where wages are lowest, there is the greatest poverty and suffering; there the condition of the laborer is most forlorn and wretched; there is the least moral and intellectual culture; and there is our race sunk into the depths of political and social degradation, incapable of raising itself to that lofty elevation attained by a free and enlightened people capable of governing their own affairs. It tends to the very opposite of everything dearest to us, for the descent carries with it not only wages, but all the high and noble qualities which fit man for self-government. This, Mr. Chairman, is no exaggeration. An appeal to the darkest pages of the history of our race reveals abundant evidences of its truthfulness. We find it in the expulsion of *three thousand* families from their little farms on the Sutherland estate, and their villages *burnt.* "Two acres *per family* were allowed them elsewhere, to be held on short leases, on payment of a rent of two shillings six pence per acre. Nearly the whole race of Highlanders has been expelled in a similar manner, and their habitations destroyed." Read the report of the Poor-Law Commissioners, who, in speaking of the pauper lunatics, tell us that "the portion of the domestic accommodations usually assigned to these unfortunates is that commonly devoted to the reception of coals, &c., namely, the triangular space formed between the stairs and the ground floor. In these confined, dark, and damp corners may be found, at this very time, no small number of our fellow-beings, huddled, crouching and gibbering, with less apparent intelligence, and under worse treatment than the lower domestic animals." Take up the history of Ireland, and refer to the records of 1847, and later. See in one single parish, *sixteen hundred* human beings with neither work nor food. Eight families, consisting of forty-seven persons, were ejected from one estate, (Sir Edward Waller's.) From another, (Lord Bloomfield's,) eight families of forty-five persons were turned upon the road without a roof to protect them from the rigors of the weather.

At the village of "Glen, on the estate of the Earl of Cork, ejectments were executed by the sub-sheriff of Cork, aided by the military and police force, on forty-eight tenants. Their houses or cabins were thrown down, and the forty-eight families, numbering about four hundred human beings, were turned out upon the high road. Of these, it is alleged, more than *one hundred were suffering from fever*. They were obliged to take refuge in a neighboring churchyard. The churchyard of Ballysally contains many flat tombstones and grass-covered graves; and among these graves the ejected families slept for four consecutive nights, huddled together. One poor woman was taken off her bed four days after confinement, and placed by the side of the ditch with her infant, both in a state of helpless exhaustion."

Search the records of France, and behold the awful results of human overwork — of a system by which one-third of those who work in mines, factories, and workshops, are under *twelve years old*. "The paupers are described as consisting of weavers, unable at times to support their families, and wholly chargeable to public or private charity in case of illness, scarcity, or discharge from work; of workmen, ignorant, improvident, brutified by debauchery, or enervated by manufacturing labor, and habitually unable to support their families; of aged persons prematurely infirm, and abandoned by their children; of children and orphans, a great number of whom labor under incurable disease or deformity, and of numerous families of hereditary paupers and beggars, heaped together in loathsome cellars and garrets; and, for the most, subject to infirmities, and addicted to brutal vice and depravity." Yes, Mr. Chairman, the history of the world praises nothing more certainly, nothing with clearer demonstration, than that, where wages are lowest, there is the greatest poverty and suffering, there the condition of the laborer is most forlorn and wretched. In 1844, out of a population of 34,400,000 in France, there were 16,855,000 persons unable to read and write; and 7,097,000 able to read, but not to write; and 6,968,000 able to read and write but incorrectly. Thus, in a population of over 34,000,000, we find about 24,000,000 without sufficient mental cultivation to comprehend the most ordinary events, while we find but 315,000 who had completed their classical studies. Surely, here are the privileged *few* and degraded *many*. What a commentary on the civilization of the nineteenth century!

Yes, Mr. Chairman, experience teaches us nothing more certainly than that the downward tendency of the price of labor carries with it not only wages, but all the high and noble qualities which fit us for self-government. The nation cannot be truly great, that people cannot be truly free and happy, where labor is poorly paid.

These evidences are from the blackest chapters of history, and the mind, horrified and disgusted, gladly breaks away from the fetters that bind it to the contemplation of scenes so appalling, and involuntarily exclaims: "Oh, is there no escape? is the great bulk of human kind doomed to eternal, unremitting toil? is there no bright oasis in all this black desert of despair, no bright star of hope to guide the toiling millions to some far-off haven?" Yes, one blessing does illuminate the scene. The chill winds which blow over the neglected wastes of social economy, bear upon their wings the glad tidings of one little green plot discovered; a voice which rose when man first oppressed his fellow-man, and has come floating upon the tide of time through all the centuries of the past, awakening at long intervals the toiling many to visionary dreams of a day of deliverance. Then passing on, leaving no track behind, the name of that voice we will call "Brotherhood," and as century after century rolled away into the ocean of eternity, it found, in later ages, by the wayside, a companion, naked, neglected, and deformed, still a companion, whose name we will call "Combination." Uniting their fortunes, with healing on their wings, and teaching, as they passed from age to age, the inspiring doctrine of "universal brotherhood,"—of hope, and love, and truth, — they reach the present century, they come down to the present age; and here, in their wanderings up and down the avenues of the world, they fall in with a third companion, strong, hale, and hearty, clad in impenetrable armor, gigantic in stature, with inexhaustible resources, ready to seize with herculean force upon the powers of mental, moral, and social darkness, and make eternal, unrelenting, uncompromising war upon these enemies of mankind. This one we will name "Co-operation." "Co-operation" says to "Brotherhood" and "Combination," Go out among the poor and lowly, teach the principles of "peace on earth and good-will to men;" unite them in one common brotherhood, combine them for one common purpose, and together we will commence *offensive* war upon the strongholds of monopoly and centralization. We will level to the ground these pyramids built of the blood and tears and groans of oppressed humanity — these monuments of perverted ambition. We will hurl from their seats each tyranny and oppression, under the sway of which the multitudes have groaned in the long days of sorrow. Sir, the work is commenced; the great gulf between poverty and competence is being bridged over, and the great artificers who dig the foundations, quarry the stone, and construct the plans, are "brotherhood," "combination," and "co-operation."

Mr. Chairman, I have not lost sight of the original proposition,—that of the necessity for action of some kind if we would escape the power that is grinding us to the dust of misery. That such a necessity does exist, who will deny.

It may be said that I have been confining myself wholly to a review of the condition of the people of older countries, and that so sad a state of affairs as I have presented can never exist on this continent, because of a more enlightened civilization, and a higher appreciation of the "rights of man." But, sir, "the same spirit which operated to the vassalage" and degradation of the toiling millions of the Old World is abroad in our land. The spirit of centralization on the one hand, and depression of the price of labor on the other. It is the same spirit that has consigned to eternal toil, with almost no remuneration, a hundred thousand American women. We find it in the vindictive spirit manifested on every occasion of difference between men and employers; we find it in the refusal of employers to accept offers of arbitration as a means for the settlement of difficulties; we find it in their refusal to meet us on equal and honorable terms, except upon isolated occasions, and then only to gain time and impose on our credulity; we find it in the "utter contempt" with which they look upon the whole laboring community, and every effort made by them for their elevation and protection. What but the same spirit has caused this universal uprising of the laboring-people of this continent, and this wide-spread and everywhere existing contest between capital and labor. It is the same spirit that with vindictive persecution would consign to obscurity the very names of those who put themselves forward as the champions and defenders of the labor movement, who are denounced as mischief-makers, demagogues, and theorists, actuated by selfish motives. This is the everyday cant of the aristocracy, the prolific source from which low-priced editors draw many a high-sounding editorial with which to tickle the ears of their wealthy patrons.

Sir, "the same spirit which dooms millions of our fellow-workmen in Europe to all the horrors of squalid poverty, in order that ONE earl, or duke, or lord may wear his coronet, riot in his castle, and wring from the hard hand of labor the last doit of his earnings," is abroad in OUR land — is everywhere to be met with in all of our relations and connections with capital.

"It is admitted on all hands, by the philanthropists of the age, that the condition of society demands amelioration. They affect to sympathize with misery, and exhort to reform the depravity of man. They call upon the laboring masses to cease their crime and study frugality; yet refuse them time and means for education, to give them a knowledge of virtue, and deny them that justice which would rescue them from beggary. The problem lies in the *insincerity* of their concern, and is solved by the pertinacity of their injustice. By imposing the compulsion to labor for a meagre subsistence, they have degraded the minds and obliterated the principles of those upon whom they make a requisition for qualities, which can only belong to intelligence and competence. If those who labor are already despised, they have little motive for virtue. If they are oppressed by the extortion of capital within the narrow confines of "keeping body and soul together," they have as little motive as room for economy. It is, therefore, a mere pretence to affect regard for the happiness of society, and at the same time deny the means by which alone it can be happy.

It is worse than pretence, to say we cannot consent to receive and pay for your labor on principles of equity, but we will provide you a poorhouse to die in. We cannot agree to treat you as equals, and furnish you education to meet us on equal terms; but we will build penitentiaries in which to incarcerate you, when you commit crime. This is the philanthropy of the age. Nor yet is it the best possible physical condition of man that can make him virtuous and happy. His MORAL state controls his destiny. As he is treated by society, so will he rise or fall in the scale of human excellence and infirmity. Contemned, despised, degraded, he sinks to the lowest level of the brute; respected, cherished, honored, he becomes ambitious of esteem, and aspires to excel in all that confers reputation or extorts applause. The virtual distinctions of rank, which too frequently extend into forms and titles, and which have for their basis injustice and extortion, which are the adjuncts of wealth, and which draw the line of exclusion where labor commences, are the cause of all that moral depravity over which the pampered men of opulence affect to shed tears of compassion, and project systems of amelioration. When the children of toil are as much shunned in society as if they were leprous convicts just emerged from loathsome cells, the most powerful obstacle is erected between them and all that can make them happy, the family tie of the race is snapped asunder, and man, thus degraded and oppressed, would be less than man if he did not feel enmity towards his oppressor, and view with resentment an order of things so contrary to the dictates of justice and humanity — so broadly in contradiction to his political and social rights, and so basely in violation of his equal attributes as a man. Here is the fountain, the sacred fountain, of all revolutions, all strikes; this is the point at which nature revolts; this is the point to which the producing classes have been depressed, and at which they now rebel, claiming their rights, and resolving to attain them.

Mr. Chairman, "the proper means of developing a nation's resources" is, perhaps, a subject upon which more has been written by political economists than any other. By them and by all capitalists it is understood to mean the best means of acquiring wealth, national and individual wealth. Acting upon this idea, co-partnerships are established, companies with acts of incorporation are organized, speculative associations of every kind and character are fastened upon the body politic, having at their disposal immense sums of money and sources of revenue, and around these are thrown the protecting arms of the law; — even the law itself becomes subject to their will. A vast network of railroads is spread over the face of the country; canals are excavated, connecting distant points by water navigation; navigable rivers and lakes are burthened with steam-vessels and other craft, and every ocean is whitened by canvas. All these are used as a means of developing the commercial, manufacturing, agricultural, and mineral resources of the country, such as bringing to the surface the vast deposits of coal, iron, lead, copper, silver, gold, and other minerals, which lie hidden in inexhaustible quantities within the bowels of the earth, and the creation and adoption of systems by which the soil can be made to bring forth the most plentiful supply of its various productions, and of converting the raw material into the most abundant supply of articles useful and useless to mankind. A nation that accomplishes these things, that is free from debts, has an overflowing treasury, that can boast of its magnificent cities, public buildings, and institutions of learning and science, with a vast system of internal improvements, and a navy of steam and sail vessels sufficient to carry its commerce to every corner of the world, with hundreds of citizens who can each boast his million or more — I say a nation that accomplishes these things many be termed rich, is termed rich by social economists — is rich in all that constitutes material wealth. But, sir, if all this vast system of improvements is owned and controlled by a few individuals, with the manufacturing and commercial interests in the hands of another few, with all the positions of honor and profit monopolized by the representatives of wealth, and the institutions of learning filled by the sons and daughters of the aristocracy, while the producing classes — a vast majority of the people — are, by low wages and long hours, depressed to the lowest social position, with sensibilities blunted, principles obliterated, minds degraded, every motive or incentive to virtue removed; with squalid poverty and all its vast train of evils and vices as an inheritance forever; with a fixed consciousness that no change can ever come, that the great yawning gulf between indigence and competence can never be bridged over, that themselves and their posterity are doomed to eternal unremitting toil, the mere living pullies of a vast machine, that nation would be poor indeed, though possessed of vast material wealth, yet poor in all that constitutes true riches, small in all that constitutes true greatness. There is, there can be, but one rule for estimating the true value of wealth; that rule is HUMAN HAPPINESS. General competence, which can only be secured by an equitable distribution of the products of labor.

> " Ye friends to truth, ye statesmen who survey
> The rich man's gains increase, the poor 's decay,
> 'T is yours to judge how wide the limits stand
> Between a *splendid* and a *happy* land."

When philanthropists and political economists turn their

attention to an equitable (not equal) distribution of the world's wealth, then will there be some hope, then can we believe that their concern for mankind is something more than mere hypocritical cant; but this they never dream of. They continue to doctor the disease without removing the cause. Hence the *necessity* we set out to prove. I think I hear the howlings of the defenders of the aristocracy as they cry agitator, fanatic, enthusiast.

Rowland Hill, in once addressing an immense congregation, raising himself, exclaimed: "Because I am in earnest, men call me an enthusiast. When I first came into this part of the country, I was walking on yonder hill, and saw a gravel pit fall in and bury three men alive. I lifted up my voice for help so loud that I was heard in the town below, at a distance of near a mile. Help came and rescued two of the sufferers. No one called me an enthusiast *then;* and when I cry aloud for men to 'flee from the wrath to come,' shall I be called an enthusiast *now?*"

I am no enthusiast, though I would thunder in the ears of every enslaved man these denunciations of that power which has covered our palsied limbs with chains. An equitable distribution of wealth would bring joy and gladness to the human race. Small capitals are productive of happiness and industry; large ones become pernicious, by giving to one great capitalist the profits of the wages of hundreds and thousands of workmen. In some immense factories of England and this country, thousands of workmen drag out a half-famished existence, whilst the capitalist, who lives at his ease, in London or Boston, perhaps rioting in all the sensuality of court life, amasses millions on millions. Here, then, we behold capital degrading and enslaving mankind, making society vicious, wretched, and ferocious on the one hand, and proud, cruel, and oppressive on the other. In this country, we are daily approximating to the same horrible inequality to be met with everywhere in Europe, owing to that tendency in capital to detract, extort, and accumulate from the wages of labor, besides legalized monopolies, grinding down industry to the scanty pittance necessary to sustain life. Man, selfish, ambitious, proud, avaricious, and vain, delights in being superior to his fellows, and even when the desire of fortune is gratified, the habit of extortion and the ambition of riches remain to torture himself and oppress the poor.

"For money, men sacrifice domestic comfort, health, character, and even hazard life itself; for it they are guilty of fraud, deception, and robbery. For money, they sacrifice friendship, gratitude, natural affection, and every holy and divine feeling. For money, man becomes a creeping, crawling, obsequious, despicable creature, instead of walking erect as the offspring of God. Mammon and manhood are incompatible."

> "Oh, cursèd lust of gold, when for thy sake
> The fool throws up his interest in both worlds;
> First *starved* in this, then *damned* in that to come."

If capital were always auxiliary to the objects of labor, and assisted in the equitable distributions of its wages, we should have so few poor, ignorant, and vicious, that almshouses, public schools, and penitentiaries would be unknown among us; whereas, under the existing system, science, genius, and philanthropy are baffled by these overgrown and bloated remedies of a spurious and oppressed method of government. If capital were not the enemy of industry, in most of its forms, we should not behold it in the shape of monopoly, nor giving birth to combinations on the part of labor to counteract its baneful operations. "Who 's born for sloth?" I answer, the capitalist — the idle, luxurious, extortionate capitalist. And as truly as the sun drinks up the morning's dew, so does the idle capitalist absorb the just substance of the man of labor, stripping from his children's limbs what should clothe them, taking from their mouths what should feed them, and keeping from their immortal souls what should instruct, enlighten, and save them. "Who 's born for sloth?" Yet how many thousands upon thousands live upon the sweat of the poor man's labor in idle pleasure and suicidal vice. Nature decrees it otherwise, justice decrees it otherwise, reason proclaims it ought not to be so; but proud, oppressive, overbearing, cruel man, while he admits the fact with feigned regret, ascribes it to "*circumstances*," and insists that wisdom and virtue are only compatible with satiety on the one hand, and starvation on the other.

Mr. Chairman, time admonishes me that I can proceed no farther in this direction. Have I succeeded in proving a "necessity" for action? Believing that I have, it now becomes our duty to inquire what course we should pursue. If we would raise ourselves to that lofty position for which nature designed us, we must accept the issue of a contest with tyranny, and strike out boldly for emancipation.

It may be inferred from what has been stated, that my remedy for the evils complained of is an equitable distribution of wealth. All people have had their Utopias; and it may be said that this is ours; but fortunately we have solid, substantial facts to take hold of in defence of our position.

But before proceeding to the consideration of combination and co-operation as remedies with which to meet the "necessity," let us look for a moment at the remedies proposed by social economists. All the writers on social and political economy previous to Mr. Malthus, may be considered as nothing more than apologists for the aristocracy. Among the foremost of these apologists of tyranny stands Adam Smith, who, in the very teeth of the starving millions of Great Britain, wrote in defence of the existing system of distribution, because it secured to "*every man the fruits of his own industry.*" He and the whole school of economists are very scientific in their classifications of society, but studiously avoid any application of the natural principles of justice to the comfort of those whose labor creates all wealth. Mr. Malthus, however, startled the world with a new theory. Admitting all that could be claimed by the most enthusiastic philanthropist, he proposed a remedy, a panacea for all the ills of society, and scared half the world into the commission of all sorts of "fantastic pranks," when he said "that the human race had a tendency to increase faster than food." "There are," says he, "few States in which there is not a constant effort in the population to increase beyond the means of subsistence. This constant effort as constantly tends to subject the lower classes of society to distress, and to prevent any great permanent amelioration in their condition." This, according to Mr. Malthus, is the *cause* of all our suffering. Having discovered the cause, of course it was an easy matter to propose a *remedy*. That remedy, we are told, is to be found in a check upon population. We are gravely informed that the great curse under which we labor, is the first commandment, "increase and multiply." And that this divine injunction must be disregarded, matrimony must be discouraged, and profligacy promoted. We are told that if all mankind were sober and industrious, and war, famine, pestilence, and crime were to cease, the world would soon become overpopulated, and men would be compelled to starve or eat each other. "Honest industry leads to starvation. Licentiousness and crime, robbery and murder, tend to render the supply of food abundant." We are taught to believe the disgusting doctrine, that we are placed here by an all-wise Providence, whose powers and attributes are unlimited and incomprehensible, who has filled the vast immensity of space with moving worlds, each held in its place by a power which knows no confusion. With the principles of reproduction fixed in our natures, and resting upon us the great command from the author of our being to "increase and multiply," while the "natural checks" provided as an offset to this commandment by the same wise God are poverty, degradation, war, famine, pestilence, murder, and whatever tends to shorten or destroy human life. We find this monstrous doctrine defended by nearly all the great economists since Mr. Malthus. McCulloch, Senior, Wakefield, Dr. Chalmers, Gregg, Mill, and a host of others, hold up a limit to population as the *only* remedy for the evils of poverty, and the hope of depressed labor; while even Mr. Carey, the ablest writer of the age, and opposer of the Malthusian theory, admits the possibility "that at some future period the world may be fully, and perhaps, overpeopled." But I cannot admit even the possibility of such an event. It is true, that were all the descendants of Adam and Eve to appear suddenly upon the earth, they could not find standing room. And it is equally true, that were the population of the earth to commence doubling at the rate of once in fifty years, the same result would soon be reached; or were the products of the earth most essential to the sustenance and comfort of man to suddenly double, great disorder would ensue; immense quantities would perish, and man would be but little benefited; and at most the benefit would be temporary, because the spirit of monopoly would soon bring it together in large quantities for the benefit of the few. But nature does not work by sudden starts. Order, regularity, and graduation, are great natural laws. The acorn does not suddenly become a mighty oak. The infant of to-day will not be a man to-morrow. The little rills that issue from the mountain-side are not at once made into mighty rivers, but go on leaping from rock to rock, or, murmuring through little nooks and quiet vales, they *gradually* find their way to the coast and mingle with the ocean. Winter, spring-time, and harvest, do not come suddenly upon us. The sun does not suddenly appear in all its noonday splendor, nor as suddenly disappear, leaving the world in midnight darkness. This is the order of nature. Were we to attempt to erect a column three hundred feet high upon a base ten feet square, we would find it an impossibility; but if we were to commence by throwing up loose dirt, the large lumps would roll off to the bottom, and the base would widen in exact proportion to the increasing height, and no difficulty would be experienced in carrying the pyramid to the desired elevation. Were we to place five hundred civilized beings upon one square mile of the richest soil, and leave them to shift for themselves, nearly all would die of hunger. But were we to place a single family in that position, understanding the powers of accumulation and production, they could go on multiplying until their numbers would reach five hundred or more; and yet the square mile could be made to supply their wants.

If man was guided solely by the natural laws under which he was created and designed to live, multiplication would unquestionably be much more rapid than it now is: but is it not reasonable, is it not Christian, to suppose that the all-wise Being who placed us here, and whose attributes are benevolence and love, could find other means of controlling population by than war, famine, pestilence, and crime in all its forms? And yet we find such men as John Stuart Mill, who is looked upon as the great leader on the *popular* side of the social question, and who ignores combination, and gives to co-operation but a passing notice, as a side issue, defending this most pernicious and disgusting doctrine, and holding it up as the only hope for the toiling millions. And even this plan does not comprehend anything beyond a mere nominal advantage.

Believing, as we do, that wages should be at least one hundred per cent. higher than at present, to accomplish this object, we must either destroy one-half the present laboring population, or stop multiplying until the present number is reduced one-half. Such is their theory. But let us look for a moment at the utter fallacy of such a doctrine. Suppose we could suddenly sweep from the face of the earth one-half the producing people, what would be the result? Would wages go up? By no means. Vast districts would become depopulated, real estate would become valueless, rents would fall to a mere nominal standard, universal ruin would everywhere exist. The productive industry of the world being reduced one-half, production would of course be reduced at least to that extent, the ability to pay increased wages would thus be no greater than previous to the change, and the condition of the remaining half would be far worse than before; and the results would be the same if we would adopt the slow process of abstaining from reproduction. Anything that interferes with the principles of production, whether it be human industry or the introduction of machinery, detracts from the aggregate wealth of the world; it is here those people mistake who oppose immigration, and the appliance of the arts and sciences to mechanical, manufacturing, and agricultural pursuits.

Mr. Chairman, believing that the question of population is one we can safely leave with the Author of our existence, whose laws, if not transgressed, will secure to us happiness and safety, and believing that this is the highest ground that can be taken, I shall not pursue the argument by showing that in all countries where the remedies have been applied, the condition of the people is more deplorable, and where reproduction has been unchecked, their condition is most comfortable and promising; nor shall I proceed to discuss the absurd theory that a given portion of the aggregate wealth of the world, or of a country, is set apart as the wages of labor, and that that sum cannot be augmented without corresponding injury to "commerce and trade." It will readily be perceived by the reflecting mind that this theory carefully conceals the idea of an equitable distribution of wealth, and is founded upon the presumed fact that the merchant is the most important individual in society, instead of being but the agent of labor.

This theory entirely ignores the idea that, as civilization advances and workingmen become more enlightened, they will see that they have a right to a voice in the fixing of the "wages fund," and that ten per cent. of what they produce is hardly a fair or just proportion to be set aside for their benefit. Time will not permit me to dwell upon these points.

We will now return to the consideration of what we believe to be the remedies for the present unsatisfactory state of society. Combination, or union among workingmen, may be looked upon as the first step towards competence and independence. Long years ago the few more intelligent among the laboring-classes saw that by individual action no change in their condition could ever come; and they also saw that, without an effort on the part of the masses themselves, their condition must forever remain the same; and they also clearly saw that an effort to be successful must be a united one.

These ideas were not long in taking practical shape in the organization of "trades-unions." Foremost among these, and one that preserved its organization, and went on increasing in magnitude, importance, and influence against the most fearful odds, breaking down every barrier and removing every opposition, and one which now, at the end of *fifty-five years*, can boast of a combination superior to any other in the world, stands the Moulders' Union of England, Ireland, and Wales, with a branch from the same in Scotland. This organization was founded in 1809. Similar organizations have sprung up in all sections of the Old World, where they are not interdicted by law. The same cause, the same "necessity," produced similar results here, and to-day we find almost every branch of labor, skilled and unskilled, with its organization. In the front rank, though not the oldest, but without a rival, stands the "Iron-Moulders' International Union." To enter upon a summing up of the good these unions have accomplished, or of the two specified, would be a herculean task; nor is it necessary that I should do so; it is sufficient to know that the most beneficial and astonishing results have sprung from them. We see a convention of moulders, assembled for the modification and creation of laws and rules for their own government, holding a session in London, last year, extending through a period of *seventy-four days*. The income and expenditure of this association amount to many thousands of pounds annually, and so completely do they control their trade, that they are now receiving as large wages, and are in the enjoyment of as many blessings and privileges as we are; while all around them we find unorganized labor occupying a position far below them in wages, mental and moral condition, and, indeed, in every respect. Another of these organizations, with a membership of over 24,000, received, during the past year, about $650,000, and of that sum disbursed about $310,000, leaving on hand, at the disposal of the members, nearly $340,000. These organizations contain both the protective and beneficial features. The amount of good accomplished by the expenditure of such large sums of money for the alleviation of distress, in cases of sickness or misfortune, is incalculable. In this country our unions, as a general thing, contain but the protective feature — that is, to force capital, by the power of numbers, to concede to our demands. Although what is termed the beneficial feature is discarded, they embrace, besides the protective, many other splendid features. The wages of labor here are fully fifty per cent. above what it would be had the idea of union never entered the brain of a man in this country, except, perhaps, in a few isolated cases. One of two things is always present when an advance of wages is given — either a demand on the part of the men, or a fear that such a demand will be made. Had no union ever been formed, and employers felt perfectly sure that no demand for increased pay would be made, would they ever have given it?

Workingmen throughout the States are now working for considerable less wages than they received four and five years ago; and how, let me ask, have we got the small advance thus far secured? By fighting for it — by making demands, and backing them up by whatever power we could command. So persistent and bitter has been the opposition to an increase of wages, that what little we have secured, has cost us very nearly as much as the amount received. It is no difficult matter to see what would now be our condition, had we no unions.

The benefits secured by *our* union, aside from an increase of wages, are beyond calculation. A strong desire for mental cultivation has infused itself throughout the entire body. Schools, libraries, reading- and lecture-rooms, and other institutions for the diffusion of useful knowledge, are springing up among us; and were it not for the opposition of the "better classes," the progress in this direction would be much more rapid. One of the most beautiful and beneficial results flowing from our organization is the universal and wide-spread acquaintance that has sprung up among the members: a feeling of brotherhood everywhere exists; an interest in each other's welfare has broken down, to a vast extent, that old feeling of selfishness that used to exist among us; a feeling of manly independence has taken the place of that cringing and crawling spirit that used to make us the scorn of honest men. Indeed, Mr. Chairman, it is impossible for the true man to cast his eyes over the past, and contemplate the present proud position our organization has attained, and the glorious future that lies invitingly before us, without being carried away by those lofty feelings of manly pride and hope which have animated the true reformer — the true friend of right — in all ages of the world.

These are but a few of the benefits and beauties of combination as applied to labor, and but briefly told. But, sir, however widely extended may be the principles of combination, with their teachings of unity and brotherhood, and however great may be their influences upon our people; yet I do not agree with those who believe that combination is *the* great idea, and that by its agency alone we can carry forward this great reformation to an entirely successful issue. No, sir. Combination is only the first great step on the road to emancipation and success. Protective combination has gone forward and marshalled the forces of the great army of labor; has caused a ray of light to penetrate the midnight darkness of the mind; has opened our eyes to a true sense of our condition; has shown us the true reasons why that condition is poor and miserable; has given us a true conception of the principles of justice and common sense, and taught us to reason upon the great issues before us, as man should reason with equal; has shed abroad in the land that great and divine principle of universal brotherhood, without which man can never rise to that lofty elevation which alone can fit him for self-government; has led us on by glittering hopes and promises to the very threshold of the promised land; and as the mind warmed into new life, animated with bright and cheering hope, reaches forward to grasp the great idea, and begins to realize the glorious future which lies just beyond, the soul enlarges, we draw nigher to the great Author of our existence, and we begin to *feel* that we are men.

A new idea has been born to the children of industry. "Co-operation" has dawned upon the world. "Co-operation" is the next great step; this taken, and we will have crossed the boundary which has so long separated man from his true destiny. This is the true remedy for the evils of society; this is the great idea that is destined to break down the present system of centralization, monopoly, and extortion. By co-operation, we will become a nation of employers — the employers of our own labor. The wealth of the land will pass into the hands of those who produce it. The idle drone, who fattens upon the substances of the poor, will be forced to seek an occupation; the rum-seller, who, with an ungodly hand, deals out ruin to mankind, will be forced to honest industry, or left to starve. "The devil won a great victory when he introduced whiskey into the world. He knew what he was about. It was his business to fill his region with souls, and he knew that whiskey was the best recruiting officer for the armies of perdition he could employ. Don't touch it; it is a vile practice in which politicians, common people, all the rest of mankind, and even editors and lawyers indulge." The vile, the vicious, the evil-doers, and the idle of every class will be driven from society. The body politic, which is now a mass of festering sores, will become clean and healthy; honesty and integrity will be rewarded; genius will be developed; the principles and powers of production will be understood and multiplied, and the wealth of the world vastly augmented; the penalties attached to a violation of nature's laws — war, famine, pestilence, and all the vast train of disturbing causes — will disappear; population and production will take care of themselves, and God will take care of the race. Such, Mr. Chairman, is destined to be the glorious future of the labor movement, wrought out by *our* remedies — brotherhood, combination, and co-operation. But let us not forget that success depends upon our own efforts. "*It is not what is done for people, but what people do for themselves, that acts upon their character and condition.*"

But, sir, we are told that we cannot succeed; that our plans and theories are chimerical, and therefore impossible of execution; that society, as now existing, is founded upon the experience of all ages, and that so firmly is it established, that to overturn it is impossible, and that none but designing and corrupt men are found advocating the cause of labor. The mind of that man must be dull indeed, who can see in this great movement nothing more than a momentary excitement, produced by the condition of the country, and the influences of ambitious and designing men. And those statesmen and journalists who pretend to ignore this the greatest reformation the world has ever witnessed, are false lights, and are doing more to retard the progress of the age, and fasten upon the masses the chains of slavery, superstition, ignorance, and moral darkness, than any and all other causes. I do not believe the doctrine taught by many, that man has, at different periods of the world, risen to the highest state of civilization attainable, and then gradually sunk back into a state of comparative barbarism, from which, after long years of darkness, he would advance; and thus rise and fall like the succeeding waves of the ocean. No, sir; I believe that man is a progressive animal, and that, notwithstanding civilization has received many and severe checks, and has been thrown back hundreds of years at different times, the march of the empire of knowledge has been steadily forward, and that we are a long way in advance of any other people of any other age. Man is a progressive animal, and has been from the beginning; or at least from the first great transgression, making steady progress upwards. Slow sometimes, to be sure; so slow, indeed, as to cause the best men, in all ages, to weep and mourn over the perverseness of the race, and even to doubt the possibility of his rising to that lofty elevation designed by his Creator. But sure, if slow; and that progress is destined to go forward until that point has been reached so devoutly to be wished — when all mankind shall be free, when the whole human family shall become united in one common brotherhood; when the broad banner of political, social, and religious freedom shall wave over every land, under whose ample folds all the nations of the earth can find protection, and when reason, directed by moral principle, shall rule all the nations of the earth.

> "Even now the half of slavery's flag is furled,
> And thought's free sunshine circles the wide world."

To some, this consummation of a civilized age may appear visionary; but let it be remembered that, at one period, all the improvements which subsequently arose were adjudged impossible. Time and mind are the creators of human destiny which accomplish more than miracles, and produce revolutions that only fail to astonish because they enlighten. As it is mind that makes the man, we have but to combine intellect with labor and the task of equal happiness is completed. It is only under the dark and hush policy of silence that abuses can expect to continue, extortion to thrive, capital to luxuriate, and monopoly to expand.

Mr. Chairman, the little hour allotted to this purpose has passed away, leaving the subject by no means exhausted. Let us remember, sir, that burning words and thrilling eloquence cannot alone accomplish our purpose, though they may do much to arouse the dormant energies of the thoughtless and indifferent. Works are what we want; great, noble, and brave deeds. Our task is but commenced; difficulties and dangers environ on every side. Many may faint and falter in the great work; others may sink beneath the strokes of tyranny, and perish by the wayside; this generation may pass away long ere this great work shall be accomplished. But let us remember that

> "They never fail who *die*
> In a great cause; the block may soak their gore;
> Their heads may sodden in the sun; their limbs
> Be strung to the city gates and castle walls;
> But still their spirit walks abroad. Though years
> Elapse, and others share as dark a doom,
> They but augment the deep and swelling thought,
> Which overpower all others, and conduct
> The World, at last, to Freedom."

And now, Mr. Chairman, in conclusion, let me ask again: Why should toiling, starving men be linked to misery forever? Labor of head and hand is man's best estate and earthly destiny, but it is at the bottom, instead of the top of the scale. Yet the time is drawing nigh — a little bird whispers it in my ear —when the laborer, the workingman, no longer ignorant, brutalized, debased, shall rise, without impeachment of the claims of any, to the highest, best elevation of nature's aristocracy. Shall he not dwell in palaces, who raises palaces? Shall she not go in rich attire, whose fingers wind the silk of the toiling worm? Shall the ruby, the diamond, and the red, red gold, not glitter on the miner's manly breast, or deck the fingers of his wife and child? Shall she not wear who spins; he eat who sows? Shall the purple juice recruit no more the fainting vine-dresser, or pictures deck or choicest harmony cheer the dwellings of the poor? Yes! By the living God shall they. By the very majesty of heaven, man, man himself, shall waken from the trance of ages, and the producer and the consumer, the creator of enjoyments and he who revels in them, shall be one and indivisible once more. Nature's glad voices shall breathe out peacefully again. The carolling birds, the whispering winds, the gorgeous clouds and perfumed flowers, the sunny earth, the mighty ocean, man's glorious beauty, speak seraph-toned his ineffable destiny, the faint foreshadowings of his final home.

ADDRESS DELIVERED AT BOSTON, JANUARY, 1867.

Gentlemen of the Convention:—I greet you, to-day, as co-laborers in the great work of reform, and hail this large representation as an evidence that our organization has extended its field of usefulness over a vast extent of country for some years divided from us by internal dissensions. I need not say that I feel gratified to know that a restoration of national harmony has removed the last obstacle to our onward march—opening up avenues of communications which will extend our lines, and eventually bring into close association the moulders of every State in the Union.

The annual return of our sessions never fails to inspire emotions of pleasure, but, on the present occasion, that pleasure is enhanced, from the fact that the participants in trials and sacrifices of no ordinary character during the past year have come together where they can shake hands in mutual congratulations over banished troubles, and rejoice that manly independence, blended with a just appreciation of individual rights, has given us strength and power to combat the wrong, and to assert and maintain the great principle of free agency, with which an all-wise Creator has endowed mankind. The present is an occasion, too, in which we can enjoy an interchange of thoughts, recount experiences growing out of the varied circumstances presented in the past, and apply them with such profit as intelligence and calm discussion may suggest.

The past year has been prolific of conventions — capitalists, those devoted to the professions, students of science and art, and the politicians of both parties, have held conventions, but none, in my opinion, have been of so much importance as those held by workingmen. None ought to awaken as deep an interest in the breast of the moulder as the one I am now addressing. Here there is no scramble for office, no selfish ends to promote, no political ambition to gratify. We constitute an assemblage of men who aim to lay the corner-stone of that proud structure of equality which defends the weak and shelters the oppressed. We profess to recognize manhood in rags or broadcloth, in poverty or riches, and claim for labor the same prerogatives accorded to capital. Our legislation is circumscribed by no narrow limits, nor is it designed to meet the emergencies of the hour, soon to be effaced by the rapid march of time. No; we are here, to-day, to act as stewards of a high trust, for which we are to render a strict account to posterity. Our acts will redound to the weal or woe of future generations, as well as of the present; and hence I claim that this convention, compared to all others, so far as moulders are concerned, involves graver interests, nobler duties, and holier trusts. All that makes life desirable, and all that gives hope to the toiler, and all that secures comfort to the fireside of millions, is intimately interwoven with the deliberations of this body. Example is the parent of influence, and in proportion as we establish wholesome precedents, to that extent will others profit by the good we accomplish; for there is such a close affinity between all classes of workingmen, that whatever advantages or disadvantages are worked out by one is felt by all.

Bear with me, then, gentlemen, if I too earnestly impress upon you the important nature of the responsibilities which cluster around your deliberations. I need not tell you that the eyes of capitalists, from Maine to California, are directed towards you. While they may be too prudent to betray anxiety, rest assured that they are keenly alive to all the actions of this body, and every mistake, every dissension, will be a source of exultation to them. But I have that confidence in the experience and intelligence here assembled, which gives me assurance that a spirit of harmony and mutual concession, as well as brotherly forbearance, will govern us in discussing the many subjects presented for our consideration. I hope to escape the charge of egotism when I assert that the moulders have, and will excel in dignity and decorum, conventions composed of those who sneer at workingmen, and who are actuated by more selfish motives. I am not insensible to the pride awakened by the fraternal relations you have exhibited on former occasions; and when I know that the honor of our organization is in your keeping, I can smile at the groundless anticipations of those who hope for, if they have not prophesied, discord.

Since we last met, many collisions between labor and capital have taken place. I have carefully watched these conflicts in both the Old and New World, and have deduced from them such lessons as, in my humble judgment, are best calculated to afford us profit.

The helpless condition of the vast majority of the producing classes in Europe and Asia, while it excites our warmest sympathy, should admonish us to guard our rights with greater vigilance, lest we suffer encroachments to steal upon us imperceptibly, that we may find ourselves bound hand and foot, helpless for resistance, before we wake from a dreamy security to find ourselves enslaved. Unfortunately for our transatlantic fellow-toilers, they have never possessed the facilities for self-defence so wisely provided for the masses by the founders of our government; and while drawing a distinction that may point to their social disparagement, we cannot but compliment them for the progress they have made under so many discouragements. Strangers to the ballot-box, without a voice in making the laws, treated as the mere inanimate machinery of society, forced to the lowest scale of social life by the aristocracy, kept in poverty and despised because they *are* poor, yet still they heave and surge against the walls of exclusiveness which wealth and power have erected—always hoping and never despairing of ultimately extorting relief. Even now, the great reform movement, which threatens to break down the proscription of wealth and power, is causing the "privileged classes" the most intense anxiety. They quail and cower before the myriads who are clamoring for justice, and cluster around parliament as the last fortress that can shield oppression; but even here they have what they esteem an Achar in the camp, in that indomitable and fearless champion John Bright, while the masses are thundering at the very gates of the citadel. God speed the right. And what has rendered these extraordinary efforts to ameliorate their condition necessary? It is the encroachments of unjust laws that foster a system of speculation, by which the rich are made richer and the poor poorer. Wealth is continually drifting into the hands of the few; the lands are monopolized by the "nobility," and all laws are framed to maintain this condition of things, because the victims of this exclusive monopoly are disfranchised, the rich make laws to protect themselves, and the poor have no remedy. While the "noblemen" hold fancy parks of hundreds of acres, workingmen and working-women are literally packed in narrow courts and alleys, reeking with filth, where they inhale the poisonous malaria of the stews and dens they inhabit. Dissipation, vice and misery of every grade, is the level they reach at last, and the two extremes of wealth and squalid poverty meet in a Christian land.

Here is a lively picture of class legislation in the Old World, and does not the same causes produce the same effects in the New? I need not tell you, gentlemen, with what aptness the capitalists of America imitate those abroad. It is a continual struggle to reach the same standard of exclusiveness, to exercise the same tyranny, and to confine our privileges to the same limits. Here, where our institutions give better means of defence, it requires greater tact and shrewdness on the part of capital to accomplish the results; hence we find it more prolific in expedients, more untiring in its efforts. In spite of all we have yet done, however, there is no denying the fact that the slow and certain centralization of wealth in the hands of the few is progressing. As this evil grows upon us, so certain will the degradation of labor follow. This has been proved in all ages of the world. But since the tendency of capital is to monopoly, and since the streams of wealth continually flow into the pockets of the few, we need not be surprised at the efforts to make the masses tributary to their gains. To accomplish this monopoly, it arrogates to itself the right to hold and control every avenue of wealth; and they do not fail to have the mantle of legislative protection thrown around every undertaking when they desire to cripple or exclude individual enterprise. Then we have the combinations of gold gamblers, money brokers, note shavers, speculators and forestallers, who place a fictitious value upon money and plunder the poor of the necessaries of life. And here, permit me to say, will be found the fruitful source of trouble between capital and labor. These money-worshipping conspirators place a tariff upon the bread we eat, which drains the last penny to satisfy the cravings of hunger. Not only from necessity, but from sheer desperation, workingmen are forced to combine in turn, and strike for wages that will relieve them in some measure from the extortion practised upon them. We know, and God knows, it was never from choice that we engaged in a conflict with our employers, but as husbands and fathers we have been compelled to seek redress from imposition that brought starvation to our doors.

But our list of monopolies does not end here. Perhaps the most extensive of these evils is to be found in coal and iron. Capitalists appear to have singled these two interests over which they claim exclusive control. They must regulate the price and the supply, and every dealer is punctual in practising the extortions of the combination which governs them. The poor may shiver, or flee as paupers to our charitable institutions, but five prices over its cost, when ready for shipment from the mines, must be maintained as the price of coal.

Who shall estimate the miseries and privations entailed upon toiling men and their families from the causes we have named? It is the old process of widening the breach between the rich and the poor — enabling the one to enjoy the luxuries, while the other is denied the necessaries of life. Now, let me ask, is it reasonable to expect workingmen to rest contented under this inequality? It was never designed that these advantages should belong exclusively to the rich, or that this oppression should be visited upon the poor. Society is never safe when such proscriptions are tolerated. Here is the fountain, the sacred fountain of all revolutions, all strikes, all flour riots, or "bread or blood" demonstrations, which so frequently darken the annals of the world; this is the point to which the producing classes have been depressed and at which they now rebel, claiming their rights and resolving to attain them. There is a point beyond endurance to which men may be driven, let their veneration for the law be what it may; for

> "To men
> Pressed by their wants, all change is ever welcome."

The extent of our public domain may, in the estimation of many, seem to render it impossible that monopoly should despoil the poor of land, but, unfortunately, capital absorbs our broad acres as fast as civilization advances. We find in the middle and seaboard States that it is gradually being concentrated in the hands of the few. Wealth owns the town lots, and, to a great extent, the farm lands. In the vicinity of all mechanical and manufacturing pursuits few men who work for a living can save sufficient to purchase a lot from the wages paid. Speculation has scarcely left a foot of land for a poor man to stand upon that he can call his own. While the homestead law may benefit actual settlers to a limited extent, it is so evaded that speculators can fasten upon it at will, and turn it to profit. The mania for monopolizing public land has invaded the halls of Congress time and again. Scarcely a session passes, but some adroitly cloaked bill is presented by speculators, who adopt every conceivable pretext for securing a grant, and holding it till it rises to many times above the original price. The questionable appropriations of land by Congress to railroads, and to further other enterprises in new States and

Territories, is another means of placing the soil beyond the reach of the poor man. These corporations are rich enough to hold it until they obtain fabulous prices, which proves that they do not need the patronage of the government. We have seen the efforts of Wall Street speculators to secure some of the most valuable mineral lands in Montana Territory, ostensibly for mining purposes, and they would have succeeded but for the interposition of the President's veto. There was no difficulty in passing the bill through Congress, because we commit the fatal blunder of selecting capitalists and their sympathizers to represent us. Nay, it has been openly asserted that some of the "Honorables" belong to the "ring" and "go snacks" with the projectors of those fat jobs, and share the profits. We have also seen 800,000 acres of the Cherokee lands sold to the "American Emigrant Aid Society," a company chartered, if I mistake not, by the Legislature of Connecticut, for one dollar per acre less than the government price, thus robbing the government of over three-quarters of a million of dollars, and placing this vast tract of land beyond the reach of the poor man. This company is composed of capitalists and fostered by capitalists, and was organized for the sole purpose of inducing workingmen to immigrate, with a view to overstocking the labor market, and thus effect a reduction of wages. This is one of the "remedies for strikes" proposed by our oppressors, and they were never guilty of a baser fraud than when they asserted that this land was designed for immigrants. Not a man at home or abroad will ever occupy a foot of that land at the price paid for it, and Secretary Harlan was never guilty of a baser act than giving it away. That whole transaction is but another scheme to legislate the land from under the feet of the masses, and to render them more dependent by closing every avenue of relief from the thraldom of monopolists. Far better for the country and the liberties of the people would it be, were the government to give the land to actual settlers in small parcels, than to have it absorbed and held by land companies, emigrant aid societies, and mining corporations; for, even now, capitalists are getting possession of all that portion of the country from which the precious metals are extracted. Thus, we find every expedient that avarice can invent is urged to cut off this last resource of industry.

Capital feels unsafe in waging a war against labor, so long as workingmen have access to land. The object is to get possession of it, and thus cut off all retreat. There is still hope for the toiler, though he be driven to the wilderness for sustenance, while he can stand upon a portion of God's footstool and call it his own. Far better for him to become familiar with the war-whoop and to brave the dangers of frontier life, than to be pent up in the fetid atmosphere of narrow lanes in crowded cities, or inhale the foul air of packed workrooms, at such wages as taskmasters see fit to pay.

It has been predicted that the population of this country will reach 100,000,000 by the close of the present century. This may not be an over-estimate, in view of the fact that a large portion of Europe's oppressed population is flocking to our shores; and many are of the opinion that the exodus will be greatly increased by the fearful revolutions which a dissatisfied population threaten. We cannot escape the conviction that the reins of power must be loosened in the Old World, if existing governments fail to ameliorate the condition of the masses, and to recognize the great principle of self-government which is now working like leaven in their midst. When that struggle comes, as come it must, society will be so disrupted that we may look for large accessions, terminate as it may. This, added to our rapid increase of population, will go far towards peopling the vast territory we possess. But, bear in mind, we are a new country, yet in our infancy, compared to those which now exhibit "the sear and yellow leaf;" and what will be our condition when we shall number half the years of those now in existence? A few centuries, at most, will find our lands absorbed to such an extent that we shall be unable to offer inducements to settlers, and land will be entirely inaccessible but to those who can command larger sums of money than workingmen can save. Hence, we cannot see the wisdom of surrendering thus early to speculators, or of forcing a population upon it to the exclusion of posterity. When we shall have reached the power and greatness of which our liberal institutions give promise, to maintain the high standard we aspire to as a nation, we shall still need a resting-place for the poor, a refuge for oppressed labor; and I regard that as short-sighted legislation which squanders blessings with a lavish hand, when they were as sacredly bequeathed to coming generations as to us. Workingmen, we are but the custodians of this treasure, given to us to enjoy, but not to destroy, and we shall be held as recreants to our trust, if we fail to shield it from the grasp of a moneyed aristocracy.

But there is a remedy for these abuses, and that remedy is with us. Unlike our struggling brothers abroad, we have the ballot-box. We can make laws and repeal laws. We possess the power, because we have the numbers to annul any oppressive act emanating from State or National legislation. We can *compel* our rulers to be just, or supplant them by men from our own ranks, whose sympathies and interests are identical with our own.

Possessing this power to right our wrongs, I blush to say that we have been too long indifferent to the means of defence afforded us by the institutions of the land. The present war, however, so earnestly urged against labor by capital, appears to be rousing the dormant energies of workingmen, who are gradually breaking the ties which bind them hand and foot to *party*. In many localities we have extorted an approval of the eight-hour law from candidates, quite a number of whom have been elected through our aid. Yet, it too often happens that we lack the moral courage to sever our political associations, and thousands of workingmen still suffer themselves to be used as hobbies, upon whose shoulders aspiring demagogues ride themselves into power and place. If we would make the ballot-box a sure weapon of defence, we must appropriate it to our own interests, instead of to strengthen parties that make use of it to enslave us.

Let me ask you, to-day, to point out a single benefit that you have derived from your years of devotion to any particular party. Not one of them ever put a loaf upon your table, a pair of boots upon your feet, or a coat upon your back. All of them stand out in bold relief as the proscriptive agents that never fail to close the door of promotion to us all. The rich are promoted, the poor are excluded. Why? Because our system of conducting elections has become so corrupt, that none but the rich possess the means to purchase power and position. The question is not upon the character or capacity of candidates, but upon the amount of money they can spend. Hence, workingmen may devote a lifetime of service to the existing parties, but they can never rise to position. Their poverty is an inseparable barrier.

If the theory of our government is the greatest good for the greatest number, why shall we not put it in practice? This government was made for the people, and we are the people, but thus far we have proved ourselves unequal to the task of self-government, because we wear the chains of party. We fail to come up to that standard of manhood, and aim not for that proud position which entitles us to the appellation of a free people. We are slaves, not because we *must* be, but because we *will* be. So long as we tolerate this condition of things we must expect to be scourged, for we merit the lash of the taskmaster. How contemptible, how belittling, to whine and complain of the very wrongs we sanction by our own indifference. It is impossible that we can long maintain the sympathy of our toiling brethren in Europe, if we voluntarily hold out our hands and suffer capital to rivet our fetters upon us. Give our struggling brethren abroad the facilities for social emancipation that we possess, and thrones would totter, the nobility would tremble, and money kings would stand aghast as they gazed upon the surging masses, while uprooting the last landmark of aristocracy, and expunging from the statutes every oppressive enactment. Not by violence, not by mob law, not by anarchy, would this work be accomplished, but by that innate yearning for social emancipation which centres around the ballot-box millions who regard it as their only ark of safety, for

> "Slaves who once conceive the glowing thought
> Of freedom, in that hope itself possess
> All that the contest calls for, — spirit, strength,
> The scorn of danger, and united hearts, —
> The surest prestige of the good they seek."

Surely, the lessons of deception we have learned from broken political promises and violated faith should be sufficient to warn us against confiding the interests of labor to demagogues. From year to year workingmen are wheedled and cajoled into supporting partisan favorites who dare not hazard a renomination by any act of political heterodoxy which might "injure the party." Even if a measure favorable to the interests of labor is introduced, there is too often a secret understanding by which other members dovetail amendments to it that render it useless or offensive. We have seen eight-hour bills strangled in several Legislatures by this very process. But it is needless to dwell longer upon these unpleasant facts. Before me are the representatives of man's handicraft, whose interests are identified with all who toil. They comprise at least eight-tenths of a voting population — each a freeman, a sovereign possessing intelligence and capacity for self-government. Then let us rise in the majesty of our strength, and resolve to rule instead of being ruled; assert our rights instead of begging for them, and occupy that proud position which a republican form of government secures to majorities.

To me, it is sometimes a matter of amazement, that we have accomplished so much for the interest of labor in this country, when we have suffered the most effective agencies of its elevation to lay idle by our side. We have passed many trying ordeals during the past few years, and manfully resisted the most formidable assaults. I can but attribute our success more to the justness of our cause, however, than to a proper use of all the means of defence placed within our grasp. Yet how much of suffering, how many privations, our wives and little ones might have escaped, had we commenced years ago to legislate for ourselves. The firmness and resolution so nobly displayed in many conflicts with capital, would, if applied to the principle of self-government, put an end to all such contests. It is with us to establish a permanent code of justice, which would concede to capital all that it can claim in equity, while it would secure to labor all that belongs to it.

It was unfortunate for labor that wages were far beneath an equitable standard, when a fictitious value was placed upon the necessaries of life by the war. As fast as we endeavored to adapt wages to the cost of living, speculators would immediately place every home comfort beyond our reach. Thus we have been forced again to try to get wages up, to try to keep pace with the advance of the necessaries of life. Capitalists would complain of our so frequently "disturbing the relations between capital and labor," while they were in the very act of buying up and forestalling everything that necessity compels us to consume.

But the war is over, and nearly two years of peace bring us no relief. The profits of capital are maintained at the war standard. The prices of all we consume are kept at the same figures, and yet we are censured because we demand a proportionate recompense. No, not proportionate, for we failed to make it so at the start, and we have never yet succeeded in equalizing it. Therefore, if capitalists desire peace, let them cease predicting an additional advance on products of fifty per cent. by labor. All we ask is reasonable wages — let them be content with reasonable profits, otherwise an advance on our part becomes necessary whenever capital attempts extortion.

Oh, then, while we have the power, let us use it to lift labor from the bondage into which it has been plunged by the iron grasp of capital. As an agent of all that is beneficial to our race, do not suffer it to remain where it is, or to sink lower and lower in the social scale. Want and misery are members of every poor man's home, bound to us by the ties of necessity. And yet in this country we possess the right and the power to appropriate labor to its legitimate purposes. How blessed we are in facilities for guarding and fostering it, compared to those possessed by our fellow-toilers in other countries. There they are hampered by oppressive laws, and deprived of every means of redress save revolution, and that is next to impossible, because large standing armies are maintained to keep the masses in subjection, and the entire military force is not only controlled but owned by the aristocracy. But even there a brighter day is dawning. We cannot be indifferent spectators to the convulsive throes caused by the industrial and political reforms now agitated in the Old World. The upheaving masses are clamorous for those rights which nature and nature's God assigned to man. As the light of intelligence spreads abroad, and gives them a clearer conception of the wrongs inflicted upon them, they pause in amazement to find themselves in social and political slavery — bound, as the Roman prisoners of old, to the triumphal car of capital. Starting from their apathy by the clanking of their own fetters, they are surging to and fro like desperate men, resolved upon emancipation.

The reaction has commenced. The cry for deliverance penetrates hall and palace, and rings in the ears of kings, emperors, and noblemen. The rights of labor are not only demanded, but they insist upon the elective franchise as a safeguard against future aggressions. At this hour a struggle is going on in the Old World, the results of which will be the social and political emancipation of enslaved millions, and the downfall of monarchy everywhere, and the building upon its ruins a more liberal government. Need I remind you of the importance of the conflict now going on in America? Need I tell you that the interests of labor are identical throughout the world? We suffer from the degradation of labor, let it occur where it will, because we are liable at any moment to meet it in competition. With but ten days distance apart by steam, and but a few minutes by telegraph, it is an easy matter for capitalists and chartered emigrant societies to arrange an exodus of labor from one country to another, to carry out schemes of oppression. Experience has taught us that capitalists are not slow to avail themselves of such facilities. It is, therefore, a matter of vital importance that an equilibrium of wages should be established throughout the world. Hence, both our sympathies and our interests are enlisted in favor of the great reform movement abroad. A victory to them will be a victory to us; and when the news of their triumph shall be heard across the Atlantic, the workingmen of America will ring out shouts of triumph from Maine to California. I trust that a knowledge of anxiety, and our hopes for their success, will cheer them on, and spur them to nobler efforts. Nor can we, in justice, refuse to accord to them unlimited praise for what they have already accomplished. Amid disparagements of every kind, under all the restrictions that tyranny could invent, they have overleaped every barrier to their progress, and are bravely pressing on to social and political deliverance, realizing the fact that

> "Men, at some time, are masters of their fates:
> The fault, dear brothers, is not in our stars,
> But in ourselves, that we are underlings."

To counteract the manifold evils of which we complain, however, it is well to view, from a rational stand-point, the relations of labor to capital. It requires no argument to show that workingmen make up the aggregate of all governments. Labor is the great fountain from which they draw all support and acquire a vital power. Upon labor is founded all of enterprise, progress, and the perfection of everything that renders a nation great and prosperous. In all these elements of national pride, capital, without labor, would be like a loaf of bread suspended over a hungry man without the means to reach it. It would be as silent and dead as the unearthed treasure embedded in the mountains. But, without capital, labor would be by no means helpless. Daniel Boone was no capitalist, neither was John Jacob Astor when he first started out as a trapper. The history of this country, from its earliest settlement to the present time, proves that labor can survive where capital would starve.

While I admit that the greatest good can be accomplished by a harmonious and equitable association of the two, I deny that labor is as dependent as capital. Combined on equitable terms, both receive an impetus which rapidly achieves great results; and all we ask is, that labor should be rewarded and ennobled in proportion to the good accomplished. It is not my purpose to depreciate capital when I desire to elevate labor. Nature designed them to work in concert, and the happiness of man is involved in their close alliance. What we complain of, is conceding to capital ninety per cent. of the total production, and robbing the producing power of its just dues. Labor has never yet received an adequate reward. As the basis of all national and individual wealth, it should receive an equitable share of what would not exist without it. Combined with mechanical skill, inventive genius, and scientific knowledge, it has brought countless blessings to mankind. It gives practical shape and utility to all things. It is the great civilizer, educator, and beautifier of the world. Labor has felled the forests, beautified the plains, built up cities, spread a network of railroads over the earth, whitened every sea with canvas, united rivers and seas by canals, controlled the elements, connected continents by a wire rope, and brought the capitals of Europe nearer to New York than Boston was a year ago. It is labor that defends a nation in war, and contributes to its wealth and glory in peace.

Upon this subject we want more of practical argument and less of theoretical speculation. I know it has become fashionable among politicians, sensation writers, and political economists, to descant "upon the dignity of labor;" and it is too often used as a hobby upon which to ride into power and place. Popularity-seekers never fail to sweeten the mental palates of workingmen with fulsome eulogies and windy panegyrics upon labor, because they have found it the shortest road to the poor man's heart. Even those who aspire to the title of statesmen stoop to flattery and noisy declamations, while they enlarge upon the rights and wrongs of labor, decking it with flowers, or clothing it in rags, as interest or fancy may prompt. But there is a wide difference between these speculative theorists and those who have practical experience. The man who sits by his comfortable fireside, with pen in hand, sketching a picture of labor such as an active brain may create, can never portray the living likeness, with its hopes and its despondency, its care and suffering, its physical and mental prostration. The workingman, who, after a hard day's work, returns to an impoverished home, shut in from pure air, and packed in a contracted street or alley, *feels* what a mere theorist, surrounded by wealth and luxury, can never comprehend. To work, and slave, and suffer, for the simple reward of what will keep body and soul together, with no hope of a respite in old age, is the real condition of millions at this hour. Therefore, I say, that no school of political economists have faithfully represented the wrongs of labor. Such men as Smith, Malthus, Mill, Carey, and the whole batch of them, only skim the surface, and never descend to the bottom of the labor question. They view it from a standpoint so far removed from the workshop and the poor man's home, that they can have no practical knowledge of the condition and wants of labor. Why, let me ask, do not these speculative gentlemen draw that comparison between labor and capital that would exhibit the misery of the one and the luxury of the other? A just God never designed that this discrepancy should exist. It was never intended that one portion of mankind should drink the dregs of misery, and the other riot in a surplus of wealth, surfeit on every delicacy, and travel a life-long round of idleness and pleasure. To this extent has avarice and oppression made a distinction between the rich and the poor, in a country where the laws concede equal rights and privileges to all. For my part, I have often wondered at the pretensions of capital, when it is so dependent upon labor. It arrogates to itself a superiority, and extorts a deference, which can scarcely be expressed in the word *presumption*. Yet how helpless, how impotent, would be capital, but for labor. The purse-proud may domineer and oppress, the millionnaire may exhibit contempt or pity, as impulse may suggest; but there is not an article of food they eat, or of clothes they wear, or shelter they own, or a convenience fashioned for their ease or comfort, that does not place them under obligations to labor.

But the train of thoughts these remarks suggest, gentlemen, will render a further illustration of the dependence of capital upon labor unnecessary. Your own observation will enable you to pursue this subject much further than I can on this occasion.

Fellow-workingmen, I cannot but congratulate you upon the many agencies of assistance your own exertions have developed within the past few years, which have worked out so much of good, and which steadily tend to our social elevation.

Within twelve months, none more than moulders have tested the utility of compact organization. During the period named, we have encountered a concentration of capitalists, who could command many millions of dollars, drawn together for the purpose of making one determined effort to break through our ranks, and subject us to the bondage of unrequited labor. They were well organized, and contemplated a simultaneous onslaught upon us throughout the land. But when the charge was made, you met it manfully. That struggle will render the annals of 1866 ever memorable among moulders. Thanks to the perfection of our organization — thanks to the manliness and liberality of our members — we breasted the storm and successfully resisted this well-concocted scheme. I will not deny that many privations and trials were forced upon us, and although we were called upon to make sacrifices, yet there was no real suffering.

Foiled in this, they next sought to break up our unions by offers of dishonorable compromise, and to demoralize our leaders by direct bribery and offers of prominent and profitable situations, which would place them beyond want, and beyond the reach of those they might betray. In these they were also unsuccessful. We had passed through too many trying scenes, and found our unions an impregnable fortress of defence on too many occasions, to tamely surrender them. And here, permit me to say, we shall ever find the point of attack from capitalists. They have *felt* the power of trade organizations, and aim at their destruction as the first step towards our subjugation. When our opponents thus acknowledge their potency, can we too highly appreciate their importance — *their necessity?* The fact that they strike terror to our foes is the strongest argument in their favor. Therefore let us cling to them as the wrecked mariner clings to a floating plank; cherish them as our strongest means of defence; honor them as the source of new-born hopes; lean upon them as the last rock upon which we can stand while drifting towards the maelstrom of social degradation.

Yet, in the face of all the good that combination has accomplished, we find those among us who are opposed to trade organizations. We cannot ascribe this perverseness to conscientious scruples, for neither their government, laws, nor usages conflict with duty, morals, or justice; on the contrary, these essential virtues constitute integral parts of all such combinations. Upon what, then, is their opposition based? Ah! I fear "in their simple show they harbor treason." It is a fact well known to all, that capitalists will use them for a convenience, and spurn them when their ends are accomplished; for however severe the conflict between journeymen and employers, a display of true manliness on the part of the former will always be respected by the latter, when the struggle is over; while the fawning, subservient creatures who betray their fellow-workmen will be loathed and scorned by those they have served. This class of men will always be found Iagos in friendship, Indians in treachery, Malays in mercy—ever ready to betray, while they infuse poison into the minds of those who listen to their fault-finding. Yet these very men are indebted to the unions they defame for the wages they receive. They share all the advantages which flow from the organization, and contribute nothing to its support. Were these same principles of rascality involved in a suit at law, these miscreants would be left to brood over their perfidy in a penitentiary.

But we leave this unpleasant part of our duty to dwell upon the more pleasing subject of co-operation.

In this country the great principle of "self-help" is yet in its infancy, although we regret to say it falls short of the fair proportions it ought to present, when we consider the date of its introduction among us. Repeated failures at first dampened the ardor of its early friends; many of these failures were caused by inexperience, and many by mismanagement. Of late, however, its success in England seems to have given birth to new efforts in America, and I am gratified to know that co-operation is gradually becoming a fixed institution among the masses. Regarding it as the most important feature of combination, I claim it as the most valuable of all the instruments for our elevation, and cannot too earnestly impress upon workingmen everywhere the necessity of adopting it. The few efforts that have recently been made have answered all expectations, and now that we have been made familiar with its practical workings, we see nothing to retard its progress but the want of energy among ourselves.

It has no doubt been a matter of surprise to you, as it has been to me, that in Europe, where the masses are kept in subjection, and hampered by restrictions and oppressive laws, they should rise superior to all these obstacles with a boldness and success that has so far eclipsed our best efforts. With all their poverty, with all the proscriptions heaped upon them, they subsist amid strikes and lock-outs, such as would sorely test our powers of endurance in this land of plenty — *the secret will be found in co-operation.* They have no credit in the corner grocery, because the employers warn the proprietors against trust. They seldom have a shilling "to the fore," because the wages paid admits of nothing "for a rainy day." But they have invested the profits of the corner grocer in co-operation. Little by little it has been accumulating in stock, and when idleness or sickness comes, they have a fountain from which to draw. In this way labor is made independent of misfortune and affliction, and the members thus possess an advantage under the system they never could obtain without it. In the ordinary lifetime of a workingman, the aggregate gain he could derive from co-operation would maintain him in old age. The profits of these associations have been frequently published in the labor press of America, and all of you are more or less familar with the history of the Rochdale Pioneer Society. At this hour it is driving on milling and manufacturing on a large scale; while it counts among its various branches of business, dry goods, boots and shoes, groceries, fresh and salt meats, and every article of domestic use.

The following statement will give an idea of its immense transactions, together with the profits of the Corn-Mill

Society. The members are 5,730 in number, being an increase of 230 for three months. The assets of the society are $444,885, being more than in March last by $17,885. The cash received for goods sold during the three months is $304,520, an increase of $17,935, as compared with the preceding quarter. The profits realized on three months' sales are $34,585, which, after depreciating fixed stock account, $1,375, paying interest, $4,730, applying $710 to educational purposes, allows a dividend of 44 cents on every $25 worth purchased at the society's store. At the quarterly meeting, held July 2, 1866, the committee was authorized to contract or make arrangements for supplying coals to the members. At the same meeting the members voted $50 to the Manchester Eye Institution, also an annual subscription of $25, to be paid on the first day in each year.

The business cash receipts of the Rochdale Corporation Corn-Mill Society for the three months are $251,030, being $43,705 more than last March quarter, which, after deducting an item termed "extraordinary receipts wholesale, $27,540," leaves an increase on ordinary sales of $16,180. The society's assets are $318,860, being higher than the preceding quarter by $15,335. The profits realized on the three months' sales is $16,965, which, after depreciating fixed stock, and paying interest on capital, gives a dividend of 22 cents on every $25.

The following statistics afford an index to the progress of the system in England: The annual returns of the societies registered under the act of 1863, contain accounts for the year 1865, relating to 417 of the 599 whose rules have been certified by Mr. Tidd Pratt.

These co-operative associations, carrying on the trade of grocers and dealers in other provisions, shoemaking and drapery, had, at the close of 1865, 148,586 members; their share capital amounted to $3,806,565, and their loan capital was $563,665. They paid $15,315,440 for goods bought in the year 1865, and received for goods sold $16,869,185. They state their profits realized in the year to be $1,396,130, out of which they paid dividends on shares and dividends on purchases made from the societies, and provided for reserve and depreciation funds. At the close of the year the value of their assets and property was $5,528,425, the money in hand, $684,615, and trade liabilities, $1,367,400.

I might present many more evidences of the utility and great prosperity of co-operation abroad, but these are sufficient to show, in bold contrast, our own indifference to this great lever of self-defence; still, I feel encouraged to hope, by the efforts already made, that we shall soon follow in the wake of our more enterprising brothers abroad. I am already gratified to witness industrial combinations on the co-operative principle, and a little pride will be pardonable, when I state that the moulders of Troy have presented the first and most successful experiment in the manufacturing line in this country. Every member of this association can better appreciate the wisdom of this movement, from the fact that they have so recently passed through severe trials, which might have been greatly lessened, if not altogether avoided, had their co-operative foundry been started a year sooner. Having been forewarned, they are now forearmed.

But even in "industrial combination" England is far ahead of us, as will be found in the plan, recently adopted, of giving the workmen a percentage of the profits in addition to their wages. The following test of this new system is derived from the Whitewood and Methley Colleries, as detailed by Mr. H. C. Briggs, the managing partner, although it has been adopted with equal success by other firms.

The profits had fallen in one year to 4½ per cent., in another year to 3½ per cent., and the constant recurrence of strikes among their workmen afforded no probability of effecting any improvement in their affairs. It was clear that there was little encouragement to run all the risks, and to submit to all the anxieties of a business so costly and so uncertain as coal-mining, and to get in return the same interest for the capital invested as it would have yielded if left in the funds or put out on mortgage. They determined to try whether, by so far taking their workmen into partnership with themselves as to make the interests of the two identical, the difficulty could not be solved. The company was accordingly registered under the act of 1862, two-thirds of the share capital retained by the members of the firm, and one-third allotted in shares of £15, with £10 called up, to their workmen and customers. The rate of wages paid was to be the average rate of the district, and the profits of the concern were to be divided in the following fashion: 10 per cent. was set aside as the dividend due to the capitalist; but all above that proportion was to be divided equally between the shareholders and the laborers in their employ. In order to encourage the latter class to become shareholders, the half set apart for them was to be again subdivided, so that the shareholders employed should appropriate one-third of the bonus, and the whole number employed the remaining two-thirds. It was agreed to try the plan here sketched, during the year beginning July 1, 1865; and in the previous May, Mr. H. C. Briggs, the managing partner of the firm, put out an address to the workmen, detailing the scheme at full length, and encouraging them to co-operate heartily with the experiment by a detailed example of the results which would follow, supposing the divisible profits of the year to amount to 12½ or 15 per cent. In the former case, a workman not a shareholder would receive, according to Mr. Briggs's calculations, 1 7-10 per cent. on his earnings, making, if his weekly wages amounted to 30s., a bonus of 26s. 6d. at the end of the year; while a workman who was also a shareholder would receive 5 per cent., giving him — supposing his wages to be the same — a bonus of £3 18s. at the end of the year. If the profits should rise to 15 per cent., the bonus divisible among the workmen would amount to 10 per cent. on their earnings, or double the preceding estimate.

Aided by the increased care and attention of the workmen, and, above all, by the absence of strikes, enabled the directors to divide 12 per cent. for the year on the paid-up capital, and to devote the sum of £1,800, (equal to 2 per cent. on the capital) to the formation of a workman's bonus fund. Thus, on the one hand, the owners of capital realized an actually larger sum during the year than they had ever done before; and, on the other hand, the workmen received from £1 to £10 in addition to the usual wages paid in the neighboring collieries. "Many had a five-pound note in their possession for the first time, and some few had two; the highest bonus being paid to a miner who, being a shareholder, received on his year's earnings of £109 8s. 9d. a bonus of £10 18s. 10d."

The justice and equity of this system are too apparent to admit of discussion. That it will tend to establish more amicable relations between employers and journeymen none can doubt; for, say what you will, there is an antagonism in fact, however ably theorists may argue against it; and it must continue to exist so long as avarice dwells in the human heart, or man struggles for deliverance from necessity, unless the producer is raised to the position of an employer; this will neutralize the effects of the one and destroy the other. We cannot hope for a real identity of interests until capital and labor become united in the same person. Make labor a participant in the profits of its products, and you create an identity that cannot be established by any other process. This will forever destroy all antagonism, and prove a sure remedy for all the unpleasant and unprofitable struggles between capital and labor.

The above statement proves that a firm under the old system had to endure all the vexations incident to its imperfections with small recompense, while under the new, their profits were greatly increased, and the year passed in harmony between employers and journeymen. Why? Because every man felt that he had an *interest* in its success. He was careful to waste nothing, destroy nothing, because every offset to the profits was his loss. In addition to this, he had an incentive to industry; for the more he made, the greater were his profits secured by the percentage derived from the aggregate earnings. With encouragement like this, workmen will be loath to idle away their time. The ambition to display that "five-pound note," as a premium for industry, quickens their ambition, and they commence and continue a race to excel each other in the amount of yearly bonus derived from their earnings. Sum up, if you can, the many domestic comforts this would bring to the families of workingmen. Estimate its value in improving the morals of the poor. Freed from the apprehensions of want, the workman no longer repairs to the dram-shop to drown his sorrows in the bowl. The fact that he is a *partner* in the firm begets a self-respect consistent with his new position, and he becomes more keenly alive to the responsibilities of manhood. The wife grows more cheerful over the improved condition and buoyant hopes of her husband, and her heart leaps with joy to find his brow unclouded with care. Even the children realize a new life in the change, and happiness, like a ministering angel, hovers around the hearthstone.

In my preceding remarks, I have presented reasons why labor should share a portion of the profit it earns. It is but equitable and just, because labor is the foundation of all wealth. I maintain that this division of profit will produce harmony in society, elevate morals, increase temperance, and spread true religion more than the combined efforts of all the moral reforms, philanthropists, missionary societies, and pulpits, in the country; because it chases despair from poverty, it removes all cause for provocation, it leaves no motive for revenge, it tends to lift mankind above their vices, gives him a higher estimate of manhood, inspires a fraternal feeling, and no longer permits him to brood over the world's injustice. In short, give to labor a fair share of the profits on its production, and you will witness a revolution in society that will shed its benign influence over the whole human race. Let us hope that the good example we chronicle of capital in the Old World will be speedily followed in the new.

Among other available instruments for the elevation of labor, I cannot fail to mention education — mental, moral, and physical. There are thousands of workingmen who have not been without many opportunities of advancement, but were compelled to plod on in the beaten track, because deficient in the rudiments of a common English education. So large a portion of the time of the working-classes is taken up by active physical toil, that mental cultivation, however strong the desire for it may be, is rendered impossible. And yet we are scoffed at for the want of cultivation, and pointed to the various institutions of learning scattered in abundance around us. It is true that churches are erected, school-houses are built, mechanics' institutions are founded, and libraries, free and otherwise, are ready to receive us, to instruct our understanding and shape our judgment, but alas! we lack *the time to use them* — time.

The vast numbers of laboring-people who are confined in our large cities, are justified in every sense of the word to bring the prolonged hours of toil within reasonable limits. Compelled of necessity to seek a dwelling-place for their families in the most remote suburbs of these vast collections of humanity, where they can most economically eke out the scanty earnings of the week, they are compelled to rise at the *first* hours of early morn, in order to reach the great gates of the capitalist, to enter upon the long hours of toil that stretch their weary length until the close of day. But the labor is not yet at an end. Again they have to exert their exhausted frames and weary limbs over many a weary mile before they can sit down to rest, or enjoy the society of wife and children. In what physical state, in what mental condition, is this exhausted laborer to enter upon the duties of the social circle, or the cultivation of the mind? Alas! his toil-worn limbs refuse their office any longer. The eyes, wearied with continued vigilance, sink blinded within their aching and throbbing sockets, and the slumberer, half fed, half cleansed, half caressing and caressed, is prostrated in a sleep that hardly knows a waking. Again, and yet again, is this process of walking, toiling, eating, and sleeping repeated — nature engaged in a fearful conflict with mind acted upon by the laws of necessity and social existence.

And this is not the end. Necessity too often forces our children from the school-room to the workshop at a premature age. The small pittance they can earn is essential to the support of the family, and poverty thus closes every avenue of education to a large portion of the rising generation. This is the experience of a large portion of the workingmen of this country; and I cannot too strongly urge the endurance of every bearable privation, or the propriety of making every possible sacrifice, to fit our children for the best opportunities of promotion. Every effort should be made to rescue the young from the evil associations by which they are surrounded. Above all, keep them from all immoral enticements calculated to instil vices which time may never remove.

We know of many great and good men who have sprung from obscurity to adorn the walks of life. The most proficient in arts and science, the most skilled in mechanism, the most ingenious inventors, the most renowned statesmen, commenced their career with no capital but their bone and muscle. But all these men owe their greatness to midnight study, and persevering search for information that overleaped every barrier to their progress.

This is the history of all self-made men, for they were strangers to colleges and all the avenues of education monopolized by the rich. The road to greatness for the toiling millions is a thorny one, and few they are who can travel it.

The workingman needs education also for other purposes than those prompted by mere ambitious motives. Intelligence, sharpened by education, often enables a mechanic to advance more by head-work than hand-work. It gives him a quicker appreciation of his art, makes him more precise in his calculations, and suggests many expedients that enable him to save time and labor. To a practical workman, it furnishes ideas that often culminate in valuable improvements and inventions; and it has often happened that a single thought applied to mechanism has worked out a fortune to the thinker. Aside from this, education fits a man for a variety of occupations the illiterate can never aspire to, when idleness or misfortune is forced upon them.

In connection with this subject permit me to impress upon you the importance of moral culture. The revolution we hope to work out in favor of labor involves an earnest preparation for the many important changes that will follow in its train. Our aim is to reach that standard in society which will enable us to be recognized as intelligent free agents — a portion of the body politic — exercising a controlling power commensurate with the responsibilities devolving upon us; and we must convince the world that we merit the exaltation. It is our duty, therefore, to combine dignity and morality with education. Every vice should be surrendered on the altar of our aspirations. You might as well deck the jackdaw with the peacock's feathers as to place a man in an elevated position, with head and heart poisoned by a passion for low and degrading pursuits.

While I am no temperance crusader, my anxiety for the improvement of workingmen prompts me to warn them against the evils of intemperance. The sober man is always a preferred workman, because he is more reliable. The sober man makes a better husband, father, and citizen. The sober man brings more happiness to his fireside, and proves a better friend and neighbor. His chances for promotion are far better than the inebriate's. We know that workingmen are as sober, moral, and upright as any other portion of the community; but it is my ambition to see them *excel* all others in this respect. Therefore let us set about a reform that will render us worthy of the amelioration we are struggling to achieve.

I need not point out to you the deleterious effects of depraved habits in a physical point of view. That dissipation tends to a prostration of the system, shatters the nerves, and stultifies the senses, none can deny. The slave to his appetite thus becomes deficient in workmanship, and renders his chances of employment more precarious, while the mind gradually relaxes into imbecility. The workman should never fail to adhere to that discipline, and exercise those restraints, which bring to his aid the greatest amount of physical energy.

I am happy to know that my suggestions in regard to

education and self-improvement have been anticipated in a few localities, by the establishment of workingmen's libraries, free reading rooms, debating clubs, etc. No surer means could be selected to facilitate the education and refinement of the masses; while intellectual and moral benefits of incalculable value are derived from these associations, they absorb the time and attention of young and old, and serve to warn the more evil-disposed from demoralizing associations.

Aside from this they constitute a school for the development of varied talent, and fit us better for contact with the world. I cannot too strongly impress upon you the importance of establishing these institutions in every part of the land. What our unions accomplish socially, they will accomplish intellectually, for we become qualified to combat, in the press or on the forum, every assault made upon the interests of labor.

I will now approach a subject to which I have given much serious thought. I allude to the financial interests of the workingmen. It has long been a custom with us to place our savings in the keeping of bankers, banking institutions, and savings-banks, under control of capitalists. We make up no trifling capital for these institutions in the aggregate, and, after making a profit upon our labor, they make another upon our savings. Nay, it frequently happens that, by mismanagement or roguery, the carefully hoarded surplus saved from years of toil is swept away by failures or embezzlement, and we are left destitute of the last means we had provided against sickness or old age.

These swindles are of frequent occurrence, and thousands of workingmen have been stripped of their last dollar by the dishonesty of these institutions.

Why need we run this risk? Will you tell me there is not sufficient financial ability among workingmen to qualify them as custodians of their own savings? They neither lack honesty nor capacity; and surely men who toil for their money, would guard it with more care than those who live upon the labor of others. If anything is to be made upon banking capital furnished by workingmen, they should make it — not the pampered drones who live upon their wits. Every encouragement given to this system is a virtual acknowledgment that we are incompetent to manage our own affairs, and is a direct assault upon the principle of self-government we are striving to establish.

In the July issue of the *Journal*, we proposed a plan for raising a sufficient capital to establish co-operative foundries throughout the country, and suggested a process by which we could establish a national bank. Time has only confirmed my convictions upon that subject; but independent of that proposition, the road is open to moulders and all other workingmen by which they can have sole control of their earnings on a safer basis than that presented by the present banking system. It is an easy matter to start one on capital furnished by labor, and to be officered and controlled by workingmen selected by the depositors. An institution of this kind would command general confidence, because the officers would not receive princely salaries, nor would the sons of broken merchants be pensioned upon it. Its profits would be increased by an economical administration of its affairs, and this would secure a liberal patronage from the public.

The experiment has been successfully tested in France, and a number of banking and saving institutions are now in successful operation in that country. Under the present banking system in this country, poor men can hope for no advantages. All the favors are bestowed upon the wealthy. All the profits go to the stock owners. What we need is a bank that will carry out the co-operative principle, by sharing the profits with the depositors, and affording facilities to struggling men making an honest business effort. In short, those who create the institution should reap the accruing benefits, and not the few who speculate upon the deposits.

Among other handmaids of help to workingmen will be found Home and Land Associations, Building Societies, etc. I commend them to your careful consideration, because I look upon them as exercising a great social influence. By small monthly instalments, such as we can spare above our expenses, a few years at most will find us the possessor of a homestead. United with one of these institutions, we always have a motive for perseverance, because we know that our yearly accumulations will place us beyond the extortion of landlords. Rent is an incessant moth upon our earnings, and is ever detracting from our substance. Oh! what a happy deliverance from the worst apprehensions, when we obtain a home of our own. Let our afflictions or our misfortunes be what they may, it is a relief to know that we are freed from the importunities of landlords and their agents.

It is by a combination of all the elements at our command, and by their proper application to our wants, that we can escape the condition of dependence which too often falls to the lot of the poor. Having so much to oppress and embarrass us, we should not hesitate to avail ourselves of every means calculated to place us upon an equality with the more favored, and to secure us those comforts which are due to honest industry. These agencies, discreetly used, cannot fail to hasten the dawning day of a happy deliverance from social bondage, and guide us in the attainment of those blessings and privileges which avarice and oppression have wrested from us.

In view of the past year's struggles to establish the eight-hour law, much might be said, but it would reflect but little credit upon the energy of the workingmen as a body. In some localities, however, there are noble exceptions to the general indifference upon this subject. Our labor organs have apprised you of the progress this reform has made, and of the untiring efforts of a devoted few to awaken a new interest in its success. When I reflect upon the advantages it would secure to the masses, and the comparative ease with which it could be made a law of the land, I am amazed at the apathy of those for whose benefit it is designed. I need not rehearse the many arguments advanced in its favor, for so ably has the subject been discussed by the many talented champions of our cause, that I have but little to add. I will remind you again, however, that the introduction of labor-saving machinery should confer upon workingmen equal benefits with those received by capitalists. Under the existing organization of society, machinery increases the profits of the latter, while the former are compelled to devote the same time to labor. Yet all these business facilities, at least a large majority of them, emanate from the brain-work and handiwork of the toiler. They are projected and constructed by workingmen, and none can present higher claims to the advantages derived from them.

We must admit that machinery lessens employment to a certain extent, and often forces mechanics to seek other avenues of labor, and but for the growing enterprise of a new country, we should often experience a disastrous stagnation. As it is, we are not free from the effects of those changes which its introduction never fails to create; and when we ask a reduction of two hours per day, the demand is a modest one, to say the least, compared to the additional gains received by the capitalist. We contend, also, that machinery destroys the necessity for so much hard labor.

It was designed to give all mankind a limited respite from incessant physical exertion, and not to benefit the few whose circumstances allow them to live upon the labor of others. We regard it as one of the instruments for ameliorating the condition of the industrial classes, as well as a means of increasing the usefulness of capital. It is one of those blessings developed by the progress of the age, and, like the air we breathe, the water we drink, or the glorious sunshine, should be shared by all in common.

The principle of reducing the hours of labor was tested in this country thirty-two years ago, when such men as Farrell, Luther, English, Hogan, and others, met with the same opposition in establishing the ten-hour system that we now encounter to make eight hours a legal day's work. Then a reduction of three hours per day was demanded — now we ask but for two. Will it be denied that this is a reasonable request, when we consider that, in 1834, labor-saving machinery was yet in its infancy, and that now it has almost reached the acme of its expansive power? Yet none of the disasters predicted by the change then fell upon the community. There was no reduction of wages, there was no curtailment of profits. On the contrary, more have since made fortunes, and made them in a shorter space of time, than ever was known before. Why? Machinery for planing and grooving boards, for making bricks, boots and shoes, and its adaptation to all mechanical and manufacturing operations, to say nothing of navigation and commerce, have not only made up the deficiency created by the reduction of three hours at that period, but the inventions of man have so multiplied that a further reduction of working hours becomes necessary, in order to give a fair proportion of employment to the increasing number of workmen incident to the rapid advance of population.

Man's propensity to evade the law, however, has prevented the producing classes from enjoying, as a whole, the advantages of the ten-hour law. In several of the Eastern and Middle States, particularly in manufacturing districts, eleven and twelve hours are still extorted from workingmen, in violation of the law, by the special contract system. Only very recently, we have noticed the efforts of mill operatives to secure a reduction to the legal ten hours. In these establishments children of tender years are doomed to a life of servitude, the severity of which was seldom felt by plantation slaves. Let us then renew our efforts to shorten the hours of labor. It may be that when we establish eight hours as a legal day's work, those now forced to work twelve will be allowed to reduce theirs to ten. But we should not fail to profit by past experience. Since capitalists will evade the law, we must throw such guards around this reform as will prevent special contracts, or agreements of any kind, that will strip it of its full force and power. The law must mean what it says—eight hours and no more, and not be framed in such a manner as to render it nugatory by such quirks and quibbles as capitalists may invent.

While considering this subject, it may not be amiss to state that we owe some relief to the rising generation as well as to ourselves. We hold that a man who works ten hours can scarcely obtain a sight of his children, certainly not by daylight, except on the Sabbath, for six months in the year. He has to start so early to the shop, and return so late, that he must leave them in bed and find them there when he comes home. Poverty compels him to live in the suburbs, and generally at such a distance from business marts that two hours of preparation and travel to and fro are added to the ten before he can rest at his fireside. He is thus deprived of all opportunity to cultivate those affections, and give that proper tone and direction to his children, which are demanded of every parent. The mother, possibly, is compelled to toil at some occupation independent of household duties, and her children are left to all the evil associations and surroundings which train them in habits of vice and crime. Could the inmates of the houses of refuge, houses of correction, and other institutions for the punishment of youthful offenders, speak, they might trace their wanderings from the path of rectitude to involuntary parental neglect.

Aside from this, children are often forced into mills and factories at a premature age, from necessity. The workman, for instance, becomes a father at 25 years of age; at 35, when his boy is but 10, the father, by incessant application, finds his energies beginning to relax. He can no longer work with his accustomed vigor, and his earnings are gradually lessened, for man, in one sense, is like a piece of machinery — constant use will wear him out; and he often fails in the meridian of life. What then? Want compels him to introduce his children into the factory to make up the deficiency. Thus we find the rising generation is deprived of education and parental control, only doomed to physical prostration, and denied all opportunities of mental cultivation. Each child in turn must follow, because the father is growing less efficient; and thus a whole family is not only enslaved but reared in ignorance, and left destitute of every incentive that ennobles manhood, or that prompts to social, moral, or religious culture. We find this point of our argument ably sustained by the following extract from "Prize Essays on the Temporal Advantages of the Sabbath:"

"The ordinary work-days of most of our operatives are necessarily so engrossed by their out-door occupations, and the time consumed in going to and fro, that whatever their inclinations may be, they seldom have opportunities to indulge in the offices of family devotion. Business, as now conducted, is so thoroughly worldly in its spirit and requirements, and so greedy of every moment it can wrest from its slaves, that no space is left between the rising and setting sun for the pious laborer to assemble his household around the domestic altar. His meal-times barely suffice to enable him to reach his home to appease the appetite of nature and to retrace his steps again. Thus the devout workman, however his soul may pant for a brief daily season which he may consecrate to the social exercise of religion, finds himself irresistibly borne onward by the tide of human selfishness, and compelled to conform to many of the customs and restrictions imposed by the ungodly."

Every consideration, then, which involves physical relaxation, mental improvement, social elevation, moral progress, and religious devotion, demands of us new efforts and cheerful sacrifices to make eight hours a legal day's work. We must unite and work in harmony to accomplish this great reform. If labor and means are required, give them cheerfully and liberally. If a sacrifice of political preferences or partisan attachments is necessary, lay both upon the altar of our hopes and desires for the success of the cause. Whenever you can nominate a candidate favorable to this measure, bear down all opposition by your numbers. Whenever you can exercise a balance-vote to accomplish the same purpose, go to the polls a unit, and make both politicians and capitalists feel your influence.

"Let not the poor
Be forced to grind the bones out of their arms
For bread, but have some space to think and feel,
Like moral and immortal creatures."

Prison labor is another subject which should arrest the serious attention of workingmen. The Labor Congress which assembled in Baltimore last August, treated it as one of the most important business features of the session, and will no doubt give it due consideration at the next session of that body. That it is an evil, and a growing one, all must admit; for there can be no surer agency for the degradation of labor. Like the eight-hour law, it can only be reached by legislation, and we must look to the ballot-box for a remedy.

Having so thoroughly discussed this question in the *Journal* for the months of November and December, we need not enlarge upon it here. In a circular dated Louisville, Ky., November 14, 1866, I find the following statement, which may be regarded as a synopsis of the practical working of the system:

"A firm in this city, extensively engaged in the manufacture of agricultural implements and machines, employing necessarily a number of workmen, has entered into partnership with the lessee of the beforenamed penitentiary, thereby, at certain reduced rates, all the labor is performed by convicts. Having succeeded in this enterprise, we understand that the same firm has made a similar agreement with the party having control of the Nashville penitentiary. And it requires little foresight to see that other capitalists will not be behind them; and thus it may come to pass that these houses of correction, which we build and sustain with our money for a specific end, may be made the means of depriving us honest men of our means of subsistence. We know, from observation, that capitalists will invest so as to realize the largest profits; and it cannot be doubted that they will gain more by employing convict workmen at the rate of forty cents per day than they will by employing us. We have learned that the same parties have made arrangements to carry on the same business in the Kentucky penitentiary."

I have long been convinced of the beneficial results which would accrue to the interest of labor by an alliance with trade organizations throughout the world. Our aims, objects, and interests are the same everywhere, and I look upon this as the safest plan to prevent an unjust competition, because it would destroy the power of capitalists to supplant workmen struggling for their rights in one portion of the world by the importation of help from another. We could hold communication at close intervals, and keep the producing-classes informed of the movements of capitalists in both hemispheres. We know that strangers have often been intruded upon us to effect a reduction of wages, when they were entirely ignorant of any existing difficulty. In many instances they have nobly refused to be made instruments of our oppression, and cast their lot with us, resolved to stand firm in our defence. But it often occurs that our poverty, and their necessities, leaves them no alternative but that of "fulfilling the bond" with those who have contracted for their labor. In addition to this, we could establish rules and regulations which would prevent capitalists from contracting for labor in any part of the world, when detrimental to the interests of labor, by the same process of warning now in practice among ourselves. In this particular, the Atlantic cable might prove as advantageous to us as it is to others.

I need not point out to you the advantages to be derived from such an alliance, so far as fraternal feelings and interests are concerned. Under existing circumstances, strangers from other countries are looked upon with suspicion, if not with fear, when they approach our workshops. Their advent among us has so often proved an injury through the deception and misrepresentations of capitalists, that we are loath to give them a cordial welcome. In this way a prejudice has been created and ill-feeling engendered which ought never to exist.

An alliance that would embrace in its membership every workingman, no matter where his lot might be cast, would ensure a hearty welcome to the toiler in every quarter of the globe. As far as trade is concerned, he would be a cosmopolitan, enjoying the right to locate where it best suited him, possessing credentials that would open the door of trades-unions, and cause the right hand of fellowship to be extended to him, no matter where he is located. Bound together by fraternal ties, having the same interests and feelings, recognizing membership in his trade organization as the only essential passport, we could build up a power that would defy the world. With eight-tenths of the civilized human race in the union, we could laugh at the assumptions of avarice, and successfully resist oppression.

This and kindred subjects, however, will be the legitimate property of the next Labor Congress. In view of the many important questions that will be brought before that body, I cannot too strongly urge the propriety of selecting for delegates our deepest thinkers and most proficient legislators. If ever there was a necessity for the convocation of the best talent, the clearest intelligence, and the greatest experience that the ranks of labor can produce, it exists now. The action of that convention, if made up of such material as workingmen can furnish, may confer lasting benefits upon the producing-classes. We require in council men of broad, comprehensive views, capable of taking in at a glance the great future, and so familiar with the laws of cause and effect that they can legislate for posterity as well as the present generation.

I need not say to you with what anxiety I look forward to its deliberations, for labor's best hope will centre there. Let us see to it, then, that a full representation is secured. The Baltimore convention was a new thing — we might say an experiment. The notice was short, and its importance not fully understood. Under the circumstances, it exceeded our expectations in point of numbers and talent, the able manner in which vital questions were treated, the interesting character of the business before it, and the favorable opinions elicited from the President of the United States in regard to many of the leading measures, left an impression, which will, I trust, awaken a deeper interest in the next Labor Congress, and render it a worthy custodian of all that labor will confide to its wisdom.

Let me congratulate you, gentlemen, upon the encouragement and aid the labor movement has received from its accredited organs in this country. It would be difficult to estimate the assistance they have afforded us in resisting that prejudice, proscription, and oppression which have drawn so broad a line between the rich and the poor. Since 1863, a number of these "silent pleaders" for the rights of workingmen have been started, and nobly did they perform their mission, so long as they maintained their vitality. But, I am sorry to say, they were suffered to languish and die for the want of proper support. One after another went down after spasmodic struggles, leaving their projectors deeply involved. Subsequent to that period, however, the progress derived from these disastrous experiments gave courage to others, and new organs have made their appearance in different parts of the country, the majority devoted wholly to the labor cause, but a few of them are obliged to blend extraneous issues with the ostensible object of their publication, in order to secure an existence. I cannot too earnestly declaim against such uncongenial association of antagonistic purposes. Particularly is it detrimental to our cause when newspapers, professing to be labor organs, lend themselves to either one of the political parties. It is this practice which gives our enemies cause for the not always groundless charge of prostituting the labor movement to partisan interests. Such impressions forced upon the public, either by necessity or design on the part of the publishers, stultifies our best efforts, and creates a prejudice that is difficult to overcome.

Let me urge you to a course of liberality and personal exertion to extend the circulation of labor organs that will place them above the necessity of occupying so questionable a position. Keep them distinct, and sanction no "entangling alliances" calculated to awaken distrust or suspicion. We must hold our cause spotless and pure if we would win public favor, and those who attempt to carry water on both shoulders, that is, "to serve two masters," cannot bring essential aid to either. He that is not for us is against us, and we want no partial advocates of the labor movement, no half-way support. To such organs, therefore, as start out wholly and solely devoted to us, give them that aid which will remove them from the temptation of wearing two faces.

I need not dwell on the importance of an outspoken press. It is ever powerful in moulding public sentiment wherever civilization and intelligence hold sway. Every interest dear to man, art, science, morality, religion, temperance, or any other cause influenced by public opinion, have their organs, and labor alone is deficient in this essential element of progress. Without them we struggled hopelessly and groped in the dark for many years. Not until their advent did we make the slightest advance towards equalizing wages with the cost of living, nor would our best efforts to establish the eight-hour law, or to accomplish any other reform, have availed us anything without their aid. Can there be any more effective weapon to guard against assault, let it come in what shape it may, whether from oppression, extortion, or misrepresentation? The time was when we were compelled to submit to the sneers and scoffs of capital, and insulting defiance hurled in our teeth; but since we have established labor organs we are treated with respect, and our opponents are slow to provoke a controversy the merits of which will be placed before the public, whom we no longer permit to make up a verdict on ex parte evidence furnished by our opponents. In view of these apparent truths, I hope I shall escape the charge of egotism, if I refer with pride to the field of usefulness occupied by our own *Journal.* But nine numbers have been issued, and I wish that you were as well informed as my position enables me to be, of the happy results derived from its publication. Since its first issue I venture to assert that the members of our organization have become better informed of the practical working of the international and subordinate unions than they ever were before. They have manifested a deeper interest, exhibited a greater anxiety, and devoted more time and attention to the work of self-elevation. The eagerness with which the *Journal* is sought after, too, gives me reason to hope that a concern and devotion, on the part of its readers, is bestowed upon the labor movement heretofore unknown.

That it has exalted our character as workingmen, both at home and abroad, is proved by the copious extracts taken from, and the high encomiums passed upon it in both hemispheres. It has made the Iron-Moulders' International Union of America a household word in Europe; and the hope and encouragement it has given to the labor cause everywhere, I leave to be estimated by others. Not the least compliment paid our *Journal*, however, is the fact that employers as well as journeymen are always eager to peruse its contents. This may be prompted more from fear than affection; but so it is, and not a few capitalists read it by stealth as a "forbidden book," while others peruse its contents with undisguised gratification.

We are pleased to see that the Coachmakers' International Union, though yet in its infancy, has issued a monthly journal, got up and illustrated in a costly manner. Thus our example has not been without profit, and it is to be hoped that the time will come when every national trade organization will have its own organ, placed above the accidents of time and circumstances by the liberality of its respective members. In such an event, our own *Journal* will be looked upon as the pioneer of labor literature, should you, in your wisdom, decide upon its continuance. I might add that the uncertainty of its future has proved a formidable obstacle to its general dissemination. The knowledge that this body could at any time suspend its publication has prevented that exertion to extend its circulation which would have been put forth under other circumstances. I have not a doubt that its expenses could be materially lessened, if it could not be made a source of revenue, were this body to decide it a fixture of our organization. Before I close my remarks, I feel it a duty to speak of the depressed condition of female labor. It is a lamentable fact, that "the fairest portion of God's creation" is left to struggle in their weakness, with no manly hand extended to lift them from the social oppression of this avaricious age.

True, spasmodic efforts have resulted in a few public meetings, where superficial theorists have been permitted to display their oratorical powers and to tickle the public ear, but no good has been gained. The efforts were ephemeral, the effect fleeting. It is but a mockery of woman's woe to draw a fanciful picture of her sufferings, and then leave her in her misery, without hope of amelioration. All laws, human and divine, point to man as her natural protector; and yet we suffer women to be made the victims of inhumanity without throwing a protecting arm around them. Why this indifference? Are we not selfish and unfeeling, to be so absorbed in our own interests as to lose sight of all that pertains to the welfare of the weaker sex?

I have often pondered upon their destitute condition since the unprecedented rise in the cost of the necessaries of life, and wondered how they could exist on the starvation wages paid them. Many have been made widows by natural causes, and more by the casualties of war, with from two to five children to provide for. How is it possible to support them on the pittance paid for needle-work or any other labor? Manhood, honor, humanity, gallantry alike revolt at the hardships women are compelled to endure through the avarice of man. All the economy they can practise, pinch and stint as they may, cannot secure them the comforts of life, though they may stitch till the midnight hour and rise at early dawn. In this land of plenty thousands of women and children go to bed hungry, while mothers toil on hopelessly, with hollow cheek and sunken eye, until their trials are ended by premature death.

What is it that drives women to houses of prostitution or consigns them to prison? The character of American women is too exalted, too pre-eminent in virtue, to suppose that they would seek either from choice. No, it is man's injustice that drives them to the alternative of starvation or a life of vice and crime. Too often it is necessity that compels her to flee from hunger and seek temporary relief in haunts and associations that awaken feelings of loathing and abhorrence. We hold that man's injustice works out more ruin for the sex than all the libertines and roues in the land, and even these never fail to parade the show and tinsel of a life of crime, and contrast its luxuries with the poverty of their victims, before the starveling flies from one misery to another.

We claim that workingmen, above all others, should wash their hands of all participation in this rank injustice. As men struggling to maintain an equitable standard of wages and to dignify labor, we owe it to consistency, if not to humanity, to guard and protect the rights of female labor, as well as those of our own. How can we hope to reach that social elevation for which we all aim, without making woman the companion of our advancement as she has been of our depression? Are we to march on to the goal of our ambition and leave her behind to drink the dregs of misery? Surely we have not paused to reflect upon this subject, or we would have higher conceptions of our duty as men.

The influence workingmen exercise in society can accomplish much for the amelioration of women. Instead of patronizing establishments for such articles as women make or manufacture, because they sell cheaper, and are enabled to do so by the pittance doled out to their operatives, purchase only from those who pay them living wages. Base your preference on the liberality of the employer to his operatives, and let them know that you will promptly make a sacrifice to maintain a principle. If they deal fairly with their workwomen, you will deal with them, and not otherwise. Remember those who labor comprise the great mass of consumers, and possess the power to punish avarice wherever it is practised. Let their goods remain on the shelf, and do not purchase them at any price, if they have been put there by the unrequited labor of women.

We can further aid workingwomen by urging and assisting them to organize trade societies. Let us place the same weapons of defence in their hands that we have found so effective. In their unions, they could keep a list of employers in any particular calling, placing the Shylocks on a black list, which would enable us to shun their establishments, and select from the more just and liberal with whom to deal. In this way we would be offering an inducement, or paying a premium in the way of patronage, to those who paid their hands living wages.

But the surest remedy for these evils, after all, is co-operation. There are many occupations which women could carry on with but a small amount of capital, such as all kinds of clothing for women, boys and girls, shirts and caps for both sexes, umbrellas, map coloring, and almost all the occupations at which they are employed. In the majority of cases no capital at all would be required, because the customer could bring the material to the co-operative depot, and have them made up. Transfer the profits from the pockets of heartless employers to the pockets of the worker, and a different state of things would exist. Workmen, however, must take the initiative, and give the women all necessary assistance at the start. Once in operation, they can "go alone," if we give them the support we can give. The experiment has been tried with but limited success, and why? Because we have given all such efforts cold neglect instead of the encouragement they had a right to expect.

Rest assured, gentlemen, we cannot go forward without marching hand-in-hand with woman. If we leave her behind, capital will not be slow to unsex her, and place her in many of those channels of labor now occupied by us. She must have the same inducements, and derive equal benefits from the reform we are striving to accomplish, to make ourselves secure. We are bound to extricate her from her present depressed condition from motives of humanity as well as policy. It will be fatal to the cause of labor, when we place the sexes in competition, and jeopardize those social relations which render woman queen of the household. Keep her in the sphere which God designed her to fill, by manly assistance, and save her as far as possible from physical prostration, and the too often demoralizing influences of the mill, the factory, and the workroom.

The proud mission of woman should place her above a mere condition of drudgery, a machine to be worked by the power of necessity on one hand, and that of avarice on the other. What would be the domestic hearthstone or the family altar without her? How desolate and cheerless the home denied the presence of woman. She it is who ministers to our wants, shares our sorrows, soothes in sickness, lessens our cares, and blunts the barbed arrows hurled by malice, envy, or slander. She is the great moral reformer who lifts us above selfishness, and points out the path of honor and usefulness. Without her civilizing and christianizing influence, man would be a savage. Essayists have written and poets have sung in praise of woman's faithfulness and constancy; but could they witness the patient endurance and long-suffering of women in the humbler walks of life, when husbands and fathers are forced from employment by tyrannical exactions, they would feel an inspiration never awakened beyond the pale of labor's circle. How they banish despondency, cheer the despairing, and strengthen the wavering in such trying hours, can be attested by many before me. Where is our gratitude, then, that we shall leave her helpless and unprotected? Unfortunately, society has long been too niggard of privileges that should be conceded to women. Her moral worth is too lightly estimated, and we consider it a foul wrong that she is not included in every progressive movement designed to benefit man.

Recently, however, by their own indomitable perseverance, the public are beginning to recognize the claims of woman. They fill professorships, receive diplomas, and master art and science with an aptness not excelled by the sterner sex. A writer in a recent issue of the New York *Tribune*, states that there is a college at Manhattan, Kansas, where the sexes are placed on an equality in the race for honors. He says: "Thus far, the girls excel their competitors of the other sex, even in composition, declamation, and the higher mathematics. This term they are to have a debating club, and learn parliamentary law. If women *will* conduct our great charities, they must hold public meetings; if they will hold public meetings, they must know the rules of deliberative bodies."

The constitution of Kansas allows every woman of eighteen and upwards to vote on every question in district and school meetings, and makes them eligible to all offices in school-boards. The same writer states that "in some districts they do not vote; in others, they turn out *en masse.* Many are elected to offices, and fill them with great zeal and practical wisdom. I learn of one district where a lady drew plans, obtained and let a contract for a school-house, and is the leading spirit of the board."

I find the subject of conferring the elective franchise upon women begins to meet with grave consideration. Senator Cowan, of Pennsylvania, and Senator Wade, of Ohio, have openly declared in favor of it in the U. S. Senate; and it has long been a debatable question with myself, whether common justice should not concede them the right to vote on all matters that directly affect their welfare. Many assert, and I fully endorse it, that they would add dignity to the elective franchise, and give it a moral power that would elevate it above the bribery, corruption, dissipation and dishonesty that now cling to it like a festering sore. Certain it is, had they the privilege of voting, they would command a consideration now withheld. Left out of legislation, denied all means of redress, and held subservient to man, they are restricted in their usefulness, and crippled in their efforts to consummate those comprehensive schemes of benevolence and charity which alone can originate in woman's heart. Why should women not enjoy every social and political privilege enjoyed by men? The time, I hope, is not far off when universal suffrage and universal liberty will be the rule all over the world.

In conclusion, gentlemen, let me remind you that it requires union and harmony to carry out the several suggestions I have made. Let us "pull together," and avoid the bickerings and jealousies often awakened by an honest difference of opinion, where men fall short of the intelligence and toleration that should govern rational beings striving to accomplish a great purpose. When men become slaves to their passions and prejudices, good results are hopeless. It is my ambition to see moulders exhibit a liberality and a charity for each other that will strengthen the ties of friendship, cement the bonds of union, and render our organization a brotherhood that will always command a cheerful obedience to its enactments. Whatever the sacrifice we may be called upon to make, or however severe the trial duty demands we should encounter, let us meet them with ready hands and cheerful hearts. Above all, let us exercise that charity and forbearance towards each other which are demanded by the great interests we have at stake. I am admonished by my own deficiencies that none of us are infallible. Let us do the best we can. "Angels can do no more."

SPEECH DELIVERED AT BIRMINGHAM, PA., SEPTEMBER, 1868.

Fellow-Workingmen:—And if I am not mistaken, this is a meeting of workingmen; assembled pursuant to a call made by the Labor Reform party of this county. We are not here, then, to praise or condemn either the Democratic or Republican parties; we are here to discuss such questions as seem to be of vital importance to the laboring-men of the nation, and if, in the discussion of those questions, we shall bear hard upon either of the parties, it must be because they have acted contrary to what we believe to be correct, viewed from our stand-point. I am not here as a politician, as a representative of any political party, but as a workingman. I have but one object in view — the success of our party, of such principles as will elevate and better the condition of the class to which I belong — the workingmen of the nation; the men whose labor has made our country what it is; the men who, when treason and rebellion reared their monstrous heads in the land, and threatened our government with destruction, rose up in the majesty of their strength, and stood like a wall of adamant between the Constitution and all the elements of destruction and desolation. When I can see the workingmen of this nation enjoying some of the fruits of their toil and some of the rights supposed to belong to freemen — some protection under the common law, and some exemption from the burdens imposed upon them — then will I be content to "shuffle off this mortal coil," for mine eyes will have beheld the day of our salvation.

When our fathers landed upon the barren shore of New England, in 1620, they did not bring with them a cargo of gold and bonds, with which to begin the erection of a new empire — their stock in trade was composed of strong arms and brave hearts, and they went to work cutting down the forests, building log-cabins, and planting corn. They were our fathers in the great field of labor; and their descendants, with hundreds of thousands of the oppressed of all nations, have gone on from that day to this, until, as a result of their toil, what was then a vast wilderness, is now the finest country on the globe, and, in some respects, the greatest nation the world has ever seen. The founders of our government intended to create a true democracy, where every man should be in the enjoyment of equal rights and privileges. They did not anticipate a time when every example and precept taught by them should be disregarded, and every landmark by them erected should be torn down, and a despotism erected here such as nowhere else exists, and yet they are scarcely cold in their graves until all these things have come to pass.

Men talk to me of our independence and boast of our constitutional government, and all that it guarantees to us; but with these spread-eagle gentlemen I do not agree. These things will do very well for Fourth-of-July orations, but not for every-day life. Workingmen do not live in imagination, but upon cold, practical facts; and the facts are, that the workingmen of this nation are oppressed more than the same class in any other country. It is true, we have no king — no political king — but here we have monopolies, banking monopolies, railroad monopolies, land monopolies, and bond monopolies, that supply the place of kings, dukes, lords, etc., and their rule is getting to be more intolerable than is found anywhere else. If we have no political king, we have money kings, and they are the worst kings in the world. We, by our labor, have been putting into motion millions of little streams of wealth, and a false financial and money system has been directing them into the pockets of a few individuals, while we remain poor and powerless. No, not powerless, for we have yet one way of escape. The ballot-box is still open. We in this State have yet no law allowing the Legislature to do our voting for us. If we will use the ballot effectively, we will soon be freed from the golden rule that now crushes the vitality out of the industry of the whole nation. This we are now trying to do. This is the object of the Labor Reform party; and we are ready to make common cause with any other party or people who will adopt our principles and get on our platform; and our platform is broad enough and strong enough to hold nine-tenths of the people of our country. So we now ask all men of all parties, who have an interest in the industrial and commercial success of our country, to get upon our platform.

What do we want? Why, we want peace, harmony, and union, from ocean to ocean, and from the Gulf of Mexico to the North Pole; we want the immediate restoration to their proper places, under the Constitution, of every State, and a reconstruction that will give immediate confidence to all the people, and put all workingmen to work upon an equal footing; we want an immediate repeal of the law that grants from $12,000,000 to $50,000,000 annually to feed and clothe the labor of one section, while the workingmen and women in another section are starving; we want those who are held under charge of treason to have a speedy trial, and, if found guilty, to be hung without further humbug or expense to the people. We want a public land system that will give the lands to actual settlers, and not one acre to any man who will not go upon and cultivate it, and a restoration to the government of every acre now held by any company or individual that is not placed in the market at once, and for all time put an end to all speculation in the public domain. We want equal protection under the flag to every man who sets his foot upon American soil with the intention of living among us, no matter where he may be from, and immediate reparation, or war with any government that will insult an American citizen, no matter where he may have been born.

WE WANT TO PAY EVERY DOLLAR OF THE PUBLIC DEBT IN THE SHORTEST POSSIBLE SPACE OF TIME.

We want "one currency for the government and the people, the laborer and the office-holder, the pensioner and the soldier, the producer and the bond-holder," the widows and orphans of the dead soldier, and the money-kings who skinned the government in the hour of its danger. We want an immediate repeal of the National Bank law, and all other banking laws, because the whole banking system, and especially the national banking system, is a swindle from beginning to end, and is sustained by a direct tax upon the industry of the nation. We want "equal taxation upon every species of property according to its real value, including government bonds and other public securities." And finally, more than anything else, we want a monetary system that will give to the people a secure, cheap, and abundant currency. Here is a chapter of wants, that constitute the platform of the Labor Reform party; and is there any man who will say that they are not reasonable wants? Is there any man who dares to say there is not justice in every one of them? If there is, let him come up here and object. We are ready to meet the issue here or anywhere.

It has become fashionable to call us and those who think with us, repudiators, because we desire to pay a certain portion of the public debt with greenbacks, and because we want to tax the bonds. Now, in reply to this, I claim that those who gave us the greenbacks are the repudiators. They claimed that it was a work of necessity. We admit it. But when they made them a legal tender, all who disputed their right to do so were called traitors. I was not one of those, because I was then, as now, in favor of a paper currency issued by the government. But, now, after they gave us the greenbacks, and we find them to be the best currency we have ever had, and want to keep them, they brand us as repudiators. They created the greenbacks, gave them to the country, forced them upon us, and now want to repudiate them. The government got into a tight place; there was no money to be had; those who had gold and silver hid it away, held on to it, looking to a higher rate of interest, a higher price for it. Congress, in this dilemma, did just what it should, just what was proper—issued a paper currency free of interest, and made it a legal tender in payment of *all debts public and private*, except duties on imports, and interest on public debts. This took the power from the money-shavers, and gave the people and government a currency independent of the gold that was hid away. What was the result? how long did this wholesome condition of things continue? Not long; for the Shylocks bought up the greenbacks at a low price, raised the price of gold and everything else so high that they made the greenbacks almost powerless. Then came another pressure. What was to be done? There was an open warfare between Congress and the money-lords, between the government and gold; gold went to Washington and dictated terms; Congress was not equal to the emergency and gold conquered; and from that day to this, the government and the people have been at the mercy of the gold board and their satellites. Wall Street, Third Street, and State Street said, issue bonds at a higher rate of interest, payable in gold, and we will buy them. The bonds were issued, and were purchased at an average rate of about sixty cents on the dollar; six per cent. interest in gold on their face value, free from tax. But even this advantage of thirteen per cent. did not satisfy them: they wanted a still further chance to speculate in gold, and skin the government and people. To do this, the national bank swindle was organized, which has succeeded in placing the whole monetary power of the nation in the hands of a few men, and to sustain which we are compelled to be taxed more than a hundred millions a year. But we are told that Congress could do no better; that an emergency existed, and that these moneyed men—these patriotic Christian bankers—came forward and saved the government. These Christian gentlemen held on to their money until they had squeezed the hardest terms possible out of the government, and then they took a mortgage on the bone and muscle of the country — on the body and soul of the nation, and to-day they are sucking the life-blood from the productive powers of our country. Why, sir, the armies of Jeff. Davis were full of such patriots, and hell is full of such Christians. I am asked, what better Congress could have done than submit to the hard terms of the bankers? Suppose the workingmen of the whole country had said, we won't go into the army, nor fire a musket, until you give us one hundred dollars a month in gold. What would Congress have done? Do you think the terms would have been granted? No; a draft would have been ordered; armed soldiers would have entered our workshops and our homes, and forced us into the army, and that would have been perfectly right. When men were wanted, they were taken, which was right; for the government has the right to lay its hand upon every citizen, and say, "You must come and help defend the life of the nation." Now, if it wanted money, could it not have done the same thing? If it has the right to take every man, has it not the right to take every dollar also? Why, sir, instead of surrendering to the bankers, Congress should have drafted the money, as it did the men; it should have filled its treasury, as it did its army. Congress should have taken this monetary power by the throat and squeezed the life out of it. This was not done, and now the bankers and bond-holders are squeezing the life out of the nation. There is but one remedy — the people must do what Congress failed to do. They must take this monster by the neck and shake the life out of it.

Our debt of $3,000,000,000 is but a small matter, if properly managed. Give us a sound currency, equal taxation upon all property, resolve to pay the five-twenties in greenbacks, reduce the interest on the debt to three per cent., and bring the expenses of the government within reasonable limits, and every department of industry will be fully employed, the productive powers of the nation will go forward as we have never seen them, and the wealth of the nation will be so largely and rapidly increased, that the payment of the debt will be but a small task. As it is, what are the prospects? Commissioner Wells issued a report, a short time ago, which led us to believe that the debt was being largely reduced. Now, what are the figures? We see that the debt has been increased over $50,000,000 in ten months. At this rate, how long will it be until the debt is paid? Just get out your slates and pencils, and figure it up.

Who is this man Wells? He is one of the worst enemies the workingmen of this country ever had. It was he who published a report, some time since, showing how well the labor of the United States is paid, and what a happy and contented people they are. I guess he had not heard of the Labor Reform movement. He is the same fellow who went over to England, and in a speech said that the girls who work in the cotton-mills in the Eastern States were so well paid that they spent a portion of each summer at the seashore.

Now, fellow-workingmen, I must close, and in doing so, let me call upon you to sever old party ties, cut loose from old party associations, and get right upon our platform. On the platform of the Labor Reform party. Vote for Burtt, send him to Congress, and you will send a man who will act with the other friends of labor in Congress, and from whose united efforts we must look for emancipation from the burdens under which we are now groaning. Mr. Burtt stands committed to every one of the ideas and principles above referred to, and will make an able advocate of the rights of labor. Vote the whole Labor Reform ticket, and where there is no labor ticket in the field, vote for the man who stands pledged to carry out the ideas contained in our platform. If we are but true to ourselves, and true to the great principles we acknowledge, and which were advocated by the fathers of the Republic, the time will soon come when we will be in fact what we have long been in name, a free, happy, and independent people.

ADDRESS DELIVERED AT SUNBURY, PENNA., SEPTEMBER 16, 1868.

Fellow-Workingmen: — I left my office this morning, and hurried from that great city on the Delaware to this beautiful town on the Susquehanna, at your call. I come not among you as a Republican or a Democrat, but as a worker in that great labor reform movement that is so rapidly developing itself over the whole land.

We have met here, not as the adherents to either of the two great political parties, but as workingmen; not as partisans, but as patriots; not as pieces of machinery, but as intelligent citizens of a common country; not in a spirit of rebellion, but to protest against the monstrous wrongs that are and have been imposed upon us and all who toil. We are not here to talk about the issues that have been buried in the past, and which will never come upon the stage again, but to discuss the living issues of the day — the great questions that are now before the American people, and which are to be passed upon in the coming elections.

As most of you are aware, I have been, for years, connected with the labor movement in some capacity. I am a workingman myself, and have been all my life. For twenty years I have been trying to discover some remedy for the great wrongs imposed upon labor—to find the reasons why a small portion of the population enjoyed ninety per cent. of the wealth of the nation while the many, whose labor produced everything, lived in poverty and want; why the millions of little streams of wealth, put in motion by our hands, run continually into the pockets of a few individuals; why one man can enjoy his millions while a thousand go hungry and naked; why one man can live in a palace while hundreds have scarcely a roof to cover them; why the costly equipage and the starving mechanic are jostled together in the same street. I believe we have at last discovered the cause; and if we are true to our own interests, true to the class to which we belong, true to our families and our country, we will soon see a brighter day than has ever yet been seen by workingmen in any part of the world.

In the discussion of the great questions of the hour—or such as them as I shall notice—I shall treat them as a workingman, viewed from a labor stand-point, and draw such conclusions as I believe are best calculated to promote the interests of the great masses of the people.

Within the last seven years we have passed through the most gigantic war the world ever saw. A rebellion such as no other government could have successfully combated. Whatever our opinions may be as to the immediate causes of that war, we can all agree that human slavery (property in man) was the first great cause; and from the day that the first gun was fired, it was my earnest hope that the war might not end until slavery ended with it. No man in America rejoiced more than I at the downfall of negro slavery. But when the shackles fell from the limbs of those four millions of blacks, it did not make them *free* men; it simply transferred them from one condition of slavery to another; it placed them upon the platform of the white workingmen, and made all slaves together. I do not mean that freeing the negro enslaved the white; I mean that we were slaves before, always have been, and that the abolition of the right of property in man added four millions of black slaves to the white slaves of the country. We are now all one family of slaves together; and the labor reform movement is a second emancipation proclamation. The second Declaration of Independence was issued by the Labor Congress, in Chicago, in 1867; and upon that platform of principles we will stand until liberty is proclaimed to every son and daughter of this great land. When the rebellion came, the workingmen from every city and town, from every hillside and valley, rushed forth to save the life of the nation; the bone and muscle of the country stood, like a wall, between the Constitution and all the elements of destruction, and hurled back the power that would destroy our government.

More than three years ago these toilworn and war-battered veterans forced the last armed foe to yield, and returned to their homes, believing that their work was done, the Union saved, and that peace and gladness would at once reign over all the land. They supposed each State, lately in rebellion, occupied just the same position as before the war. They believed that a number of the leading rebels would be hung for treason. They believed that the war establishment would be reduced to a peace-footing. They believed that the freed negroes would, like themselves, be compelled to go to work and earn an honest living. They believed that the expenses of the government would be reduced to what they were before the war, and that, in a short time, all traces of that great contest would be wiped out, and we would at once begin to pay off the debt. This was the general belief.

Not a single one of these expectations has been realized.

More than three years ago the war ended, and we are now farther from a true peace than we were then.

I do not intend to discuss the several plans of reconstruction, because it is foreign to my object, and I do not believe in any of them. I first desire to state a workingman's idea of the matter.

The Southern States undertook to secede — to get out of the Union. We went to war to prevent them from seceding. We whipped them; consequently they never were out. Secession never was an accomplished fact.

I hold that if, at the end of the war, there was but one loyal man in the State of South Carolina, that man was the State. The words "reconstruction" and "restoration" are the wrong words. Reorganization, under the State Constitutions, was all that was needed. It is just as impossible to take a State out of the American Union as to make the Susquehanna River run over the Allegheny Mountains. Every man, woman, and child might be hung for treason or blown from the cannon's mouth as rebels and traitors; but the territory would be there still, and any man setting foot upon it would be just as much under the laws and the Constitution as in any other spot. But we will leave this. I said that the soldier, when he returned to the field or the workshop, expected that the negro whom he had set free would be made to work for his living the same as the white workingman of the North, but he was mistaken.

The Freedmen's Bureau was established, and still continues, and there seems to be but little prospect of its repeal under present management. How much money that institution has cost the people we will never know, for the reason that there is nobody who does know. It has been variously estimated at from $150,000,000 to $300,000,000, and it is now costing from $12,000,000 to $20,000,000 annually. For salaries alone it costs almost a million of dollars — a vast army of Federal officers, and worthless, ignorant negroes feeding from our labor. I pronounce the Freedmen's Bureau to be a stupendous fraud upon the labor of the nation. It has been feeding and clothing the negroes while thousands of white workingmen and women in the North, within the past two years, have been suffering all the pinchings of poverty and starvation, with no bureau to go to; and a portion of every dollar they have earned has gone to feed these people at the South, who are abundantly able to work. Here in this part of the world, where men are compelled to work, we find no such sympathy. While we have work, we receive just wages enough to buy the commonest necessaries of life, and when dull times come, and we are thrown out of work, we must get along as best we can; if we have no money, buy on time — must mortgage the future, and if we cannot get credit, we must beg or starve.

We have no Bureau to go to, and many of us are compelled to sell our *bureau* to get bread, if we are fortunate enough to have one. But we do not want to be clothed and fed at public expense. All we ask is an opportunity to work. We want the labor of the whole country to be put upon the same footing. While we are willing to work, we are not willing that a portion of our wages should go to keeping other men in idleness who are as able to work as we are. But it is said that some provision had to be made for those people. Very true; but they should have been put to work and made to earn their living. "Oh, but," says some fellow, "the planters, their former masters, had no money, and everything was disorganized; they could not pay for labor." Very true; but a reorganization would have been an easy matter; and would it not have been much better to loan the planters a few millions of dollars, at a reasonable rate of interest, taking a mortgage on their real estate as security. $20,000,000 loaned in this manner would have done more to "reconstruct" the South than a thousand millions spent upon the Freedmen's Bureau. At the close of the war the whole South was in ruins. Grim-visaged war had desolated the whole land. Not only was their substance eaten up, but their currency became suddenly worthless and labor unmanageable. Had order been restored, as it should have been, and capital furnished to employ labor, the whole South would this day be in a prosperous and flourishing condition. These people, who have been fed and clothed at our expense for three years, would, by their industry, be paying a large portion of the taxes necessary to carry on the government, and the labor of the rest of the country would be relieved of a great burden.

We now come to the greatest question before the American people — a question of the very first importance to every producer in the land — a question in which is involved the freedom or slavery of every workingman in America — a question that must destroy the power of a monster moneyed aristocracy, or bind the whole labor of the nation, white and black, in fetters of gold — that question is one of finances. A great noise is being made by the bond-holders about the national credit, national honor, the plighted faith of the nation, and so on. They do not pretend to place their claims to gold upon the broad grounds of right and justice. To alarm the people, and draw attention from the merits of the question, they raise the cry of *repudiation.* Now let us consider this matter for a little while, and see what there is in it. The whole amount of bonds now out were purchased at about sixty cents on the dollar, *in greenbacks.* They draw six per cent. interest *in gold,* on one hundred cents to the dollar; that is, they draw ten per cent. in gold, on the sixty cents in greenbacks invested. When these bonds are paid, it will not be at the same price they were purchased, but at their full face value. Now, don't you see, if they are paid in greenbacks, the holder will get forty cents on the dollar more than he paid. If a man holds $100,000 of these bonds, he will make $40,000 by the operation, besides his interest for the time he holds them. Don't you think he ought to be satisfied with that? Yes; but he is not. He demands gold. Suppose he is paid in gold, at the present rates he would get one hundred and forty-four cents for every sixty cents paid; or, for his $60,000 he would get $144,000 — a net gain of $84,000. The interest at ten per cent. in gold would be 14 4-10, say fourteen per cent. in greenbacks, or $8,400 per annum. If he holds the bonds five years, this would be $12,000 more, or a total of $126,000 made in five years on an investment of $60,000, and without one hour's labor. Just look at these figures, fellow-toilers, and see how much justice there is in this demand for gold. We will not pay gold. Forty cents on the dollar and fourteen per cent. on the investment is all the premium we *will* pay, or *can* pay. There is not an honest man in the country who will tell you that this debt can be paid in gold. The gold coin now in the country is estimated at $250,000,000. Our debt is $3,000,000,000. Can we pay the larger sum with the smaller? And the amount of gold is growing less each day. The sum sent abroad to pay interest on bonds, and the sum required to settle balances of trade against us, is greater than the supply. The payment of the debt in gold means repudiation. The people will never stand it. These bond-holders, having raised the cry of repudiation to frighten the people, are now frightened at the monster they created, and are trying to find refuge in a funding bill. You know a funding bill passed Congress just before it adjourned. The President refused to sign it, and it failed. This bill provided for a new bond at 3.60 per cent., *principal* and interest payable in gold, bonds to run forty years; the old bonds to be converted into the new. This was the bond-holders' bill. They were perfectly willing to sacrifice two and one-half per cent. of interest to secure a mortgage on our labor for forty years, and then get gold for their whole claim.

We are told now that this bill would have amounted to nothing; that nobody would have been fool enough to exchange a six per cent. for a 3.60 per cent. bond. That is a mistake. Bond-holders are alarmed at the rising wrath of the people; the word "repudiation" comes up before them like a grim monster — a spectre that haunts them at every turn; they see that the people have penetrated the thin armor that covered their rascalities. This funding bill was a dodge to deceive the people, to take the whole matter out of our hands for forty years. Did you ever stop to consider what a funding bill means? Suppose we issue a new bond at four per cent., with forty years to run, four per cent. on $3,000,000,000 would be $120,000,000 per annum; for forty years $4,800,000,000 — or nearly $2,000,000,000 more than the whole debt, leaving $3,000,000,000 still unpaid. At the end of forty years this and the rising generation will have passed away, and what will we have left our posterity? The children of the bond-holder will hold a mortgage on our children; our children will be slaves to them, as we are now slaves to the bond-holders to-day. The funding system is one of the parents of the unequal distribution of property — a fungus on the body politic. In itself, the funding system, of all the provisions of our Constitution, is especially oppressive to labor. It is the parent of the banking system—that fruitful mother of unutterable affliction to the sons of industry —which brought us, at one fatal step, into the vortex of a moneyed aristocracy, overgrown fortunes, and hopeless poverty, taxation through all the elements of existence, and speculation to the utter grinding down of labor, to pamper the fortunes of the rich. Thus far, then, we see our boasted *equal rights* to be the merest skeleton of liberty, which by its *letter* declares that equality shall be guaranteed to all; but by its *operation* creates aristocracy, privileges, extortion, monopoly, and the *legal* robbery of those who toil. Shall these bonds be paid in gold? Shall this incubus of uncounted millions be fastened upon us and our posterity forever? Our answer at the ballot-box must settle the question. When the greenbacks were issued as a legal tender, many men in both parties opposed it as dangerous legislation, and contrary to the spirit of our Constitution. The friends of the measure were compelled to defend it. I remember the debates very well. I was one of its friends, for I thought I could see through it the dawning of the day of deliverance for labor. I remember that it was common to raise the cry of rebel, traitor, etc., against all who opposed it. We, who favored it, said the greenbacks would be as good as gold; that they would take the place made vacant by the withdrawal of the gold and silver by these patriotic bankers; that we would have no more use for gold as money — no more use for bankers and brokers — and that we would be free from the grasp of the money power. If any of you, fellow-working-men, are fortunate enough to have a greenback in your pocket, just look at it, and you will see on its back the words — "This note is a legal tender for *all debts, public and private*, except duties on imports and interest on the public debt, and is receivable in payment of *all loans made to the United States*." From this we draw the most conclusive proof, that it was the intention of the makers of the law that these greenbacks should be the currency of the country, and that no law should be made recognizing contracts for the payment of any other kind of money. So careful were they not to be misunderstood as to the public debt, that they said, in large letters on the back of each note, "And is receivable for *all* loans made *to* the United States." Not only do we find this clear proof on the backs of the original legal-tenders, but if you will look up a national bank note, you will see upon its back these words: "This note is receivable at par in all parts of the United States in payment of all taxes and excises, and all other dues to the United States, except duties on imports; and also for all salaries and *other debts owing by the United States to individuals, corporations, and associations* within the United States, except interest on the public debt." These notes were issued after every denomination of bond was authorized. Does any man want any stronger evidence than this, that those who framed these several laws never intended the public debt should be paid in gold? The only exceptions made were duties on imports and interest on the public debt. If they intended to pay the principal in gold, would they not have excepted that also? If it was not the intention to pay the principal in greenbacks, then every note issued by authority of Congress bears a lie upon its back, and those who authorized their issue are fathers to the lie. But we have further evidence: Senator Sherman, of Ohio, a leading man in all our financial measures for years past, said in a speech the other day in Ohio:

"Now, when we come to look at the law, which is the essential part of the contract, we find a provision that a kind of money defined in that act, and called *lawful money*, shall be a lawful tender in payment of *all debts*, public and private, *except the interest of the public debt*, which must be paid in *coin*. Now, I have reasoned about this matter very often, in public and private discussion. I have made and answered collateral arguments in speeches and reports; *but my mind always comes back to this conclusion:* that under the law the contract between the creditor and the United States was, that the creditor should loan the United States *lawful money,* or paper money — that the United States would pay the interest at six per cent. in coin, and that the United States might, at the end of five years, return to the creditor his principal sum, *in the same money loaned to the government.*"

Senator Sherman is stumping the West for the Republican party. He says the law means greenbacks. Senator Morgan is stumping the East for the same party. He says the law means gold. Who is right, Sherman or Morgan? The secret of the difference between these two great men is not to be found in men, but in the atmosphere. In the West, the plough-holders predominate; in the East, the bond-holders control the political machine. The operations of the atmosphere upon the human system, and especially upon the human pocket, are altogether different in the two sections. Shall these bonds be paid in gold? Not if the people have the power to prevent it. What do you say, you man, out there in the crowd, with one leg, and a prop under your arm, did you get your wages in gold? Do you get your pension in gold? No. If you did, you might buy a new leg. But there is no gold for you. The blood that flowed from your veins on some hard-fought field in the defence of the old flag, was coined into gold for the bond-holder. There is no gold for the widow and orphan. Their tears and sorrows have been made into gold-bearing bonds, and sold to the worst enemies this country ever had. What do you say, workingmen of Northumberland County, are you going to allow yourselves and your children to be chained to the car of this monstrous Juggernaut— this gold power? Are you going to receive wages in greenbacks and pay taxes in gold? Your answer is one universal NO. But election-day will tell whether you are honest or not. But we are told that these bond-holders loaned their gold to the government when it was in a tight place.

They never did any such thing. They held on to their money-bags until the government, to save itself, was compelled to issue greenbacks. They then run down the greenbacks and bought them up with their gold, and bought bonds with the greenbacks. As soon as they had got the bonds, they had both the government and the people in their power. The next step towards absolute power was the creation of the national banking system, by which we are taxed $50,000,000 a year, which we pay to these banks for furnishing us with $300,000,000 of bank-notes — the printing of which could be done for a few hundred dollars. Why did not Congress issue $300,000,000 of greenbacks, instead of these national bank notes? Greenbacks are free of interest. But the $50,000,000 of interest is but a small portion of what the government and people are swindled out of by the speculations and dishonesty of these banks. One of the ablest writers in America says of this greenback question:

When the Legal-tender Act was passed in 1862, all our Republican friends declared that greenbacks were as good as gold. Governor Todd, in a speech which elicited great attention, insisted that they were better than gold. They actually did pay all debts, debts that had been contracted in gold to be paid in gold. There were plenty of instances where debts of $1,000 in gold were paid with $1,000 in greenbacks, which were worth but $400 in gold. They liquidated all contracts of every description; they cancelled mortgages; they satisfied judgments and stopped executions. All the business of trust funds was conducted in them. The debts of the infant creditor, the widow, and the orphan were discharged in them. They paid the soldier and the pensions for the price of their blood. They satisfied all bonds of every description — town, city, county, and State. The Republican legislatures of the States paid the interest of debts contracted in gold with legal-tenders. Did our Republican friends see any repudiation in all this? None in the world. The legal-tenders were money, the people's money, and to question it was to be disloyal in the highest degree. But, presto! what a change! When the bond-holder of the United States is to be paid — that privileged and aristocratic class, which has been exempt from all taxation for years — then, for the first time, we are informed by the radicals that greenbacks will not answer. They have paid everybody else's debt, but they can't pay the bond-holder. He stands on a more elevated plane than the rest of the community. No offerings can be burned at his shrine but the solid and bright gold. Now, we are told, after greenbacks have liquidated thousands of millions of debts—after they are in everybody's pocket — they are not money, but mere promises to pay, of no particular account. By a magic wand, the bond-holder seems to have converted all the radical leaders and newspapers to his opinions; and the latter immediately proceed to unsay all that they have said, and to undo, financially, all they have done. To pay the bond-holder in the same currency that pays every other debt, in the same currency with which he bought the bonds, is now, forsooth, no payment at all — it is repudiation.

Most happy and patriotic bond-holder! you are the preferred of the preferred, the very elect of the elect. The people lent gold, and had to take legal-tenders; you lent legal-tenders, and must have gold!

But another objection raised to the payment of the 5.20 bonds in greenbacks is that most of the savings-banks hold them as security or on deposit, and most of the depositors are poor men — workingmen; and to pay in greenbacks would be an injustice to these people. This, the gold people think, is a strong point, and thousands of workingmen think it is a sound and just argument. Let us see how much truth there is in it. A savings-bank holds $500,000 in bonds. It draws six per cent. in gold, or nine per cent. in greenbacks, and pays to its depositors five per cent. in greenbacks — a clear gain of four per cent. Nine per cent. on $500,000 would be $45,000; five per cent. to the depositors would be $25,000 — a net profit to the bank of $20,000. But this is not all. The poor depositor must pay tax on his income, while the bank pays no tax at all. This, with other advantages in favor of the bonds, makes the interest about twelve per cent. Thus you see, while the depositor gets but five per cent., the bank gets seven per cent. Twelve per cent. on $500,000 would be $60,000; or, in other words, the depositors would get $25,000 and the bank $35,000. Do you see how this is done? Do you see how labor is robbed? You pay your money to these banks and get five per cent. in greenbacks; they take your money and buy bonds, and get interest in gold, and pay no tax. Some may say no wrong is done the depositor, because he gets what they agree to pay him. Very true; but a great wrong is done to the people, to the tax-payer, to the producer. The $35,000 pocketed by the bank is stolen from the people. It is added to the millions more that are ground out of your bone and muscle by the tax-gatherer's machine.

Three years ago the war ended, and every heart was filled with joy. The soldiers returned to their homes, the ships were laid up, and every one expected a large contraction of expenses. What has been the result? $600,000,000 a year is squeezed from the industry of the nation in the shape of taxes, and yet the debt is increasing at the rate of $10,000,000 a month; and one of the leading papers of our country stated, a few days ago, that the last report of Mr. M'Cullough showed that the revenue laws were not quite productive enough. Taxes must be raised. "Oh, but," says John Covode, and other gold men, "no man pays any tax whose income is not over $1,000!" What do you say to that? How much more do you pay for the necessaries of life than you did before the war? I make the assertion here, without fear of contradiction, that not one dollar of tax is paid, or can be paid, that does not come out of the workingman — the producer; not indirectly, but directly out of the producer's sweat and toil; and the man who will endeavor to deceive the people by a contrary argument is a fraud upon the country. We pay fifteen dollars a barrel for flour that we used to get for six, from four to eight dollars per ton for coal that we used to get for less than one-half of that. Rents have advanced more than one hundred per cent., and everything we consume has gone up in like proportion; and yet, in the face of these things, men have the impudence to say the workingman pays no tax! I find very great efforts making to convince workingmen that the high price of coal and flour is owing to a short supply. We are told that the Western farmers are holding back their crops, and that coal is scarce because the miners have been on a "strike." Let us see how much truth there is in this The entire production of anthracite coal this year is 8,340,173 tons against 8,116,832 tons last year, a gain of 223,341 tons. If this increase is kept up to the end of the year, the whole amount will be about 14,000,000 tons. So you see there is no short supply there. The eastward movement of flour and grain through Buffalo, from January 1st to September 1st, shows an increase over last year of 163,407 barrels of flour, and 4,050,932 bushels of wheat; and the season for the shipment of flour and grain is just opening. So we find no short supply there; and so we would find it through the whole catalogue. I only call your attention to this to show you the folly of some of the arguments of our opponents.

It is claimed that the national banks should not be disturbed, because they furnish a safe currency. Is it any safer than greenbacks? Again, we are told that by the creation of the national banks the government obtained an *immediate* loan of $300,000,000. This is not true. It is well known that, for the first year after the adoption of the system, not more than $40,000,000 of bonds were purchased from the United States treasury. The most of the few banks that did adopt it during the first year had on hand a sufficient amount of bonds, which they handed over to the treasurer for currency. It was nearly two years before the system was generally adopted, and not more than fifty or sixty millions' worth of bonds were ever taken by the national banks; and this sum being spread over a period of two or three years, what becomes of the immediate loan of $300,000,000?

A man wanting to start a bank, buys $100,000 worth of bonds, takes them to Washington, deposits them with the secretary of the treasury, gets $90,000 in national bank notes, comes home, and opens a bank. He draws six per cent. interest in gold on his bonds, besides what he makes on his circulation and the speculations banks indulge in. The profits made by these banks can be judged from the magnificent palaces they build. The operation, in all its naked deformity, is a simple one. The government furnishes the bonds upon which the circulation is based, and pays six per cent. in gold for the privilege of allowing them to remain in the treasury department; then it furnishes the notes for circulation; then it issues a charter, — more properly called a license to swindle the people, — and the bank is complete. The only thing that the banker furnishes is his own worthless carcass. The interest of the nation requires that the $300,000,000 of national bank currency be called in, and $500,000,000 of greenbacks be issued; with these take up $500,000,000 of 5.20 bonds. This will give us a good currency, and will pay off nearly one-fifth of the national debt, and save, in interest alone, $30,000,-000 per annum, besides breaking up the greatest nest of public robbers ever organized in any country. I am frequently asked by workingmen, what has this question of interest to do with us? we are not borrowers, neither have we money to lend. Let us see: the natural increase in the wealth of the nation in seventy years is less than four per cent.—say four per cent. per annum. Then it follows that any rate of interest above four per cent. is too much, and is running the nation in debt. While the increase of wealth was at the rate of four per cent. per annum, interest has averaged at least eight per cent. for seventy years. But if we take the last seven years, we will find that the increase in wealth has not been over three per cent., while the rate of interest has averaged fully fifteen per cent., making an actual loss to productive industry of twelve per cent. per annum. This matter of interest is the source of all our financial panics. The man who spends more than his income must go to the wall sooner or later; and the nation that spends more than it produces must come to ruin. No nation on the globe ever did, or ever can, carry a rate of interest above the natural increase of wealth, without coming to financial ruin. The manufacturer, the farmer, the mechanic, and the common laborer each run in debt, or each have a load of debt accumulating upon him, an ever-increasing mortgage upon his energies, upon future labor to make up present deficiencies. The money-lenders and the whole horde of bankers, speculators, and other gamblers are, day by day, accumulating additional liens upon labor. This condition of things lasts about ten years, when labor breaks down under the load. Its resources are exhausted, the rate of interest can no longer be paid, the creditors begin to crowd the debtors, a "money panic" ensues, and financial ruin sweeps over the land, prostrating everything before it; debts are settled at a small per cent. on the dollar, bankrupt laws are enacted, we become a nation of individual repudiators — all the figures on the slate are wiped off. In this general ruin and mixing up of things, the bankers gather up all there is, and labor must make a new start. This operation is repeated every ten or twelve years. Interest acts like the tax-gatherer; it enters into all things, and eats up the profits of labor. Labor marries a wife and supports a family; labor needs food, clothing, and rest; labor works but six days in the week; labor gets sick, and has doctor's bills to pay. Interest works all the time; interest never gets tired; interest needs no clothing; interest never gets hungry; interest never gets sick; interest has no family to support, and needs no almshouse when it gets old; interest produces nothing, but it consumes everything; it gathers together the products of labor, making the rich richer and the poor poorer. Interest produces nothing; all it does is to transfer the products of industry to the pockets of the money-lenders, bankers, and bond-holders.

One word more about these bonds: they should never have been issued; there was no necessity for it. If the government has the right (and it has) to make every man enter the army, has it not also the right to take every dollar? Is money more sacred than life? When the government wanted men, it drafted them. Why did it not draft the money also? When it sent a file of soldiers into the workshops to look after us, why did it not send them into Wall Street to look after the money-bags? When these bankers refused to give up their money, they should have been put into the front ranks, and their money taken to pay the expenses. Had this just policy been pursued from the start, we would not now be cursed with this vast gold-bearing debt, and a bond-holding, privileged, untaxed aristocracy, that is squeezing the life out of the nation and people.

Jefferson tells us that "a wise and frugal government, which shall keep men from injuring one another, shall leave them otherwise free to follow their own pursuits of industry and improvement, and shall not take from the mouth of labor the bread it has earned, is the sum of good government." How far we have departed from this simple plan of government every man can judge for himself. Nowhere in the world is there such powerful monopolies; nowhere in the world is there so rapid a centralization of wealth; nowhere are the rich becoming more rapidly richer and the poor more surely poorer, than here in our boasted land of liberty. Our dearest rights are being stolen from us by the power of gold. Bonds and banks are the Alpha and Omega of the devil's alphabet, and unless we arrest them in their work of ruin, our government will soon be but the shadow of itself, and our liberty the lingering memory of a dream.

I ask for what I have said, a careful consideration. I have considered each question from a labor stand-point as they affect labor and laboring-men. Let us be true to ourselves, true to our country, and true to the principles that must prevail in this nation, or it must cease to be the land of the free. If each man will do his duty in the coming struggles, we will soon be in *fact* what we have so long been in *name* — a free people.

EXTRACTS FROM REPORT TO THE TORONTO SESSION OF THE I. M. I. U.

TORONTO, July 8, 1868.

To the Officers and Members of the 9th Session of the Iron-Moulders' International Union, in Convention assembled:

GENTLEMEN: — It again becomes my duty to submit to your honorable body a report of my official actions. I shall, therefore, in accordance with the law, proceed to detail, as briefly as possible, the more important events of the past eighteen months, and make such recommendations as may seem to me calculated to promote the best interests of our organization.

The Boston Convention left the proceedings and revised Constitution in the hands of a committee, to be prepared for publication. The custom, at all previous conventions, was to leave the printing of these documents in the hands of the president, who was supposed to be sufficiently honest and trustworthy to be intrusted with a matter of such importance, and who would be most likely to get them out in the shortest possible time, so that all the members could read for themselves what was done by their representatives.

The action of the convention in this matter retarded the publication of the documents, and seriously injured the organization by keeping the members in ignorance of the laws under which they were supposed to be working, and to which they were to be held amenable. Within my official experience, I can think of nothing that caused so many complaints and so much dissatisfaction as this delay in the publication of these documents; and I must here express the desire that in whatever you may do in this matter at the close of this session, you will have in view the earliest possible publication of all documents necessary for the successful carrying on of the organization.

STRIKES OF 1867–'68.

It will be remembered that during the sitting of the Boston Convention, a telegram was received from Pittsburg, giving notice of a reduction of twenty per cent., and asking instructions as to what course to pursue; an answer was returned that the reduction should be resisted. The men had been out of work for some time; and it was supposed by the employers that their means were exhausted, and no resistance would be made to a reduction of wages.

I need not detail the circumstances connected with the strike, but will say that it was one of the most bitter and protracted strikes we have ever had; it continued during almost the entire year of 1867, and resulted in almost a complete victory. I deem it a matter of justice to the members of No. 14, to say that no strike was ever better conducted. The law was strictly complied with in all cases, and the men were ever ready to pursue whatever course was best calculated to ensure success.

As early as October, 1866, it became evident to my mind that we were about to enter upon a severe industrial prostration, and I began looking around me for the best means of defence from the threatening storm.

I went to the Boston Convention with my mind fully made up as to the proper and only safe course to pursue. In all my conversations with delegates, I endeavored to show the dangers by which we were surrounded, and to point out the true policy to be pursued. The last words I spoke to the convention, previous to its final adjournment, were words of warning and caution. After the final adjournment, I consulted with many of the delegates, especially those from the Ohio Valley, and we parted with the understanding that the policy pursued should be a voluntary reduction of prices to seventy per cent. in all those places where the advance was 100 per cent. above the bill of 1861. The first vice-president, representing in part the whole of the West and Northwest, gave me his solemn pledge that he would advocate that policy on his return home. I was well aware of just what was going to happen. I knew that before the first of February the employers would demand a reduction of wages, and I also knew that, if it was refused, a long and serious struggle would be the result. My object was to make a voluntary reduction of wages before the employers demanded it, and before they could come together to consult upon the matter. The combination of 1866, which resulted in the great lock-out of that year, had been completely broken up, and a feeling of estrangement existed between some of them. My object was to keep them apart, and prevent a new combination, and preserve a good feeling between both parties.

On the 17th of January, the first vice-president wrote me of his safe arrival home, and of trouble in Louisville. I also received unfavorable news direct from Louisville. On the 19th I telegraphed him to go to Louisville immediately, and there receive instructions by mail. I wrote him full and explicit instructions what to do. For some reason, unknown to me, he did not reach Louisville until the 22d. On the 24th, he telegraphed me in these words: "Bridgeford refuses all compromise; other shops accept Cincinnati prices." I immediately returned this answer: "Put the men in Louisville to work at thirty per cent. off, and return to Cincinnati immediately." Instead of carrying out these instructions, or doing nothing, he got the men in Louisville to agree to the Cincinnati bill of prices — a reduction of about five per cent. — and gave them a solemn pledge that Union No. 3 would make no reduction; and all this was done, not only in direct violation of my instructions, but without even asking my advice, or notifying me of what had been done. I had already learned of the beginning of trouble in Cincinnati, and determined to go there. On the 31st of January, I received a telegram from a secret agent in these words: "Danger of losing everything. O'Brien embarrassed. St. Louis lost. Come, or order immediately." I started, and reached Cincinnati on the 5th of February, and found a communication had passed between the union and the employers; that the employers had met, formed an association, and adopted the following preamble and resolutions, which were posted up in all the shops:

CINCINNATI, OHIO, February 2, 1867.

The past two years' experience having fully satisfied us that there is no reliance to be placed in the repeated promises made to us by the "Moulders' Union Association," for the regulation and equalization of prices East and West, and that certain rules adhered to by each section of said union are operating to the decided injury of both employers and employés in the West; therefore,

Resolved, 1st. That from this date we will allow no dictation from said union; that we will pay only 40 per cent. above old prices, instead of 100 per cent.; this reduced price still exceeding prices paid in Buffalo, Albany, and Troy for similar work; these places coming into direct competition with us in sales.

2d. That we will at all times determine, in connection with the foreman, the prices that we will pay for new work not on the price list; adhering to the same rates as fixed for similar work, without dictation from any shop committee; and that we will be governed by our interests and judgment as to the character and number of apprentices we will employ.

WM. RESOR, *President*.

S. R. BURTON, *Secretary*.

On the evening of the 7th of February a meeting of Union No. 3 was held, and after a very free discussion of the whole matter, a committee of conference was appointed, with myself as chairman. The following note was sent the employers:

CINCINNATI, February 7, 1867.

WM. RESOR, *President Employers' Association:*

Sir: — Union No. 3 having appointed a committee to confer with the employers, with a view to effecting a settlement of the present difficulty, we respectfully ask you to notify us whether or not you will consent to an interview. If favorable, state time and place. WM. H. SYLVIS, *Chairman.*

The following reply was received:

CINCINNATI, February 8, 1867.

Mr. WM. H. SYLVIS:

Dear Sir: — Your communication in regard to the difference between the Moulders' Union and the employers, asking a conference, has been received.

In a communication written to the Moulders' Union, January 19th, we fully stated the position we occupied, and owing to the low price of labor in the Eastern cities, and the facilities of transportation, we must either abandon the prospect of a remunerative and large stove business in the West, for the benefit of ourselves and our employés, and work against the competition that would not remunerate for the capital employed, or resist the oppression, and endeavor to work outside of the union sooner than sacrifice what we have invested.

You are fully aware that the difference in the prices of moulding is from 60 to 70 per cent. higher here than at the points above mentioned that come in direct competition with it. As a single example, we may mention that Eastern stoves are sold in Columbus, Ohio, and at other points near us, that defy competition from us, although the difference in *our* favor, as to transportation, is from 600 to 800 miles.

We believe the cost of living is as low or less here than in the East, and there is no reason why we should not be entitled to obtain our labor at the same price, and thus be enabled to compete successfully for the trade that legitimately belongs to the West.

We have repeatedly made the same statements by communications and committees of conference of Union No. 3, and always with the same result, viz., a disbelief in our statements, and an increase of price.

The reply to our communication of January was an almost unanimous vote (as we are informed) that no reduction would be acceded to until they had time to equalize prices.

Having already defined our position fully in the preamble and resolutions unanimously adopted by us, February 2d, we see no good to arrive from a discussion by any committee.

Should your committee wish to submit any communication or proposition to us in writing, it will be received and respectfully considered and replied to.

STEPHEN R. BURTON, *Secretary.*

In answer to this, the committee agreed to the following, which was adopted in a joint meeting of Unions Nos. 3, 20, and 50, previous to being sent to the employers:

CINCINNATI, February 12, 1867.

S. R. BURTON, Esq., *Secretary.*

Sir: — Your letter of the 8th instant was duly received, and we will answer it as briefly as possible. You say the prices for labor should be the same in the West as in the East. We think a difference of 20 per cent. between the East and the West would be no disadvantage to the employers of the West. Your argument as to the unfair competition, at present, we admit as true; rents in the East are at least 50 per cent. less than in the West, while many of the necessaries of life are higher in the West than in the East; and material (coal and iron) is cheaper in this city than in Albany, Troy, and many other points East.

The statement you make, both in your letter and in your printed circular, that the interest of the West demands an equalization of prices, we admit as correct; but when you say we have made no effort to effect such an equalization, we must differ. You will not fail to remember that when we made an effort to raise wages in the East, last spring, we were defeated as to a question of wages by *your* opposition. You, not us, are responsible for the present difference in wages. We beg leave to submit the following propositions:

1st. The status of the union, so far as your shops are concerned, shall be the same as before the present difficulty.

2d. We will work at 70 per cent. above old prices.

3d. The committee on equalization, appointed by the Boston Convention, shall report on or before the first day of May next.

Should you decide to accept these propositions, please send reply to 479 Race Street. WM. H. SYLVIS, *Chairman.*

CINCINNATI, February 13, 1867.

Mr. W. H. SYLVIS, 479 Race St., City.

Sir:—Your favor is received and contents carefully considered. We do not, at this time, wish to enter into particulars on the various speculations contained in your communication, as the *first* proposition determining the control of our shops and business, *by the society*, precludes the discussion of the communication in the other *particulars.*

STEPHEN R. BURTON, *Secretary.*

To this we returned the following:

CINCINNATI, February 14, 1867.

S. R. BURTON, Esq., *Secretary.*

Sir:—The statements made in our communication of the 12th instant, were *correct* answers to the "*speculations*" contained in your favor of the 8th. We must again call your attention to the important fact, that the preamble to your printed circular of the 2d instant is a misstatement—known to be such by you. In that preamble you say: "There is no reliance to be placed in the repeated promises made to us by the Moulders' Union Association for the regulation and equalization of the prices East and West." At the beginning of last year, we undertook to raise prices in the East. The work was begun in Troy. We wanted an equalization of prices, taking the highest shop as the standard, and an advance of 25 per cent. upon the equalization. This would have given us an advance of 50 per cent. in Troy. We were obliged to give up the advance, because you made common cause with the Eastern employers in an attack upon the life of our organization. But for your opposition, prices would now be fully 50 per cent. above the present standard in Troy and other points East, and you would have no cause for complaint. And in this case you have made a direct attack upon the union, and opened our eyes to the fact that a reduction of wages is not the question. You refuse to discuss the question of wages, unless we abandon our organization. *This we will never do.* We are willing to go before the world upon such an issue, and the results will depend upon who can pound the longest. If there has ever been any imposition by shop committees, you had at all times the remedy in your own hands. A notice to the union would have corrected all abuses.

WM. H. SYLVIS, *Pres. I. M. I. U., Chairman.*

This ended all efforts at negotiation, and the struggle began. It was not until after a most severe struggle that I succeeded in getting the union to come down to 70 per cent., and there make a stand. As my determination on that point was the cause of much hard feeling and severe criticism, I desire to state my reasons for my actions.

First. I did not believe the 100 per cent. could be maintained, because a voluntary reduction to 70 per cent. had already been made in Quincy and St. Louis; and while the reduction might have been restored at Quincy, it could not have been at St. Louis, for reasons well known to every gentleman present.

Second. I was in possession of the most positive evidence that a strong party existed in No. 3, who were opposed to making a strike to maintain the 100 per cent., and that if a stand was made on that ground, the union would be divided against itself, which would have resulted in defeat almost before the struggle began.

Third. Having a struggle before us, it became our duty to have all the advantages on our side, so far as we could command and control them. Public opinion is a powerful weapon, and had we stood for the 100 per cent., that would have been against us.

For these and many other reasons, I deemed it madness to attempt a strike for the 100 per cent. So firm was I in this conviction, that I determined there should be no struggle, so far as the I. M. I. U. was concerned, until it could be upon safe grounds.

In my opinion, the strike was prolonged for months after it could have been brought to a successful termination. For this, those who had the immediate management of affairs are responsible. Many of my letters, containing advice, counsel, and encouragement, were suppressed, and never read to the union; and up to this hour the then Corresponding Representative (Neall) refuses to give up the correspondence, although called upon by a vote of the union to do so. It is a most unpleasant task to complain of any one, but this much I considered it my duty to say.

It is not necessary for me to refer particularly to the strikes at Covington, California, Dayton, and Louisville, because the men in each of these places were out under precisely the same circumstances as those in Cincinnati. I will say, however, that the strike in each of these places was well managed, and a continual desire shown to embrace every opportunity to effect a settlement. Every attention was paid to pay-rolls and every requirement of the law.

Being impressed with the full force of the struggle that was about to come, I prepared a "Secret Circular," setting forth my views in full, and detailing what I considered it our duty to do; a copy of which was sent to each union, and a copy of which is herewith transmitted, marked "A," and I ask that it be inserted in its proper place in the printed proceedings, that it may become a part of the record, because in it is to be found a clear justification of my course.

SECRET CIRCULAR.

OFFICE OF THE PRESIDENT OF THE I. M. I. U.
PHILADELPHIA, February 2, 1867.

To the Officers and Members of the several Subordinate Unions:

GENTLEMEN: — My object in the issuing of this circular is to have a very serious talk with all of you. We started together in this good work years ago, and together we have labored to the successful building up of an organization far superior to any other on this continent, and, taking into consideration all the circumstances, equal to any in the world. Together we have passed through many trying scenes, and made many sacrifices, to reach this advanced position; but all the trials through which we have passed sink into insignificance compared to what is now before us. Dark, portentous clouds are gathering around us in every direction, and the future is gloomy enough to create in our minds the most lively apprehensions. These, indeed, "are the times that try men's souls." If ever there was a time when we should reason together, and take counsel against the coming storm, that time is now. Last year our employers made a direct assault upon our union; in that effort they expected to drive us into such a position as would exhaust our resources, demoralize our members, and break up the great body of our union. The return of good times, and the wise policy pursued, brought us complete victory. Although successful at that time, the struggle has by no means ended. The attack now comes from a new and far different direction: fertile in expedients, with plenty of time to concoct and devise new plans, they have resolved upon a new system of attack, determined, if possible, to drive us to the wall before the close of the present year. They believe that if there is any one thing we will resist more than another, it is a reduction of wages; and their plan now is to involve us in a general strike, and break up our union, or a great portion of it, before the return of good trade. Will we allow them to do this is now the question. Remember that the strength and power of our organization does not exist so much in our great numbers and our determination to resist at all hazards, as in our ability to adapt ourselves to all surrounding circumstances. The giant oak, conscious of its great strength, may stand erect and defy the blast, but a single stroke of the hurricane may lay it prostrate upon the earth, and its power of resistance has passed away forever; while the tiny twig will bend before the blast to stand erect again when the storm-cloud has passed away. Are you ready to learn a lesson from this example? Are you ready to submit to a temporary reduction of wages to head off the schemes of those who seek our destruction? I know full well the unpopularity of urging such a course, and I expect to bring upon myself the taunts and jeers of the unthinking by making these recommendations; but my deep solicitude for the welfare of our noble organization prompts me to this course. I am willing to be called a coward, willing to sink into oblivion, and be utterly forgotten, if by so doing I can save the organization. Before heaven I can say that my motives are pure, and that I am making these recommendations from a perfect knowledge of the dangers by which we are surrounded, and with full confidence in the wisdom of the policy herein set forth.

I have said that the reduction would be temporary; I say this, because I look upon a reduction of wages now as a wise means of defence. A war measure, if you please, only to be submitted to until the return of good times; then, when the advantage is on our side, we can demand and get an advance. The reduction should be something like this: in those places where the advance is 100 per cent. over 1861, let the reduction be 30 per cent., and where the advance is 50 per cent. over 1861, let the reduction be 15 per cent., and in like proportion throughout the organization. This would bring us nearer to an equalization of prices than we have ever been yet. This is not only a wise measure of defence, but it is a measure of protection to the men in the Ohio Valley and up the Mississippi. For some time past a competition, ruinous to the West, has been going on between the East and the West, the results of which are now being felt all over the Western country. Work made in the East is flooding the Western market, while the Western shops stand idle for want of trade. Let the men in the West take a broad view of this matter, and insist upon a reduction now as a matter of self-protection, and when trade will warrant it, let them demand of the men in the East an advance of wages, and insist upon it until it is done.

If this course is adopted, the time is not far distant when every member will rejoice that it was so. If we cannot pursue a course of policy sufficiently far-sighted to head off and outflank our employers, then we must take the consequences, and the responsibilities shall not rest upon me. If the organization goes down in the coming struggle, I can say that I warned you of the dangers, and pointed out the road to success, and you heeded me not. There never was a time when we had so good a chance to make a master-stroke as now; and if we have the necessary discipline, good judgment, and moral courage to do it, we will prove ourselves superior to our enemies, and bring to our organization a degree of success never before attained.

You are aware that a strike is now going on in Pittsburg against a reduction of twenty per cent.; it is not the intention that this circular shall apply to that city. My plan is to maintain peace everywhere else, and fight it out in Pittsburg. The question may be asked: "Why pursue a different policy with relation to Pittsburg from that pursued during the great 'lock-out,' when it was considered wise to keep the men in that city at work?" I will make it plain. Pittsburg lies at the head of the Ohio Valley, with a water navigation of many hundreds of miles, running directly by Cincinnati, and all the manufacturing towns on the Ohio River. During the "lock-out," the struggle was confined to Cincinnati and vicinity. It was important to keep Pittsburg to work, because of the bearing it would have upon the issue in Cincinnati and vicinity. With Pittsburg at work, the towns below could not long remain idle. The employers made a mistake by not forcing the issue in Pittsburg. We took advantage of that mistake, and won by it. Now, the tables are turned; they have forced the issue in Pittsburg. They have done this because they believe that to be our weak point, and expect to break up No. 14 in a short time; the effects of which would be, in their opinion, the demoralization of the union all over the West. They now demand a reduction of twenty per cent. If on that issue they should succeed in defeating the union, a further reduction of twenty per cent. would soon follow. By this means they expect to run wages down to the standard of 1861 before the middle of the present year. We should now make Pittsburg the battle-ground, because a reduction of thirty per cent. down the river, with our present standard at Pittsburg, would still leave that city behind in prices. If we fight it out in Pittsburg, and maintain our present rate of wages there, we can, on the return of good times, demand an advance of thirty per cent., and get it, or drive the trade further West; in either case, there would be no trouble to get an advance throughout the West.

One of the strongest arguments in favor of carrying out the policy herein recommended, is the fact that our employers admit that if we adopt such a course, they are defeated; but, at the same time, they say we cannot do it, for the reason that we are not sufficiently well organized to control our members in so important a matter as a reduction of wages. They urge, that to resist will involve us in a general strike, exhaust our means, and destroy the union; and they say that if we do not resist, a reduction of wages will demoralize our members, destroy confidence in the International Union, and so weaken us that our power will be destroyed. That they are correct in their first view, I think no one will question; whether they are correct in the second point, depends entirely upon ourselves. If we have not sufficient of manhood and moral courage to adopt a line of policy looking to our own preservation, and carry it out to the furthest extremity, without destroying ourselves, then, in my opinion, we are not worth saving. In fact, it is just this that should create confidence, and make the union a power it will never be so long as we rely upon mere brute force to carry our point.

Again, let me ask you the plain question — are you ready to stand by your Executive in this emergency, and assist him in carrying out the policy which he deems necessary for our preservation? Would you rather go on a strike for an indefinite period, with no money to support you, and the prospect of an extremely dull time ahead, than to remain at work at a reduction of wages? By which of the two would you lose the most, and in which is involved the least danger to the union?

Already there is a reduction of thirty per cent. in St. Louis and Quincy, and a reduction to Cincinnati prices in Louisville; while in Cincinnati the bosses demand a reduction to Albany and Troy prices, and the movement on the part of the bosses everywhere West is to a reduction. The hour of trial is upon us, and unless the recommendations herein made are adopted, and a voluntary reduction proposed by ourselves, we will soon be involved in a storm, such as we have never heard of in this part of the world. The greatest dangers by which we were ever threatened are now upon us. Resistance is sure defeat; a reduction of wages is victory. Give this matter your immediate consideration. Let no quarrels or hard feelings interfere with your good sober judgment. Meet the issue like men forced to retreat in the face of the enemy, and remember that our only hope depends upon the manner of this retreat. We must take it as a matter of course, and rely upon the return of times when we will have them in as close a corner. By proposing a reduction, we will disarm the bosses, and maintain peace on better terms than we otherwise can expect, and in the end we will not only save money by it, but, what is of much more importance, we will save our organization. Report to me your action in this matter at the earliest possible moment.

Yours, truly,

WM. H. SYLVIS, *President.*

NEW CARD SYSTEM.

The Boston session "resolved that the president be authorized to remodel the card as he may deem best." After a thorough consideration of the whole matter, and a comparison of the card systems in use by various organizations, both in America and Europe, I decided upon the system of numbers now in use. The system is a new one, and has been attended with some trouble; but it is now fully understood, and I am of opinion that it will prove a great benefit. It is not near so complicated as the Scotch system, and yet it accomplishes the same purposes. I think it will prove all we desire.

EQUALIZATION.

A series of resolutions were adopted at Boston looking to an equalization of prices in the different parts of the country. On the 2d of May, 1867, a circular was issued in accordance with these resolutions. Some of the unions returned them properly filled up, and some did not. The committee was never called together. It was thought that it would be incurring a useless expense, as the condition of trade was such that no good could result from it. But the strongest reason in my mind, and many others, was that the Western employers did not receive our efforts to bring about a more equal standard of wages between the East and West in a friendly spirit. But instead of lending us their aid and sympathy, as we had a right to expect they would, they made a bitter attack upon our organization. Judging of their opinions by their actions, we must suppose that the Western employers are and have been opposed to an equalization of prices, unless it be a general levelling down to a point that will just provide the necessary subsistence.

In 1866, when we attempted to raise wages in the East, the Western employers made common cause with those of the East, and the great lock-out ensued. So, in 1867, when we attempted to effect an equalization throughout the country, a fierce struggle ensued, by which they hoped to totally destroy our organization. Perhaps the time may come when employers will have brains enough, justice and honesty enough to admit that moulders have feelings, rights, and honesty. When that time does come, there will be another opportunity to offer conciliatory measures; until that time does come, I shall favor a line of policy looking only to our own interests without regard to the interests of our enemies.

NATIONAL LABOR UNION.

I was instructed by the Boston Convention to attend the Labor Congress, at Chicago, in August, 1867, which I did. The Congress was well attended, and business of a most important character was done; the most important of which was the adoption of a Platform of Principles, a copy of which is herewith transmitted. This document I consider one of the most important ever issued in any age of the world. It is the second Declaration of Independence, and contains the principles upon which must be fought out the great battle for the emancipation of labor. The proceedings of that Congress have never been printed, consequently I cannot present you a copy. The next session of the National Labor Union will be held in New York City, on the — day of September, 1868, and I would earnestly urge upon you the necessity for selecting a man to represent our union in that body.

STRIKES.

From my earliest connection with our organization, I have been opposed to the whole system of strikes, as a remedy for the evils we suffer, and have favored them only because I could see no better way, and hoped, by experience, to discover some plan by which they could be abolished, and we secure our rights. A strike means open war between us and our employers, and war means a knock-down argument, at which both parties are likely to be seriously hurt.

I gave it as my opinion years ago, that we could never accomplish our complete emancipation from the power and tyranny of wealthy employers by a simple combination. This is evident from the fact that we can see no time in the future when our work will be complete — when we can say the objects for which we started have been reached, and *permanent* relief secured.

It is true, the work of combination could go on until a thorough union was established; but no matter how perfect that combination might be, permanent security would not follow. All the wrongs and hardships imposed upon labor have a cause. The present unsatisfactory condition of labor is the effect produced by some great, all-pervading cause, and the effects cannot be removed without first removing the cause.

Combination, as we have been using or applying it, makes war upon the effects, leaving the cause undisturbed, to produce, continually, like effects. If wages are reduced, combination may force an advance; but they will go down again, because the *cause* of the reduction remains. If labor is deprived of privileges, and forced to submit to insults and impositions, these wrongs may be removed by combination; but they will be repeated at the first opportunity; the cause that produced them once will produce them again. Under no circumstances can combination bring more than temporary relief. We may strike this year to force a raise of wages, and next year we will have to strike to prevent a reduction. And a hundred other things are continually coming to pass which furnish cause for strikes — all being the effects or results of a cause which combination can never reach.

The cause of all these evils is the WAGES SYSTEM. So long as we continue to work for wages, so long will we be imposed upon by those who buy our labor, so long will we be subjected to small pay, poverty, and all of the evils of which we complain. Therefore, if we desire permanent relief, we must strike at the root of the evil; we must adopt such measures as will strike down the whole system of wages for labor. We must adopt a system that will divide the *profits* of labor among those who produce them — a system that will drive the vast army of non-producers — paupers upon the producers of wealth — into honorable employment or starvation, for no man has a right to live who does not produce what he consumes.

When we started this movement, we had but a vague idea of the work before us. We felt we were the victims of a heartless tyranny, but just how to escape from it was not so clear. The most simple means visible was combination, concert of action, oneness of purpose, the power of numbers. This we adopted, not that we supposed it would bring permanent relief, but because we considered it the first step in a great reform movement—because we hoped there would grow out of it such measures as would work out our complete emancipation — because we expected it would be a school to educate us for the great work we had to do.

In the year 1866, immediately after the successful termination of the great lock-out, I gave it as my opinion that we had accomplished all that we could hope for by simple combination. I was fully convinced then, as I am now, that we had reached the end of all we could do, or hope to do, by the means we had employed. And I also believed that we must adopt a new plan of operations, or consign ourselves to an eternal warfare to maintain our position, with the prospect of ultimate defeat continually before us. Like two armies in the field, we and the employers stood face to face, each seeking for an opportunity to do the greatest amount of injury to the other. In good times we would take every advantage — we would enforce our rules, curtail the number of apprentices, force wages up as far as possible, abolish harsh and obnoxious rules, and do many other things, because we had the power. In dull times the employers would reduce wages, put on apprentices, discharge men because they were active members of the union, and do many other things, because they had the power. During these times our members would become discouraged and demoralized, our membership would decrease, and our power would be destroyed, and it would take us months to build up again and get ready for another encounter. All this time our members would be under a heavy tax, and the demoralizing cry for funds to sustain ourselves would be continually heard. I could see no prospect before us but that of continual trouble and taxation; and I stated in the New York and Boston Conventions that, unless we could adopt some plan that would show to our members a reasonable prospect of ultimate and *permanent* success, and relief from strikes and taxation, they would, after a time, become discouraged, give up the fight, and allow the whole thing to fail. The experience of the eighteen months just closed has confirmed these convictions, and I came to this convention with feelings of the deepest solicitude for the welfare of those whom we have the honor to represent on this floor. From all parts of our widely extended organization the cry comes up — *something must be done;* our organization will fail unless we can see a streak of daylight somewhere in the future; the exhaustive strikes of the last two years must not be repeated; and here, upon this floor, with a full and clear knowledge of the status of our union, and what its requirements are, I re-echo this cry — SOMETHING MUST BE DONE; and it must be done by this convention. Should we adjourn without such legislation as will restore confidence, renew hopes, and give a reasonable promise of ultimate and final success, and freedom from strikes and taxation, more than fifty unions will return their charters before the close of 1868.

This feeling of opposition to strikes would not be so strong, and the dissatisfaction so serious, had all our strikes been justifiable or unavoidable; but the great body of our membership has come to see and understand that the exhaustive and terrible strikes we have had in the past two and a half years, were wholly uncalled for, unnecessary, and could have been avoided by the exercise of a reasonable amount of caution and common sense. They have come to see that the circulars posted in the shops, which caused the troubles of 1866, contained nothing but a *threat*—that the employers had committed no *act*—only threatened what they would do, and that there were no grounds for action on the part of the unions until an effort was made to put those threats in force, which, in all probability, would have never been done. They also very clearly understand, that had a wise and reasonable policy prevailed in the early part of 1867, the terrible strikes of that year would have been avoided, wages would be higher than at present, and many thousands of dollars would have been saved. They also know that a large number of smaller strikes were brought about by hasty and unwise action; and it is a knowledge of all these facts that has produced the condition of things we now find, and made it imperatively necessary that we adopt a new line of policy for the future.

I have dwelt at length, and very plainly, upon this subject, because I desired to give full and candid expression to my views, and endeavored to impress it upon the minds of all present that we are in the midst of great and pressing dangers, and to show you that upon the action of this convention depends the full and final success of our organization, or its speedy downfall.

CO-OPERATION.

The question that forces itself upon our minds, as we dwell upon the prospect before us is, that if our organization, as it now stands, is a failure, what can we do to make it a success? My answer to this question, here and everywhere, is — CO-OPERATION.

Twenty years ago I had made myself somewhat familiar with the principles of co-operation in Europe, and when I joined this union, it was with the firm conviction that through our efforts at combination we would succeed in establishing the great principles of co-operative industry, and ultimately get control of the whole foundry business of the country, and thereby break down the wages system, become our own employers, end strikes, and put the profits of our labor into our own pockets.

When I accepted the presidency, in January, 1863, I did so with a firm resolve that I would use every means, and make every sacrifice necessary, to build up a combined family of moulders on this continent, and through that combination establish co-operation; and from then to now, it has been my daily study, how to convince the members of our unions that in co-operation was to be found their only hope, and to induce them to take hold of it. It was a long time before the seeds sown began to exhibit signs of life.

Immediately on learning of the serious troubles in Albany and Troy, N. Y., which were the beginning of the strikes of 1866, I went to Troy with my mind made up to stay there, if necessary, to start a Co-operative Foundry Company. After a few days' talking, a company was formed, a charter was secured, a location was fixed upon, and the buildings pushed rapidly forward, and, long before the end of the year, one of the most complete foundries in the country was in successful operation. It is now one of the most solid and successful concerns in the country. In November of the same year, a company was organized in Albany, and the shop put in operation early in 1867. They have been eminently successful; they have two shops, and have, or soon will have, one hundred and thirty moulders at work, which places them among the largest foundry establishments in the land. I refer particularly to these two companies, which were organized in 1866, because they were the beginning of a new era in our trade. Since then, there have been two more shops started in Troy, one in Rochester, two in Cleveland, one in Chicago, one in Quincy, one in Louisville, one in Somerset, and one in Pittsburg, making *eleven in all.* All of these that have been in operation long enough to furnish a test, are completely successful. Besides these, a number of companies are in course of organization, and many more being talked about. The system seems to have taken a deep hold upon our members generally, and, with the proper encouragement, will soon spread itself all over the land.

I desire to call your special attention to the Pittsburg enterprise. Early in the summer of 1867, when it became evident that our strikes were going to continue throughout the year, and perhaps terminate unfavorably, I began considering the expediency of organizing a Co-operative Foundry Company, under the direct supervision of the I. M. I. U. The subject was a very important one, because it would be the first effort ever made to establish co-operation upon so broad and liberal a basis, in the world, and because, if undertaken and failure should follow, it would retard the co-operative movement for years to come. Having implicit faith in the correctness of the principle, and a firm conviction that, unless such a movement was begun, defeat and disaster would come sooner or later, I, on the 16th of August, 1867, issued a circular, making a brief argument in favor of the movement, and setting forth the following plan:

1st. This Association to be known as the "International Co-operative Foundry Association, of Pittsburg, Pa."

2d. The capital stock of the Association shall be one hundred thousand dollars, to be divided into twenty thousand shares, at five dollars each.

3d. No individual or union shall hold over four hundred shares, or two thousand dollars.

4th. The Association shall not be bound to redeem any share of its capital stock within two years from the date of subscription, and in no case without three months' notice.

5th. Whenever a shareholder desires to sell or transfer his stock, he shall first offer it to the union of which he may at the time be a member; and in no case can stock be sold or transferred to any person not a member of a Moulders' Union, without the consent of the Board of Directors.

6th. No shareholder can have more than one vote on any question.

7th. Five per cent. of the actual profits, after paying all expenses, shall be set aside as a sinking-fund, upon which to draw in case of an emergency. But said sinking-fund at no time to exceed ten thousand dollars.

8th. Fifteen per cent. of the profits (after deducting the five per cent. for the sinking-fund) shall be divided among the shareholders, in proportion to the amount of stock held by each, as interest on capital.

9th. The balance of profit shall be divided among the shareholders employed by the Association in proportion to the amount of wages earned by each, as interest on labor.

10th. The unions in Pittsburg, or their members, must subscribe for at least five hundred shares.

11th. The annual meeting of the stockholders will be held on the first Monday in February, of each year, in the city of Pittsburg, at which meeting a President (who shall be Superintendent,) Secretary, Treasurer, and a board of thirteen Directors shall be elected.

12th. The President and Treasurer of the I. M. I. U. shall be members of the Board of Directors, to represent the interests of the shareholders who cannot attend the annual meeting.

13th. Subscriptions for shares shall be paid to the Treasurer of the local Union to which the subscriber may belong, to be held by him until called for by the Treasurer of this Association.

This plan was decided upon after long and anxious thought. It was to be an experiment never before tried by the workingmen of any country, and upon its success or failure hung the fate of many of the brightest hopes I had ever indulged.

While the response to this call was not all that it might have been, yet it was much more than I had reason to expect. Times were exceedingly dull; at least one-half of our membership were out of work, and the prospect of a terrible winter was before us. Besides this, we had on hand the severest strikes we had ever been called upon to support. Nearly the whole of our membership was very poor; still the movement progressed, and on the 2d of October a permanent organization was effected, and the work of erecting buildings, etc., begun. On the 20th of January, 1868, a charter was procured from the State of Pennsylvania, and everything was in a legal shape. A Constitution and By-Laws were adopted, based upon the thirteen rules above given, a copy of which is herewith transmitted.

The shop is now in running order, the first "cast" having been made on the 18th of May last. Everything about the establishment is of the most complete character. The moulding-floor is 100 by 120 feet, with a self-supporting roof, and is the finest moulding-floor in America. Thus far everything has been managed in a manner eminently successful. There has never been put up, in this country, a foundry capable of holding fifty moulders, with everything complete for running it, at so small a cost.

I do not deem it necessary to give a detailed statement of the present standing and prospects of the association. The treasurer and secretary are now on this floor, and have prepared, with a view of submitting it to this body, a full, detailed report of everything connected with the establishment. This report will show the aggregate cost of the shop, as it now stands, the number of shares subscribed for, the amount of money received from subscriptions to stock, the debts of the association, and all its present wants; and they are prepared to give any information concerning their shop to all who desire it.

This is the most important movement ever undertaken, and I ask for it a very careful and candid consideration, believing, as I do, that the adoption of this plan, and its general application throughout our jurisdiction, will soon relieve us from all our present embarrassments, and bring final and permanent relief.

From the foregoing remarks upon strikes and co-operation, you will not fail to see that I am in favor of incorporating the principles of co-operation, as embodied in the rules above given, into our organic law. I believe the time has come when we should abandon the whole system of strikes, and make co-operation the foundation of our organization, and the prime object of all our efforts.

Nine years ago, almost to a day, this union was organized. After a fierce struggle, vast labor, and many and great sacrifices, we have succeeded in building up the finest organization of laborers on this continent, and as good as any in the world. By it we have maintained a higher standard of wages — established a feeling of friendship and brotherhood throughout the land — broken down old prejudices and jealousies — established acquaintances highly beneficial to all — raised the social and moral standard of a large portion of our members — taught many of us to place a higher estimate upon true manhood and self-reliance — and done much in helping our fellow-laborers in other departments of industry to push along the great work of reform. All must agree that we have done much. But it was not to accomplish these things that we started in this movement; these are only the natural results of a movement made to accomplish a much higher object. We are the victims of a soulless money power — of a false social system — of a heartless tyranny. We desired to free ourselves from these; we saw the thousands of little streams of wealth put in motion by our labor wending their way into the pockets of a few men; we desired to change the course of these little streams, that they might flow into our own pockets; we desired to work out our complete emancipation from that power which compelled us to toil eternally without a recompense. These were the primary objects for which this union was organized nine years ago. Have we accomplished these objects? To this there can be but one answer — no, we have not. So far as reaching the point started for is concerned, our organization stands to-day an almost total failure. True, we have made a nine years' journey on the way, but we have now reached a point where the road makes a short turn to the right, and on a finger-board we see the word — CO-OPERATION. This road is a broad, straight, and well-made highway, and leads to prosperity, success, and happiness; while directly ahead, in the direction of the road we have travelled for nine years, is a small, crooked, thorny path, leading to a wilderness of perplexities, trials, and difficulties. Which of these will we choose? This is a question that must be answered by this convention.

In closing this important part of my report, let me express my firm conviction that, if we continue on in the future as we have done in the past, long before the end of another nine years this organization will cease to exist, or, if it lives at all, it will be only in name, and upon the memories of the past; and, in giving expression to this conviction, I am but reiterating the settled opinion of three-fourths of our members.

EIGHT HOURS.

The agitation of the eight-hour question was very great during the greater part of 1867, and several organizations became involved in strikes to enforce it. Some of our unions were unfortunately drawn into those troubles. The strikes to enforce the eight-hour rule, whether in our own unions or others, were entered into against my earnest protest. While I am in favor of the eight-hour system, I have always held it to be unwise and eminently foolish to undertake to enforce the system by strikes. What we want is agitation, education, and legislation. Convince the people that it is right, and then demand the necessary legislation. If our representatives refuse to give it to us, turn them out and put somebody in who will. The universal adoption of the eight-hour system is only a question of time. If we want it, we can get it.

ANNUAL SESSIONS.

I would again call your attention to the very important subject of extending the time between our sessions. You are aware that as early as 1864, I favored the holding of our sessions but once in two years. No action was taken on the recommendation until the Boston Convention, when the term was extended to eighteen months. This action of the Boston session was a very wise measure. Had the time of meeting not been changed from January to July, it would have been impossible to have held a session last January, for the reason that there could not have been raised money enough to pay the expenses, and nearly all of the unions were too poor to send delegates. In view of these facts, it is a very fortunate circumstance that the time of meeting was changed. But, aside from this, there are very strong reasons why we should meet but once in two years, the strongest of which is that of economy. It will cost very near as much to hold one convention as it will to pay the necessary expenses of the union for two years. Thus, it would be a very great saving in money. Besides this, we have too much legislation when we meet every year. It is an old saying, and as true as it is old, that the world is governed too much. We have been governed too much. Let us abate it by one-half, and if we do not succeed, we can go back to annual sessions. The amount to be saved is certainly worth the experiment.

BENEFICIAL FEATURE.

The question of incorporating a benevolent feature into our organization has been prominently before the unions for a long time. In 1866 a committee was appointed, who, after much labor, made out and submitted to the Boston session a report containing a comprehensive plan for putting a beneficial feature into operation, and making certain necessary recommendations. This report was read in the convention, and referred to the committee of the whole, where it was debated with considerable interest; the committee rose, reported progress, and never sat again; consequently the whole thing was killed. I was surprised at this disposition of it. The measure had many warm friends, or, at least, I supposed it had; but not one of them made an effort to have the matter finally and properly disposed of. It was my desire that the report of the committee be adopted by the convention, and referred to the subordinate unions, to be by them adopted or rejected; and in case it should be adopted by two-thirds of the unions, it should become a law; but as it was allowed to stick in committee of the whole, I supposed it was considered a matter of minor importance. I find a large number of our members are in favor of some plan by which men who are out of work, either by sickness, discharge, or inability to get work, can receive some benefits. The whole matter is an important one, and I ask for it a careful consideration.

In closing this report, let me again call your attention to the important business that will come before you. There never was a time when we were surrounded by so many dangers as now, and the worst feature of these dangers is that they are within our organization. We have very little to fear so long as all our trials and dangers come from the outside, and we can present a united front to whatever opposition we may meet; but a house divided against itself cannot stand. Let our business here be to remove dissensions, jealousies, prejudices, etc., and bring about a universal feeling of brotherhood. Let us bring to the consideration of every question a determination to do what will be for the best interests of the whole organization; remembering that if we fail to heal all our differences, and restore harmony, and bring confidence and unity to the union, we will admit ourselves incapable of self-government, and upon our heads must rest the responsibilities of whatever may happen.

I am no alarmist. The dangers I have tried to point out to you are not creatures of my imagination, but real, tangible facts, and we *must meet them.* The legislation I have recommended is the result of long and careful consideration, and founded upon what I believe to be the wish of a large majority of our members. Should you, in your wisdom, decide upon some other means to overcome our present troubles, let it be sufficiently broad and comprehensive to embrace the whole union, and it must point to a time when we will be permanently secure. Any legislation short of this, will only aggravate the matter, and lead to speedy and disastrous defeat.

WM. H. SYLVIS, *President I. M. I. U.*

A SPEECH OF RECEPTION TO SENATOR SPRAGUE, AT THE CONTINENTAL HOTEL, PHILADELPHIA, WITH MR. SPRAGUE'S REPLY.

MR. SYLVIS'S SPEECH.

Senator Sprague: In tendering you the compliments of a serenade, the working-people of this city are moved by no ordinary motives. We have read your late speeches with lively satisfaction, and recognize in you the only man who has had the wisdom, moral courage or honesty to stand up boldly in the United States Senate on the side of the people. When men in the humbler walks of life raise the cry of danger and reform, the cry of "demagogue" is raised, followed by persecution, and every means known to tyrants for stilling the murmurings of discontent. But when senators speak, the "hush policy" cannot be applied. The people will hear: they have heard you, and indorse every word you have spoken. It is true the cry of "ambition" has been raised against you, and all the curs, large and small, are barking at your heels. But the people — the millions of mechanics, laborers, farmers, manufacturers, and merchants — are at your back to drive the curs away.

A subsidized press in the interests of the moneyed power call you ambitious and dishonest. We do not stop to ask or answer such questions. It is enough for us to know that you are right. Knowing this, we will sustain you to the end.

These people whom I represent — these millions of producers who are sending you words of encouragement from all parts of the country — are the "malcontents, disorganizers," and persons who, like Micawber, are "waiting for something to turn up," referred to by the Washington *Republican.*

They are the people who, by their energy and industry, have developed the resources of our country, fought our battles, and placed us in the front rank of nations. These are the "malcontents" who are "waiting for something to turn up," that will give profitable employment and stability to commerce and industry.

The "National Labor Union," of which I have the honor to be president, is an organization extending to every corner of the country. Our object is, and has been, to make war upon a moneyed power that is corrupting every channel of legislation, and making the people tributary to it. We believe that our institutions and liberties are in much more danger now than in the darkest hours of the rebellion. A moneyed aristocracy—proud, imperious, and dishonest—has grown up in our midst. This aristocracy, few in numbers, of vast wealth, controls the financial policy of the government, and through the money controls the government itself. This power is blasting and blistering everything it comes in contact with. The policy of the government has been such as to draw hundreds of millions of dollars from productive industry, and lock them up in non-productive investments.

The rate of interest on money is so high that but few branches of legitimate business can use it; by it labor is robbed — all wealth is being gathered together in large piles — the rich are becoming richer, and the poor poorer. Thousands of workingmen are without profitable employment, general despondency everywhere exists, and there is no confidence in the future. Extravagance on the one hand, and abject poverty on the other, has filled the land with crime, and national demoralization is the result.

Vast accumulation of wealth in individual hands has ever produced the extremest poverty among the many; corruption, decay, and final ruin are sure to follow. The

Roman Republic fell when government and people became corrupt. The stability of our government must rest upon the virtue and intelligence of the people. No republican government can long exist after the abandonment of sound moral principle. Money and monopoly, with the power they give to the few, are dangerous elements in a free government; and it is against these that we and you, sir, are making war; and we congratulate you upon the brave and manly words you have spoken in defence of the rights of the people. Go on with the good work. Let this monster squirm and shake its forked tail; let the dogs howl and show their teeth. The people are with you, and will be with you to the end.

The remarks of Mr. Sylvis were well received, and at their conclusion Senator Sprague stepped forward, amid the most tumultuous greetings, and spoke as follows:

SPEECH OF SENATOR SPRAGUE.

I thank the Union Labor men, and their fellow-citizens of Philadelphia, for this exhibition of their approval of the words I have uttered in their behalf.

Where, away from the national capital, could I better reiterate those words, and where better pledge myself to a continuance in the course I have adopted, in the interest of the nation and the people, than on this sacred spot, under the shadow of Independence Hall, where were gathered those noble patriots who, by their immortal declaration, hurled their grand words of defiance at monarchical power, and, by a steady and courageous adherence to their great principles and purposes, gave self-government and a nationality to a brave and heroic people?

What better hour than this to associate that grand idea which gave birth to a nation with one no less grand, and equally sure of consummation, which alone can preserve and perpetuate a nation — the idea of consolidating and so operating the accumulated debt, wealth, capital, and currency of the government, as to antagonize, check, and regulate the power and despotism of private and associated capital, a vitiated partisan press and secret caucus dictation?

These designated and combined agencies have waxed fat and strong throughout our vast domain, and in their operation and effect on the business interests and social condition of the masses of the people have become far more vicious and oppressive than the worst form of British tyranny was ever likely to have been.

On this subject there is nothing to conceal, nothing of local or sectional interest. What is for the benefit of the workingmen of Pennsylvania will be of equal advantage to the workingmen of South Carolina, Kentucky, New York, New Jersey, Rhode Island, New England, and the great West and Southwest. All will stand on common ground.

The principle enunciated and the grievance recited by the Declaration of Independence, unheeded, unredressed, proved messengers of destruction, devastation, and war. Those I propose, once in operation, whilst reforming unnumbered abuses and corruptions, will result in establishing permanent peace and prosperity throughout the land.

As a salutary warning, let those who wield and control the resources of the country in the interest of the few, be not unmindful of the historic character of that *latent power* always residing in the people, which, when their reasonable demands are met with ridicule and resistance, invariably wields the torch and axe with irresistible force to accomplish desired reforms.

From all quarters the acknowledgment comes up that Sprague has uttered some unquestioned, wholesome truths, and I am constantly congratulated for brave words bravely spoken.

Has truth, then, become the exception, not the rule? Does it require an extra amount of principle and courage to tell the truth? Is not all I have claimed proven true, when one cannot speak the truth to his peers and the people without creating such criticism and remarks? How low in our own estimation must we have sunk, when we are obliged thus to speak and feel!

What food for reflection and regret when plain truths plainly spoken, clear propositions broadly enunciated, instead of being met manfully, with frankness, fairness, and well-sustained opposite views and arguments, only bring forth defamation and threats, ridicule and revilings.

Labor and the workingman are the corner-stones and foundation of society. If broad, massive, and secure, the superstructure of governments, religious creeds, education, and business, standing on a firm basis, and are built on the rock. All else forms but a shifting, sandy foundation, changing and unsteady, finally tottering to the ground, covering all in one common ruin.

For the consideration of the people of Pennsylvania, I declare that by the plan I advocate there will certainly be secured a reduction in the cost of money, production, and living. If this prove true, then I add, indefinitely, to that protection of house capital and labor, which will enable you to develop to their fullest extent the untold resources of the Keystone State.

Gentlemen, as I do not propose to inflict a speech upon you, I will not detain you longer. Again thanking you for your kindness and consideration, I bid you good-night.

Throughout the delivery of the address the senator was frequently interrupted, and cheer upon cheer was given for the Rhode Island advocate of the interests of the workingmen. Music by the band concluded the pleasant ceremonies of the evening, and the senator, upon retiring, was taken by the hand and warmly congratulated. His remarks were attentively listened to and appreciated by the large audience present.

PLATFORM OF PRINCIPLES OF THE NATIONAL LABOR UNION,

ADOPTED FRIDAY, SEPTEMBER 25, 1868.

We hold these truths to be self-evident: that all people are created equal; that they are endowed by their Creator with certain inalienable rights; that among them are life, liberty, and the pursuit of happiness; that to secure these rights, governments are instituted among men, deriving their just powers from the consent of the governed.

That there are but two pure forms of government—the Autocratic and the Democratic; under the former, the will of the individual sovereign is the supreme law, under the latter, the sovereignty is vested in the whole people,—all other forms being a modification of the one or the other of these principles, and that ultimately one or the other of these forms must prevail throughout all civilized nations, and it is now for the American people to determine which of those principles shall triumph.

That the design of the founders of the republic was to institute a government upon the principle of absolute inherent sovereignty of the people, and that would give to each citizen the largest political and religious liberty compatible with the good order of society, and secure to each the right to enjoy the fruits of his labor and talents; that when laws are enacted destructive of these ends, they are without moral binding force, and it is the right and duty of the people to alter, amend, or abolish them, and institute such others, founding them upon the principles of equality, as to them may seem most likely to effect their prosperity and happiness.

Prudence will indeed dictate that important laws long established should not be changed for light and transient causes; and experience has shown that the American people are more disposed to suffer, while evils are sufferable, than to change the forms and laws to which they have been accustomed. But when a long train of legislative abuses, pursuing invariably the same object, evinces a design to subvert the spirit of freedom and equality upon which our institutions are founded, and reduce them to a state of servitude, it is their right, it is their duty, to abolish such laws, and provide new guards for their future security. Such has been the patient suffering of the wealth-producing classes of the United States, and such is the necessity which constrains them to put forth an organized and united effort for maintaining their natural rights, which are imperilled by the insidious schemes and unwarranted aggression of unscrupulous bankers and usurpers by means of unwise and corrupt legislation.

We further hold that all property or wealth is the product of physical or intellectual labor employed in productive industry and in the distribution of the productions of labor. That laborers ought of right, and would, under a just monetary system, receive or retain the larger proportion of their productions; that the wrongs, oppressions, and destitution which laborers are suffering in most departments of legitimate enterprise and useful occupation, do not result from insufficiency of production, but from the unfair distribution of the products of labor between non-producing capital and labor.

That money is the medium of distribution to non-producing capital and producing labor, the rate of interest determining what proportion of the products of labor shall be awarded to capital for its use, and what to labor for its productions; that the power to make money and regulate its value is an essential attribute of sovereignty, the exercise of which is, by the Constitution of the United States, wisely and properly granted to Congress; and it is the imperative duty of Congress to institute upon such a wise and just basis that it shall be directly under the control of the sovereign people who produce the value it is designed to represent, measure and exchange, that it may be a correct and uniform standard of value, and distribute the products of labor equitably between capital and labor according to the service of labor performed in their production.

That the law enacting the so-called national banking system is a delegation by Congress of the sovereign power to make money, and regulate its power, to a class of irresponsible banking associations, thereby giving to them the power to control the value of all the property in the nation, and to fix the rewards of labor in every department of industry, and is inimical to the spirit of liberty, and subversive of the principles of justice upon which our Democratic Republican institutions are founded, and without warrant in the Constitution; justice, reason, and sound policy demand its immediate repeal, and the substitution of legal-tender treasury notes as the exclusive currency of the nation.

That this money monopoly is the parent of all monopolies — the very root and essence of slavery — railroads, warehouses, and all other monopolies, of whatever kind or nature, are the outgrowth of and subservient to this power, and the means used by it to rob the enterprising, industrial, wealth-producing classes of the products of their talents and labor.

That as government is instituted to protect life and secure the rights of property, each should share its just and proper proportion of the burdens and sacrifices necessary for its maintenance and perpetuity; and that the exemption from taxation of bank capital and government bonds, bearing double and bankrupting rates of interest, is a species of unjust class legislation, opposed to the spirit of our institutions, and contrary to the principles of sound morality and enlightened reason.

That our monetary, financial, and revenue laws are, in letter and spirit, opposed to the principles of freedom and equality upon which our Democratic Republican institutions are founded; there is in all their provisions manifestly a studied design to shield non-producing capital from its just proportion of the burdens necessary for the support of the government, imposing them mainly on the industrial, wealth-producing classes, thereby condemning them to lives of unremunerated toil, depriving them of the ordinary conveniences and comforts of life, of the time and means necessary for social enjoyment, intellectual culture, and moral improvement, and ultimately reducing them to a state of practical servitude.

We further hold that while these unrighteous laws of distribution remain in force, laborers cannot, by any system of combination or co-operation, secure their natural rights. That the first and most important step towards the establishment of the rights of labor, is the institution of a system of true co-operation between non-producing capital and labor. That to effect this most desirable object, money — the medium of distribution to capital and labor — must be instituted upon such a wise and just principle that, instead of being a power to centralize the wealth in the hands of a few bankers, usurers, middlemen, and non-producers generally, it shall be a power that will distribute products to producers in accordance with the labor or service performed in their production — the servant, and not the master of labor. This done, the natural rights of labor will be secured, and co-operation in production and in the distribution of products will follow as a natural consequence. The weight will be lifted from the back of the laborer, and the wealth-producing classes will have the time and the means necessary for social enjoyment, intellectual culture, and moral improvement, and the non-producing classes compelled to earn a living by honest industry. We hold that this can be effected by the issue of treasury notes made a legal tender in the payment of all debts, public and private, and convertible, at the option of the holder, into government bonds, bearing a just rate of interest, sufficiently below the rate of increase in the national wealth by natural production, as to make an equitable distribution of the products of labor between non-producing capital and labor, reserving to Congress the right to alter the same when, in their judgment, the public interest would be promoted thereby; giving the government creditor the right to take the lawful money or the interest-bearing bonds at his election, with the privilege to the holder to reconvert the bonds into money, or the money into bonds at pleasure.

We hold this to be the true American or people's monetary system, adapted to the genius of our Democratic Republican institutions, in harmony with the letter and spirit of our Constitution, and suited to the wants of the government and business interests of the nation; that it would furnish a medium of exchange, having equal power, a uniform value, and fitted for the performance of all the functions of money, co-extensive with the jurisdiction of government. That with a just rate per cent. interest on the government bonds, it would effect the equitable distribution of the products of labor between non-producing capital and labor, giving to laborers a fair compensation for their products, and to capital a just reward for its use; remove the necessity for excessive toil, and afford the industrial classes the time and means necessary for social and intellectual culture. With the rate of interest at three per cent. on the government bonds, the national debt would be liquidated within less than thirty years, without the imposition or collection of a farthing of taxes for that purpose. Thus it would dispense with the hungry horde of assessors, tax-gatherers, and government spies, that are harassing the industrial classes, and despoiling them of their subsistence.

We further hold that it is essential to the happiness and prosperity of the people, and the stability of our Democratic Republican institutions, that the public domain be distributed as widely as possible among the people—a land monopoly being equally as oppressive to the people, and dangerous to our institutions, as the present money monopoly. To prevent this, the public lands should be given in reasonable quantities, and to none but actual occupants.

We further hold that intelligence and virtue in the sovereignty are necessary to a wise administration of justice, and that as our institutions are founded upon the theory of sovereignty in the people, in order to their preservation and perpetuity, it is the imperative duty of Congress to make such wise and just regulations as shall afford all the means of acquiring the knowledge requisite to the intelligent exercise of the privileges and duties pertaining to sovereignty, and that Congress should ordain that eight hours' labor, between the rising and setting of the sun, should constitute a day's work in all government works and places where the national government has exclusive jurisdiction; and that it is equally imperative on the several States to make like provision by legal enactment. Be it therefore unanimously

Resolved, That our first duty is now to provide as speedily as possible a system of general organization in accordance with the principles herein more specifically set forth, and that each branch of industry shall be left to adopt its own particular form of organization, subject only to such restraint as may be necessary to place each organization within line, so as to act in harmony in all matters pertaining to the welfare of the whole, as well as each of the parts; and that it is the imperative duty of each individual, in each and every branch of industry, to aid in the formation of such labor organizations in their respective branches, and to connect themselves therewith.

CO-OPERATIVE.

Resolved, That in co-operation, based upon just financial and revenue laws, we recognize a sure and lasting remedy for the abuse of the present industrial system, and that, until the laws of the nation can be remodelled so as to recognize the rights of men, instead of classes, the system of co-operation carefully guarded will do much to lessen the evils of our present system. We, therefore, hail with delight the organization of co-operative stores and workshops, and would urge their formation in every section of the country, and in every branch of business.

WOMAN'S LABOR.

Resolved, That with the equal application of the fundamental principles of our Republican Democratic government, and a sound monetary system, there could be no antagonism between the interests of the workingmen and workingwomen of this country, nor between any of the branches of productive industry, — the direct operation of each, when not prevented by unjust monetary laws, being to benefit all the others by the production and distribution of the comforts and necessaries of life; and that the adoption, by the national government, of the financial policy set forth in this platform, will put an end to the oppression of workingwomen, and is the only means of securing to them as well as to workingmen the just reward of their labor.

Resolved, That we pledge our individual and undivided support to the sewing-women and daughters of toil in this land, and would solicit their hearty co-operation, knowing, as we do, that no class of industry is so much in need of having their condition ameliorated as the factory operatives, sewing-women, etc., of this country.

CONVICT-LABOR.

Resolved, That we demand the abolishment of the system of convict-labor in our prisons and penitentiaries, and that the labor performed by convicts shall be that which will least conflict with honest industry outside of the prisons, and that the wares manufactured by the convict shall not be put upon the market at less than the current market rates.

IMPROVED DWELLINGS FOR LABORERS.

Resolved, That we would urgently call the attention of the industrial classes to the subject of tenement-houses and improved dwellings, believing it to be essential to the welfare of the whole community that a reform should be effected in this respect, as the experience of the past has proved that vice, pauperism, and crime are the invariable attendants of the overcrowded and illy-ventilated dwellings of the poor, and urge upon the capitalist of the country attention to the blessings to be derived from investing their means in the erection of such dwellings.

INTELLECTUAL IMPROVEMENT.

Resolved, That the formation of mechanics' institutes, lyceums, and reading-rooms, and the erection of buildings for that purpose, are recommended to workingmen in all cities and towns, as a means of advancing their social and intellectual improvement.

REMEDY FOR INSUFFICIENT WORK.

Resolved, That this Labor Congress would most respectfully recommend to the workingmen of the country that, in case they are pressed for want of employment, they proceed to become actual settlers; believing that if the industry of the country can be coupled with its natural advantages, it will result both in individual relief and national advantages.

Resolved, That where a workingman is found capable and available for office, the preference should invariably be given to such person.

ADDITIONS TO THE PLATFORM, ADOPTED BY THE NATIONAL LABOR UNION SINCE 1868.

Resolved, That the claim of the bond-holders for payment of it — gold of that class of indebtedness known as 5-20 bonds, and the principal of which is legally and equitably payable in lawful money,—is dishonest and extortionate; and hence we enter our solemn protest against any departure from the original contract, by funding the debt in long bonds, or in any increase of the gold-bearing and untaxed obligations of the government.

Resolved, That justice demands that the burdens of the government should be so adjusted as to bear equally on all classes and interests; and that the exemption from taxation of government bonds, bearing extortionate rates of interest, is a violation of all just principles of revenue laws.

Resolved, That Congress should modify the tariff so as to admit free the necessaries of life, and such articles of common use as we can neither produce nor grow; also to lay duties for revenue mainly upon articles of luxury, and upon such articles of manufacture as (we having the raw material in abundance) will develop the resources of the country, increase the number of factories, give employment to more laborers, maintain good compensation, cause the immigration of skilled labor, the lessening of prices to consumers, the creating of a permanent home-market for agricultural products, destroy the necessity for the odious and expensive internal taxation, and will soon enable us to successfully compete with the manufacturers of Europe in the markets of the world.

Resolved, That the public lands of the United States belong to the people, and should not be sold to individuals, nor granted to corporations, but should be held as a sacred trust for the benefit of the people, and should be granted, free of cost, to landless settlers only, in amounts not exceeding 160 acres of land.

Resolved, That the treaty-making power of the government has no authority in the Constitution to "dispose of" the public lands without the joint sanction of the Senate and House of Representatives.

Resolved, That as labor is the foundation and cause of national prosperity, it is both the duty and interest of the government to foster and protect it. Its importance, therefore, demands the creation of an executive department of the government at Washington, to be denominated the Department of Labor, which shall aid in protecting it above all other interests.

Resolved, That the protection of life, liberty, and property are the three cardinal principles of government, and the first two more sacred than the latter; therefore, money necessary for prosecuting wars should, as it is required, be assessed and collected from the wealth of the country, and not be entailed as a burden on posterity.

Resolved, That we are unalterably opposed to the importation of a servile race, for the sole and only purpose of tampering with the labor of the American workingmen.

Resolved, That the rights and interest of all useful industries are unitary, and, to be successful, must make common cause against their common enemies — unprincipled capitalists, dishonest legislators, and all monopolists of the products of human labor.

Resolved, That we cordially invite and entreat all classes of workers, common, agricultural, and skilled laborers, and all persons who sympathize with our efforts to protect and improve the condition of the producing-classes, to unite heartily with us in placing in office men who truly represent the substantial interests of the whole country.

Resolved, That we view with apprehension the tendency to military domination in the Federal government; that standing armies are dangerous to the liberties of the people; that they entail heavy and unnecessary burdens on the productive industries, and should be reduced to the lowest standard.

Resolved, That the Union was sustained in the late struggle by the working-classes, the citizen-soldiers of the republic, who, when the battle was over, returned to the private walks of life and the productive industries, whereby the expenses of the war are being paid, the government supported, and the wealth of the country increased; that the officers of the army who receive the highest pay and do the safest work, get all the honors and the highest pensions; do the least and get the best accommodations, and are now clamoring for positions which are sinecures, resisting the efforts to retire the surplus and to reduce their pay, demanding the continuance of a standing army beyond our necessity; and that all this shows that patriotism is in the people, ambition and plunder in the officers, injustice and ingratitude in the government.

Resolved, That we recognize in agricultural labor the base of all our supplies; and this interest is second to no other; and that we specially and heartily invite the farmers and workingmen to unite with us in our efforts to improve ourselves and the country.

Resolved, That what we call common or unskilled labor is an essential and indispensable element of support and wealth, and we cordially invite its co-operation in our efforts to improve the condition of the productive classes.

Resolved, That inasmuch as both the present political parties are dominated by the non-producing classes, who depend on public plunder for subsistence and wealth, and have no sympathy with the working millions beyond the use they can make of them for their own political and pecuniary aggrandizement; therefore, the highest interest of our colored fellow-citizens is with the workingmen, who, like themselves, are slaves of capital and politicians, and strike for liberty.

Resolved, That the Indian has the same normal rights as any other type of the people; that he has an original and inalienable right to maintain his tribal condition; and that any attempt on the part of government to force on him an unwilling citizenship is grossly unjust, and a blow at individual liberty.

Resolved, That the management of our Indian affairs is wasteful, abortive, and destructive of its own objects, and demands an immediate and radical reformation.

Resolved, That women are entitled to equal pay for equal services with men; that the practice of working women and children ten to fifteen hours per day, at starvation prices, is brutal in the extreme, and subversive of the health, intelligence, and morality of the nation, and demands the interposition of law.

Resolved, That we reaffirm our position in favor of the necessity and justice of the reduction of the hours of labor as well as the obligation of all able-bodied persons to contribute to useful labor an equivalent for their support.

LETTERS.

NATIONAL DEBT, BANKS, CURRENCY, BONDS, TAXATION, AND PUBLIC LANDS.

PHILADELPHIA, January 17, 1868.

GEORGE BABER, Esq.,

Editor Evening Advocate:

There are several questions of vital importance to the workingmen of the country, that must come prominently before Congress during its present session, and will demand a large share of public attention hereafter.

It is a matter of the highest importance that the industrial classes should discuss and fully understand the relation that each of these questions holds to labor, that they may be prepared to vote for their own interests, and so dispose of each particular question as to secure to industry its rightful dues.

Believing it to be the duty, as well as the right, of every workingman to express his sentiments upon all matters of general importance, I propose to give your readers the conclusions I have reached after a careful consideration of some of the great questions now before us. I do this the more freely because I have been requested to do so by many friends in all parts of our State.

The contest that is now stirring up the people from one end of the country to the other is simply a struggle between the productive powers of the nation and a powerful moneyed aristocracy. And if, in this contest, the people are defeated, it will be because they deserted their own standards, and went over to their enemies. With these remarks by way of preface, I shall proceed directly to the questions before us.

NATIONAL BANKS.

The point upon which Mr. Jay Cooke rested his strongest arguments, in his recent letter defending the national banks, was, that these banks were "the great necessity of the government." Some deny this on the ground that there was a sufficiency of greenback currency previous to the creation of the banks; but they comprise only the small class who have money to lend at two or three per cent. a month. If more money was needed — and I think it was — greenbacks could have been issued, and they would have given us a much better currency, and, at the same time, saved many millions of dollars, paid to these banks, all of which the people must pay in the shape of taxes!

It is claimed that the national banks should not be disturbed, because they furnish a safe currency. And why safer than that of the old State banks? Simply because it has the indorsement of the government. But have not the greenbacks the same indorsement, besides being a legal-tender, and non-interest bearing?

Again, we are told that, by the creation of the national banks, the government obtained an immediate loan of $300,000,000. This a very great mistake. It is well known to all who have made this question a study, that, for the first year after the adoption of the national bank system, not more than $40,000,000 of government bonds were purchased from the United States Treasury, and most of the few banks that did adopt the new system, during the first year, had on hand a sufficient amount of bonds, which they handed over to the treasurer for currency; and where new banks were organized, it was done in nearly all cases by men who already held large amounts of government bonds.

It was nearly two years before the system was generally adopted, and not more than fifty or sixty millions were ever taken by the national banks; and this amount, being spread over a period of *two years*, what becomes of the *immediate* loan of $300,000,000?

The defenders of these banks tell us that to discontinue them would be a violation of contract. There can be no truth in this, for the bill creating them provides that "Congress shall have power at any time to alter, amend, or *repeal* this act," viz., the act making them. And for the privilege of having these banks, the laborer—the productive power of the nation—must pay not far from one hundred millions of dollars annually in taxes! There is no necessity for these banks; there never was a necessity for them; and, therefore, every workingman in the land, independent of party ties, should demand the recall of the national bank currency, and the issue of greenbacks in its stead. This brings us to the consideration of a proper national currency, and a remedy for the present distressed condition of the entire country.

NATIONAL CURRENCY.

In my opinion, we want

First. — No contraction of the currency.

Second. — Legal-tender notes — greenbacks — to be declared lawful money for the payment of all debts *public* and *private, and to remain the legal currency of the country for all time.* As has been well said, "It is the duty of the government to institute and regulate the medium of exchange; but that this duty has been imperfectly performed, appears from the fact that, where specie is made the only tender in payment of debts, neither the government nor the people have had nor can have any adequate control over it."

Capitalists control the money, and, through the money, control the government. The defective character of the present monetary laws further appears from the *variations in the rates of interest* on government stocks perfectly secured at all times, but constantly fluctuating in value. If a government cannot secure a uniform value to money for its own use, how can it be said to regulate the currency of the country? It is impossible to secure to labor its earnings, under a system by which the government and the people are made to depend upon a few capitalists who furnish the medium and standard for the distribution of the productions of labor. The system, however, above proposed, can be put into operation to the very great advantage of all the people, without consulting capitalists, bankers, or brokers.

Third. — The country needs the unconditional repeal of the law authorizing the national banks, the calling in of the whole national bank currency, and the issuing of $700,000,000 of greenbacks to take its place. This, with the amount of greenbacks now in circulation, would give the country a little over one thousand millions of greenbacks as a circulating medium, which, apportioned among the people, *per capita*, would be about thirty dollars to each individual, which is just about equal to the apportionment in France and England. We need a little more than France and England do, owing to the greater extent of our country, and the scattered condition of our population.

Fourth. — The redemption of the five-twenty bonds, as they fall due, in greenbacks, or at the option of the holder, in other bonds, at one per cent. interest, convertible at the pleasure of the holder into greenbacks.

Fifth. — Holders of greenbacks to the amount of $50 to be entitled to receive bonds as aforesaid at their pleasure.

Sixth. — That neither gold nor greenbacks be permitted to accumulate in the treasury beyond the immediate wants of the government, the surplus to be applied to the payment of the national debt.

Using the language of the Hon. Samuel F. Cary, I hold that "a currency constantly fluctuating in value, by varying rates of interest, is no more suitable as a medium of exchange than an elastic yard-stick is fit for a measure of cloth. Justice requires uniformity of value." A currency, to be of uniform value, must be limited only by the *wants of business.* Any monetary system that will give us too much money at one time, and too little at another, is not sound, and should be discarded. So long as gold and silver are our legal currency, so long will our whole monetary system be controlled by capitalists — a few rich men. And while such is the case, "fluctuation," "expansion," "contraction," "financial panics," &c., with all their attending evils, will continue to curse the land.

With a currency such as is here proposed, all these evils will be avoided, because there can never be too much nor too little money, if regulated by the needs of the country. Supply and demand will at all times determine the amount of the circulating medium. When money should be abundant, it would be absorbed by the government in its bonds; and, when scarce, and in demand, the bonds would be converted into greenbacks.

The government should issue all the currency, with branches wherever the demands of business required them, the money to be loaned to the people direct on *real estate security,* and the rate of interest should be just what it would cost to furnish the currency, say one per cent. With this system, the occupation of bankers and brokers would be gone, and society would be freed from one of the greatest curses that was ever inflicted upon the body politic.

Labor would receive its just reward, and stability, peace, and plenty would bless the land. At present, our currency rests upon a specie basis. When that basis is gone, the currency is worthless. That basis is comparatively small in quantity, easy of transportation or concealment, and, therefore, at the mercy of speculators. Under the proposed new system, the land of the country would be the basis of the currency; greenbacks would represent *real* value — would rest upon land; *that* can neither be concealed, shipped from one section to another, nor taken out of the country.

As has been clearly stated, the question to be settled then is this: "Can a currency be founded entirely of paper, which will buy the productions of labor as readily as gold and silver coins; not whether a silver spoon can be made out of a paper dollar, or whether a gold watch-case can be made out of a ten-dollar greenback as well as it can be made out of an eagle? We do not want money to make utensils and ornaments. We want money for a *medium of exchange.*"

After having made these provisions, let us reduce the interest on the whole of the national debt to *three per cent.*, the difference between three per cent. and the interest now paid to be set aside as a sinking-fund, for the payment of the national debt as fast as possible.

I am well aware that the proposition to reduce the interest on the national debt will be met by the bond-holders with the plea that the government has no right to do such a thing. The right to reduce the interest could be sustained, however, by numerous precedents; but, as precedent is but a poor argument, at best, I shall rest my demand, for a reduction of interest, upon the broad plea of *justice to the industry of the country.* Any rate of interest over three per cent. is a direct robbery practised upon the producers of wealth.

Is it not a well known fact, that, when money is plentiful, and interest low, the country is prosperous, and labor fully employed? And when money is scarce, and interest high, prostration and idleness are the sure result. When money is worth two and three per cent. a month, brokers and bankers get rich, and workingmen starve!

NATIONAL DEBT.

The interest-bearing debt of the United States is about $2,500,000,000, upon which the interest value, in currency, is about $225,000,000. By reducing the rate of interest to *three* per cent., we would save at the end of one year nearly $150,000,000, to place to the credit of the sinking-fund, for the redemption of the national debt.

Thus, by constituting from a portion of the present rate of interest a sinking-fund for the payment of this national debt, the whole debt might be ultimately paid, without any other provision.

But I believe it to be the duty of the government to pay off the debt as rapidly as possible, and, therefore, I recommend the calling in of the national bank currency, and the issuing of $700,000,000 in greenbacks, with which to take up a like amount of five-twenty-bonds about due. This would wipe out more than one-fourth of the interest-bearing debt at once, and relieve the labor of the nation of nearly $50,000,000 of taxes, besides furnishing a better currency, and relieving the country of one of the worst monopolies ever imposed upon any people.

I am no believer in the new idea promulgated by Jay Cooke, that "*a national debt is a national blessing,*" *and that* "*the funded debt of the United States is, in effect, the addition of* $3,000,000,000 *to the previously realized wealth of the nation — it is* $3,000,000,000 *added to its available capital. To pay this debt would be to extinguish the capital, and to lose this wealth would be an inconceivably great national misfortune.*" That is, the more a man is in debt, the richer he is.

We are told that "to pay this debt would be to extinguish the capital;" that is, if a man pays his debts, he wastes his money! This is not a very moral view to take of the subject of debts; but, aside from its immoral tendencies, there is no truth in it as applied to our national debt. If it were possible to pay off the national debt in one day, it would at once relieve the country of the entire load of taxation, except what would be necessary, in addition to the receipts from customs, to pay the current expenses of the government. Surely this would not be a very serious loss to anybody, except to the bond-holders. At present, hundreds of millions of capital are withdrawn from the industrial pursuits, and tied up in government bonds, which, at present rates, afford to the holders about ten per cent., besides relief from all the cares, troubles, and risks of doing business. Pay off the national debt, lift this load of taxation from the people, and give the country a cheap, safe, uniform, and abundant currency, and, instead of the nation losing $3,000,000,000 of capital, instead of the universal prostration of business, and a degree of privation and suffering among those who toil, such as we have not had for thirty years, we should behold cultivation extending, the arts flourishing, the face of the country improving, our people fully and profitably employed, the public countenance exhibiting tranquillity, contentment, and happiness, a ready market for all the surplus productions of our industry, innumerable flocks and herds browsing on ten thousand hills and plains, our cities expanding, whole villages springing up, as it were, by enchantment, our exports and imports increasing, our tonnage, foreign and coastwise, swelling and fully occupied, and our rivers animated by the perpetual thunder and lightning of countless steamboats.

GREENBACKS.

The bill by which the five-twenty bonds were authorized, says that they shall be paid in lawful money. Greenbacks are lawful money. And Mr. Stevens tells us that when "the bill for the issue of the five-twenties was on its final passage, the question was expressly asked of the chairman of the Committee of Ways and Means, and as expressly answered by him, that *only the interest* was payable in coin." Other members of Congress have expressly stated that they voted for the bill with the understanding that the principal should be paid in greenbacks. They who insist upon the payment of these bonds in coin, have no better argument than that there is an *implied* promise to pay them in gold. This is no argument at all. It is clearly shown that the ten-forties are made payable in gold by the law creating them. Why should there be an *express* promise in one case, and an *implied* promise in the other? On this subject, George H. Pendleton very pointedly says:

"It is said that those who purchased these bonds believed they were to be paid in gold. I cannot aver, my friends, that they did not believe it, but I do aver that they had no reason to believe it. The law was open to their inspection, and was plain. They knew well that the government of the United States paid every other debt that it owed, except only the interest upon the bonds, in legal-tender notes. They knew that they themselves discharged every debt that they owed in legal-tender notes. They knew that they themselves, when they bought these bonds, paid for them in legal-tender notes, and they had no reason to believe that an exception would be made in their case alone."

It seems to me to be very clearly settled that there is no *legal* obligation to pay these bonds in gold. But there are those who insist that there is a *moral* obligation.

If greenbacks are good enough for the people, are they

not good enough for the bond-holders? For instance, Mr. Jones has bonds to the value of $100,000; he owes a like amount to sundry persons; the people pay taxes to the government in gold, or its equivalent; the government pays Mr. Jones in gold, and he pays his debts in greenbacks, realizing by the operation $40,000. He paid for these bonds in greenbacks, at the rate of about sixty cents on the dollar; or, in other words, he paid $60,000 for what he now gets $100,000, thus realizing $40,000 more, making $80,000, besides six per cent. interest in gold, while he held the bonds, in all about $125,000, or a clear profit of $65,000 in five years. Is there any injustice to Mr. Jones in this?

But the bond-holders tell us that they came to the aid of the government in a critical moment, and made sacrifices to save it, by furnishing the sinews of war; that the government would be ungrateful not to pay them in gold! Let us see how the case stands when we look at it from the workingmen's stand-point. Bond-holders paid the government sixty cents on the dollar, and received credit for one hundred cents. They tell us that there was a great necessity existing — the government could not have carried on the war without their money. I admit the necessity, but I do not forget that they, taking advantage of that necessity, made the people pay very dear for the accommodation. But was not the labor of the workingmen who built the steamboats, and, by their incessant toil, supplied the material of war, just as necessary as money? and were they not paid in greenbacks? were they not as much entitled to payment in gold as are the bond-holders? and was there not as great a necessity for soldiers as for purchasers of bonds? and were not the men who did the fighting paid in greenbacks, and a very small quantity of them at that?

Go ask the tens of thousands of poor widows doomed to

poverty and toil who made the sacrifices. The government, when paying a pension — a mere trifle — to the widows and orphans of our dead soldiers, pays them in greenbacks. Are the claims of the bond-holders to payment in gold better than theirs? Go visit the battle-fields, and tread among the little hillocks beneath which sleep thousands of brave men who had no money to buy bonds, but who left their wives and their little ones to go to the front and die for their country, and ask yourselves who made the greatest sacrifices for the nation? *They* were paid in greenbacks; and are the claims of the bond-holders to gold better than theirs?

The man who lost his life in battle made a vastly greater sacrifice than the whole national debt would be, were it all given to the government as a free donation. The crippled soldier gets a pension; but he gets it, I repeat, in greenbacks, and never thinks of asking gold. If all the bonds in existence were gathered in a pile and consumed by fire, and the bond-holders consumed with them, the sacrifice would be but as a drop in the ocean compared with the sacrifices made by the workingmen of the nation. They did the actual work, did the fighting, won the victories, saved the nation, and are now paying the taxes necessary to pay the bond-holders! The workingman who went into the army, and served four years, received in wages $864. To do so, he gave up a job worth, say $2 a day, which for four years would be, say $2,000, making a net loss of $1,136. There would be much more justice in his demanding the payment of this loss than there is in the bond-holders' demand for gold at the existing premium rate. In fact, there exists no moral obligation to pay these bonds in coin.

The bond-holders are few in numbers compared to the laboring masses; but they constitute a powerful and dangerous moneyed aristocracy — an aristocracy dangerous to the rights and liberties of the people, and opposed to the very spirit of a truly popular government. The result is, we see a war of interests—the people against monopolies. And this war can never end until, by our power at the ballot-box, we shall have voted them out of existence. The great industrial classes of this State and of this nation must take hold of these questions with a firm grasp, and resolve to vote for no man, and to act with no party, that will not openly and honestly stand upon the labor platform, viz., a speedy payment of the national debt, equal taxation, opposition to all monopolies, a sound currency, and one kind of money for all the people.

TAXATION.

The opponents of a paper currency, and those favoring contraction, tell us that the present high prices of all the necessaries of life, and the wide-spread stagnation of business, are due to an inflated currency.

Another class tells us that the present condition of things is due to speculation and over-production; while others lay it to a defective tariff system. Now, while I am willing to admit there is *some* truth in all of these reasons, and *much* in some of them, I do not think that we can find the true cause in any of them.

Next to a false money system, our system of internal taxation may be looked upon as the great cause of the present dull times. To these two things alone can we look for all our troubles.

The sum required to meet the ordinary expenses of the government for 1866, including the interest on the public debt, was $551,000,000, and the income from all sources was over $600,000,000, which imposes on each individual a higher rate of taxation, perhaps, than is paid by any other people on the globe. Divided among the people, it would be over $17 to every man, woman, and child in the country. In England the rate is $11, in France $8, and in Austria $5.

To make it clear to the mind of every workingman,—and it is for such that I am writing,—I will try to show just how this taxation is levied, and why it is unjust. For instance, the duty on a pound of coffee, when it is imported into Philadelphia, is *five cents per pound* (all coffee is imported); this is added to the price. The wholesale dealer must pay a *license* to do business; when he buys, and the bill is receipted, it must be *stamped;* if he gives a check on the bank, that must be *stamped.* A dealer in Pittsburg goes to Philadelphia and buys some of this coffee; he, too, must pay a *license.* A part of his fare over the road is *tax.* When he pays for his coffee, the receipt must be *stamped.* A part of the freight to Pittsburg is *tax;* and the freight bill must be *stamped.* A part of his fare home again is *tax.* The fare and freight are raised because everything is *taxed.* Well, a merchant in Brownstown goes to Pittsburg to buy goods; he buys some of this coffee brought from Philadelphia, and takes a bill, which must be *stamped;* and he, too, must pay a *license;* and a part of his fare both ways and the freight on his goods are *tax.* The importer in Philadelphia and the merchants in Pittsburg and Brownstown must pay higher rents because everything is *taxed,* and all these taxes are added to the price, and paid by the consumer; and hence we are paying fifty cents a pound for coffee that we used to get for fifteen cents!

It has been demonstrated by publishers that books pay some fifteen separate taxes before they reach the reader. This unjust system is the same in its operations throughout all the ramifications of industry. The hat on your head, the boots on your feet, the clothes on your person, the food you eat, the tea and coffee you drink, the pot it is cooked in, the cup you drink it out of, the implements on your farm, the tools you work with, the paper upon which you write, the pen and ink you use, the papers and books you read, the furniture in your house, the gas or oil you burn, the coal you consume, the stove you burn it in, the medicines you take, the tobacco you smoke, the pipe you smoke it in, the match you light it with, the dishes on your table, and all you eat off them — all, all are subject to the same unjust system of accumulated taxes, and all are paid by the consumer. This system is so adjusted that the tax is virtually apportioned *per capita* among the people. The poor man, with a family of six, pays as much tax in the prices he pays to feed and clothe them as his neighbor worth his millions, with a family of equal numbers. There are a hundred poor men to one rich man. So it is easy to see who pays the taxes. The accumulated labor of the country pays nearly the whole of the taxes, while the accumulated capital of the country is almost entirely exempt. We have a national debt of $3,000,000,000 held by a comparatively few individuals. Nearly the whole of the capital thus held is free from taxation, and yet nearly every branch of industry is paralyzed in a time of general peace. To these two causes, viz., a false money system and a system of internal taxation without a parallel in the history of the world, must be ascribed the present deplorable condition of every branch of toil.

A hundred millions of gold, and nearly forty millions in greenbacks, lying idle in the vaults of the United States treasury, and one thousand millions more locked up in bank vaults and the safes of corporations or individuals, with seven hundred millions of paper money resting upon a basis as uncertain and shifting as the sands upon the seashore — with all this money in the country (nearly or quite two thousand millions of dollars), we hear the cry everywhere in the land: "*Money is scarce.*" "*There is no money.*" "*The mills, the foundries, the factories must stop for want of money;*" and interest ranging from ten to thirty per cent!

The total amount of money in the country bearing the stamp of the United States or State governments, if divided equally among all the people, would give to every man, woman, and child about seventy dollars; and yet we see one-half the entire population without money to buy bread from day to day, many of them living on credit or public or private charity, three-fourths of the other half holding a very small portion of the whole currency, and the other fourth, or one-eighth of the whole population, holding the balance. I suppose that of the two thousand millions of money now in the country, nineteen hundred are in the hands or under the control of two million persons, out of a population of thirty-five millions! Truly, our present monetary system is as a house built upon the sand. We have a country that may truly be called the garden of the world. With agricultural, manufacturing, and commercial resources superior to any other portion of the globe, blessed by Providence with every element necessary to the highest success, prosperity, and happiness attainable by man; and yet, in the midst of all this, want fills the whole land; millions of men are forced into idleness, denied the sacred right to toil, and compelled to beg or starve. What a sad commentary upon the intelligence of American legislators! Taxation in any form is obnoxious, but of all the systems that curse the workingmen of the world ours is the most odious. From these false systems there is but one way of escape; let every workingman resolve to use his power at the ballot-box.

REPUDIATION.

The efforts to fasten the odium of repudiation upon those who favor paying the *five-twenties* in greenbacks, and the withdrawal of the national bank currency, are so transparent that it seems like a waste of words to refer to it at all. The cry of repudiation is raised by the bond-holders and their friends, and is done for no other purpose than to *blind the people, and assist themselves in getting gold!* I am in favor of paying every dollar of the national debt. All we ask is that this debt, which is the debt of the people, be paid in the same kind of money that the people must take. We are willing to give one hundred cents on the dollar in payment of this debt, although it cost the bond-holders but sixty cents on the dollar; but we want to give it in the *same kind of money with which these bonds were purchased.* While we receive pay for our labor in greenbacks, we do not think it just that we should pay taxes in gold. In this cry of repudiation there is neither truth nor sense. There are those, however, who do favor open repudiation. With such, workingmen have no sympathy. At the same time, the least said about it the better for the bond-holders, because arguments can be used in favor of it — such as would raise a storm against which all the wealth of the bond-holders could not successfully contend. Let them take a friendly warning, and cease their unjust and senseless cry, or repudiation *may* come.

THE PUBLIC LANDS.

The proper disposition of the public lands is a subject of vital importance to the workingmen of the nation. No republican government has withstood the blighting and withering influences of land monopoly. History demonstrates this at every turn. In the ownership of the soil lies the foundation of manhood, independence, liberty, and civilization. In the first stage of her existence, with "lands to all," Rome prospered, and rose to the zenith of her glory; while, in the second phase, "lands to the few" was the cause of her total destruction. Lord Bacon says: "Let States take heed how the landed aristocracy multiply, for thus is the dignity of the people lost, and serfdom established." Aristotle says: "When the lands become concentrated in the hands of the few, the balance of power in a commonwealth is destroyed, and is an occasion of sedition, which ends in monarchy, to prevent which confiscation had been adopted in several of the States of Greece; but it were better to prevent the growth of such an evil rather than, when it has got head, to seek the remedy." Machiavel says that "he who goes about making a commonwealth where the lands are owned by the few, unless he first destroys them, undertakes an impossibility, and he who attempts to destroy a commonwealth where the condition of the people is equal, shall never bring it to pass." John Adams says: "The lands of New England were generally in the hands of the people, but the policy of the British politicians was to change this by putting the titles to the lands in the hands of a few aristocrats, as fixing a firm foundation for their form of government."

John Bright tells us "that one-half of Scotland is owned by twelve persons, and one-half of England by one hundred and fifty persons." Jefferson, Madison, Monroe, and Jackson have told us that "every citizen should have an interest in the soil;" that "the lands should not be sold;" that "there is no power in the Constitution by which special land grants can be made." And Sir Edmund Burke tells us that "the only interest which the government can have in the public lands is in securing their early occupation and settlement." Thus we find the opinions of the greatest men recorded against land monopolies.

Wherever we find the land in the hands of the few, we find the masses of the people reduced to poverty and want; and wherever we find the rights and privileges of the people equal, and the land divided fairly among all, we find prosperity, contentment, and happiness. In England and Scotland the lands are held by a very few persons; and yet these countries are densely peopled, and the toiling millions constantly seeking an outlet. Thousands of acres of the finest land are uncultivated. Wheat and corn are imported, and thousands of people die of hunger and want annually.

Look at Ireland. Cast our eyes in whatever direction we may, and nowhere can we find such a poverty-stricken, heart-broken people, as the Irish are. Poverty and wretchedness are their daily companions, from which they are fleeing, as men flee from pestilence and death. For three hundred years, the Irish people have groaned beneath the blighting influences of land monopoly and aristocratic government. Every effort of this great but unfortunate people to shake off the deathlike grasp of these monsters has been met by confiscation, banishment, and death, until now we find the whole of the land in the hands of a few individuals of professed loyalty to the British crown — most of whom do not even live in Ireland; while the people, to whom the land rightfully belongs, have been literally driven from the soil, and forced to a condition of servitude. English statesmen are seeking a remedy for discontented Ireland, but fail to find it; and yet the problem is easily solved. Let them destroy this monster, Land Monopoly; repeal unjust laws, divide the land equitably among the people, and cease to treat the Irish people as a nation of slaves, and there will be no more of Fenianism and its consequences.

But, monstrous and pernicious as are the land monopolies of England and other portions of Europe, they are as nothing compared to the landed aristocracy rapidly building up in the United States.

It is but a few years since Congress began the work of giving away the people's inheritance, and already near TWO

HUNDRED MILLIONS OF ACRES have been granted to railroads and other monopolies. The land thus given away from beneath the feet of the masses, equals in extent Virginia, Maryland, Delaware, Ohio, Pennsylvania, New Jersey, New York, Connecticut, Vermont, New Hampshire, Maine, Massachusetts, and Rhode Island, with more than fifteen millions of acres left, which alone would give to each head of a family, in Pennsylvania and New York, about sixteen acres; or, taking the whole two hundred million acres, it would give to every head of a family in the United States about forty acres, the whole being in extent of territory about equal to England, Ireland, Wales, Scotland, France, and Belgium, whose present population is about 75,000,000. The land thus taken from the people, without their consent, and without the shadow of a right in the Constitution, would make an empire capable of sustaining a population of three hundred millions of people.

These statements will serve to show workingmen the enormous extent and power of land monopoly in the United States. Land, like air and water, was given to man as a free gift. God did not sell it, but gave it for the use of *all* his children. He never intended that the ownership of the soil should be vested in a few persons, and the many denied a habitation. As air and water are free to all, so also should land be. The improvements upon a piece of ground should give the person who put them there the right to use the ground. There being no ownership in the soil, it could not be sold. The sale of the improvement should convey to the purchaser the right to use the land, and no man should be allowed to hold more land than he could properly cultivate. All land should be held by the government for the use of the people, to be given to whomsoever would improve and cultivate it. The credit of the government, and the currency of the nation, should rest upon every acre of the soil. But as these ideas will be looked upon as utopian, I will pursue the point no farther now.

The question before us is the distribution of the lands now held by the government in trust for the people. The government has no right to dispose of these lands except to actual settlers. The object of Congress should be to people the lands as rapidly as possible; but instead of adopting a policy that would secure this end, they have actually prevented their settlement to a very great extent. As an illustration, we will take the grants made to the Illinois Central Railroad. Two million five hundred thousand acres were given to this company. Of that number, over fifteen hundred thousand acres have been disposed of at from six to twenty-five dollars an acre. Taking ten dollars as the average, we find the huge sum of $15,000,000. Although the company has not, and never did have, one dollar invested in these lands, yet they sell them to be paid for in instalments, so much each year, and add *six per cent. interest*, principal and interest to be *paid in advance*. From this six per cent. interest, the use of the money paid in advance, and the forfeits of money and improvements, they have realized about $4,000,000 more. This would make $19,000,000. They have one million acres yet to sell, and as this land will be worth more because of the improvement of that already sold, it will average, say twelve dollars per acre. This would be $12,000,000. Add to this the interest, use of money, and forfeits, and it is a safe calculation to say that the company will realize at least $35,000,000. These two million five hundred thousand acres at government price (one dollar and twenty-five cents per acre) would be three million one hundred and twenty-five thousand dollars, leaving a balance in favor of the company, and against the people, of $31,875,000 — a tax paid by the purchasers of these lands to this railroad company and land monopoly.

Had these lands been sold to actual settlers at government price, and the proceeds pledged to the company, or, what would have been still better, had Congress appropriated to the company the sum of $3,125,000 (if they *must* give away something), and given the lands in small parcels to actual settlers, we would see to-day, instead of the 25,000 people now upon these lands, a population of at least 100,000.

The policy of the government is just the reverse of what it should be. Instead of giving the land to railroad companies, it should be given to the people, who would build the roads themselves. Had the 2,500,000 acres given to the Illinois Central been given to actual settlers, in parcels of not less than forty nor more than one hundred acres, and the $3,125,000 been given to poor but deserving workingmen, to assist them in getting to the land and getting a start on it, every acre of that land would now be occupied and under cultivation, sustaining a population of at least 200,000 thriving, industrious, and happy people, and they would have had a railroad, built by themselves, taking to market the products of their labor at half the present rates for freight, and doing ten times the business done by the present road.

I have selected the Illinois Central to illustrate how this thing is done, and the same statement will hold good as applied to all other grants to railroad companies, other corporations, and individuals. Enough, however, has been said to show to every workingman the extent of the injustice that has been thus practised upon the industry of the country.

WHAT WE WANT.

We now want:

1. A new department at Washington, to be called The Department of Labor, the head of said department to be called the Secretary of Labor, and to be chosen directly

from the ranks of workingmen. To this department should be referred all questions of wages and the hours of labor in the navy-yards and all other government workshops, the registry and regulation of trades-unions and co-operative associations, the disposition of public lands, and all other questions directly connected with and affecting labor.

2. The unconditional repeal of all laws bearing upon the disposition of the public domain.

3. The adoption of a plain, unvarnished law for the giving away of the public lands to actual settlers in parcels of not less than forty nor more than one hundred acres, no man being allowed to hold in his own name, the name of his wife, nor any other name, more than one tract.

4. Every man taking up land to be required to proceed to live upon, improve, and cultivate it within one year, or forfeit his claim.

5. Appropriations to be made from the United States Treasury to assist workingmen who desire to locate upon the public domain, but who are destitute of the means to do so.

6. No grants of public land to be made to railroad companies or to other corporations, nor to individuals, except actual settlers, under any circumstances, nor for any purpose.

7. All lands granted to railroad companies or other corporations, or individuals, remaining unoccupied and uncultivated at the end of five years from the date of said grant, to revert back to the government, and be sold at government price ($1.25 per acre), the proceeds to go to the person or persons to whom the grant was made. This provision should apply to *all* grants that have been made.

8. All uncultivated lands held by grant of Congress, by any person or persons, shall pay a tax of *ten cents per acre* into the treasury of the United States until said lands are cultivated, or have reverted to the government.

9. All uncultivated lands now held by grant of Congress, by any person or persons, shall be immediately placed in the market at one dollar and twenty-five cents per acre.

Anticipating the opposition that will be made to the proposition to give the public lands away, and pay the expenses of the poor workingmen who desire to move upon and cultivate these lands, upon the ground that they cost the government something, I will answer, that whatever these lands did cost for surveys, etc., came out of the public treasury; and all the money that is or ever was in said treasury was put there by *the labor of the country.* The lands belong to the people, were paid for by the people, and the people have a right to enjoy them without paying for them a second time. And, all things considered, the proposition to assist the very poor in getting to these lands is a very modest one. We only ask that a very little of the taxes paid by labor be returned to those who paid it, while hundreds of millions are being appropriated for other purposes. And we declare the Freedmen's Bureau to be a stupendous fraud upon that portion of the labor of the country that has produced nearly all the wealth, paid most of the taxes, and preserved the life of the nation.

The hundreds of thousands of honest, industrious workingmen, who, through bad legislation, are now out of employment in the manufacturing districts and large cities, and who are now suffering all the horrors of extreme poverty, do not ask to be fed and clothed out of the public treasury. All they ask is an opportunity to *feed and clothe themselves.*

CONCLUSION.

Let Congress adopt a law embracing the foregoing propositions, and the agricultural interests of the nation will largely increase; the surplus population of our overcrowded cities will be drawn off; crime will rapidly disappear; rents and all the necessaries of life will be cheapened; many of our prisons and almshouses can be turned into agricultural colleges; the aggregate wealth of the nation will be largely augmented; the ability of the people to pay taxes will be vastly enhanced, and the untilled wilderness will blossom as the rose!

WILLIAM H. SYLVIS.

THE EIGHT-HOUR LAW.

CONGRESS had enacted a law making eight hours a legal day's work in government workshops, arsenals, navy-yards, etc.; but the pressure of those who feared that this dreaded eight-hour principle would spread, was sufficient to induce the secretary of the navy, and other government officials, to misinterpret the intention and the wording of the law, by deciding that the reduction of the hours of labor to eight per day was intended to be followed by a reduction of twenty per cent. in wages. Mr. Sylvis was a firm believer in the eight-hour principle, and had been among those most active in securing the passage of the law alluded to; and when Attorney-General Hoar rendered his decision sustaining Secretary of the Navy Borie's interpretation of that law, by which the wages of government employés were cut down one-fifth, he grew naturally indignant, and wrote to Mr. Hoar, plainly telling him that he had done the workingmen who had asked the passage of the eight-hour law, the members of Congress who voted for it, and the people it affected, a gross injustice. Mr. Hoar was evidently somewhat nettled to be thus "bearded in his own den," and answered Mr. Sylvis, accusing him of misunderstanding his decision. But Mr. Sylvis was not the man to yield in an argument when right was so plainly on his side, even though his antagonist was an austere attorney-general of the United States. He again wrote to Mr. Hoar, this time such a letter as indicated that the writer meant just what he said, and, not having taken the position he did without due consideration, was in no mood for abandoning it. We give the correspondence entire, feeling sure that it is well worthy of the room it occupies, and will reflect no discredit upon the one of the parties to it in which our readers are most interested.

PRESIDENT SYLVIS TO ATTORNEY-GENERAL HOAR—REVIEW OF HIS DECISION.

OFFICE OF THE NATIONAL LABOR UNION,
PHILADELPHIA, May 3, 1869.

E. R. HOAR, United States Attorney-General.

SIR:—Your late "opinion," giving a construction to the eight-hour law, approved June 25, 1868, has caused considerable excitement and much inquiry throughout the country. You say the effect of the law reducing the hours of labor was to reduce the wages. I have given this matter a very careful consideration, with an earnest desire to arrive at the truth; but I have failed to find a single justification of your course. I have read, very carefully, the debates in both houses of Congress, while the bill was under consideration, and I can find nothing upon which to base the opinion that the reduction of hours was intended to work a reduction of wages. It seems to me that some respect should be paid to the INTENTION of those who, from all parts of the country, petitioned for the passage of the eight-hour law, and those who advocated the bill and voted for it.

Among the millions of workingmen throughout the country, who have discussed this question, and asked for the passage of an eight-hour law, not one can be found who intended or believed a reduction of wages would follow a reduction of hours. We have further the most positive evidence that not one, in either house, who voted for the bill, intended a reduction of wages; and when we turn to the opponents of the bill, we find that even they did not expect a reduction of wages would follow its passage. The speeches of Sherman, Fessenden, and others, show that the ground of their opposition was because the effect of the bill would be to shorten the day and not the wages, thus discriminating in favor of government employés and against those in private employment, which they held would create an antagonism between the government and private employés, and between the workmen employed by the public and private employer. So fully convinced was Mr. Sherman, the champion of the opposition, that this would be the result, and so anxious was he either to kill the bill or destroy its effect, that he offered the following amendment:

"And, unless otherwise provided by law, the rate of wages paid by the United States shall be the current rate for the same labor for the same time, at the place of employment." — Page 3424, *Congressional Globe.*

This amendment was ably debated by both sides, and defeated by a vote of 24 to 15. If, as you say, the bill as it passed the house would work a reduction of wages as well as a reduction of hours, where was the necessity for Mr. Sherman's amendment; and on the other hand, if the senate intended to reduce wages as well as hours, why did it not adopt the amendment? The defeat of this amendment furnishes the most positive evidence that the senate did not intend there should be a reduction of wages.

As a still further evidence of this fact, we find that immediately after the passage of the bill in the senate, Mr. Sherman suggested that "the title of the bill ought to be changed to read, "A bill to give to government employés twenty-five per cent. more wages than employés in private establishments receive." This facetious proposition of the senator was laughed at. As a still further evidence that the house did not intend a reduction of wages, we have the fact before us that the house, just before its final adjournment, unanimously adopted a resolution attesting the fact that a reduction of wages was not intended to follow the passage of the law.

I think I have said enough to prove that the friends of the eight-hour bill never intended a reduction of wages should follow its passage.

In your opinion, you place great stress upon the assertion that Congress failed to repeal the Act of December 21, 1861, as amended July 16, 1862, which reads, —

> "That the hours of labor and the rate of wages of employés in the navy-yards shall conform, as nearly as is consistent with the public interests, with those of private establishments in the immediate vicinity of the respective yards, to be determined by the commandants of the navy-yards, subject to the approval and revision of the secretary of the navy."

And you have labored hard to impress the President and the Cabinet with a sense of your position. So weak is your position on this point that the whole country ridicules it, and believes you have resorted to it simply as a subterfuge to maintain a position utterly untenable by any honest course of reasoning.

That the eight-hour law does repeal the Act referred to, there is not the least doubt in the mind of any candid man. The eight-hour law as it stands, reads, —

> "That eight hours shall constitute a day's work for all laborers, workingmen, and mechanics now employed, or who may be hereafter employed, by or on behalf of the government

of the United States. AND THAT ALL ACTS, AND PARTS OF ACTS, INCONSISTENT WITH THIS ACT, BE AND THE SAME ARE HEREBY REPEALED."

"Shall constitute a day's work." Does this mean what it says, or is there a hidden meaning, invisible to everybody but yourself? If it means what it says, then it simply fixes the length of the day. Under the old law, the length of the day was to be measured by the standard outside of government shops, and the wages to be the same as in outside shops. Neither the employés of the government, nor those outside, worked by the hour, but by the day, and the length of the day and the wages were to be the same. The eight-hour law reduces the length of the day, but is silent on the subject of wages. It simply strikes out that part of the Act of July 16, 1862, which refers to the hours of labor, leaving the standard of wages for a day's work remain as before. "Shall constitute a day's work," not four-fifths of a day's work, measured by the day in private shops, as you would have us believe, but a DAY'S WORK, the wages to be the same as before for a day's work.

But we can sustain our construction of the law upon other grounds. The government in its past policy has at all times recognized and indorsed our view of this question. When Mr. Van Buren issued his order making ten hours a day's work in all government workshops, no reduction of wages followed, although most employés in outside establishments worked eleven and twelve hours. Again, in October, 1866, the hours of labor in the government printing establishment at Washington were reduced to eight, and an advance of wages made at the same time. I might call your attention to several other cases bearing directly on this point, but I think enough has been said to fully sustain my position.

It is a sad spectacle — in a country like ours — to see the

legal adviser of the President yielding to the demands of a few men to defeat the will of the people, as expressed by their representatives. There seems to be no desire on your part, nor among your superiors at Washington, to do anything for the people. Congressmen and Senators can raise their wages with impunity. Men in government employ, whose daily labor does not average six hours, get large salaries, and no fault is found. Swindling railroad corporations, land-rings, gold-rings, whiskey-rings, bond-holders' rings, and the representatives of all other kinds of swindles, can receive kind words and special privileges, but workingmen must be insulted and take back seats. Eight thousand dollars a year, to say nothing of perquisites, are not too much for a Cabinet officer, but six hundred dollars are enough for a workingman. The President gained the popularity which put him where he is by the hard knocks of the workingmen of the nation upon many a hard-fought battlefield; but now he and his advisers are ready to kick away the ladder by which they reached their present high positions. We still hold the ballot in our hands, and by a judicious use of it we can ultimately gain what is justly due us, but now withheld by those placed in official positions by our votes.

W. H. Sylvis.

Washington, May 18, 1869.

My Friend:—From the tenor of the letter which you addressed to me on the 13th, I am led to conclude that you have never read my opinion to which your letter refers—certainly you do not understand it, as the second sentence in your letter is exactly contrary to fact.

Will you allow me to express a hope, as I have not the pleasure of your personal acquaintance, that in the progress of time you may become, if not wiser, at least less abusive.

Your obedient servant,

E. R. Hoar.

REPLY OF THE PRESIDENT OF THE NATIONAL LABOR UNION.

OFFICE OF THE NATIONAL LABOR UNION,
PHILADELPHIA, May 21, 1869.

E. R. HOAR, United States Attorney-General.

SIR: — Your note acknowledging the receipt of my letter of the 3d inst., is received. You have adopted the easiest way in the world of replying to an unanswerable argument, namely, by throwing yourself upon your dignity, and telling me I never read your opinion, and did not know what I was talking about. But let me assure you, sir, that I am not to be silenced in that way. It was not my intention to be "abusive;" but if anything I said hit you, or hurt you, the fault was not mine, for my remarks were intended for where they belong. It seems to me that your note of the 18th places you in a very ridiculous position. You say, "The second sentence in your letter is exactly contrary to the fact." Now the second sentence in my letter reads, "You say the effect of the law reducing the hours of labor was to reduce the wages." You say that this assertion of mine is "exactly contrary to the fact." Do you mean by this that your "opinion" was against any reduction of wages. I charge you with having decided IN FAVOR of a reduction of wages. You say that "is exactly contrary to the fact." "Exactly contrary" to what I said would be that you decided AGAINST a reduction of wages. If this be true, if your "opinion" was against a reduction of wages, because of a reduction of hours, then Secretary Borie's order is in direct conflict with and in direct opposition to your legal opinion.

But what are the facts in the case? Secretary Borie issues an order reducing the wages of employés in the government workshops twenty per cent., because of the reduction of the hours of labor from ten to eight. This action was protested against, and the question was referred to you. Your "opinion" sustained the action of Secretary Borie, and the order of the secretary reducing wages stands to-day unrevoked. Either the order of the secretary "is exactly contrary" to your opinion, or your opinion "is exactly contrary" to your letter to me. If your statement to me is true, then the order of the secretary reducing wages is contrary to law; and if said order is not contrary to law, then your statement to me that my assertion was "exactly contrary" is not true.

"Will you allow me to express a hope, as I have not the pleasure of your personal acquaintance, that in the progress of time you may become, if not wiser," at least more consistent.

Yours truly, W. H. SYLVIS.

THE PRESIDENT OF THE NATIONAL LABOR UNION TO PRESIDENT GRANT.

OFFICE OF THE NATIONAL LABOR UNION,
PHILADELPHIA, May 27, 1869.

To His Excellency U. S. GRANT, President of the United States.

SIR: — When the attorney-general, adversely to the interests of those intended to be benefited by the enactment of the eight-hour law, decided that under it workmen employed in the government shops are entitled to but four-fifths of a day's pay for what that law constituted a full day's work, we almost despaired of securing justice until after the reconvening of Congress; but your proclamation, under date of 21st instant, has pleasurably disappointed us. Though this is prepared as a letter of thanks, we do not feel it a duty to accord express thanks to government officials, who, in remembrance of their obligation, faithfully interpret or administer the law. We regard government officials as public servants, selected because of their honesty, sagacity, wisdom, and affection for the country, and an equitable execution of the law as a duty, to the faithful performance of which they have made a solemn pledge, and not as a favor meriting special thanks. The proper discharge of a pledged duty is certainly incumbent upon the servant of the public equally as upon him who occupies the same relation to the individual, who is meritedly punished for an improper, though not specially thanked for a proper, performance of his pledged or implied promise.

The history of our country during the past several years has proven, however, that the faithful fulfilment of official pledges, the rigidly honest construction and administration of law, is not the rule but the exception; so that it has become customary to especially thank officials when, in a moment of aberration, they condescend to equitably legislate, administer, or interpret.

In your inaugural address to the country, you pledged yourself to the enforcement of all laws just or unjust, which you very properly told us were enacted for the government as well of those who opposed as those who favored them — and by reason of that pledge we had a right to expect just such an order as was contained in your proclamation of the 21st inst. But you will pardon us, sir, if we say, that, accepting official conduct during the last few years as an index of that to come, we seriously doubted that, in the face of the attorney-general's very learned opinion, you would render to the laborer of the nation — we say of the nation, for a mighty principle is involved — that which the eight-hour law has declared to be their due.

But your order came, and coming unexpectedly is doubly welcome, and we experience augmented pleasure in thanking you for it.

We plain people believed the provisions of the law to be plain enough. Their being so, perhaps, accounts for the egregious error committed by your learned legal adviser in his interpretation of them. Your practical mind divined its intent; while to his acumen — the accumulated wondrous wisdom of years of varied experience—it was an occult problem, from the solution of which he emerged defeated — which was worse for his legal reputation than for his material condition, seeing that he is still your attorney-general.

My position, as official head of the National Labor Union, has brought me into contact with many "malcontents," who, deeming that the government deals inequitably by them, attribute it to too much law and a superabundance of lawyers. Whether they are correct or not, they seem determined to combat from that position, and their ranks are numerous. Their success or defeat, the progress of time alone can develop; but a multiplication of instances wherein (as in the one that has just passed into history) the learned decision of a self-puffed lawyer is compelled to give way to the unvarnished rendering of a practical citizen unread in Blackstone and unversed in the technicalities of Coke or Littleton, will make the former extremely probable.

If thanks are due for simple justice, the National Labor Union thanks you for your order.

Trusting, sir, that your actions throughout your official term may be gauged by the rule of justice that impelled you to treat Mr. Hoar's opinion with the indifference its utter silliness deserved, I am, very respectfully, your obedient servant,

W. H. SYLVIS.

THANKS TO SENATOR WILSON.

OFFICE OF THE NATIONAL LABOR UNION,
PHILADELPHIA, April 27, 1869.

HON. HENRY WILSON, United States Senate.

DEAR SIR: — Your efforts in behalf of the Eight-Hour Law, and your able and timely letter on the proper construction of said law, render it incumbent upon me to officially and specifically thank you in behalf of the National Labor Union, of which I have the honor to be the representative head. The construction put on said law by Secretary of the Navy Borie — with the advice of Attorney-General Hoar — is so manifestly unjust and contrary to the intent of the majority who voted for it, that, if persisted in, it will place Secretary Borie in the rather equivocal position of asserting that those who framed and adopted the law did not know its intent and purpose, whilst your letter proves conclusively that those who voted for the bill did so with the full understanding that eight hours were to be a legal day's work, WITHOUT A REDUCTION OF WAGES.

Yours truly, W. H. SYLVIS.

LETTERS FROM THE SOUTH.

RICHMOND, Feb. 11, 1869.

ON the afternoon of the 6th inst. we took leave of our little family, — a sad task for any true man, — and took the cars for Wilmington, Del., where we met some thirty or more friends in a cosy room waiting our arrival. After a very interesting meeting of more than three hours, and a free interchange of views, a committee was appointed to make arrangements for a mass meeting, to be addressed by Mr. Trevellick, and to take the preliminary steps for the formation of a labor union. Mr. Samuel J. Wood is the member of the National Executive for the State of Delaware, and it is to be hoped the work will go on well from this time forward. After the meeting we started for Baltimore, where we arrived at four o'clock Sunday morning. We passed the day in resting both body and mind, and in the evening we went to church, and were entertained by a very able and interesting missionary sermon. The greater part of the next day we spent in a most pleasant and profitable manner with our old friend, General Duff Green. Mr. Green is a most remarkable man; though almost at the close of a long and eventful life, his mind is as clear and active as ever. His head is a vast storehouse of knowledge gathered from a close relation to and connection with the political affairs of the country for more than fifty years. He is preparing a most able and exhaustive article on "money" and finances. He intends it as a memorial to Congress, and a defence of the money plank of the platform of the "National Labor Union." While he does not go over the ground taken by Cary and Butler, he reaches the same conclusions. His argument in favor of a paper currency, and our convertible and reconvertible plan, is powerful, and bears every impress of a giant mind. After leaving friend Green, we called at the shop of the Co-operative Carpenters, and had a chat with our friend Cather. In the evening he very kindly took us to a meeting of the Carpenters' Co-operative Society, where we were introduced to quite a number of those present, who had met for the purpose of paying their weekly instalments. This society is founded somewhat upon the plan of a building society, and is in a very flourishing condition. We were so much pleased with what we saw of it, that we shall, some day, refer to it at length, and give our readers the benefit of their plan of operations.

After a social talk with the carpenters, we attended a meeting of moulders. There was a joint one of Unions Nos. 19 and 24, and such non-union men as saw fit to attend. Of this meeting we will not speak particularly, as we met our attentive correspondent there, who, we suppose, will give our readers the benefit of what he saw of a public nature, and of what was private of course we cannot speak. Union No. 24 is a reorganization of an old union, just made. As we never found better material for a union, we expect to find No. 24 at the head of the heap. No. 19 is in a flourishing condition, and we will be disappointed if her future is not far ahead of her past. There is in Baltimore a considerable number of the animal called "scab," besides some of the weak-kneed sort who get shaky in the joints when the "boss" frowns. It is hoped, however, that many of these "critters" will turn from their evil ways, join the union, and live an honorable life the rest of their days.

From Baltimore we went to Washington, where we had the pleasure of meeting our old friends Whaley, Cary, Cavis, Puett, Day the irrepressible, Maguire, and several others. About noon we wended our way to the capitol, and through the kindness of General Cary were admitted to the floor of the house, where we witnessed a portion of the ceremony of counting the electoral vote. After exhausting our patience and much of our strength, we withdrew in disgust at the farce being enacted or performed by the assembled swindlers of the nation. We supped with friend Whaley and his good family, and at seven in the evening bade adieu to that sink of national iniquity — Washington, and started for this city, where, after a *very* slow ride by water and rail, we arrived at 4 A. M. yesterday.

This being our first visit to Richmond, we will give it and the surrounding country a careful consideration, and give our opinions and impressions of what we see in our next.

W. H. SYLVIS.

WILMINGTON, Feb. 13, 1869.

Our previous letter was from Richmond, Va., and we closed it by a promise to give our impressions of that city. First, we will state that on the evening of the 11th inst., we attended a meeting of Iron-Moulders' Union, No. 128. The meeting was quite large, and a very deep interest was manifested by all present. We feel sure that very good results will come from that meeting, and that before long No. 128 will stand in the front rank of first-class unions. We found as good men in Richmond as it has ever been our pleasure to meet anywhere; in their hands the union is safe. The union had delegated our old friend, its worthy treasurer, Mr. James Kendlar, to meet us on our arrival, and show us the sights; we therefore spent the most of the 11th in looking over the city. We first visited the several foundries, and was pleased to find trade good in all. The only drawback is low wages. Times have been so hard, and work and money so scarce since the close of war, that wages have been kept down; if the present good trade continues, there will be a chance for a raise. We found one shop where there was no admittance. The name of the firm is Ellenger & Edmond. If any one desires to see a person in their employ, they must make application at the office, the person is sent for, and "docked" for the time he remains out. We mention this by way of a free advertisement for said firm.

After "doing" all the foundries, we visited the State House, from the top of which we had a very fine view of the city and the surrounding country. The location of the State House is very fine, and the grounds about it have at one time been beautiful; but, like the house, they are in a very dilapidated condition. In the State House, but not in use, we saw what to us was a curiosity, in the shape of a heating-stove made in 1770, ninety-nine years ago. It is called the Buzaglo, but we could find nothing about it to indicate where it was made. Its shape was simply three square boxes set one upon another, the lower box being the largest, the second smaller, and the third still smaller; the boxes being connected by flues, and the fire being made in the lower box, which would take about a four-foot stick of wood. Its height was about eight feet, and every plate and piece about it had been moulded in "open sand," a term every moulder will understand.

We next visited the State prison, which, like everything else we had seen, was in a shocking bad condition. Such dirty yards and upsidedown workshops, we never before looked upon. Aside from the filthy grounds and confused condition of things generally, the institution seemed to be well managed. A considerable amount of mechanical work is done, and quite a large amount of it for contractors, who pay the State *fifty cents* a day for the labor of the convicts. This work, furniture, etc., is sold in the market in competition with the work of honest men, the tendency of which is to reduce wages for the same kind of work outside of the prison to fifty cents a day. We believe that there are no moulders in that prison, but we know of some who ought to be there. After leaving the prison, we went to see that huge swindle upon the honest workingmen of the country known as the "Freedmen's Bureau." The officer in charge kindly invited us into the institution, where we had an opportunity to see the inside of the machine. A large number of people received "rations" while we were there; one quart of "soup" and a pound of corn-bread were served out to each one. We were invited to taste the soup, which was pronounced "excellent;" but as we espied a huge specimen of a "freed man," with his sleeves rolled up, stirring the soup with his arm in up to the elbow, the sweat running down his arm and his face, and a suspicious-looking drop hanging on the end of his nose, which might not drop outside, we very politely declined "tasting." The officer in charge of the books informed us that, on the day previous, rations had been served to 2163 persons, 89 of whom were white, mostly women and children. As we had heard many stories about these people who are thus fed at the public expense, while other men must work for a living or starve, we made many inquiries, and learned that hundreds of able-bodied men had come in from the country to get rid of work, and live from the "Bureau." Hardly a day passes but men are in from the country in search of hands to work on farms, chop wood, etc., and cannot get them. One man wanted forty hands to chop wood; after much trouble, he succeeded in getting ten; half of them ran away before the end of a week, the balance remained until they got their week's pay, and then left. In every direction men are wanted to work at all kinds of work, but they prefer to remain in Richmond, and live at the expense of the tax-payers. The idea that one class of workingmen shall be fed at government expense, while others must work or starve, is preposterous — it is a swindle; an outrage practised by government, that no people should stand. We go for "smashing the Bureau," and making these lazy loafers work for a living, as other men do.

The amount of damage done by the burning of Richmond at the time of the evacuation, cannot be realized without seeing it just as it is. The city is slowly recovering, but it will be a long time before it is as it once was. The location is a very fine one for a beautiful city. Richmond will never have any commercial importance, but the time is not far distant when it will be one of the first manufacturing cities in the country; for this its location is all that could be desired. Running along its whole front is one of the finest water-powers in America running to waste. What is wanting is money, labor, energy, and enterprise; all these must come there from other sections: there are none among the people of Richmond. Back of Richmond, towards the mountains, there is one of the finest countries in the world, unsurpassed for wheat, corn, tobacco, fruit, and every description of agricultural production, and vast deposits of iron-ore and coal are found along the eastern slope of the mountains, within convenient distance. Railroads are being opened up, and all this vast wealth will become tributary to Richmond, as a great manufacturing city. Besides this, the day is not far distant when the greatest commercial city on the Atlantic coast will be located where Norfolk and Portsmouth now stand, at the mouth of James River. Here are Hampton Roads and Lynn Haven Bay, constituting the finest harbor on the Atlantic coast, if not in the world. Two lines of railroads and canals are about to be built, which will connect Norfolk with the great West; the one running to the southwest connecting with the Mississippi by the Tennessee River, and with the Gulf of Mexico by the Mobile River. The main line of this route will be both by rail and water to the Mississippi, and will constitute the eastern division of the Southern Pacific Railroad, which will place Norfolk nearer to San Francisco than New York is, and by a route uninterrupted by ice or snow. This route is destined to become the most important of all the Pacific routes.

The other line will connect by rail and water with the Ohio River, 401 miles from Norfolk. This will place Omaha about fifty miles nearer to Norfolk than to New York, and grain can be loaded at any point on the Mississippi or Missouri Rivers, and landed at Norfolk without breaking bulk. It may be said that the same can be done to New York by a canal from the Mississippi River to Lake Michigan; but the distance is much greater, and for at least five months in the year that route is closed by ice. This south-western route from Norfolk will connect with over

16,000 miles of navigable rivers, and more than 21,000 miles of railroad in the Mississippi Valley. By this route grain will be sent to Norfolk much cheaper than to New York. Estimating upon present rates, the saving would be sixteen cents a bushel cheaper than by the Pennsylvania Railroad; twenty-three cents by the Baltimore & Ohio Road; and an average of twenty cents a bushel cheaper than on present roads, on every bushel raised in sixteen States. These sixteen States produced in 1866, 1,090,000,000 of bushels. This would be a saving of $218,000,000 in a single year.

But, lest I weary the reader, I will drop this subject. Whatever others may think of it, we are convinced that Norfolk will one day be the greatest commercial city on the Atlantic coast; and as Norfolk grows in commercial importance, Richmond will grow as a manufacturing city.

We left Richmond on the 12th inst., and reached here on the 13th. This city is built upon a sand-hill, and is in a very dilapidated condition. The people move about as if their only desire was to while away the time — to see how long it would take to go from one place to another. The city is completely under the control of the negro; there is no money, consequently no business, no enterprise. All men are idle because there is nothing to do. The rate of interest is so high that business men cannot pay it; and the financial policy of the government is to furnish Wall Street with money to speculate upon, while the industry must languish and die, and workingmen must starve and go naked, as plenty of them do in this country.

There is a vast timber country back of this, and this city should be one of the best lumber and turpentine markets in the world.

Since here, we have had a very interesting meeting of those connected with the Labor Union. We find some of the very best kind of men here, and never met with a more cordial welcome anywhere. We conversed with a number of intelligent negroes, who were present at the meeting; they expressed themselves well pleased with our views, and in a short time there will be a second Labor Union in this city, composed exclusively of colored men. If we can succeed in convincing these people that it is their interest to make common cause with us in these great national questions, we will have a power in this part of the country that will shake Wall Street out of its boots.

W. H. SYLVIS.

AUGUSTA, GA., Feb. 19, 1869.

WE left Wilmington, N. C., on the morning of the 14th inst., and reached Columbia, S. C., the same evening, distant one hundred and ninety-six miles. Columbia is the capital of S. C., and before the war was considered the most beautiful city in the South. Four years ago, this month, General Sherman's army passed through Columbia, and almost totally destroyed the city; over one thousand three hundred houses were burned, the only buildings left standing were a few of little account in the outskirts of the city. Although four years have elapsed since "grim-visaged war has smoothed his wrinkled front," the city may still be termed a mass of ruins. Some new buildings have gone up, and some are going up; but the place is recovering very slowly. We spent two or three hours in looking over the grounds of the State House, and through the building. The building was commenced several years before the war; work was suspended when the war broke out, and the building left in an unfinished condition. It is not a very large structure; but if finished according to the original design would be one of the most handsome in America; over $3,000,000 had been expended on it when work was suspended; the material, South Carolina granite, Italian and Tennessee marble. We counted six places where shot or shell had struck the western end, and the heat of a burning building somewhat damaged the southwest corner, but the main building is very little damaged. The damage done was to a large amount of finished material lying under the sheds in the yard, all of which was destroyed by the heat from the burning sheds. Considerable pains seem to have been taken to render useless all the costly material and machinery in the yard.

The location of Columbia is the most beautiful we have ever seen in any part of the country, the climate is all that could be desired, and is surrounded by a country that will produce almost everything the heart of a man could wish for. The river running along its western side furnishes as fine water-power as can be found. We understand Governor Sprague, of Rhode Island, has purchased this water-power, and intends erecting cotton-mills. When capital takes advantage of this water-power, Columbia will become an important city. From Columbia we went to Charleston, where we remained two days, the first day we spent in doing business, and in visiting the several foundries, and looking over the city.

Charleston presents the saddest sight it has yet been our lot to look upon. The great fire of 1861 swept clear across the city, from northeast to southwest, burning the heart entirely out; and it remains in almost that condition to-day. We walked over the greater portion of the city, and saw but one building in course of erection; on this, the only men we saw were some half dozen bricklayers. I could best describe the appearance of the city by saying that it looks as if the people had all moved out, and returned after an absence of five years, to find grass growing in the streets, and moss and mould gathered upon the houses. There seems to be but little business, and many idle people. On the second day, we went out to see Fort Sumpter, which is simply a mass of ruins, made up of brick, granite, sand, and oyster shells. We went out in a small boat managed by two negroes, who did not understand their business, and were afraid to run any risks. The wind sprung up to a stiff breeze, and we could neither coax, scare, nor buy them to take us to Morris and Sullivan's Islands, Fort Johnson, and other places of interest; so, much against our will, the boat was headed for Charleston, distant five miles in a straight line. As we had to sail directly against a sharp wind, a strong tide running out, a very rough sea, and two men who knew little more about a boat than two mules, we had a *very* serious time of it. We came near upsetting several times, and were finally obliged to turn in and help work the boat ashore. When we reached the wharf, we were tired, hungry, and completely soaked with salt water. The foundry business is slowly reviving in Charleston, and we succeeded in reorganizing Union No. —. There is a Mechanic's Union — a union of all trades in that city — which is quite strong, and bids fair to accomplish much good. There is also a very successful co-operative grocery store, which has been in operation nearly one year. They started with less than $900, and their present capital is $10,000. The store is large and well stocked, and managed with good ability. The Constitution provides:

SECTION 1. "This Association shall be titled the Palmetto Pioneer Co-operative Association."

SECTION 2. "The business shall be conducted strictly on cash principles."

The capital stock is five hundred shares, of $260 each, payable in instalments of one dollar per week, and all profits are credited to shareholders on account of stock. After each stockholder shall have to his or her credit, from the weekly payment of one dollar and the profits standing to his account, $260, payments will stop, and dividends will be paid in cash. Each stockholder has but one vote, and no person can hold more than one share; one-third of profit is paid to capital, and two-thirds to shareholders on account of purchases made. Two hundred and nineteen shares of stock have been sold. The plan is a simple one, and we believe a very good one.

The number of mechanics in Charleston is very small; but the work they are doing shows them to be good men, and far ahead of the mechanics of many other cities, where the chances to get on well are much better.

Last evening we took the cars for this point, where we arrived at half-past six this morning, eleven hours to travel one hundred and forty miles. This is a very fine city; the streets intersect each other at right angles, and are very wide, and well shaded with fine big trees. We have not yet looked about the city, therefore cannot speak of it. This place is, by the way we travelled, nine hundred and sixty-eight miles from Philadelphia, and the fare for the whole distance very near six cents a mile. Financiers tell us that where money is plenty, everything is high; and where money is scarce, everything is cheap. That assertion does not hold good in this country. We never saw so little money; indeed, there is no money in these parts, and it cannot be got. And everything is high: six cents a mile railroad fare; ten cents to ride in the street-cars in the cities; twenty-five cents for a shave; twenty-five cents to get your boots blacked; twenty-five cents for a glass of lemonade; twenty-five cents for a drink of whiskey, but as we do not drink it, we are not interested in the prices of that article; ten cents for a newspaper; $4 a day for board in almost any kind of a hotel; and all other things in proportion. We have not said anything yet about the state of the South, socially and politically. We think it best not to until we have gone over the whole South, and from the people get their views, learn their wants, and see Southern life in all its phases. We are keeping our eyes and ears both open, and we are conversing with men in all the walks of life, white and black, and we promise the readers of the *Advocate* that, when we have gone over the country and made a thorough examination of everything, we will give them a *true* account of things here as we see them, and our opinions of the situation. The National Labor Union is but little known in this country, but everybody we come in contact with is delighted with it. Careful management, and a vigorous campaign, will unite the whole laboring population of the South, white and black, upon our platform. The people down here will be a unit on the great money question, because everybody is poor, and ours is a war of poverty against a moneyed aristocracy. W. H. S.

MOBILE, March 8, 1869.

ON the evening of the 26th of February, we had a very good meeting of the moulders of Atlanta, Ga., and succeeded in reorganizing the union. We met some first-class men, and we have no doubt the union will go on uninterrupted in the future. A want of a proper understanding as to the objects to be accomplished, and the good that has been done, with dull times and no work, had been the cause of the suspension. From Atlanta, we went to Columbus, Ga., distant one hundred and fifty-six miles south. Here we found Moulders' Union, No. 174, in a flourishing condition, and business slowly reviving. The Columbus Union is among the best in the country. Though surrounded by many difficulties, the members have done their duty faithfully. Their corresponding representative deserves the thanks of all good men.

Columbus, Ga., is a very pretty city, located on the eastern bank of the Chattahoochie River, which is navigable to this point at all seasons. Directly in front of the city, and for a considerable distance above, the river forms one of the finest water-powers we have ever seen. Columbus will some day be one of the first manufacturing cities in the South. There are now three cotton-mills there in very successful operation, and others are being built. It is in the midst of a fine cotton-growing country. The raw material can be delivered at the mills from first hands — directly from the planter to the manufacturer — without an army of middlemen to feed at the expense of the planter, the manufacturer, and the consumer.

The city bears the marks of the burning given it by the Federal troops under General Wilson. Just previous to the surrender, a large amount of private property was destroyed, which has not been rebuilt. Augusta, Macon, and Columbus are three very important cities, as they furnish sufficient water-power to spin all the cotton grown in Georgia.

Our esteemed friend, Thomas Casey, First Vice-President of the International Union, met us at Columbus on the day of our arrival, and remained with us until the 2d, when in company we left for Montgomery, Ala., distant ninety-six miles west, on the Mobile River. Here we found an old-fashioned welcome from as good a set of men as we have ever met; there are not many of them, but they are the right sort. Union No. 154 stands, and always has stood, in the front rank. On the evening of the 3d, we were called upon to speak at a mass meeting, gotten up for the purpose of using us. The night was an extremely bad one; the rain came down in torrents, and but few could get out. We talked of the benefits of trades-unions, co-operation, the National Labor Union, etc., and the people seemed much interested. On the evening of the 4th, we attended a meeting of the "Montgomery Mutual Building and Loan Association;" it was the first regular meeting, and we thought they had things considerably "mixed." We do not like their plan; in fact it is not co-operation, as we understand the term. The par value of the shares is $200, payable in monthly instalments of $1; the money is sold to the highest bidder: thus far it is all right. The number of shares is limited to four thousand, and no man can hold more than two hundred shares; and *every share* has one vote, and any shareholder can vote his whole number of shares by proxy. In this it is all wrong. Eleven men can hold two thousand two hundred shares, and the other one thousand eight hundred may be divided among two hundred; yet the eleven men could outvote the two hundred men by a majority of two hundred of all the votes. Here is too much chance for the big fish to eat the little ones. The result will be a failure, so far as helping the helpless is concerned.

During our stay in Montgomery, friend Casey remained with us, and took all pains to show us the sights. We visited the court-house, where, for the first time, we saw a "mixed" jury, nine blacks and three whites; from the verdict rendered, we concluded it was a "mixed" jury. The case on hand was that of a villanous-looking loafer, charged with arson. He keeps the lowest kind of a negro dance-house, where he dispenses bad whiskey and other refreshments. There was no doubt as to his guilt, but he belonged to the right side, and was acquitted. The judge failed to make the jury comprehend the meaning of "arson," or of circumstantial evidence. This is the way justice is dispensed in this part of the world. The readers of the *Advocate* have often heard of what are known in the South as "carpet-baggers." There are many bad stories told of these men that are not true. Many of them are good men, and are esteemed and respected by all the people here; but there are many bad ones. We met two of them in Montgomery; one of them, a fellow by the name of Barber, from Saratoga, N. Y., is sheriff of Montgomery County. He is a man without brains, education, or character. He is a common drunkard, and his looks stamp him as a common blackguard, and excludes him from all respectable society. The other is John C. Keffer, from Philadelphia, Pa., who is Commissioner of Internal Improvements, a man that could not get a position as engineer of a train of night-carts at home. He came down here a practical adventurer, destitute of brains, honor, or honesty, and by worshipping his superiors — negroes — he obtained position. He has a family of daughters, who entertain young negro gentlemen in their parlors. It is just such low scoundrels as this Barber and Keffer, that has been the cause of so much bad feeling between the two sections of our common country; and one of the very best evidences to be found, that there is no such organization as the Ku-Klux Klan, and that the people are orderly and well disposed, having patience, charity, and sincerity, desiring peace and harmony, is the fact that such scamps are permitted to live here unmolested.

Montgomery is a very pretty city, well located upon high ground, and surrounded by a good country. Before the war, it was a very rich and fast place. At present, like all other Southern cities we have yet seen, money is scarce, rents and provisions high, business dull, and the people apparently broken down in confidence and spirit.

From Montgomery we went to Selma by water, distant one hundred and ten miles west. We remained in Selma but a short time, and found business very dull; but the journeymen moulders were at work, though the prospects are not very good. The city is located on a bluff; but the country around it, in every direction, is flat and swampy. The city is too sickly to amount to anything as a manufacturing place; still, it is quite an important point as a railroad centre, and will one day be a great shipping-point for the iron and coal of northern Alabama.

On Saturday afternoon, the 6th inst., we embarked upon board the steamer *C. W. Dorrance*, Capt. B. Meaher, for Mobile, distant four hundred miles by water, nearly due south, where we arrived at 10 A. M., Monday morning. The *Dorrance* is a first-class boat, and Capt. Meaher is one of the very best types of a "fine old Irish gentleman." He is a man all over, six feet four inches high, weighs two hundred and forty pounds, well built, with a great big head filled with a large store of good common sense. He belongs to that class known the world over as "a good fellow." If any of our readers stray down this way, let them hunt Capt. Meaher, and they will find a friend. Of this place we will speak in the future. W. H. S.

MEMPHIS, TENN., March 22, 1869.

WE wound up our last letter with our arrival at Mobile, and since then we have been so much occupied with the business of our mission, as to make it impossible to write previous to reaching this point, and even now we can only hurry over the field we have travelled.

We found considerable business in Mobile, and quite a fine city. Our old friend and shopmate Lineham, Corresponding Representative of Moulders' Union, No. 137, remained with us during our stay in that city, and very kindly took us to all the places of interest in and about the place.

We went out to Whistler, six miles from the city, where the Mobile and Ohio Railroad Company have their shops. It was raining very hard at the time, and we had but little opportunity to see the place. The impressions we formed were not very favorable, and we failed to see why the shops were located there. It looks to us as if the interests of the company, and the health and convenience of the workmen, were sacrificed for the sake of cheap ground upon which to build. Perhaps the company thought by isolating the workmen from the rest of the world, they would not be troubled so much by those odious institutions known as "trades-unions," which have become a terror to all evil-disposed and tyrannous capitalists. Whatever their object may have been, they have failed. The Iron-Moulders' Union, which has become such a monster in size and strength within a few years, is gradually reaching out its arms into every nook and corner of the land; long ago found its way even to Whistler, and some of the very best members of that organization are to be found there. We had the pleasure of shaking these men by the hand, and wishing them God speed. Union No. 137 has had a hard struggle; but it has lived through it all, and is now one of the very best.

They have a shell-road running along Mobile Bay for several miles that is one of the finest drives we have ever seen. We fancy it to be a magnificent place in the warm summer weather. Mobile will never be a great city until, by artificial means, a good entrance and a good harbor can be provided, which we think will never be done. From Mobile we went to New Orleans by water, distant 190 miles. We remained in that city four days, and in that time went pretty well over the whole place. After visiting every foundry, and talking to nearly every moulder (fifty or sixty,) we succeeded in getting about a dozen to attend a meeting, and after much talk we succeeded in re-organizing the union, which had been suspended for some time. We sincerely hope there will be no further suspension, as we have found no place where a union is so much needed, and, with a very few exceptions, we found the moulders the most miserable set of creatures we have met in the whole land. Morally, socially, and intellectually, they are a long way below the standard. Our only hope is in the few good men we found among them; they may improve soon and rapidly. New Orleans is a great city; in some respects the greatest in the country, if wickedness can be called greatness. But it is a great city in point of commercial importance, and one day it will be the metropolis of America.

The great drawback to its progress is its unhealthy location. The ground upon which it is built is very flat; indeed, it is a basin, and in many places lower than the Mississippi River on the one side, and Lake Pontchartrain on the other. The water runs back from the river, and this makes a good healthy drainage almost impossible. The distance from the river to the lake is about seven miles, and there are two or three canals cut from the lake almost to the river. These carry off most of the drainage of the city, while the balance finds its way to the swamps, or is taken up by the atmosphere and breathed by the people. But New Orleans can be made quite a clean and healthy city. A channel must be cut, and the whole body of the Mississippi River turned into the lake. This will lower the water in the channel below the turn-off, and give a good drainage to the whole city. It will also avoid the difficult passes and dangerous sand-bars at the mouth of the river, and give a safer and shorter passage to the gulf. This is a bold and gigantic work, but it must and will be done; and the quicker the people stop speculating about and spending money upon a system or systems of drainage that can never accomplish the object sought, the better it will be for all.

We will not attempt a description of what we saw in that city: we have neither the time nor the space. It was very refreshing to read of snow-storms and the thermometer marking zero and below that in the North; and then walk out in the streets and see ladies dressed in spring goods, orange-trees with ripened fruit, green peas, ripe strawberries, and the most tender flowers. We enjoyed it, because to us it was a strange sight for the first of March.

From New Orleans we went to Vicksburg, Miss., by water, a distance of 400 miles. Reaching that city, our first duty was to find out the amount of foundry business done. We found two shops, one employing one moulder — a white man — getting $3 per day, the other employing one moulder — a black man — getting $2 per day; trade *very* dull. Comment is unnecessary. Take it all in all, we consider Vicksburg the meanest place we have found in the whole country, except, perhaps, Crestline, Ohio. The ground upon which the city is built is a series of high bluffs and deep gullies. The country around is good. From the top of one of the highest hills at the upper end of the city, the view looking west is very fine.

From Vicksburg we went to Jackson, the capital of Mississippi, distant 45 miles east. Jackson is a very pretty little town, but of no importance at all. There is no foundry there of any kind, and very little of anything in a mechanical line, or indeed in any other line.

From this point we went to Water Valley, Miss., distant 142 miles north. This is quite a busy place, made so by the railroad-shops there located. We found our old friend John R. Iserall hard at work, and as sound a man as ever. Here we had the pleasure of organizing the first and only moulders' union ever in Mississippi. Long may it live. It is in good hands, and, though small, will be a success.

From thence we came to this city by way of Grand Junction, distant 120 miles. W. H. S.

TO THE READERS OF THE ADVOCATE.

The undersigned having associated himself with Mr. A. C. Cameron as one of the publishers and proprietors of the *Workingman's Advocate*, it may not be out of place to bow to the readers of the *Advocate*, and make a "little speech."

At no time within the history of the Labor Reform movement in this country has the need of a first-class paper, devoted to the reform movement, been so keenly felt as now; and it becomes the duty of every man to contribute what he can to the building up of such a paper. Seeing and feeling this great need, and being willing to contribute our share to the desired end, we have joined hands with Mr. Cameron, not because of any want of energy and ability on his part, nor of any superior advantages upon our part, but upon the principle that in a multiplicity of heads there is wisdom. The *Advocate* being the official organ of the National Labor Union, of which we have the honor to be president, we believed that, by bringing the two into close relationship, we could so co-operate as to very largely increase the usefulness of each.

While we shall endeavor, by every means within our power, to strengthen the hands of Mr. Cameron, and increase the circulation and usefulness of the *Advocate*, we shall endeavor to use that paper as a means for disseminating our ideas among the masses of the people, and building up the National Labor Union.

Our most earnest desire and highest ambition is to see the greatest success of the Labor Reform movement, and we shall lose no opportunity to push along the good work. We have been actively engaged in the labor movement for many years, and it has always been our aim to assist the toiling masses in every effort to raise themselves from a condition of dependence upon capitalists. We have been, and will be, an earnest advocate of trade-unions among all branches of laborers, and of the principle of co-operation in every form by which it can be applied to productive industry and the distribution of wealth.

Whatever experience, knowledge, or ability we may have, shall be devoted to this reform movement; and while we are willing to make any and all sacrifices necessary to accomplish the objects in view, we expect the readers of this to go to work at once and do all they can to increase the circulation of our paper, and thereby increase our ability to serve the cause.

WM. H. SYLVIS.

ESSAYS.

WHAT IS MONEY?

[THESE articles first appeared in the *Workingman's Advocate*, of Chicago.]

What is money? is a question so frequently asked, especially by workingmen, and so many different answers have been given, all based upon the idea that gold is the only material out of which money can be made, that I have determined to add one more answer to the long list.

In taking up this question, I do not expect to present any new idea, or to say anything new. My only object is to present the matter in a plain, common-sense light; and in doing so, I shall use such arguments and illustrations as will be easily understood by every one who reads. What I have to say will be the plain words of a workingman addressed to workingmen.

Money made of gold is a monarchical and aristocratic institution. Kings adopted it as a sure means of keeping the people in subjection, by taking from them all power to control or in any way interfere with the currency. Princes and nobles were created—special privileges were bestowed upon a few; these few were rich, and were of course interested in maintaining the king's money. Thus the king, with his well-fed few, succeeded in robbing the masses, keeping them poor, ignorant, and wholly dependent.

When our ancestors ran away from Europe to escape religious persecution, they came here and set up for themselves; unfortunately for us, they did not leave behind them their prejudices and false notions on many of the most vital points in the science of government.

Reared amid the hardships and dangers of a new continent — separated from the "parent government" by a great ocean—thrown upon their own resources, they learned lessons of self-reliance and ideas of self-government that served them well when the struggle for independence came, and for the change in civil government about to take place. It was left for them to present to the world, for the first time, a self-formed government, whose basis was the equal rights of man, civil equality, and common privileges, and whose end was to be the general prosperity, virtue, and happiness of the people. Independence gained, it was natural that joy and satisfaction should be inspired, upon having escaped some of the oppressions of European systems, without feeling much curiosity to ascertain whether the new government was actually so founded as to secure the *happiness of the many instead of ministering to the benefit of the few.* This could only be learned after a considerable experience, and after that class out of which came bankers, brokers, bond-holders, usurers, and other plunderers of labor, had time to find out and take advantage of the weak places in our system of government.

This point was soon reached, and then began that scramble for wealth and power that has resulted in creating among us a moneyed aristocracy that is fast sapping the foundation of our government, and destroying the liberties of the people.

It is true that, compared with the wretched population of despotic Europe and Asia, the people of this country, even under existing unjust relations of man to man, enjoy many things not common to the people of other countries. But comparative superiority may still be a condition fraught with much misery to the human family, and not less repugnant to benevolence than revolting to justice. Even in Europe and Asia, this superiority forms the boast of one nation over another, throughout the long-continued chain of comparative wretchedness among the great mass of the population.

We might run without end through a scale of comparative physical misery and enjoyment, and corresponding moral dignity or degradation, and never attain a principle of justice to reconcile ourselves to a wrong and oppressive system from such examples.

The question is not what people endure the least misery, but which enjoy the most happiness and real comfort; and having found that point, we are irresistibly forced to another, based upon the susceptibility of the social compact to yield the full amount of happiness to the mass of the people, and to inquire into the reason why this object is not accomplished by our institutions, when it has been so bountifully provided for by a paternal Providence.

The slightest observation will satisfy the most obstinate mind that nature has abundantly supplied the industry of man with the means of universal comfort. We behold it in every form of luxury — every object of magnificence — every refinement of pleasure — every waste of riot and sensuality — every monument of pride — every display of vanity — every gorgeous decoration of wealth, power, and ambition. We behold the proof in the lordly millionnaire, tortured on his sick-couch by agonies of repletion, while the *laborer* famishes at his door. We behold it in the luxurious capitalist, swelling with the pride of pampered opulence, while the hearts of those who *labored* to produce his wealth, shiver and faint with misery and want, or drag out a protracted life of endless toil. What God has spread before us as the reward and property of him whose labor shall bring it into use, government—unjust, despotic, proud, all-grasping government—has ordained shall belong to those who never labor, and for whose exclusive benefit the laborer shall toil forever. Thus do human institutions, founded on tyranny, or turned from their original principles of justice, destroy the beneficence of heaven, robbing the poor and giving to the rich.

Thus do we find our boasted institutions of equal rights to be the merest skeleton of liberty, which by their *letter* declare that equal rights and privileges shall be guaranteed to all, but by their *operation* create aristocracy, special privileges, extortion, monopoly, and robbery.

Such are the defects of organic law, practical government, and property, which are thrown as obstacles in the path of the workingman.

The great mistake made by the founders of our government was in retaining the king's money, — in ingrafting into our republican institutions monarchical and aristocratic ideas of currency and finances,— in setting up, in our temple of liberty, the golden calf. But the time has come when this idol shall be removed.

Fellow-workingmen, prepare for the fight. The world's greatest revolution is now at hand.

My first article was general or preliminary, intended to show, *First*, that money made of gold was a kingly, despotic invention. *Second*, that it has been continued in use because it provided the surest way to rob the many for the benefit of the few. *Third*, that it was the most dangerous element of despotic governments ingrafted into our republican institutions; and, *Fourth*, that its use is wholly incompatible with the spirit of our form of government, and has entirely subverted the designs, intentions, and desires of the authors of our Constitution.

We come now directly to the subject: "What is money?" Kellogg says that money has four properties or powers. *First*, to represent value. *Second*, to measure value. *Third*, to accumulate value by interest. *Fourth*, to exchange value.

As a discussion of either one of these four powers would involve a partial discussion of all, and prolong the discussion, I shall consider them in a general way, giving the greatest prominence to *interest*, and the material of which money should be made.

Money is the measure of value, and the rate of interest fixes the standard of measure; therefore, the standard should be the same everywhere. Government has decreed that sixteen ounces shall make a pound, and thirty-six inches will make a yard. Suppose Congress should repeal this law, and say that the people in each State or city shall have the right to regulate these matters to suit themselves, what would be the result? We would soon have yard-sticks and pound-weights of various capacities. There would be just as much reason and justice in this, as there is in allowing everybody to fix a measure of value to suit themselves. The necessity for uniformity in weights and measures is no greater than for uniformity in the rate of interest; but it is said that a uniform rate of interest cannot be maintained, no matter what the law may be. That this is true under our present monetary system, I freely admit; because bankers and brokers monopolize the lending of money. The law of Pennsylvania says that six per cent. shall be legal interest; and yet it is impossible to borrow money at that rate, because Congress has fixed a higher rate, and because the business money-lending is confined to a few persons, whom neither the law of the State nor the law of conscience can control. All borrowers must go to them; therefore, they can fix their own terms; that is, they make their own measure of value, which amounts to the same thing as if it was cloth they were selling, and had the making of their own yardstick.

"The government reserves the right to fix the length of the yard, the weight of the pound, the size of the bushel, and the value of the dollar. Money is the public measure of value, and the government is bound to make it just and uniform, that it may correctly determine the value of all commodities. Measures are definite quantities of length, weight, size, and value. The pound-weight, yardstick, and bushel are measures of quantity, and the dollar or money is the measure of value."

"When the yardstick measures cloth, it does not determine its own length, and when money measures property, it does not determine its own value." The law fixes the length of the one and the value of the other. To alter the length of the yardstick is a high crime, and subjects the person guilty of it to severe punishment, while the power of the dollar to measure value can be altered with impunity; and yet the fraud practised upon labor is a thousand times greater than would be the shortening of weights and measures at the option of every seller in the land. "The government reserves the right to fix the measuring power of the dollar to bankers, brokers, and other gamblers."

The man who will interfere with the measure of value is just as guilty of crime as he who defrauds his customers by light weights and short yardsticks.

One of the most silly and absurd notions of the day is that each State should have the right to give to money a legal standard — to fix a legal rate of interest. The government should issue all money, giving to every dollar the same legal value — the same power to measure value in all parts of the country. Money, properly considered, can in no case be an article of barter and sale. It was never instituted to be bought and sold; its only functions are to buy and sell the products of labor. The laborer does not buy money, but he sells his labor *for* money. The farmer does not buy money, but he sells his wheat *for* money. The manufacturer does not buy money, but he sells his wares *for* money; and the consumer buys what he wants *with* money; thus is money simply a medium of exchange. The making of money an article of commerce is a prostitution of the currency of the country, and is simply legalized robbery.

A false monetary system, and the unwise financial policy pursued by the government from the beginning of the war to the present time, has built up a moneyed oligarchy such as the world never saw; and the whole nation is completely under its control. Congress has so legislated as to fix a standard of value, or a rate of interest that is absolutely ruinous — six per cent. in gold is about nine per cent. in greenbacks; and the bonds being exempt from taxation, and considering all other things to their advantage, we find that the rate of interest is fully thirteen per cent. If this was really the *fixed* standard, it would not be so bad; but it is only the rate *below* which it cannot go; but it goes far above that nearly all over the country.

Money was instituted by the government for no other purpose than to be a measure of value and a medium of exchange. We see that the law in nearly every State recognizes this principle by fixing some legal rate of interest; and the government has recognized it by fixing six per cent. in gold as the legal standard. These legal rates are not uniform; and if they were, it would make no difference, because the whole matter of interest, and everything connected with money, is in the hands of a few persons, whose only study is how best to bring to themselves the wealth produced by the labor of the nation. They rob alike the government and the people.

The Constitution of the United States declares that Congress shall have power to coin money *and regulate the power thereof*, and of foreign coin, and to fix the standard of weights and measures.

Congress has definitely fixed the length of the yard, the size of the bushel, and the weight of the pound, but it has not fixed the value of money. Under our present monetary system, the value of money is no more fixed by congressional action than is the price of coal, iron, or any other article of commerce.

Money is the legal standard of value. The rate of interest fixes the value of money. Its value is no more fixed by the quantity or quality of its material, than the size of the bushel is fixed by the quantity or quality of its wood. It would be thought unwise or unjust, if Congress should provide that the yardstick should be made of a rare and costly material, and to authorize a few merchants to regulate its length; and yet it would not be half so injurious to the public good as to empower a few bankers and usurers to regulate the value of money. In the former case, the merchant would be brought face to face with the purchaser, the fraud would be seen, and the buyer would have the means of self-protection; while in the latter case, the power operates silently and unseen, and the oppressor is seldom brought in contact with the injured party.

The rapid centralization of the property of the nation into our large cities, and into the pockets of the strictly non-producer, is plain to every mind. The wealth-producing classes have sought to avert this evil, and better their condition, by almost every means but the true one. Labor-saving machines have been invented to increase production, and every possible means of improving the quality of the various productions of the soil and labor have been introduced, and new avenues of transit have been multiplied to cheapen transportation, but all to little or no avail. These classes are still compelled to toil on in comparative poverty — the increase in production, the improvement in quality, with the increased means of transportation, have but tended to augment the wealth of the few and impoverish the many.

With the present accumulative power of interest, there is no more chance for the laboring-classes to gain their rights by combining their labor to increase production, than there would be hope of success in combining their labor to reverse the course of the rivers, and make them run to the tops of the mountains, and pile up their waters on the summits. The law of gravitation, in the latter case, would not be more sure to overpower all their labor and frustrate all their plans, than the present governing power of interest on money is sure to gather up the increased production and add it to the wealth of the capitalist. The fault is in the law which governs the distribution of property; and combinations to increase production would no more effect any general change in the distribution, than combinations against law of gravitation would effect a change in its general governing powers. The evil is legislative, and the remedy must be legislative, or something worse.

It was my intention, in the beginning, to have finished this subject in three articles, but I have found it impossible to do so to my own satisfaction. I must, therefore, ask the indulgence of the reader; if I grow tedious, and if these articles are extended beyond what may seem necessary, it must be attributed to an earnest desire to make the whole matter plain to the understanding of every reader.

The power of money to accumulate value by interest is a vast power; so great, indeed, that it is hard to bring it into such proportions as to be easily understood by ordinary minds. When we begin to talk of thousands of millions, and billions, etc., the mind of the workingman, who but seldom has more than a week's wages to count over, becomes bewildered, and he don't care to listen. I have already said that interest acts like the tax-collector; it gathers up the products of labor — taking them from the laborer and giving them to the capitalists. Money loaned at ten per cent. will double in seven years, three months and five days; at nine per cent. in eight years and fifteen days; at eight per cent. in nine years and two days; at seven per cent. in ten years, two months and twenty-six days; at six per cent. in eleven years, ten months and twenty-one days; at five per cent. in fourteen years, two months and thirteen days; at four per cent. in seventeen years and eight months; at three per cent. in twenty-three years, five months and ten days; and at two per cent. in about thirty-five years. The average rate of interest for seventy years has been about eight per cent. per annum. At the beginning, property was more equally distributed than it is now. We will suppose one-eighth of the population to have owned one-fourth of the value of the property, and to have loaned it on interest, or rented their property at this rate; collecting and reloaning the interest annually for the seventy years, the amount would be $54,639,310,632, or over three times the amount of the value of the whole property of the nation in 1860.

Now, cannot the simplest mind see something wrong in this? The rate of interest amounting, in seventy years, to more than *three times* the value of all the property in the nation. All that labor produced went to the capitalists — a few men — all non-producers, and this balance of interest over production is a lien upon labor — productive labor, physical labor — a vast load of debt heaped upon the backs of the toiling millions — a mortgage upon the bone and muscle of the nation — the very heart's blood of the workingman is mortgaged from the cradle to the grave.

Had the rate of interest been *three per cent.* instead of *eight per cent.*, it would have amounted, in seventy years, to $1,980,000,000, or less than one-twenty-seventh part of the amount at eight per cent. Thus, it will be seen that, at three per cent., labor would have retained over *seven-eighths* of all it produced; while at eight per cent., capital got over three times the value of all the property in the nation, besides ALL that labor produced. This seven-eighths, which would have been labor's share, would have been divided among the producers in the shape of wages, and every workingman in the nation could be in possession of a comfortable home, and in circumstances entirely independent. We would have no Vanderbilts, Drews, Astors, Stewarts, Belmonts, and Cookes, worth their hundreds of millions, and exercising an influence and power over the government and people such as was never before known since creation, while the dismal cries of poverty-stricken labor, shivering with cold and hunger, come up from every part of the land. Just think of it, fellow-workingmen, there are ten men in the city of New York whose combined wealth is over *three hundred millions of dollars*, and in the same city there are over one hundred thousand workingmen and women whose daily wages do not bring them the commonest necessaries of life, and during last winter many honest, industrious workingmen and women were compelled to apply for public or private charity to keep themselves and their loved ones from starvation, and many died from want of proper food, clothes, and shelter. While these ten men were worth millions, there were nearly 63,000 paupers supported by the city of New York during the year 1867, and a much larger number during 1868. Let it be remembered that a large proportion of these poor people, called "paupers" by newspapers and officials, are honest workingmen and women, the profit of whose toil goes to make up the fortunes — the millions — of the few whose costly equipages jostle the starving mechanic in the same street.

Nowhere in the world is so high a rate of interest maintained; nowhere in the world is labor more completely under the control of the money power; and nowhere in the world is all wealth so surely and so rapidly concentrating in the hands of the few, as in the United States.

It is a first principle that no man can become rich without making another one poor, and that all accumulations of great fortunes necessarily produce poverty somewhere. The course is plain. It is not in the power of man to produce a sum of labor so immense as to make every one rich, but he does produce enough to make all comfortable. If some, therefore, acquire large fortunes from the pile produced by labor, it must leave others without any. To make this still plainer, we will suppose there are one hundred men whose combined or aggregate production is $100,000; an equal division would give to each one $1,000. If one of these men got one dollar more than his share, ninety-nine would get less. But suppose *ten* of them got $5,000 each, then there would be but $555.55 apiece for the other ninety; but if twenty of the ninety take $2,500 each, then seventy would be left without any. A truth so plain requires no further demonstration.

Wealth, seated in the midst of her golden paradise, often sends her attendant, false benevolence, among the wretched, who are famishing from hunger and cold, to exhort them to economy and temperance; or, alarmed by their cries of anguish and suffering, she gathers the poor into almshouses, and eases her conscience by feeding them upon offals, and selling their dead bodies to the dissecting-rooms to defray a portion of the expense. The most pernicious character in society is the miser — the accumulator — the man who will gather up the products of labor beyond his needs; the man who steals from honest toil and leaves the toiler to starve. He is one of the moral extremes that meet us on the verge of misery, worthlessness, and non-production. The accumulator is a tyrant, whose every step inflicts anguish, crushes the heart, or slays his victim.

I am frequently asked by workingmen, what has the question of interest to do with us? we are not borrowers, neither have we money to lend. The natural increase in the wealth of the nation in seventy years is less than four per cent.; that is, the aggregate wealth of the nation increased at the rate of four per cent. annually; then it follows that any rate of interest *above* four per cent. is direct robbery upon labor, and is running the nation in debt.

While the increase in wealth is at the rate of four per cent., interest has averaged at least eight per cent. for seventy years. But if we take the last six years, we will find that the increase in wealth has not been over three per cent., while the rate of interest has averaged fully fifteen per cent.; making an actual loss to productive industry of twelve per cent. Right here the question may be asked, how can this thing called interest consume more than is produced? the answer is plain. The three per cent. consumes all that is produced, after feeding and clothing the producers; and the twelve per cent. is a lien upon future labor. It is a mortgage upon the productive industry of the country.

That this may be clearly understood, I will put it in another form. I have said that three per cent. is a lien upon *present* labor. That is, if a man has an income of $3,000 a year, and spends $15,000, how long will it be until he is bankrupt? He is running behind at the rate of $12,000 a year, providing his debts are such as bear no interest; but if they are interest-bearing debts, the matter is still worse. This, I think, will make it perfectly clear to every workingman.

Interest acts like the tax-gatherer; it enters into all things, and eats up the profits of labor. Labor marries a wife and supports a family. Labor needs food, clothing, and rest. Labor works six days out of every seven, and but ten hours out of every twenty-four. Labor gets sick, and has doctor-bills to pay. Interest works twenty-four hours in a day and seven days in a week. Interest needs no clothing. Interest never gets sick or tired. Interest has no family to support, and needs no almshouse when it gets old. Interest produces nothing, but consumes everything; it gathers together the products of labor into large heaps, making a few rich and many poor. Labor erects a house, and then pays from ten to one hundred per cent. for the privilege of living in it. Labor produces bread, and then pays from ten to five hundred per cent. for the privilege of eating it; every dollar labor can raise goes for interest; labor remains poor and the Shylocks become rich. Interest produces nothing. All it does is to transfer the products of labor to the pockets of the money-lenders, bond-holders, &c.

While this question of interest is the most important of all the questions connected with the political and social relations of the people, yet it is less understood, perhaps, than any other. The poor man, while he toils from year to year, but little dreams that it is interest that is robbing him of all he produces.

This matter of interest is the source of all our financial panics and business prostrations. The man who spends more than his income will go to the wall sooner or later, and a nation that spends more than it produces must break down. No nation on the globe ever did or ever can carry a rate of interest above the natural increase of the national wealth without coming to financial ruin. The manufacturer, the farmer, the mechanic, and the common laborer, each run in debt, each depending upon future labor to make up present deficiencies. A vast system of credits is built up throughout the land. The money-lenders, and the whole horde of bankers, speculators, and gamblers, are day by day accumulating additional liens upon the productive powers of the nation. This condition of things lasts for about ten years, when labor breaks down under the enormous load. Its resources are exhausted; the rate of interest can no longer be paid; the creditors begin to crowd the debtors; a "money panic" ensues, and financial ruin sweeps over the country, prostrating everything before it; hundreds of millions' worth of property change hands at great sacrifices — debts are settled at a small percentage on the dollar — bankrupt laws are enacted — we become a nation of individual repudiators, and there is a general balancing of accounts, which simply means transferring all there is from labor to the pockets of the money-lenders and financial gamblers. The bottom is reached; a lull takes place; labor renews its energies for a new start, only to have the same operation repeated over again. And this same operation has been repeated about every ten years, ever since we have been a nation, and will continue to be repeated so long as we are cursed by our present monetary system.

The manufacturer, the farmer, the business man of any kind, needing money, must pay from ten to thirty per cent. for the use of it. In many cases the profits of his business are less than the rate of interest demanded. To borrow would be ruinous; therefore his business must languish, or, what is very frequently the case, a reduction of wages is made. This reduction does not always, as is supposed, go into the pocket of the employer, but into that of the money-lender. Thus do employer and employé suffer from this system of legal robbery called interest on money.

I have already said that Congress has, by a violation of the Constitution, delegated the power to fix the value of money to a few bankers, brokers, and usurers. It is true, that Congress has fixed a rate of interest on its bonds — six per cent. in gold or about nine per cent. in greenbacks — considering that they are exempt from taxation, and have certain other special advantages, the rate is very nearly thirteen per cent. This may look to many as if Congress had fixed the rate of interest which determines the value of money, and it may be said that the fact that this does not control the rate of interest is a sufficient answer to my argument. That this does not control the rate of interest is evident from the fact that the usual or average rate is far above thirteen per cent. Would it be otherwise, if the rate of interest on the bonds was but three per cent.? While the average rate of interest would be less than now, the system would remain the same, for the reason that while Congress says that one hundred cents shall make a dollar, it has allowed a few men to monopolize the lending of money, and to fix their own measure of value. To these all borrowers must go, because there is nowhere else they can go.

By reason of speculation in gold, and the high rate of interest maintained, a very large proportion of the whole currency of the nation is centralized in the great commercial centres of the East, leaving the West and South without money to do business. While money is worth from thirteen to twenty-five per cent. in Philadelphia, New York, Boston, and other points East, it is worth much more West and South; indeed in many places it is not to be had at all. In many of the manufacturing and mining districts of the interior there has been an almost universal return to the old order system; and private scrip, such as due bills, &c., is made to answer as currency. Why? Because the profits of business are less than the rate of interest on money; and because men cannot borrow money, they are compelled to do without it — to provide their own currency, or close up altogether. In many instances, the employer, to keep his works going, must borrow money, and must pay more interest for the use of it than his return in profit; to save himself, he reduces wages; the workmen, not being able to see where the true difficulty is, go on a strike—the works are closed, and employer and workmen go to ruin together.

"Money creates no wealth; it only gathers up and appropriates to its owner things already produced."

Money is not wealth; it only gives to its owner power over the productions of labor. Wealth is accumulated labor. Money creates nothing, and has no value whatsoever to its owner, except as he exchanges it for what labor produces. A man may have a million of dollars, and be very poor; if he keeps it in his possession, he will starve, he will be destitute of food, clothing, and shelter. Money has no value, only as we part with it for something we need. This is, of course, plain to every mind.

A centralization of wealth is a centralization of power. When the few possess themselves of everything, and the many are reduced to that condition of dependence when it is compulsory to work or starve, then it is that the power of wealth and the rule of the few is absolute.

The most pernicious effect of wealth is, that it hardens the heart, blunts the sensibilities, deadens the conscience, deforms the moral nature, and makes a tyrant of its possessor.

For money, men sacrifice domestic comfort, health, character, and even hazard life itself. For it, they are guilty of fraud, deception, and robbery. For money, they sacrifice friendship, gratitude, natural affection, and every holy and divine feeling. For money, man becomes a creeping, crawling, miserable thing, instead of walking upright, as God intended he should. Mammon and manhood are incompatible.

When wealth accumulates in the hands of the few, the spirit of vindictiveness — a desire to rule, to get more, to reduce labor to a condition of vassalage, and to make pliant tools and helpless, obedient slaves of all who toil at physical labor — develops itself more and more, and widens the breach between the rich and the poor. As the one goes up, the other must go down. The one feels secure in its power, the other grows restless under fraud and persecution.

Here is the fountain from which flow all the social eruptions that blacken the body politic. Here is the cause of all strikes and revolutions. So tight has the hold of these money-changers upon the industry of the country become, that we will find it a hard job to shake them off. We must not waste our time in parleying, in trying to coax them to let go, or thinking we can frighten them away. All this has been tried. There is but one way left. We must take them by the neck with a grasp like a vice, and squeeze the life out of them.

There are but two ways by which this can be done. The first is by our power at the ballot-box: we can vote them out of existence, if we will. If we fail to do this, they will continue to suck at our vitals until, in a fit of desperation, we cut their heads off with the sword.

If, out of the vast wealth we produce, we are to receive but a miserable subsistence, and no prospect before us but eternal toil, and starvation or an almshouse in old age; if the ballot-box is not a sufficient remedy for these evils; if a few men will appropriate all to themselves, while labor toils and starves, then the time will come when an outraged and enslaved people will rise in their physical power, and force a more equitable division of the products of their labor by other means than a lower rate of interest.

What we want, and what we propose to have, is a general

levelling up. I do not mean by this that we desire to pull anybody down, not even if they are up with a rope around their necks—as a considerable number of them ought to be; but we do desire and intend to get up.

The work of accumulation on the one hand, and degradation on the other, *must stop*. The millions of little streams of wealth, put into motion by our hands, must find their way into other and a larger number of pockets. We have no desire to disturb any man in the possession of what he now has; we are willing the thieves shall escape with their plunder; but we say the work of plunder must stop. This is what we mean by a levelling up; and this levelling up must be effected by a lower rate of interest, and an entire change in our monetary system. This change we will have by one means or another. The bleeding operation has been going on long enough; the patient is tired of it, and demands that it be abandoned. We are for a peaceable solution of this problem; but if there must be blood-letting, it shall be on the other side.

Confiscation or organism is no part of our plan; but it does not require a very great stretch of the imagination to picture the lamp-posts in Wall Street ornamented with the bloated carcasses of the money-shavers, gold gamblers, and land-sharks, who are robbing the government and the people. Labor is forced into an unnatural and degrading position. It is at the bottom of the hill instead of at the top. The products of labor are sifted like corn through a ladder — labor gets what sticks to the rungs. Out of this unnatural position we desire to get — through the ballot-box, and by peaceable means, if possible; but we mean to get out, even if to do so involves the cutting off of a few heads. If this is a digression from the subject, I ask the reader's pardon.

Up to this point in the discussion of this question, I have

dwelt almost entirely upon the power of money to accumulate value by interest. Having, I trust, made this part of the subject clear to every reader, I shall now offer a few remarks on the "material" of money.

The reader will remember that I have already said that only the precious metals are fit to make money with is a fallacy, and has been adhered to by those who have taken upon themselves the management of financial affairs, for no other reason than because it furnished the surest and most secure means of controlling and enslaving the productive industry of the world.

For the first time in the history of civilization, we find a wide-spread and earnest effort in favor of a currency made exclusively of paper; and it is not surprising that these efforts have been opposed by many workingmen. We have all been educated to the idea that money could only be made of gold. In fighting this battle against the centralizing power of "gold money," and against the whole monetary system as it now exists, we have to combat the accumulated prejudices of thousands of years, a vast amount of ignorance and indifference, besides the combined power of the worst moneyed aristocracy in the world.

There are very few men, outside of those who control financial affairs, who have given the subject of money any consideration, and all who have written upon it have viewed it from a gold stand-point.

Workingmen, as a general thing, have given the matter no attention whatever. They have taken it for granted that the subject was so deep and mysterious as to be entirely beyond their reach. They have supposed that only men educated in all the arts and mysteries of financial problems could handle it; therefore they have given it the go-by, allowing bankers, brokers, and other swindlers to do their thinking for them.

One hundred and fifty years ago, Bishop Berkeley wrote a pamphlet called the *Querist*, in which he took strong ground against gold, and in favor of paper money. So fierce was the denunciation of his work and of himself by the wealthy, and so ignorant and indifferent were the working-people, that his little book soon became obsolete, and for nearly a hundred years the idea slept: men who entertained the same idea were not bold enough to proclaim it. It was not until the great work of Edward Kellogg made its appearance that any definite shape was given to it, or that men began to study and comprehend it. This work made a deep impression on the minds of a few men, while the many cast it aside, and the newspaper press almost universally denounced it as the production of a lunatic. In 1864, Hon. Alexander Campbell, of Illinois, issued a pamphlet called the "Free American System of Finance," which was a powerful defence of the Kellogg theory of money. This work was widely read in the West, and made many converts.

During the winter of 1865, Mr. Kuykendall, of Illinois, introduced a bill in Congress, providing for a national currency to be exclusively paper, and made a very able speech on it. These were widely circulated, and did good work. In 1868, Mr. Cary, of Ohio, the only workingman's Congressman ever elected, presented a bill looking to the same end, and made a powerful speech upon it. These, too, were scattered broadcast over the country.

In the meantime, others had taken up the subject, and it began to make slow but certain progress. It was left for the National Labor Union, at its second session, August, 1867, to be the first public body to adopt it, and proclaim it to the world as the central idea of their platform and organization. So rapidly is this idea of a people's money being spread, and so deep is its hold upon the people, that its enemies — all who are interested in swindling labor —

are becoming alarmed, and beginning to denounce it. This is the point we have long been desiring to reach, knowing very well that just so soon as a fair hearing could be had, our ideas would prevail.

The accumulation of a vast public debt, and a system of taxation the most odious in the world, with a national bank monopoly, and the gigantic swindles going on in all parts of the country, even in the treasury department at Washington, have opened the eyes of the people. Workingmen are taking hold of the question, and find it no difficult matter to unlock the whole mystery, and are astonished to learn how they are being swindled, and wonder why they never discovered it before.

Just now the world is being agitated by a cry for an international currency. The wise men who arrogate to themselves the right to do our thinking on financial matters, have not condescended to tell us what this cry means, nor do I believe one of them could give a satisfactory explanation if put upon the witness-stand. They might tell us that it meant a money that would go in all countries at a fixed value. But as the world has, and always did have, such a currency, there is neither sense nor reason in the cry or the explanation. Bullion — gold in the lump — has always been an international currency. That it may be improved upon, I admit; and the best way to improve it is for the world to make its money out of paper, and reduce gold to an article of merchandise.

When we talk of an exclusive paper currency, the question is asked, "How are we to settle balances of trade, and what are men to do who desire to travel in foreign countries where your paper money would not pass?"

Balances of trade are never paid with money. If, in our dealings with England, we find, at the end of the year, a balance against us of $50,000,000, this balance is paid with *gold*, but not with *money*. They take our gold coin at its weight, without any regard to the legal stamp upon it; and they would much sooner have gold bars than gold dollars.

By establishing paper money, we would in no wise alter our manner of doing business with other countries. As money does not in any way enter into our foreign dealings now, it would not then. As all business between us and foreign nations is now carried on by a simple exchange of commodities, so it would be then. We export cotton, corn, and wheat, and import sugar, coffee, and cloth; that is, we trade the one for the other. If we get more than we give, we settle the balance with something else. If they want no more of the produce of our farms or workshops, we give them the production of our mines—iron, copper, lead, silver, or gold; and when they take our gold it is no more money than is our wheat; the quantity of wheat they take is measured by dollars, so is the quantity of gold. If our merchants desire to settle balances with gold, let them buy it, as they do cotton and corn. If our people desire to travel in foreign countries, they will do just as they must do now—secure a sufficient amount of gold, which they will convert into money that will pass where they are going.

But we are told that to establish a paper currency, will be to undo the experience of six thousand years, and go back upon every established principle of political economy. Well, suppose it is. If men have worshipped a golden idol for six thousand years, is that a good reason why we should continue it? If the people have been robbed, and kept in poverty and wretchedness for six thousand years, is that a good reason why they should still permit it? If gold is the god that has always ruled and ruined in despotisms, is that a good reason why it should do so in a republic? We think not. Therefore the cry, Down with this false god; clean out Wall Street and the treasury department, as Christ cleaned out the temple, and let the betrayers of the people do as did Judas their illustrious predecessor — go and hang themselves.

Must we stick to gold because all the theories of political economists are built upon it? We think not. This is an age of reform; this is a time when old things are pulled down, and new things are built up; and if the "established principles" of political economy are wrong, and are in the way, they must come down.

The whole system of political economy, from beginning to end, is an apology for tyranny, and the whole tribe of political economists are humbugs; they are such because they have humbugged the people, and at their head stands the prince of humbugs, John Stuart Mill.

I desire to show how the flow of gold from the United States has affected the currency.

In 1855, there were $90,000,000 of gold in the Bank of England, and the rate of interest fell to four per cent. By the close of 1856, the amount of gold in said bank had fallen to less than $50,000,000, and the rate of interest rose to seven per cent. Immediately, gold began to flow towards England. In 1857, the amount of gold in the Bank of England fell to $35,000,000, and interest rose to ten per cent. — the highest point ever reached. Within a very short time, over $30,000,000 of gold left New York. This thirty millions of gold had been the basis of at least one hundred and twenty millions of State bank paper, besides many millions of commercial credits.

This sudden departure of gold unsettled all financial arrangements; credits and value were alike disturbed; confidence was destroyed; a panic seized the people, and a run on the banks commenced. "The regular discount of bills by the banks had mostly suspended, and the street rates for money, even on unquestioned securities, rose to three, four, and even five per cent. a month. On ordinary securities of merchants, such as promissory notes and bills of exchange, money was not to be had at any rate." The Commercial Agency of New York reported the debts of the country merchants to be *two thousand two hundred and eighty-two millions* of dollars, and the debts of the whole country to be over *twelve thousand millions* of dollars,— a sum four times greater than our present national debt. This vast system of credits and utter financial rottenness was the result of a vicious system of paper money — "wild-cat"— based upon gold, and its offspring, a high rate of interest. With such a load of accumulated debt piled upon the back of productive industry, it only required the first brick to fall to knock down the whole row.

I have said that the sudden departure of $30,000,000 of gold took away the basis at least of $120,000,000 of bank paper. The holders of these notes were swindled. The notes purported to be the representatives of money, when, in fact, they represented nothing. They rested upon gold; the gold was taken away, and the whole structure fell to the ground, involving the whole industry of the country in disaster and ruin. The same thing was repeated in 1861, when the amount of gold in the Bank of England fell to less than $60,000,000, and the rate of interest rose to eight per cent. It was not until the adoption of the greenback law, in 1862, that relief came. Immediately on the passage of that law, confidence was restored, new life and energy were infused into every department of industry, and although involved in a gigantic war, the people started upon a period of prosperity without a parallel in the history of the nation. This high degree of prosperity was the result of a partial divorce of the government from gold money.

The government's necessities compelled Congress to adopt

the greenback law. Our armies were in the field, but there was no money to feed and clothe them. Congress asked for money, and instantly the vault-doors of the banks were closed; the patriotic and Christian bankers hid away their gold, and left our soldiers to shiver and starve, and the industries of the country were almost entirely suspended. Not only had inactivity paralyzed the nation, but a feeling of alarm, bordering on despair, was rapidly taking hold of the people; and the more urgent became the necessity, the tighter did these patriotic and Christian bankers draw the strings of their money-bags. To save the life of the nation, Congress was compelled to make a new money.

The great mistake made was, that the greenbacks were made payable in gold; they should have been separated entirely from gold, and made money absolutely. The perpetuity of the government should have been their corner-stone. Upon their face should have been written: "This is *the* money of the United States, and is receivable for *all* debts, public and private." But, unfortunately, Congress made two kinds of money—one for the government and one for the people. It made gold — its worst enemy — the corner-stone of the greenback; and it made two classes of debts, one payable in gold and the other in greenbacks. Immediately there began a war between greenbacks and gold; and just as soon as the war closed, there began a cry from Wall Street — that den of thieves — for a return to specie payments. This cry was taken up by bankers and brokers all over the country. Pretty soon it was given out that the Supreme Court would declare the greenback law unconstitutional. But for this, there would have been no pause in the prosperity of the country. If, in 1867, the sudden flow of gold out of the country caused the panic of that year, why did not the same result follow in 1866, when the rate of interest in the Bank of England rose to ten per cent., and large amounts of gold left the country?

All will remember that in the latter part of 1866 we had a general prostration of trade, from which we have not yet recovered; but we had no real panic. Why this difference? It was because we had got rid of the local or State banks. Previous to 1857, we had a paper currency based upon gold, and issued by irresponsible parties; and when in that year it was discovered there was no gold to redeem this "wild money," the paper became suddenly worthless—a market-basketful would not buy a breakfast. The gold having disappeared, and the paper being good for nothing, the country was without any money at all; and for nearly five years the nation was involved in utter financial ruin, and want, misery, and squalid poverty stalked through the land. If these results did not follow a suspension of specie payment in 1862, nor at any time since, it was because our greenbacks were issued by the government. They rested upon a foundation stronger than gold—they remained good when there was not a dollar of gold to be had. In this fact we have a more powerful argument in favor of a paper money based upon the credit of the government, and entirely separated from gold; for, even though they were a promise to pay in gold, the absence of gold did not destroy their value.

The greenbacks carried us safely through the war, and saved the life of the nation; and, after the close of the war, nothing saved us from such financial ruin as the world never saw, but our greenbacks. And had Congress separated them from gold entirely, and given us enough to do the business of the country, the industrial and commercial interests of the nation would have remained undisturbed.

In these instances of a sudden flow of gold out of the country, and the fact that for a long time past there has been more gold going out of the country than was produced or being brought into it, we find the strongest argument against gold as a material for money. If our money was all made of paper, and gold was reduced to a simple article of commerce, the same as iron, wheat, cotton, corn, etc., the Bank of England might raise her rate of interest to fifty per cent., and every ounce of gold in the country might be taken away, it would have no effect whatever upon our country.

The advocates of a metallic currency, or "gold money," tell us that the material out of which money is made must have a value within itself equal to its legal value. That is, a twenty-dollar gold piece must weigh enough to make its commercial value as gold as much as its legal value in money, so that if the legal stamp were removed, it would still be worth twenty dollars. This, they tell us, constitutes the basis of a sound currency — that is, it is money, and rests upon itself; is dependent upon no other thing to give it permanent value.

Instead of this being a good argument in favor of gold as a material for money, I consider it one of the strongest arguments against it, and for the same reason that gold is not a fit basis for money made of paper, because it is small in quantity, easily concealed or taken out of the country, and when it disappears it takes with it its value as money as well as its value as gold. When gold goes to Europe to settle balances against us, it does not go as money, but as gold — as bullion; the moment it crosses the border it loses its legal value; but it does not leave its legal value behind it to circulate as money. Its power as money dies; as money, it is entirely wiped out of existence, and its place is filled by nothing else.

A democratic money, a people's money, a money fit for a republican form of government, must be cheap, safe, convenient, abundant, an inexportable. Cheap in the material out of which it is made, and that material must belong absolutely to the government; that is, it must be a material in which there can be no possibility of speculation, a material that nobody will have except for its legal value. It must bear a low rate of interest, that it may be cheap to all who desire to use it.

It must be safe. It must rest upon something that has positive and permanent value; something that cannot be destroyed without destroying the government; something that cannot be collected together in small heaps, in a few hands, and hid away out of sight; something that cannot be carried out of the country. Money must be as a house built upon a rock; the foundation upon which it stands must be indestructible and immovable; permanent as the government itself. These are the elements of safety.

It must be convenient. It must be easy of transportation, small in bulk and of little weight, so that it can be sent from place to place at little cost, and be carried about in the pocket for every-day use, without hindrance or inconvenience. Lycurgus money, that took a yoke of oxen to pull a hundred dollars, was too cumbersome; it was just the opposite of a convenient currency. It must be convenient to get; all who desire to use it must be able to get it without bar or hindrance, by a simple compliance with the law.

It must be abundant. There must be no limit to its quantity, except the laws of supply and demand. To limit the amount in dollars, and say no more shall be issued, is to create a monopoly; to place much in the hands of some, and none in the hands of others, is to create borrowers and lenders, and place the borrowers at the mercy of the lenders. If a few men can control all the flour there is, they can fix their own price, and the people must pay it. If a few men can control all the money there is, they can fix their own rate of interest, and the borrowers must pay it.

Money — *all* money — should be created by the government, out of a material that will admit of no speculation. The government should be the only lender, and should lend at the same rate of interest to all borrowers, and the government rate of interest should never exceed one and a half per cent. They would secure an abundant currency at all times and under all circumstances.

It should be inexportable. That is, it should have no value outside of our own country. A money that can be taken out of the country, either to settle balances of trade, to purchase goods or property in other countries, or for any other purpose, is not a safe, a reliable currency; because every dollar taken away lessens the quantity, creates a vacancy, and to that extent unsettles values and disturbs the whole business of the nation.

When we have secured these five necessary qualities — cheap, safe, convenient, abundant, and inexportable — we will have a democratic money; we will no longer present to the world the inconsistency of a republican government with a monarchical currency.

One of the very best results of the late war is the practical demonstration of the utility of paper money, and its many and great advantages over gold. In nothing is this so clearly shown as in the fact that the same cause (a flow of gold from the country) which produced the financial panics of 1847, 1857, and 1861, has not disturbed us since the passage of the greenback law.

We see that in 1847 the rate of interest in the Bank of England rose to eight per cent., in 1857, to ten per cent., and in 1861, to eight per cent. At each of these periods a large amount of gold left the country, and a panic ensued. In 1862 the greenback law was passed, and a paper money was substituted for gold. In 1863 the rate of interest in the Bank of England rose to eight and a half per cent., in 1864, to nine per cent., in 1865, to eight per cent., and in

1866, to ten per cent.; during the whole of this time — from 1862 to the present time — the flow of gold from the United States has been very great, most of the time more than was produced by our mines and that imported, that is, there was more gold went out of the country than came in; and notwithstanding this almost continuous flow of gold from us — sometimes in quantities greater than ever before — so little did it affect our currency or the business interest of the nation, that no one stopped to inquire whether gold was going out or coming into the country.

Practically, there has not been a gold dollar in the country since 1862, because none were in circulation; and for the purpose for which it has been used, it would have been better in the shape of bars, than in the shape of dollars. The reason why this continual and heavy flow of gold from the country did not affect our currency or our business, was because it did not go from us as money; it did not take a single dollar from our circulation; it did not disturb the value of our greenbacks, because the greenbacks rested upon something stronger than gold, something that the people valued more highly than gold; they rested upon the credit and stability of the government.

Our experience since 1862 has proven that there is a security, a reliability in paper money, that "gold money" never did and never can have; and it furnishes the most incontestable proof of the correctness of our position, that gold is not a fit material out of which to make money.

We must not lose sight of the fact that all this experience, all this accumulated mountain of evidence against gold, is the result of a paper money only partially separated from gold. Greenbacks are a promise to pay gold; they are not a legal tender for all things, therefore they are not absolutely money. They are not receivable by the bond-holders for interest on the public debt, nor by the government for duties on imports.

The great mistake made by Congress was that it did not make the greenback *money* instead of a promise to pay, and a legal-tender in payment of all *debts* to the people by the government, and to the government by the people. There should have been a total separation from gold.

The New York *World* — the organ of the gold gamblers — tells us that such a currency would create "a prodigious inflation of the currency. Supposing the natural rate of interest [*natural* rate of interest is very good] to be seven per cent., if men can borrow at half that rate, they will be likely to use double the quantity of money," that is, if industry is prostrated because of a high rate of interest; lower the rate, and men will borrow money, and business will revive; or to put it in plainer terms, if a manufacturer can only run his shop with half his usual number of employés, reduce the rate one-half, and he could borrow money to fill up his shop and run full time. At a high rate of interest, the builder is not willing to embark in new enterprises; reduce the rate one-half, and he would put up whole rows of new houses. At a high rate of interest, the farmer cannot afford to make improvements; but lower the rate one-half, and he will build a new barn, make new fences, underdrain his swamp lands, and put his farm in complete order. But, according to the *World*, to stimulate industry by plenty of money and a low rate of interest, would be a national calamity.

A high rate of interest is the mill-stone about the neck of labor; it cripples the energy of the whole people, and retards production; because of it thousands and tens of thousands of workingmen are out of employment, and want and misery are abroad in the land. Reduce the rate of interest to three per cent., and give us a *national* currency made of paper, and new enterprises will be started, machinery now idle will be put in motion; there will be work for all, and peace and plenty will bless the land. This, the *World* thinks, would be a disaster. Perhaps it would to the *World* and its backers, but not to honest people.

Why is the rate of interest so high? Because it is but a limited quantity in the country, and that is controlled by a few men who control the rate of interest. The borrowers are many and the lenders few. If one thousand barrels of flour come to market, and there is no more to come, and everybody wants flour, a few men will buy it all up, and charge whatever their conscience will allow.

All monopolies are wrong, and especially monopolies of the necessaries of life; but the most infamous of them all is a monopoly of money, and a government that will permit it is not a government of the people.

Expansion and contraction are terms very much used, and it would be well if workingmen understood their full meaning.

Inflation, in the sense in which it is used, does not mean a plentiful supply of money. It means too much money — money lying around loose — a quantity of money above the wants or demands of the people. Inflation, as used by the *World* and its masters, means *too much*. There cannot be too much money, until everybody has enough. There can be no such thing as an inflation of flour, until everybody has as much as they can eat. There is just as much sense in saying there is too much flour in the country, when half the people were hungry for bread and could not get it, as to say there is too much money in the country, when half the people have none, and no way of getting it. This word inflation is held up before the people as a hideous monster, and is one of the scarecrows used to frighten the ignorant and unsuspecting. We also hear a great deal of talk about an irredeemable currency. We are told that a purely paper currency would be an irredeemable currency, therefore good for nothing. Why, workingmen, there is no such thing as irredeemable money. Whenever it ceases to be redeemable, it ceases to be money, because it has lost all the qualities of money. It is redeemable so long as it circulates, and whenever it ceases to circulate, that is, whenever people refuse to take it, it ceases to be currency. Money is a lien upon every dollar's worth of property in the nation; money will buy anything that is for sale, even congressmen; money is being redeemed continually; it is redeemed whenever it is paid out for value received.

The same $10 bill may be redeemed a dozen or fifty times in a day. One man pays it out for flour, another for rent, a third for coal, a fourth for clothes, and so on; and it is redeemed every time it is paid out. But, say these croakers, paper money must be redeemable in *gold*, that is, it must be exchangeable for "gold money." A man must be able to swop dollars; but money was not made to buy money, and I fail to see the sense in trading one dollar for another. But paper money is redeemable in gold. Greenbacks will buy gold watches, or any other articles made of gold, or gold in the lump or bar. Thus are they redeemable in gold, as in flour.

If workingmen will just stop and think a little, they will see that all the greenbacks they can get are redeemed for rent, clothing, provisions, just about as fast as they can get them.

Expansion and contraction. The one means a low rate of interest, plenty of money, labor fully employed, high wages, no credit, cash for everything, and the general prosperity of the people.

The other means a high rate of interest, no money, low wages, store pay, idleness, poverty, and want. Wall Street and the *World* go for contraction, honest people go for expansion.

The Cary bill proposes to reach the same point, but by a different road. It provides for the issuing of a paper money to be called "Treasury Certificates," the notes to be in denominations of $1 upwards to $1,000, not bearing interest, and to be a legal tender for *all* debts public and private; this includes all taxes, duties on imports, interest on the public debt, except that portion the interest of which is made payable in gold, and all other debts due the government.

It further provides for the issue of bonds in denominations of not less than $100, nor more than $10,000, said bonds to bear three per cent. interest. The bonds to be convertible into money, or the money into bonds, at the will of the holder.

Let me illustrate this.

Mr. Jones has a $1,000 bond bearing three per cent.; if he holds this bond one year the interest will be $30. If he wishes to borrow money he deposits his bond with the government, and gets $1,000 in "Treasury Certificates." This money he keeps one year, then returns it and takes up his bond. For this year he receives no interest on the bond, or, in other words, while he holds the bond, the government pays him three per cent., when he converts the bond into money the interest stops. So long as he can make more than three per cent. out of the money he will keep it, and when his profit falls below three per cent. he will return the money and take up the bond.

This is the monetary system proposed by the National Labor Union, and is emphatically a people's monetary system.

There could be no speculation in these bonds, because they are issued by the government, directly to the people, and every person with a hundred could buy a bond, and every person with a bond could borrow money directly from the government, at three per cent. The government would be the only lender, and the whole people would be the borrowers, and between the borrowers and the lender there could be no middlemen — brokers, money-changers, and skinners — to swindle the people by high rates of interest, as there is now under our present monetary system.

This would, of course, abolish all banks of issue, and leave the present national banks merely banks of "deposit, loans, and discounts."

This bill further provides that the national banks shall return their notes to the treasury department within six months, the notes to be returned in sums not less than $1,000, and for every $1,000, or more, of these notes returned, a just and proper amount of bonds pledged for their redemption shall be returned to such bank. And should any bank fail to return its notes, or any part of them, within six months, the interest on the whole amount of bonds deposited with the treasurer by such bank shall cease; and in case the whole or any part of the notes of such bank are not returned within two years, the bonds, or other securities in the hands of the treasurer, shall be forfeited to the government, and used to redeem the outstanding notes. It also provides that all debts, bonded or otherwise, of the government, contracted to be paid since July 1, 1861 (except such as are made payable in gold), and all debts which may hereafter be incurred, shall be paid in "Treasury Certificates," or in three per cent. bonds, at the option of the creditor.

It authorizes the secretary of the treasury to give notice to the holders of bonds, or other obligations of the government, to present the same for payment or exchange, when due and payable, or redeemable at the option of the government, within five months, and, failing to do so, the interest shall stop. The holders of the bonds or other obligations to have the right to exchange them for the three per cent. bonds, or receive in payment the "Treasury Certificates," at their option.

With this I will leave the subject for the present, and if I have succeeded in making it plain to the mind of a single individual, I am amply paid for my labor.

[The following Essays are taken from the *Iron-Moulders' International Journal*, without regard to date.]

CO-OPERATION.

Of all the questions now before us, not one is of so great importance, or should command so large a portion of our consideration, as co-operation.

In the darkest hours of the Revolution, Tom Paine said, "These are the times that try men's souls." What was true of the immortal patriots of that day is true of the moulders of this day, for so many of them are walking about that it not only tries their *soles*, but many find it hard to keep them in repair.

Many who, in the days of prosperity, were deaf to the voice of reason and wise counsel, blind to the ways that lead to competence and independence, heedless of all warnings of danger ahead, and unwilling to contribute a small portion of their wages against the days of adversity, are now being convinced by the most powerful argument in the world — a hungry stomach.

During the war, when there was an artificial demand for almost everything, and when a large portion of the workingmen of the country was in the army, those who remained in the workshops had things pretty much their own way; and when warned that then was the time to prepare for the universal prostration of trade sure to follow upon the heels of the war, they laughed at those who pointed to the future, and acted just as though dull times were so far off that they would end their natural existence before they would arrive. All the teachings of history were disregarded, and those who preached and taught co-operation were hooted at as alarmists, old fogies, and weak-kneed prophets. But the car of time rolled on, the war ended, armies were disbanded, emigration increased, every avenue of industry was over-run, unwise legislation destroyed confidence and drove capital out of the industrial pursuits into gold, interest-bearing, untaxable bonds; money ceased to circulate among the people, the "bottom dropped," and ruin, want, and misery filled the whole land. With this came sober reflection; men began to see that when they could they did not, and when they would they could not.

Time, that severest of all teachers, is now teaching us one more lesson; but this time it is finding more willing scholars than formerly. It is very instructive, as well as amusing, to watch the course of events, and note the many little incidents that go to make up the great things of every-day life; and among the many things that occur from day to day none are more interesting than the new face co-operation has put upon many things in our trade.

As long as we can remember, it has been the custom among our employers, whenever trade was dull, to demand a reduction of wages, upon the ground that they were making no profit; were only running their shops out of charity for us poor devils, and that, to enable them to run without loss, we must "come down." A case in point in this city will illustrate where this "loss" on their part comes in. One firm asserted, in justification of a reduction of wages, that they had lost $25,000 in 1867. When the truth became known, the case stood as follows: at the first of the year 1867, they made calculations as to what their profits should be for the year,— it was set down at

$128,000. After taking account of stock at the end of the year, it was found that they had made but a trifle over $103,000, — therefore they *lost* $25,000. What a pity!

We poor silly fools used to believe these stories about no "profit," etc., and out of charity for our employers would submit without complaint to a reduction of wages. But a change has taken place. Those of us who used to insist that all this talk about "loss," "no profit," and so on, was the same as the talk of the spider to the fly, "Come into my house, little fly," and little fly went in, to have the meat picked off his bones, are no longer laughed at.

The sworn statements of several of our co-operative foundries have opened the eyes of many of our members to the fact that there is money in the foundry business. The employers, seeing that the thick wall that has so long surrounded their business, and secured it from the vulgar gaze of common people, has been penetrated, are becoming alarmed. Some of them go so far as to say these sworn statements are false; others endeavor to account for these large profits in various ways. They have received a severe "dig" in the short ribs, and, seeing that these "digs" are to be repeated, they don't know what to do, nor which way to turn.

A meeting of the employers of this city and vicinity was held in January, to consider the subject of a reduction of wages. The measure was strongly opposed on the ground that it would drive the men into co-operation. This was ridiculed by one or two; but when it was shown what had been done elsewhere, it had the effect to cool down the angry passions of those who wanted to "go the whole hog." Straws show which way the wind blows.

Two years ago, co-operation with us was an unsolved problem; now it is a practical fact. The first company was organized in April, 1866, during the great lock-out; now, there are eight shops in operation, all successful. There are four other shops nearly ready to start, and about twenty companies organized or in course of organization, and the sound of preparation for co-operation comes from every quarter. For years I have been teaching the doctrine, that under the system of paying *wages* to labor and *profits* to capital, there never was nor never could be any identity of interest between employers and employed. Both were actuated by the same motive and controlled by the same principle — to buy in the cheapest and sell in the dearest market. The result of this could be nothing but antagonism.

For teaching this idea of universal war between those who worked for wages and those who pocketed the profits, I have been fiercely assailed, not only by capitalists, who get ninety per cent. of the whole product of labor, but by many laboring-men, who get but ten per cent. of what they produce. Ten years ago I was universally denounced as a dangerous man, a revolutionist, an agrarian. It was an innovation upon the established principles of political economy taught by all the old fogies and apologists of tyranny from Adam Smith to John Stuart Mill. To-day, the labor of this country is acting upon this idea of antagonism, fully satisfied that there can be no identity of interests between laborers and capitalists until the whole system of *wages* is broken down, and labor and capital are made to share the *profits* in just proportion.

Co-operation is the only true remedy for low wages, strikes, lock-outs, and a thousand other impositions and annoyances to which workingmen are subjected. Let us move steadily forward on the line of co-operation, and in ten years from now our troubles will have an end.

THE USES OF CO-OPERATION.

To the laboring masses of the Old World belongs the credit of first making manifest the advantages of co-operation. Oppressed to a greater degree, necessity seems to have driven our transatlantic brethren to new experiments, which were better calculated to fortify them against the power of capitalists. Reforms were started to check the progressive social degradation which threatened enslavement, and to secure such political rights as would place the weapons of self-defence within their reach. Years of labor and sacrifice, marked by the most commendable zeal, were devoted to many of them; but not until the clarion-notes of "self-help" rung out from Rochdale did a gleam of sunshine light up their pathway.

Had the oppressors of labor dreamed that, from co-operation, the toilers of England would derive an irresistible power, and place within their grasp the *means* to meet their adversaries in social conflict, the outcry against that experiment would have been just as fierce as that raised against any other reform. But, unconnected with strikes, lock-outs, and wholly distinct from the question of wages or hours of labor, they considered it a "hobby," which would divert the masses from other efforts to ameliorate their condition, and afford capitalists a happy respite from the "unreasonable demands" of workingmen. Hence, co-operation met the approval of nearly all classes of society.

But they have lived to learn that from the root of this new system of self-protection spring many branches, which are destined to overshadow various reforms. It is the corner-stone of a superstructure which will be the harbinger of social and, it may be, of political emancipation in Europe, — and everywhere its influence for good will be felt, for, like the banyan-tree, where it branches it takes root.

It has been but a few years since an offshoot of the parent stem was transplanted in this country, and already there is a glorious promise of abundant fruit. That it can be made more effective and more productive under our free institutions, none can doubt. All the system needs here is, that it shall be subjected to the same tests. It is possible, however, that the indifference of American workmen may require an experience of the same stern necessities which forced co-operation into existence in Europe. We hope not. God forbid that we should suffer the tortures of that travail which gave the system birth abroad. We know what it has done — what it can do — and we must be incredulous, indeed, if we hesitate for one moment to give it our full confidence and support, in view of the great results it has accomplished. Richly will we merit all the evils it can remove, if we fail to make use of it.

Co-operation has enabled the workingmen to provide against the necessity of strikes. In one sense, it is a savings-bank, in which they can deposit spare earnings, however small. The little capital invested is scarcely felt, and all the time it is increasing, until the dividends amount to a small annuity — whether in the shape of increased stock, money, or goods. It is a *relay* which can be depended upon in trouble, affliction, or any misfortune that may come upon us. We need not enumerate the many additional comforts thus secured to the poor man's home. Its genial influence shines with brighter lustre around the domestic hearthstone, while it renders the workman independent of necessities which often compel him to submit to hectoring, domineering, and insults of every kind that tyranny can inflict. Against all these he is protected, because the employer is conscious that he possesses the *means* to resent imposition. And should he be forced to that last resort — a strike — his ability to endure idleness will not depend upon the amount of trust he can obtain of the corner grocer, of the baker, or of the butcher. He falls back upon the "nest-egg" deposited in the co-operative store, and when that is exhausted, he meets with a confidence and a sympathy that will save himself and family from want.

Why is it that the workingmen of England, more depressed, subjected to more unreasonable exactions, and, as many suppose, occupying a lower social standard, have become so successful in their efforts to advance wages, secure privileges long denied them, and become so perfect in their trade organizations? These questions are all answered by the simple compound word — co-operation. Just in proportion as that lever of self-help was used to pry off the load of oppression which weighed them down, to that degree have they burst the bonds which bound them to a degrading servility; and now they are gradually emerging from despondency to that state of manhood which enables them to assert and maintain their rights. To have made this happy progress in the face of laws which discriminate in favor of wealth, against the frowns of an aristocracy ever jealous of the slightest innovations upon customs held as sacred as the statutes, proves that co-operation possesses a power and an elevating influence which should make the system a part of every workingman's existence.

Workingmen of America! if co-operation has accomplished such grand results abroad, what can it not do here? With liberal institutions, every man a law-maker, farther advanced in social and political rights, the uses of co-operation are of fourfold value to us. Make the system as perfect here; let capitalists see that we possess all the advantages the system will confer, and, our word for it, there will be no necessity for strikes or conflicts of any kind. There will be no attempts to reduce wages, no lock-outs, no offensive rules posted up in workshops, no display of tyranny.

Every reasonable demand will be conceded, and a greater degree of equality will be established in society. The *power* which co-operation confers will be respected, and capitalists will be slow to engage in a tilt at arms with men doubly armed for the struggle. Let us urge our toiling brethren, then, to give this subject their *immediate* attention. The work it has already accomplished in this country, even in its infancy, gives promise of a glorious future; but if the system is adopted, and pursued with the same zeal and ardor which marks its onward career abroad, who shall estimate the blessings which co-operation will confer upon American workingmen in all coming time?

THE POOR MAN'S HOME.

Poets and essayists have sung and written a great deal about the beauty and simplicity of the poor man's home, and theorists have employed the aid of art to prove that contentment and poverty are inseparable; but "The Cotter's Saturday Night," "The Village Blacksmith," "The Flat-Boat," etc., as *illustrations*, are far more welcome to the rich man's parlor than would be the living *realities* which they represent. The whitewashed cottage, the clean-swept hearth, the creeping vines, the fresh-budding flowers, and "the moss-covered bucket," afford themes for highly-colored pictures of humble life, which never fail to captivate romantic misses and sentimental young men, whose ideas of "love in a cottage" form a part of their youthful dreams. Those who enjoy wealth and luxury too often derive their impressions from the artist's pencil or the fine-spun theories of magazine writers, and settle down in the belief that the poor are exempt from many cares incident to riches, and that it's "all moonshine" to prate of the distress and privations of the toiling poor. This outside view of poverty is very apt to satisfy the conscience, and shut out from the heart those feelings of charity which make us "feel each other's woes."

But there *is* an inside view of poverty which the true Christian and philanthropist will sometimes pause to gaze upon. The smile of cheerful greeting, as wealth passes the door of poverty, is not always an index to sunshine within. The canker gnaws none the less when pride places the "best foot foremost," and many a weary and worn soul struggles hardest to keep up appearances in the darkest hour of adversity. If the poor man is blessed with a thrifty wife who turns his weekly pittance to the best advantage, his condition, and that of the family, are proportionately benefited; but what can the affluent know of the pinch and stint, the self-denial and privation practised to "make both ends meet"? What one throws away as mere offal, the other dishes up in various ways to tempt the palate; for nothing must be wasted in the poor man's home. One selects the rib or juicy surloin, the other must be satisfied with the neck and other cheap pieces; one can have his pick, while the other must be content with the refuse of the market. The toiler must put up with nourishless soups and frequent meatless meals. Deteriorated tea and coffee must suffice, when it can be afforded at all; and, as to clothing, a change of inferior domestic fabrics is all that he can aspire to.

This is the difference between rich and poor, under the best management; but it as often occurs with one as the other, that want of experience, indolence, or incompatibility of temper, proves the curse of the household. Such a condition of things is, indeed, a calamity to the poor. The former can provide against this misfortune by hiring help — but not the latter. With them it sometimes happens that the husband is idle, intemperate, or improvident, and, on the other hand, the wife may be thriftless, slovenly, and wasteful. She may be broken down by excessive labor, or crushed by the despondency of her hopeless condition. Under such circumstances, there is a life-battle with want and suffering, uncheered by one ray of hope — with no prospect of deliverance. No word of encouragement is given — no helping hand is extended. They are shunned because they *are* poor, and proscribed because they show it. Is it any wonder that despair drives many such to vice and crime? for there is nothing before them but hunger and want in the meridian of life, or the almshouse in old age.

But, in the brightest phase of poverty, look at the incident "pull backs" in the shape of lost time, sickness, medicine, doctors' bills, etc. — perhaps a periodical increase of the family, adding other mouths to be fed, other backs to be clothed. What the rich would consider a blessing, is often a calamity to the poor, in multiplying household care. Let that rich lady, lounging on her cushioned ottoman, perusing the last novel, with her children consigned to servants in the nursery, take a peep at the poor man's home. She will find the mother laboring at the wash-tub, a baby crying in the rude cradle, another, a little older, tied in a chair, and the next crying for bread, perhaps. That mother may be weak and feeble, working beyond her strength. It may be that she is getting through with the week's wash of the novel-reading millionnaire, and depending upon the hard-earned pittance for necessary comforts. And what if the husband and father should be sick — the body prostrated by racking pain, and the mind frenzied with apprehensions of a starving family? Who shall describe his agony — who can comprehend his misery?

This, reader, is the other side of the picture which has never been looked upon by poets and sensation writers, who cater for the public. But these painters of fancy scenes in poverty are too sensitive to gaze upon the reality; and, besides, it would not comport with their mission, to "draw from nature" or to paint "the living truth." It would grate too harshly upon the public ear, which needs a sweeter melody; and shock eyes which require all that is unlovely to be veiled from sight. They place the garb of romance around suffering and poverty, and deck the poor man's home in flowers, while they plant thorns in his pathway, and render him helpless for self-elevation.

There is a hidden purpose, however, in all this flattery bestowed upon humble life. It is designed to make poor men contented with their lot, and to blind them to the necessity of making proper exertions to extricate themselves from the slough of despond into which the odious distinctions of society have plunged them. It would be the height of imprudence — the extreme of presumption — on the part of a class whose condition in life is painted in such gaudy colors, to express dissatisfaction, or to make an effort to place themselves higher in the social scale. So contented — what need is there for combinations, trade-unions, strikes, etc.? These scene-painters of the poor have satisfied wealth that it has no duty to perform — that there are no claims upon the rich — and that the preposterous pretensions of the poor are entitled to no consideration. Hence, any attempt on the part of workingmen to ameliorate their condition is met with opposition at the outset, and they are looked upon as a "never-satisfied" class.

But, happily for the cause of labor, its oppressed victims have awakened from their long sleep of lethargy, and begin to fearlessly assert their claims to an equality which is not measured by dollars and cents. They have mounted the car of progress, and are determined to ride until they reach the goal of a new manhood, if they have to seize the ribbons and drive the drivers. Caste, distinctions, prejudice, proscription, must clear the track, or be run down, for they have taken off the brakes. "Upward and onward!" is shouted along the whole line; and the time will soon come, we hope, when the poor man's home may merit some of the fulsome praise bestowed upon it.

FEMALE SUFFRAGE.

STOP, gentle reader! Don't throw up your hands and roll up your eyes in holy horror, as you exclaim, "What! the *Journal* in favor of women voting?" Or, "has the editor gone clean stark mad?" Have patience, and read this article through before you pass judgment. After hearing what we have to say upon this subject, and then you should not think as we do, there will only be an honest difference of opinion.

Now, the man who does not love the ladies, should be ashamed to own he had a mother. We hope no such misanthrope — no such libel upon human nature — lives, who is so impious as to hold God's masterpiece, woman, in contempt. We *do* love the ladies, and the dear creatures must not blame us for what we cannot help. It is our love for them that prompts us to condemn the follies and extravagances of the present day, which go far to undermine health and morals, if they do not, to a great extent, divest her of all that a good man holds dear. The *fashions* of the age are doing much to drag her from the exalted position she occupies, and must, if pursued, lessen women in the high estimation in which they have ever been held by American gentlemen. We say it is *because* we love them, that we venture upon this short homily as a prelude to our answers, which we design as a plea for justice to woman; for slavery to fashion is a vice, though of a lesser grade than those we shall name, which calls for reform. While pointing to the beam in the eye of the sterner sex, we hope they will pluck the mote from their own. But we do not intend to dodge the question.

Shall women vote? We answer, *yes*. We are in favor of *limited* female suffrage. We think our wives, sisters, and daughters should have a vote on all questions involving a moral issue. Upon all laws relating to Sunday labor, granting license to sell rum, the use of tobacco, a reduction of working-hours, or any question intimately connected with the domestic and social happiness of women, they should have a vote. Give them the right to set their seal of condemnation upon rum-selling, the filthy use of tobacco, or any other vice, and very soon these skeletons of too many households, which bring upon mankind untold misery, will disappear from the land forever.

Women are deeply interested in all reforms which tend to better the condition of the human race, and why should they not have a voice in the eradication of acknowledged evils? What class of the community suffers more from the curse of intemperance? They do not visit groggeries or indulge in bacchanalian revelry, but the misery which such vices entail comes home directly to the hearthstone. Who can estimate the deprivation, the suffering, the mortification, brought upon the loveliest portion of God's creation by whiskey drinking? And are women to be silent spectators of their progressive ruin, powerless for resistance, without the right to act or protest? The first law of nature — self-defence — is denied them, and they must remain passive victims of a curse which plucks every joy from the home circle, plants life's pathway with thorns, and sends them sorrowing to a premature grave. Give to women the right to emancipate themselves from a bondage which such vices fasten upon them, and, our word for it, they will prove as potent in reforming society as they are efficient in bringing happiness to the domestic circle. To this extent we are in favor of female suffrage.

BRAIN *vs.* MUSCLE.

THE Philadelphia *Ledger*, in contrasting the effects of mental with physical labor upon the system, endeavors to prove that the professions are more liable to infirmities of the body, from excessive toil, than those who follow agricultural or mechanical pursuits. It cites Drs. Baillie, Hunter, and Dupuytren, as examples, who often devoted sixteen hours per day to mental and physical labor in the hospitals, to private practice, correspondence, etc. There is this difference between them and workingmen: In one case, they were not *compelled* to labor for a bare subsistence; in the other, they are forced to work or starve. While the professions are laboring for wealth and fame, workingmen toil for bread. One is a voluntary sacrifice on the altar of wealth and ambition, the other is the involuntary servitude exacted by the stern laws of necessity. Hence, the *motives* which govern the two classes are vastly different; and who will deny that upon the impelling *cause* of devotion to either science or labor hangs all of content and happiness in its pursuit?

The extreme cases mentioned by the *Ledger* by no means warrant the conclusions arrived at by the editor. These distinguished professors seem to have overtaxed their mental powers for the double purpose of gratifying professional ambition and to accumulate wealth. Neither their professional duties nor their poverty required a risk of life and health; and if they placed both in the venture for fame, it proves that the highest intellectual attainments are not always blended with common sense or good judgment. By the editor's own showing, a portion of their time was occupied in correspondence and other duties, which some needy assistant could perform; but the greed of gain closed their doors against help; and the fact that they allowed themselves no relaxation —attending to a large private practice, independent of their hospital duties — evinces a spirit of monopoly and avarice, if not jealousy, which was no ordinary barrier to the progress of their rising brethren. As well might a mechanic, after performing a fair day's work, continue his labors far in the night, to obtain wages beyond his wants, or to exclude others from the shop. There is selfishness in either case, and a man is entitled to but little credit for industry, and far less of sympathy, for bodily infirmities brought upon him from excesses prompted by either one of these motives.

All must admit that the prices which govern professional services are such as to secure a princely income, when based upon a daily occupation of sixteen hours; and few workingmen, however skilful, can earn in a week the physician's fees of a day. The mechanic is continually harassed to make both ends meet, and oppressed with the constant dread of idleness and want. None of these apprehensions weigh against the efforts of the professional man, and he can always bring to his labors a serenity of mind which renders them a source of pleasure instead of a burden. With them, scientific research in the allotted hours of rest, *pays*. With the workingman, it is a struggle to gain information only.

But we now come to the "brain-work," which the editor considers so very prostrating to the system. Starting out with the fact that these gentlemen were privileged to cease their labors at any period of the day — bound by no law of contract or necessity—it is fair to presume that they derived a certain degree of pleasure in the pursuit of their profession, which was nearly, if not quite, as highly prized as their profits. This is not the case with workingmen. The one obtains *all* the profits of his exertions, the other but a fractional portion. One is constantly adding to his intellectual acquirements from the very nature of his duties, while the other is debarred from increasing his store of knowledge from the necessity of close application to labor; and, if the latter were physically competent to devote a portion of the needed time for rest to the culture of his mind, his poverty denies him all facilities to make the attempt. But when a mechanic works hard ten hours per day, the mind is too often so stultified, by prostration of the body, that he has no inclination for intellectual pursuits. Thus, while the profession of one is gradually drawing him upward, the occupation of the other is proportionately depressing.

Brain-work, however, is not confined to the professions. The mechanic, the agriculturist, — aye, the laborer, — is often forced to draw quite as heavily upon his brain as upon his muscles; and upon this point we place the practical knowledge of workingmen against the incredulous smile of professional theorists. The skilful artisan, in the majority of occupations, must be well versed in mathematics, to make the nice calculations and unerring apportionments essential to their respective callings. They must devote "head-work" as well as body-work to the business; and in many instances, the difficulties and perplexities to be mastered are quite as trying to the brain as the most intricate problems which require the aid of scientific research. There is this difference, then, between the professional man and the workingman: one receives a princely compensation for pleasing intellectual pursuits, with but little bodily exertion; while the other receives a mere pittance for nearly the same degree of mental effort added to bodily prostration from overtaxed labor.

EIGHT HOURS.

HE WHO IS NOT FOR US IS AGAINST US.

No question of greater magnitude than the eight-hour law can be placed before the American people. Theorists and philosophers may prate of social and political economy till doomsday, and rack their brain for chimerical or practical hobbies; but, in our opinion, nothing of more vital importance, or more deeply interesting, could possibly claim public attention. Much that we could hope for in humanity, and still more that is due us on the broad principles of justice, is involved in this struggle. Upon the issue depends the existence of present wrong, or incalculable blessings to a large portion of the human family. We want a precedent in this great work of mercy — a landmark — beyond which avarice or oppression cannot go — a data, a fixed fact, upon which to base the amelioration of workingmen in all coming time.

Although the time is comparatively short since this great reform began to claim public attention, we already find it in the legislative halls of almost every State, as well as in the national Congress. City and town councils are importuned by petitions, immense mass meetings are being held all over the land. The forum, the pulpit, the workshop, and the family circle, are alike invaded by the agitation of this vital question. The surging masses are disciplining their numbers by forming organizations in village, town, and hamlet; and a demand has already gone forth for a national congress of workingmen, with the view of concentrating our forces, and creating a parent body, which shall bring together and unite all the fragmentary efforts now in progress. If we are correctly informed, this movement is designed, when completed, to make one *general* and simultaneous effort throughout the country. We need not say that this proposition meets our cordial approbation, and that we shall omit no opportunity to advocate it.

It is somewhat singular to witness the rapidity with which this great idea of shortening the hours of labor has penetrated every avenue of society, even to the remotest corners of our country, if we except our own State of Pennsylvania; for, more singular still, we find that three millions of people in this commonwealth, the interests of a vast majority of whom are directly and intimately connected with this movement, appear to be unconcerned, or wholly indifferent to the result. Centrally located, unsurpassed for its manufacturing, mechanical, and mineral wealth, possessing every facility for sea and inland commerce, rich in its resources, and furnishing a broad field for enterprise and labor; yet, *here*, where the deepest interest should be felt in the eight-hour movement, we find a coldness that almost amounts to opposition.

This is a strange position for the State of Pennsylvania to occupy; and none can regret more than ourselves, that she contrasts so unfavorably with her sister States. Truth, however, compels us to allude to the want of energy, and the spiritless efforts, which lock the wheels of progress in this State. If we are mistaken, we shall be happy to receive some assurance, some *evidence*, to warrant us in changing our estimate of the *home* zeal manifested in this cause.

The motives and desires of men can only be known by

their words and actions; and as we deem it impossible that a question of such vital importance can admit of either indifference or neutrality, we hold all those who are not for us to be against us. We believe the workingmen of Ohio, Massachusetts, and elsewhere, to be in favor of shortening the hours of labor, because we find them earnestly at work, using every means to further the cause; but how can we come to the same conclusion, as far as Pennsylvania is concerned, when we see her workingmen silent and inactive amid all the surrounding excitement?

The workingmen of Philadelphia, but very recently, had a splendid opportunity for the display of their zeal, when one of their representatives introduced an eight-hour bill before the Legislature, granting this special privilege to that city. But there was no meeting — no demonstration — no enthusiasm — *no gratitude!* It fell upon the community as a still-born, listless event, powerless to create a ripple on the social surface. Without stopping to question the honesty or sincerity of the member who presented the bill, we should give him credit for no small degree of moral courage, when he fearlessly braved consequences to forward a reform, although uncheered and unsupported by that portion of the community which it was designed to benefit. Under such discouragements, legislators will be slow to incur responsibilities which render their best efforts a thankless office on the one hand, while it brings upon them censure and proscription on the other.

And more recently still, an eight-hour bill, which embraces the entire State, passed the lower house by a large majority, without the slightest manifestation of joy. Having yet to pass the ordeal of the Senate, *now* is the time to recognize the faithful services of those members who were true to our interests, by enthusiastic expressions of approval, and such ovations as will strengthen our friends in the Senate. In the meantime, pour in the petitions. Let them come from foundry and furnace, from forge and loom, from manufactory and workshop. Be earnest, active, and prompt.

THE PRINCIPLE OF EIGHT HOURS RECOGNIZED.

It is a grave inconsistency on the part of our legislators in some of the States, when they dodge or openly oppose the eight-hour system. Several of our Legislatures have reduced the hours of voting two hours, thus recognizing the *principle* which workingmen seek to establish.

In most of the large cities — we know it was so in this — when the hours of labor amounted to twelve and fourteen, the polls were kept open until ten o'clock at night. This seemed to be consistent with the time exacted from workmen, for it gave them an opportunity to reach their homes, partake of the evening meal, and then exercise the privilege of freemen. Some years after the ten-hour system was adopted, the law closing the polls at eight o'clock in the evening was enacted; a very wise measure, since it gave workingmen the same opportunity to deposit their votes without any sacrifice of time, and lessened, to that extent, the arduous labors of the election officers. The humanity of this law, therefore, was highly appreciated by all classes.

Now, however, the polls close at six o'clock in the evening, and why not work out the rule by shortening the hours of labor, and still keep in harmony with the hours of voting? Politicians manifest a selfishness, in this particular at least, which is at war with that popularity they all aim to reach. They will enjoy the benefits of a reduction of time — the ward and township election officers reap the advantage of it; but the poor man, compelled to labor for bread, is "left out in the cold," so long as he is forced to labor ten hours; for when he ceases to labor, the polls are closed.

Is it right — is it *just* — that honest industry should meet with a proscription like this? He must lose both time and money to exercise a privilege dear to every man, or be disfranchised. Deny to him a reduction of two hours, and the act abridging the hours of voting becomes a pure specimen of class legislation, designed to benefit the idle and the rich, while it robs the poor industrious man of a sacred right.

We contend that all restrictions upon free access to the ballot-box are antagonistic to the letter and spirit of a republican form of government. It has justly been termed "the palladium of our liberties," because it is the great leveller which places all upon an equality, and it is the only channel through which the oppressed can speak their wrongs with trumpet-tongued force — the last weapon a poor man can wield in self-defence. Can it be that capitalists, looking at this proscription of the toiler in the light we do (it admits of no other interpretation), suggested and effected this alteration of the hours of voting, in order to render the masses powerless to check the special legislation their oppressors seek? We know that our law-makers are ever ready to lend a willing ear to wealth and influence; and the moment the voice of labor is silenced, or their power lessened, by restrictions which demand a sacrifice that many of them cannot afford, that moment politicians will "claim as large a charter as the wind," and spread their sails to every favoring gale, utterly regardless of workingmen and their interests. A vote is the only *rod* which a poor man can hold over demagogues. Deprive him of this, and he is helpless indeed.

Then, all other classes of the community having recognized the *principle* of eight hours, by shortening the time of voting, it is clearly the duty of workingmen to keep pace with this progressive reform, and *follow it,* as they did when it fell from ten o'clock to eight o'clock, P. M. And now that it is shortened to six o'clock, eight hours for labor becomes a necessity. The opponents of this measure must concede this, or merit the double charge of inconsistency and proscription. They have unwittingly given us an argument in favor of the eight-hour law, which proves that their *instincts* are correct if their cunning is at fault; and workingmen should press it home. The question now assumes a new shape, for it involves the *right* to the elective franchise, and workingmen will thus have a double incentive to action.

"OUR HEROES."

In every contest, be it revolution or reformation, involving principles of justice and truth on one side, and wrong and tyranny on the other, where men are required either to take a bold stand, assume every responsibility, make every sacrifice, and run every risk necessary to establish and maintain the right, or to bow in base submission to tyranny, we always find men with brave hearts and iron nerve to meet the crisis. While some libels upon humanity will grovel in the dirt and mire of self-abasement, yielding like cravens, we have men who, for the sake of principle and a just cause, are willing to sacrifice home, comfort, wealth, health, and even life itself. These are justly called heroes.

Every good cause — every great contest — has produced its heroes. We, too, have *our* heroes. For four years we have been engaged in a bitter struggle against a tyrant whose right to rule the world has scarcely ever been "contested since commerce set the signet of its all-enslaving power upon a shining ore and called it GOLD." A tyrant, in whose heart gold is a living god, and rules in scorn all earthly things but virtue. This contest has been all the more fierce and bitter, because we were obliged to build up our organization, and to devise means of attack and defence in the very face of the enemy, and because many of our own men, destitute of every attribute of manhood, were willing to sell themselves to a common enemy.

All these trials and obstacles were known to the capitalists with whom we were in conflict, and this knowledge culminated in the widely extended organization of foundrymen; and the great lock-out of last spring brought within its pale almost the entire foundry interest of the country, with a combined capital of $60,000,000. The country was divided into four districts, each presided over by the ablest financiers of the age, with mutual pledges to enforce laws and rules of the most unjust and obnoxious character. This formidable array of capital and capitalists was sufficient to appall the stoutest hearts and make the weak-kneed quake with fear. To this struggle we must look for *our* heroes — not that we were without evidences of heroism in the past, but that this was *the* contest, upon the issue of which depended our manhood or our degradation. To those who stood in the breach and upheld the banner of right against wrong — inspiriting the timid while they led the brave — belongs the credit of achieving a glorious victory. Their *deeds* have won for them the title of "our heroes."

The names of the men who so unflinchingly met all these trials and privations should be inscribed upon a roll of honor, to be placed in the archives of every union, and at the fireside of every true man, that his children may know to whom they are indebted for the additional comforts secured by the victory. Side by side should be placed a second roll containing the names of those who, in the darkest hour of the struggle, cheerfully and unmurmuringly contributed small sums, the aggregate of which gave us the necessary means to "carry on the war." The place assigned to Robert Morris, in the history of the Revolution, will be assigned, in the history of the labor movement, to those who displayed equal liberality in proportion to their means, during the struggle of the moulders for their rights.

But, as truthful historians of the times, we must demand a third — a "*Black* Roll." Upon this should be written the names of those who were too base and cowardly, too selfish and parsimonious, to pay the poor pittance of five per cent. These documents should be handed down to posterity together, that when the time arrives in which the moulders will be masters of their occupation, and when the great ideas of the present will be realized, those who write the history of these times may give to each his proper place; for it is the contrast between honor and infamy which induces men to aim for the one and to shun the other.

There is, however, still another class, of whom it would be the greatest injustice not to speak, reluctant as we are to approach the task; for "he who handles pitch will become defiled." Yet their names should be printed in large capitals, and hung up in every honest man's house. They should be daguerreotyped, and duplicated, till a "Scab's Album" should be furnished every union in the country. This class is composed of the two-faced, truckling, snarling crew, who act the part of puerile wiffets, by barking at the heels of those who consider them beneath contempt. Cowardly by nature, fault-finding by habit, and treacherous by instinct, they fill the position of go-betweens and lickspittles — sponges, to swab up every loose word or expression made in confidence, to squeeze it out in secret before employers. Each playing the part of Judas in friendship, and Arnold in fealty — their proudest mission is to *betray*.

These fellows are always the first to cry "strike!" when an advance of wages, or any other reform, is agitated by the unions. Yet they are the first to plead poverty, and in the hour of trial seldom fail to propose compromise, and are continually running to the office to ascertain when work will be resumed. Each day they have some startling news to report, as the result of a confidential communication with the wife, cousin, brother, or some influential individual, each of whom pump the messenger dry, and then inform the employer of all that passes in our unions. They meet the boss on the corner, and protest that *they* were always opposed to the strike and to the union; and were it not for Bill, or Tom, or Pat, the whole thing would have gone up long since.

After hanging around a strike for a while, like so many crows around a dead carcass, gnawing its vitals out and eating up the substance of the honest and deserving, they denounce the union as a humbug, and its leaders as so many swindlers. After securing all these benefits conferred by the labor of others, as the thief obtains goods under false pretences, you will next find them at work "scabbing." From this class come our bummers, news-carriers, eavesdroppers, swindlers, growlers, traitors, scabs, and other vermin. From this class, Lord, deliver us.

GRAND JURIES ON INTEMPERANCE.

Grand juries, as far back as we can remember, have never failed, in their presentments, to charge the vast majority of crime to intemperance. We are treated to periodical diatribes against this alarming vice, and still there is no abatement. Prisons, almshouses, hospitals, and a thousand charitable institutions, bear witness against this human destroyer; while our tax-payers are drained, and every stream of benevolence is made tributary to its exactions. The best efforts of the ablest reformers, the restrictions of law, and woman's tears, have alike failed to repress the ravages of, or check the appetite for, intoxicating drinks.

Whiskey-drinking, unfortunately, has become a *fashionable* vice. It is the example in high life which has enabled it to take such a strong hold upon society; for all mankind are imitators, and the force of example permeates every social avenue. We therefore hold those who "move in a higher sphere" to a strict accountability. The reform should begin with *them*, because their indorsement of an evil gives it double power; and their condemnation of it would be equally potent for its suppression.

On workingmen, however, we would impress the necessity of sobriety above all others. It is the first step towards self-elevation. A temperate man wins confidence, he is trusted and depended upon, and is always the first to gain confidence and promotion. This fact is evidenced in every workshop. And now, while pleading for two additional hours of rest for mental culture and rational enjoyment, it is important that we convince our opponents that this time will be well spent. It has already been predicted that this leisure will be devoted to the dram-shop, or to other improper associations. We can at least relieve public apprehension in regard to this objection, by promptly abstaining from intoxicating drinks. And where is the man who lacks the moral courage to make so trifling a sacrifice, if it assists in the smallest degree to silence a single argument against the eight-hour law? We trust not one can be found so selfish, or so wedded to a vice which, under any circumstances, "makes the poor poorer." Aside from this, sobriety will enable you to feed better, dress better, and live better. It will cheer the domestic circle, bring the smile of content to the careworn wife, and afford a wholesome example to your sons and daughters.

DRINKING WHISKEY.

What do you drink whiskey for? Do you know? You don't know. Well, we would like to know who does. It is a vile practice in which politicians, common people, all the rest of mankind, and even editors and lawyers, indulge. It is a very mean practice. It destroys the intellect, kills the body, and damns the soul. The kindest, truest, best-hearted men in the world drink whiskey. God, and God alone, knows the struggles of men to resist temptation. Oh, how many we know, kind-hearted, true men, who are rapidly passing down to death on the rushing tide of intoxication. Do you drink whiskey? Stop to-day, for your own sake. Do you know a friend who sometimes drinks to excess, but who is trying to lead a sober life? You do. Well, don't tempt him. It is a great crime to use your influence for the destruction of a fellow-creature. If you will injure yourself, do so; but don't be instrumental in the murder of your neighbor.

PRISON LABOR.

We have heard and read a great deal about "the dignity of labor." It is a prolific theme with demagogues, politicians, and occasionally attracts the attention of our most profound political economists. It also serves to ventilate the overcharged wisdom of many an egotist, who uses it as a stepping-stone to gain notoriety or promotion. It is a remarkable fact, however, that those who flatter workingmen most, and hypocritically chant "the dignity of labor," are the active agents in sinking it far beneath scientific and professional occupations, both of which are dependent upon and intimately connected with labor. But let labor reach what standard of respectability it may in the estimation of effeminate non-producers, one thing is certain, it is the germ from which springs a nation's prosperity, and the only true fountain from which the masses can draw social happiness. It is the motive-power which keeps the machinery of society working in harmony. It is the base upon which the proudest structure of art rests—the leverage which enables man to carry out God's wise purposes—the source from which science draws the elements of its power and greatness. In short, labor is the attribute of all that is noble and grand in civilization.

All who speak or write of labor concede these truths, yet what shall we say of the disgrace which society inflicts upon labor, when it is forced to inhale the pestilential air of State prisons? Could a greater *indignity* be heaped upon it, than that which associates it with convict competition? Of what use is it to exalt labor, when we use it as a punishment for *crime*, and make it the companion of thieves, robbers, and murderers? It is a notorious fact, that those who profess to hold its honor dear deliberately legislate it into our State penitentiaries, and wield it as a weapon to strike down the honest man's wages. The thief may rob a workingman of years of toil in a single night, and the next court will sentence him to a prison where the contract system enables him to underwork the man he wronged. The law thus makes him a double robber—

for he first steals the poor man's savings, and then steals his wages by a competition which forces his victim down to prison prices.

Need we say that this outrage is inflicted upon labor by legislators who owe their election to workingmen? It is a humiliating fact, that the producing classes have placed this sin at their own doors; for they possess the power to strike down any man or party which inaugurates or upholds a system that has proved a curse to every man forced to compete with prison labor. Our indifference to this subject has suffered an infant evil to grow upon us, until it has assumed a giant's proportions, and now seriously threatens the *moral character* of labor. All the professions of garrulous theorists amount to nothing. It is the workingmen themselves who must maintain the dignity of labor. *The men who work* can alone save it from the degradation which reckless legislation has fastened upon it, and the sooner we get about it the better. The longer this reform is delayed, the more difficult will be its accomplishment, because every year it is becoming more closely wedded to the affections of our truckling law-makers.

"But," says one, "how shall we punish our prisoners? how support them? What greater punishment can you inflict upon a felon than to consign him to close confinement *in idleness?* Leave him destitute of employment to divert his mind, where thought will be busy, and the stings of serpent-tongued conscience will constitute the refinement of cruelty. The only argument we could advance in favor of prison labor would be the severity of this mode of punishment; for none are so hardened as to be insensible to the harrowings of silent reflection over past errors.

"How shall we support them?" If no other means offer, *tax workingmen for their support.* They had better pay a tax from their weekly earnings to maintain convicts in prison, than have their wages brought down to the penitentiary standard. One per cent. of their earnings would feed and clothe the prisoners, and save the honest man from a reduction of ten, perhaps twenty, per cent. Aside from this, in all conflicts between capital and labor, prison work is a weapon which legislation places in the hands of the former to overcome the latter. Without this formidable ally on the side of employers, journeymen would have a more equal chance in any struggle for their rights.

The resolution of the Labor Congress upon this subject, contemplates, in case prison labor cannot be abolished, an advance of convict prices equal to those paid outside. This is asking too much of modern legislation. There are always a score of speculators awaiting the proposals which solicit the most profitable bids for the articles manufactured by convicts. Some States sell their time, or hire the entire prison force to the highest bidder, and suffer the contractor to wring from them the best profit he can. In either case, the sum realized to the State is so tempting, that it blinds tax-payers to the evil. What do legislators care for wages inside or outside the prison! Their object is to make the most out of the convicts, and to point to it as an evidence of their proficiency in political economy, regarding it as so much capital invested in the chances of a re-election.

Another strong objection to prison labor is to be found in the fact that felons are often taught trades in our prisons, and, after having served their time out, become contestants for the employment which rightfully belongs to honest men. Thus the convict is often brought into double competition with workingmen, by absorbing work at a cheaper rate when *in* prison, and by claiming a share of the poor man's labor when *out*, although he never served a day of honest apprenticeship. Labor and the laborer are alike wronged, and yet the authors of this disgrace inflicted upon both, with parrot-like repetition, are continually prating about "the dignity of labor." Equitable legislation from demagogues, however, like dignity from jail-birds, is not to be depended upon.

Perhaps we should not close this article without alluding to the views expressed by President Johnson on this subject in his interview with the Labor Congress Committee. When the Executive ruler of the nation declaims against the system, workingmen must be destitute of moral courage, indeed, if they longer hesitate to devote their best energies to its extinction. The President's official position gives his sentiments upon this subject an importance that cannot be too highly appreciated. Encouragement from such a source brings hope to every heart, and "spurs the will to action."

THE SPIRIT OF MONOPOLY.

THE American people, if they would profit by the experience of other countries, should wage unrelenting war against every species of monopoly. It is a remarkable fact, that a spirit of monopoly is invariably developed in proportion to the accumulation of wealth in all nations. Pride is the parent of selfishness, and prosperity is a sure tributary to that vanity which begets notions of superiority; for the estimate of mankind is measured by bank accounts, rent rolls, or broad acres; and "the more we have the more we want," is a truthful adage which exactly fits the craving instincts of avarice. Hence, the many stratagems, speculations, and combinations, on the part of capitalists, to increase their possessions. The mania for wealth has taken such complete possession of the people, that but few money-makers have any scruples in regard to the means used to obtain it.

This is all very well, so long as the laws of competition are kept inviolate, and an equal chance is offered to all for advancement. We claim that the road to wealth should be left open to all, and that those who are foremost in the race should place no obstructions in the path of those struggling on behind them. We want no special privileges, no favoritism, no legislation that singles out the few for fortune's bounty, while the many are suffered to toil on in cold neglect. We regard equal laws as the only safeguards that can be thrown around the people — the surest basis upon which social happiness can rest — the best guarantee against political inequality. We contend that, in the broad field of enterprise presented by this country, no possible contingency can arise which would warrant the bestowal of special privileges upon capital in either an individual or collective capacity; but, above all, none should be extended to a company which is denied to an individual; for it creates a combination of power which crushes private effort, breaks down wholesome competition, and absorbs all surrounding elements of prosperity.

We might point to the Old World for the sad effects of class legislation, where the masses are denied all participation in the making of laws. None but the noble and the rich are permitted to govern, and every enactment is framed with an especial view to the advancement of their own interests. Legislation, with them, is but another facility for making the rich richer and the poor poorer. Thus classes are recognized and distinctions made which create a degree of dissatisfaction and hatred that require standing armies to suppress. Under such a system, tyranny and oppression become part and parcel of the government, which must be made *strong* by the centralization of power in the hands of the few, to keep the many in subjection.

Look at the East India Tea Company, which overleaped

the bounds of endurance, to impose upon the colonies. Presuming too much upon the power delegated by government, they cut up such mad antics as to provoke the people to violence; and, by the tyrannical exercise of authority derived from legislation, hastened a revolution which lost to Great Britain her colonies. For many years this ponderous monopoly had control of the market, and made individual enterprise tributary to its wealth. What could Stephen Girard have accomplished, had he been placed in competition with the East India Company? He would have been interdicted by *law* from engaging in the tea trade, and compelled to lay up his ships, or seek other channels of commerce.

We might refer, also, to the Hudson's Bay Company, which nearly obtained the entire monopoly of the fur trade at one time. How would John Jacob Astor have fared as a citizen of Great Britain, had he dared to contend against this chartered monopoly? He might have lived and died in obscurity, for the exclusive privileges of this company effectually closed the door of enterprise to all. Yet, to both Girard and Astor, the people of Europe and America are indebted for individual efforts which placed tea and furs within the reach of the poor. Had the markets been exclusively supplied by these powerful corporations, two great comforts — aye, luxuries — would never have been accessible to the masses. As it was, the power bestowed upon these monopolies by legislation, enriched the stockholders at the expense of the consumer, thus tending to the two extremes of pampered wealth and social degradation.

In the face of such examples, we regret to see the spirit of monopoly in this country approximating to that of the Old World. The same causes will very generally produce the same effect; and who of us can contemplate it without emotions of horror? In our infancy, when the simplicity of the people more closely assimilated to our institutions, we were comparatively free from class legislation. Our poverty gave rise to no aspirations inconsistent with republicanism; but as our resources became developed, and as we acquired wealth, we became more grasping. We began to court the very agencies of oppression and inequality which drove our fathers to revolution; and we have progressed in the wrong direction, until individual enterprise is made subordinate to legalized monopoly. Railroads, turnpikes, steamboats, banks, insurance, land companies, manufactories, mining operations, oil companies, street cars, etc., down to poudrette companies, must be fostered by legislation. The example is injurious in many ways. It fetters progress, stultifies enterprise, and creates a passion for speculation and forestalling, which places a fictitious value upon the clothes we wear and the food we eat. While the rich revel, the fetters of poverty are riveted upon the poor.

The spirit of monopoly was well ventilated by President Johnson in a former message, in which he expressed the views of a statesman and philanthropist. The remarks he applies to the unwarrantable power conferred upon railroad companies, is equally applicable to all the ramifications of business. If the system can confer the power to monopolize our public thoroughfares, and extort from the travelling public such charges as avarice may prompt, our freedom is an empty boast. The worst kind of slavery is that which retards ingress and egress to and from one State to another, and which gives a license to chartered companies to place a limit to transit and travel by excessive charges. A man's personal liberty to go and come at will, without hindrance, is a sacred right, and all legislation that conflicts with it is rank oppression. It is at war with civilization, and against the genius of our institutions, and must result, as in other countries, in the establishment of classes in society, while it will create a fearful gulf between the rich and the poor. When the rapid strides of monopoly shall have reached such an extreme, it will be a dark day for this country. The hatred, malice, and envy that follow glaring wrong may awaken a terrible retribution, and, at any moment, the volcano of public vengeance may burst upon us, and send forth a consuming fire through the land.

The position taken by President Johnson against monopolies is prolific of hope and encouragement to the producing classes. Words of warning from the chief ruler of a nation ought to inspire confidence and infuse courage into the most timid heart. Familiar with every phase of society in his passage from the work-bench to the highest social and political position in the known world, he *knows* and *feels* the importance of guarding the interests of honest industry as well as those of capital. He has fought the battle of life well, and carved his way from obscurity and poverty to prominence by hard knocks. He has graduated in the high-school of a sad experience, and hence he can appreciate the obstacles thrown in the way of individual enterprise by chartered monopolies. Away, then, with all special privileges. Let the people heed his warning, and sanction no legislation designed to rob the toiler of an open field and a fair fight for self-elevation.

A PLEA FOR REST.

It is asserted that every age shortens the life of man. Philosophers and theorists have in vain attempted to ascertain the cause; and although many have been assigned, no one of them has been accepted as a satisfactory explanation. In our opinion, there are several agents which work in harmony to abridge the longevity of the human family, forming a combination of extremes wholly at war with the laws of nature; and we all know that as surely as the thunder follows the lightning, so sure are we to meet the penalty of such transgressions, which are called down upon us by a Higher Power than that wielded by judge or jury. Nor can we plead ignorance of the law; for there is scarcely a human being of mature years who does not know, and has not felt, its retributive justice, when he eats, sleeps, and works too much or too little. The gourmand is punished with gout, the inebriate with mania a potu, the idler with dyspepsia, overtaxed labor with physical prostration; and even the miser, when guarding his gold, can be frightened by the chirp of a cricket in his wakeful hours. The laws of nature wisely place a limit to excesses of any kind; and when overstepped, the offender must suffer.

We have but little sympathy with those who violate natural laws to gratify a sensual appetite or to indulge in their miserly instincts; but we do complain of the *system* which authorizes *one* man to be the instrument of forcing *many*, while powerless for resistance, to render themselves liable to the penalty prescribed for such offences as tend to curtail man's allotted time on earth. And who will deny that excessive labor is one of the most fatal agents for shortening the life of man? Do not the necessities of nine-tenths of our race place them at the mercy of one-tenth, who direct, control, and render the vast majority amenable to the consequences of extremes forbidden by the natural law? Under existing circumstances, the innocent are made to suffer for the guilty, since the offenders are *compelled* to be offenders.

We have observed, too, that as machinery has been introduced, the workingman's condition proves that he is denied a fair share of the advantages secured to society. The few still reap the benefits of those labor-saving inventions, and still the muscles of the poor are taxed to their utmost tension. As fast as labor saving machinery is introduced the toiler is made to "change his base." True, new channels of labor are developed, which he is yet to become familiar with, before he can apply his labor with profit; and in the course of his short lifetime "progress" fates him to be a novitiate in three or four departments of mechanism. Few of those who served an apprenticeship twenty years ago, work in the same manner, with the same tools, or at the same branches, which ushered him into manhood. He is too often kicked about like a foot-ball, and made to take up the odds and ends, the shreds and patches, to work up into shape. He is only permitted to do what the machine *cannot* do. The capitalist, the dealer, the consumer, may be benefited, but what does the producer gain? His wages are not increased, his labor is seldom lighter, he still lives in the fetid atmosphere of a crowded court, his hours of rest are not prolonged; and his lot still the same, to toil on for a bare subsistence, with aching limbs and overstrained muscles, until the grave claims him as a victim to satisfy the violated laws of nature, perhaps in the noontime of life.

It is asserted that the wisest statesman could frame no law which would prove equal in its operation. We are so differently situated in life that, in its general application, some must suffer temporary inconvenience at least. So with the progress of science and art. The many inventions, the introduction of vast machinery, while they add to wealth, and develop the ingenuity of man as well as the resources of our country, still rich in fields of enterprise, the laboring population, who work the machinery and run all the risk of losing life, limb, and health, and brave the dangers incident to all kinds of machinery in its profitable working, are not proportionately benefited, but "left out in the cold," while all else is progressing.

Look at the peril attendant upon the occupation of an engineer. If a train is wrecked, the engineer and fireman are sure to be among the wounded or killed. The steamboat, the locomotive, the stationary engine, may send a man in the air, an arm may be torn off by a belt in the factory, a circular saw may cut off a hand, and a hundred accidents might occur, with as many different kinds of machinery, to cripple, or shorten a man's life. Well, suppose he is sent skyward, crushed beneath a locomotive, or ground into livid matter by ponderous machinery, his place is promptly supplied, and the profits of the company or the capitalist are still accumulating. The fact that a widow may be wailing, and her orphans crying for bread, don't disturb society— there is too much of it.

We contend, therefore, that all these improvements, necessary as we admit them to be, increase the risk, and multiply the chances of accident to the workman; and while he alone encounters all these dangers, his wages remain the same, and he works just as hard, just as long, with greater responsibility and care added to his labor. He alone is made to suffer a social martyrdom to benefit every class of society save that in which *he* moves. What, then, shall be the reward worthy of his sacrifices? He is modest in his demands. He only asks the small boon of *two additional hours of rest.*

"Ah," you say, "he asks too much: he should be contented with a reduction from sun to sun to ten hours. That is the legal day's work, and one of his own seeking." He admits it, but feels that it is too much, now that machinery has placed new cares upon his mind, new vexations upon his labor, and new dangers upon his life. He is not avaricious, for he labors for wages far disproportionate to the cost of living. He would not monopolize labor, for he proposes to add just one-fifth to employment by that reduction of time. Aside from this, many mechanics, who work ten hours per day, must make some preparation outside of working hours. The period of rest is often devoted to deep thought in planning for the best advantage to be derived from the coming day's work. He must put tools in order, make calculations, and conjure up many little facilities of assistance; for machinery forces him to be a mathematician us well as a mechanic, and he must learn to comprehend the practical working of the whole, of which he may only be a part, in order to employ his mind and his labor profitably.

Hence, we claim the two additional hours of rest for the workingman as his share, and a small one at that, of the benefits which labor-saving machinery has secured to society. Give him time to cultivate his mind, that latent talent may be developed, and our word for it, that acquired theoretical knowledge, applied to the practical, will add to the improvements and inventions which will place this country ahead of all others in the perfection of its machinery, the skill of its mechanics, and the excellence of its fabrics. It will do more. All grades of society will be more closely allied in good fellowship, a feeling of equality will break down the dividing lines which mark the boundaries of classes, justice will be more evenly distributed, and intelligence become more wide-spread. Rest, *rest* — humanity, justice, the laws of nature, demand more rest for the worker.

ABUSE OF THE ELECTIVE FRANCHISE.

The demoralizing tendency of our popular elections must be apparent to every reflective mind. Old men cannot fail to notice the vast difference between the elections of the past and present; and none can view the change without painful emotions of sorrow. The time was when the elective franchise was looked upon as the most sacred agency of liberty and law — the true source of power — from which the just principles of a free government were derived. But it is a sad truth to confess that, as time progresses, we are prostituting this proud privilege to the basest purposes. Instead of being used to obtain a fair expression of opinion, the ballot-box has become an instrument of fraud and unworthy ambition — a mere engine in the hands of designing men to secure place and power, at the sacrifice of every manly principle.

It is useless to deny the fact that office is struck off to the highest bidder, in spite of all the guards that have been thrown around the ballot-box. Money is the power which influences primary meetings, delegate elections, and nominating conventions; and money enters the canvass as the most potent element of success — for in its train follow lying, gambling, defamation, whiskey-drinking, and untold vices. To this evil may be traced the many defalcations and swindles which yearly deplete State and National treasuries. The honest poor man is excluded from position, and reckless demagogues fill our offices because they have money to squander on elections; and, when elected, instead of legislating for the best interests of the masses, they only pander to the whims and caprice of the depraved and purchasable, to whom they are bound hand and foot. The question is seldom asked as to morals and capacity; but it is requisite to know how much a candidate is worth, and how much he will spend—the last two essentials overriding all considerations of merit and capacity.

Look at the men who are generally nominated for the higher places, such as congressmen, sheriffs, and other profitable offices. Show us *one* poor man — a workingman — who occupies such a position. True, there may be such exceptions as bankrupts in business, or those made poor by corrupting the ballot-box; but where can you point to one thus honored who came direct from the ranks of labor? Yet it is conceded, and history proves it, that many of our wisest statesmen, in the early history of this country, came from the plough, the anvil, the loom, and the workshop. And who will deny that the same degree of talent, the same adaptation to public affairs, can be found to-day in agricultural, manufacturing, and mechanical pursuits? If this class of men, in the past, could make better laws, and administer them with greater satisfaction — if there was less of sectional animosity and more of general harmony under their rule — why would not the same character of men in the present age, having the same feelings and interests, prove just as beneficial, and accomplish the same amount of good? It is a change in the *character* of the men we elect to office which produces and has produced more than half the troubles that have fallen upon us.

But who is responsible for these abuses? We answer: the very class which this political corruption proscribes — the *producers*. If workingmen were to withdraw their support from demagogues who make a *trade* of politics, and bestow it upon those whose feelings and sympathies are with them, they would not to-day be petitioning in vain for those reforms which are denied by the present heartless occupants of our National and State legislative halls. With the remedy in their own hands, they refuse to use it. Led away by the siren song of party, flattered by the ambitious, and cheated by the successful, they repeat the same folly every year, and heed no warning, let it come with what force it may. Is it not time that we look more carefully to the *first cause* of our grievances — *partial legislation?* While we elect the rich "clever fellows" to office, steeped in fashionable vices, and wedded to opposing interests, can we hope to obtain that just consideration to which our *votes* entitle us? From year to year these men use us as stepping-stones to power; but where can we point to an act, or an effort, emanating from one of them, which looks like gratitude, or expresses a reciprocal feeling for all the favors we bestow upon them? We have talent, integrity, and sobriety in the ranks of labor sufficient for all offices, from the highest to the lowest; we are competent to make suitable selections; we possess the numerical strength to elect them, and can do so without committing ourselves to the dogmas, or participating in demoralizing practices of any party.

If we resolve to do this, we resolve to accomplish another great reform. We shall no longer patronize grog-shops and restaurants, contribute to "refreshments for head-quarters," and come home to our families, at late hours, in a questionable condition. We shall set a better example to our sons and daughters, elevate the moral standard of workingmen, maintain a purer ballot-box, and convince the world that popular elections involve duties too solemn to be made the pretext for gambling, bacchanalian revelry, or a display of the more brutal instincts. Let the workingmen win the glory of eradicating the abuses of the elective franchise, and they will also win the respect and admiration of every good citizen in the land. They will do more, — for they at once place themselves in a position to administer to their own wants without detracting from the interests of others, while coming generations will hail them as their deliverers from a thraldom which "rendered our elections a curse instead of a blessing."

PLAIN TALK.

All organizations have their troubles, and ours cannot expect to escape its full share. In all society we find a class of men possessed of a superabundance of self-esteem, some brains, much cheek, and a little learning. These men are ambitious and intensely selfish, and, as a general thing, either too lazy or too proud to work; and when possessed of a good share of energy, become dangerous members of society. Owing to the entire freedom of our institutions, a large majority of them rise to the political surface. They are confined to no soil, climate, or locality, but can be found everywhere — all societies, all organizations, all people are cursed with their presence, and the Moulders' Union must expect to come in for its full share. Years ago, some of the worst type of this species drifted to the surface; and, although most of the original stock have sunk into oblivion, their followers and adherents have been keeping up a continual commotion. In 1860, this element was largely represented in the Albany Convention, where we had the honor to be elected treasurer. Being possessed of a watchful and suspicious turn of mind, we were not long in discovering the true character and *motives* of these restless and dangerous men; and immediately a contest sprung up between us, and before the first six months of the year 1861 had expired, there was open and bitter hostility. Nothing was more natural than for these men to affiliate, and before the close of that year a thorough understanding existed among them, and a clique was formed for the purpose of controlling the Cincinnati Convention, and dividing the profits and honors among themselves. To make themselves perfectly secure, it was thought necessary that we should not go to that convention; knowing that we were extremely poor, and believing that, should we not be elected a delegate, we would, for the want of means, be compelled to remain at home. To accomplish this object, a collusion was formed to secure our defeat. Then, in that, the darkest hour of our life, we were deserted by all but a handful of firm and devoted friends, who had confidence in our integrity, and our defeat was secured. In the meantime, accounts were being trumped up, and every arrangement made, to prove us a defaulter at the next convention. We had, however, early in the year, decided upon a course of action that should be followed to the end, and silently resolved within ourself that all these schemes should be defeated. Over $6,000 had passed through our hands during the year, and we were not to be kept from the convention. We went there; and the result was a triumphant vindication of ourself, and the entire overthrow of all the pet schemes of this clique, whose objects were to provide for themselves positions, and make the organization a stepping-stone to their political advancement. Though defeated and exposed, they lost none of their venom. At the Pittsburg Convention, in 1863, nothing was heard of them, for the reason that our union had almost ceased to have an existence; and, like a ship in a sinking condition, was deserted by all but a few brave men, willing to sacrifice all to prevent a total wreck. In one year the union was again placed upon a firm basis, and in the front rank of the union movement. The rats took to the ship again, and in the Buffalo Convention, in 1864, we found a revival of the same old faction, as intensely bitter and selfish as ever. The harmony of the convention was marred by it, and many unpleasant feelings created; but it was again crushed and silenced, but by no means defeated. At the Chicago Convention, in 1865, it raised its malignant head with a bitterness never before manifested. But there had been a change of tactics; efforts had been made to create dissatisfaction with our administration; supposed and imaginary wrongs done to the Western unions were talked about, and many of the unthinking were led into the snare, and were made to believe that injustice had been done, and that, if we were again elected president, it would be best for the West to split off from the East, and set up an independent union. These views were openly expressed in Chicago, but it is only since the adjournment of that convention that any very serious movement was made to bring about a separation. Within a few months communications have been widely circulated, filled with all the elements of dissolution, and imputing to us, and other officers of the International Union, dishonesty and dishonorable motives; hinting that money was being used for individual aggrandizement, and that we were determined to hold on to the office of president indefinitely for the purpose of keeping out of the foundry, and arguments calculated to inflame the minds of the Western men, and create a powerful movement in favor of a separation of the West from the East; all these things are well known to us. Until very recently, all these movements were conducted below the surface; but, growing bolder as they became hardened in sin, they have lately openly proclaimed in favor of secession. We penetrated the secret objects of this faction when it was first organized in 1861, and we have never for a moment lost sight of it. We determined then to stand between it and the union at all hazards, and, without any regard to our own safety, we have done so, and shall continue to do so to the end. They started out to rule the union and use it; failing in that, they would now divide it, and rule and use one-half of it. "Rule or ruin" is now their watchword. Thus ends a chapter from the secret history of our organization, and in giving it we have had but one object in view — the good of the cause. For years we have been fighting these elements quietly. Our official connection with the union will soon cease, and we have determined that, for the few months yet remaining of our administration, we will openly and fearlessly proclaim the truth, and call upon all good men everywhere to come to the rescue, and crush out of existence, now and forever, these infernal influences that would destroy the last hope of the workingman. We have been accused of dishonesty and of ambition. As a refutation of the first charge, we have only to point to our past record as an officer, and we defy any one, our most bitter enemy, to point to a single official act that will not bear investigation, or to a single dollar that has not been satisfactorily accounted for. To the charge of ambition we plead guilty; and if to be ambitious to do good is a crime, then have we sinned. We aspired to the honorable position that we now occupy, thinking that we could better serve the cause in this capacity than in any other, and we would long since have left it had it not been for our enemies, and the enemies of the cause in whose interests we have been fighting; and when we leave it, it will be with feelings of profound gratitude for the many favors received, and the proud consciousness that we have performed every official duty to the best of our ability, and frustrated the schemes of those who would sacrifice everything good and holy to gain their own selfish purposes.

THE CONSPIRACY.

Our remarks under the head of "Plain Talk" have created quite a commotion, and the very worthy gentlemen who are engaged in the laudable enterprise of destroying our union have changed their tactics. They have slunk away into dark places, and from the noxious vapors surrounding them are manufacturing a hurricane for future use, with which they expect to annihilate everybody but their own precious selves. We imagine that when the storm does break, it will make about as much noise and do about as much harm as the bursting of a soap-bubble.

These men have been quietly endeavoring to poison the minds of the union men in the West, and elsewhere, too, by insinuations of dishonesty on the part of the officers of the International Union, and by charging that gross injustice has been done to the Western unions. They say that partiality has been shown to the Eastern unions by the president, and that all the favors that officer has to bestow, he gives to the unions of the Eastern and Middle States, and that the West can ask, but ask in vain for her rights.

It is not our purpose to deny these charges in this article; we simply wish to ask a few plain and simple questions, and expect the authors of these charges to answer them.

In the first place, gentlemen, if there are any grounds for the charges you make, why do you not come out boldly before the world and publish your views? If you have good grounds for saying the officers of the I. M. I. U. are not honest, why do you not make your charges openly, and give the evidence upon which they are based? If injustice has been done any union anywhere, why don't you say so openly? let the world know in what way this injustice has been done. If partiality has been shown to any union or unions, let us know what unions, and all the particulars connected therewith. If the rights of any union have been withheld, why do you not specify what rights they are, and in what way they have been withheld? Now, gentlemen, if you are honest, and have the good of the organization at heart, step out into the daylight, make your charges and specifications, and, if you can prove your position, the guilty parties will receive the reward their perfidy deserves; the union will be saved, and you will receive the praises of all good men. The *Journal* is the mouth-piece of the organization; it is as much yours as ours, and anything you have to say will find a prominent place. Will you come? We are waiting for an answer. The men on our side of the fence are not afraid to speak. Witness the action of No. 4 and No. 14; besides these resolutions for publication, we are in receipt of protests against your infernal plot from all parts of the organization. Words of encouragement come to us from every quarter; some even go so far as to implore us not to get frightened and run away from our post, but to stand firm to the end. We don't happen to belong to the runaway kind, and will only leave when our work is done. We are watching this movement with two eyes open, and will give all particulars as they develop themselves.

THE EVILS OF PIECE-WORK.

THE evils of piece-work begin to assume an alarming shape, and must become fearful in their magnitude, if the present condition of trade be an index to that of the future. If so seriously felt at the very commencement of the dawning depression, what mischief will it not work ere we witness a revival of trade, or behold our social equilibrium restored after the disbanding of the army? We admire industry, we commend prudence and economy, and love to see a man provide for his own household, so long as his efforts are marked by a due consideration for the welfare of others; but we do object to the overstraining of these virtues, until honest ambition is transformed into the basest kind of selfishness.

When work is plenty and workmen few, there may be some pretext for working to the utmost tension of a man's physical endurance, whether suggested by sordid motives or a desire to oblige the employer. Under such circumstances, none are injured but those who violate the laws of nature; but when the reverse is the case — the many idle and the few employed — we hold it to be ungenerous, if not inhuman, for half a dozen men to transcend their physical abilities by working late and early, to monopolize all the work in the shop, when that labor divided would give as many more employment, and furnish food for their destitute families. Such a course can result in but temporary advantage to those who pursue it, because they know not how soon "the tables may turn." If they were guaranteed life-long employment in the same shop, they might escape the consequences of their folly; but no employer will do this. Promising as their prospects may be, a mistake, a neglect, a hasty word, or a capricious whim of the employer, at any moment, may send them adrift on the sea of uncertainty, where they will meet those to whom they denied a helping hand. In turn, the outs may get in, and how hard it will be for them to encounter the very selfishness of their own creation.

The maxim, "Get all you can, and keep all you get," is one against which journeymen mechanics have never ceased to declaim; but it seems that piece-workers have learned to overcome their scruples, and are carrying it out to the most selfish extreme. Surely, were they to reflect upon the danger, and consider the evil tendency of this flagrant abuse of piece-work, they would speedily abandon it. For what do we combine, but to establish rules and regulations for the observance of a uniform *system*, which was designed for the good of all. The aim of our unions is to secure equal advantages to every member; and, to retain the power of self-protection, we must be a *unit* in heart and purpose, tolerating no innovation which secures a benefit to one at the expense of another. Least of all should we suffer avarice or selfishness to wean us from an *association of interest*, to band in half-dozen squads or more, for the purpose of robbing our companions in toil of their share of work. When employers find us conflicting, and set the example of "every man for himself," can we blame them for dosing us with our own medicine? In short, piece-work must eventually lead to the monopoly of labor by a few to the detriment of the many. This will produce heart-burning, and arouse a spirit of retaliation, which will induce men to work for what they can get. It will destroy confidence, render our unions weak and impotent by contention, and leave us at the mercy of employers. We need not name the advantages which an abandonment of the practice would secure to us. It is enough to say that, by abridging the hours of labor when work is scarce, and sharing it with our needy brethren, we take the initiatory step towards legalizing, by precedent, the eight-hour system. We strengthen the bonds of union and friendship by acknowledging our mutual dependence. We establish harmony in our unions, and invest them with a strength and power which render them doubly strong for our defence. We win the esteem of workingmen of all trades, and give them hope by the force of example. We convince employers that "we know our rights, and knowing, dare maintain them." We might add, that the magnanimity of sharing employment and sustenance with our associates, in times of great depression, must exalt the workingmen of America to the highest standard of refinement and humanity. Reader, gaze on both sides of the picture — see what we must eventually lose by piece-work, and look at what we will surely gain by its abandonment.

WE BIDE OUR TIME.

THE present beclouded condition of the producing classes discloses a phase of human character peculiar to all social changes. Those who feel that they possess power, seem disposed to use it, as if in revenge for a check to their arrogance during the brief period when workmen were scarcely sufficient in numbers to perform the increased amount of labor made necessary by the war. Now that there is a lull and an excess of hands, the manner, tone, and feeling of many employers are quite different. In their intercourse with journeymen they are more dictatorial, and exhibit a brusqueness which almost amounts to offence, because they know that others are ready to take their places. Wages are lowered, new rules established, and perceptible encroachments are daily attempted, well calculated to irritate and annoy. To all reasonable men, this must be a source of sincere regret. During the past three years, it was our pleasure to witness a closer assimilation of feeling and interest between employers and journeymen, and, in proportion as this equality was recognized, we saw old prejudices vanishing, and harmony and true sociability growing. We had hoped, as the reward of labor increased, to see the workingman lifted up to the social standard of the employer, without detracting one iota from the position or the interests of the latter, and no one more than ourselves rejoiced in the prosperity of master mechanics during the period alluded to, because we based our hopes of the workingman's elevation upon their success, and looked forward to the time when every dividing line would be obliterated by congenial association, and a mutual recognition of each other's rights. But we are mistaken, and all our hopes are dispelled by the inauguration of repulsive and oppressive measures against workingmen.

How different with us when hands were scarce and work pressing upon which fortunes hung. Journeymen mechanics took no advantage of the dilemma in which employers were placed at the time. They simply asked an advance of wages, sufficient to meet the additional cost of living—nothing more. Indeed, very generally, they neither asked nor received an equalizing compensation, and, in many instances, they were compelled to strike for what they did get, although employers were receiving almost fabulous prices. All of us know how we applied ourselves to meet the sudden demand for workmen. Over-work, night-work, and, we regret to say, Sunday-work, were too often required of us. Those who would now oppress us, cannot so soon forget how we responded to every call made upon us. Thousands, to oblige their employers, taxed their physical energies to the utmost, that a contract might be completed in time, or to finish one job to open the door for another. It is useless to say "we paid you for it," for no wages can pay any man for violating the laws of nature so far as to rob himself of necessary rest and sleep.

Thus, when employers were perplexed by *success*, when overburdened with work at *their own prices*, when the chance of enriching themselves offered, and their suddenly-made fortunes depended upon the fidelity of journeymen mechanics, we slaved and toiled to serve their interests, actuated by the hope that their prosperity would inspire feelings of gratitude and liberality, which would forever lift us above the position of suppliants for *simple justice*. All obligations ought to be reciprocal, and now that we are perplexed by *poverty*, arising from the scarcity of employment, are we not entitled to the same wages, when our past services have increased the ability of employers to compensate us better than ever? After enriching them, are we to be proscribed? After placing them beyond financial care by the labor of our hands, is it manly, is it right, that they should now higgle, and chaffer, and cheapen us down to starvation wages? These are questions for honorable employers to answer, and upon their decision, in our opinion, depend the peace and harmony which ought to exist between the two classes; for should a season of prosperity again dawn upon us, we hope we may have no feelings of revenge to gratify, no enemies to punish. But, if forced to occupy the position of a "stag at bay," we should be loath to predict the consequences. Till then, however, we bide our time.

TO YOUR TENTS!

We need not remind members of our union, and all other mechanics, that the present is a critical period in our history. The lowering clouds of adversity are visible everywhere around us; and the threatened storm of persecution may burst upon us at any moment. If we would avert the force of the blow, let us be prepared for its coming. "Prompt to duty" should now be the watchword of all, and each should exercise the vigilance of a faithful sentinel; for if misfortune should come upon us, if we should "go under" at last, let not the pangs of defeat be imbittered by the reflection that we failed to discharge a single duty which might have saved us from the mælstrom of a monetary panic.

We have been so long accustomed to glide upon an unrippled surface, that we have placed too much confidence in imaginary security. Our perils have been so few of late that we have become insensible to danger, and grown careless and apathetic in all that is essential to our safety. Fatal delusion. The struggle for existence is at hand. The war of Capital against Labor is raging in the Old World, and the clang of preparation rings out upon the still air in the New. To your tents, then, workingmen, and show a steady front to the foe. The man who wavers or falters now is lost. Every mental and physical effort should be devoted to our trades-unions; for if ever we needed combination in its perfection, harmony in its excellence, and union in its strength, we need it now. The moral power of numbers is as essential to our safety as food and raiment are to our comfort. He who deserts his union now, when danger threatens, is both a coward and an ingrate. A coward, because he refuses to defend a position to which he was exalted by the sacrifices of his fellow-toilers; an ingrate, because he has enjoyed all the advantages won by others, and deserts them like a thankless drone, when only his *presence* is required to secure a continuance of blessings he never knew until his benefactors bestowed them upon him.

Our readers must excuse us if we grow warm upon this subject. We can tolerate almost any *crime* with more complacency than that of ingratitude among workingmen. Bound together by over-taxed labor, long-suffering — common victims of injustice and oppression — who, of all God's creation, should act together, think together, and move together more than workingmen? One in purpose, one in sympathy, one in destiny, they should also be a *unit* in every effort that tends to their social elevation; for we must rise or fall together. These convictions having been the guide of our individual and official connections with the union, we cannot express our regret, our mortification, at the apparent indifference manifested towards the unions by many members. Few attend, many plead frivolous excuses, and many more never show their faces until a threatened reduction of wages drives them to their only ark of safety. Yes, we have members who are prompt to come up, and poach upon our funds, when the wolf howls at the door, but never take a part in the movement unless they are *personally* interested. This species of selfishness is the great stumbling-block to our progress. We regret to add, also, that not a few who have long been considered faithful, are gradually absenting themselves from their unions. Need we say, that a once zealous member, who relaxes in the discharge of his duty or becomes apathetic, sets a more pernicious example than though he had never been among us. He is held up as a criterion by those who *seek* an excuse for their own base desertion.

Workingmen must remember that our unions are the last refuge of persecuted labor. If they fall, we fall; and every man who refuses to support them wrongs his neighbor as well as himself. Employers are already informed of the apathy we complain of, and how they gloat over this abatement of interest on the part of workingmen. They hail it as an evidence that the last barrier between them and the complete mastery of the producing classes will soon be removed, and exult over the fact that the supineness of workingmen is doing more to effect their own ruin than capitalists could hope to accomplish.

Finally, we ask members to attend their unions *every meeting night*, for the sake of example as well as of interest. The *principle* involved should be the impelling motive. Crowded unions show strength, determined purpose, and the discipline of combination. They strike terror to the oppressors, and give hope to the defenders, of labor. In short, every consideration of duty, the highest motives that can actuate man, self-preservation itself, demands, in this crisis of the labor movement, a prompt and regular attendance at our union meetings. Workingmen, to your tents.

LARGE AND SMALL ROGUES.

THE discrimination in favor of large rogues, and the rigor with which the penalty of violated law is visited upon small ones, has long been a source of complaint. Justice is as unerring as truth, and, when properly administered, gives majesty and dignity to the law; but when perverted by prejudice, or controlled by favoritism, it is natural that public confidence should be shaken. The difference between rogues in ruffles and rogues in rags is daily widening, if we are to draw correct conclusions from our civil and criminal annals; for, in nine cases out of ten, the lightest sentence demanded by the grade of crime is placed upon the most flagrant offender, while that of the severest character is visited upon the transgressor in petty cases. The man who can abuse public confidence to the amount of ten or fifty thousand dollars, is a *respectable* rogue; and if justice is bold enough to strip him of his hoarded plunder, society will sympathize with him over a fate that reduces his social status and style of living, because "he has never been used to it." But let some poor mechanic, robbed, perhaps, of his wages by the same aristocratic rascal, driven to desperation, steal a loaf of bread or a rasher of meat, and how prompt the law, how impulsive is justice. The station-house one day, the Quarter Sessions the next, and the prison the next. There is no habeas corpus, no bail, no influential friends, no public sympathy, to come between the victim and his inevitable doom. A large rogue can enjoy the benefit of all these influences, and have postponements, obtain writs of certiorari, new trials, and by all manner of legal subterfuge hold justice at bay until the case is dropped from the calendar or erased from the docket.

Then look at the difference which public estimation has established between the two offenders. The large rogue still maintains his position in society, because he has filched sufficient from the unfortunate to maintain his style of living, and to *purchase* homage by princely benevolence or ostentatious charities. Liberal to the Sanitary Committee, generous to Dorcas Societies, a life-member of Bible and Missionary Societies, he passes as current coin in the community he has robbed. But how is it with the small rogue? He emerges from prison broken-spirited, crushed to the earth with the burden of his own shame—it may be to find his home desolate, his family scattered, and every tie that bound him to earth severed. He is despised by the rich as a *common* thief; he is shunned by old friends, and feels that he wears a brand of infamy which attracts every eye. While the big rogue is taken by the hand, the little one is kicked aside with loathing. Re-entering the world as an outcast, he must possess a remarkable degree of moral courage, indeed, if he pursues a moral and upright course of life amid the persecution and proscription he is forced to encounter. In too many cases, such injustice drives despairing men to reckless habits of life, and a career of crime which destroys all hope of reformation. These are some of the differences, reader, between large and small rogues.

THE ARISTOCRACY OF INTELLECT.

IF ever one absurdity exceeded another, it was when a class of self-constituted savans set themselves up as the sole custodians of all intelligence, which is to be eked out, as they see fit, in small doses, to those who hunger and thirst for knowledge. It is really a matter of wonder, in a land of equality like this, that these pretenders should have been so long tolerated, and conceded a superiority to which they were never entitled. In monarchical governments, cursed with a titled nobility and privileged classes, whose wealth is permitted to elevate them in the social scale, high above the producing millions, we are not surprised that these assumptions should lead to the acknowledgment of an aristocracy of intellect; because the masses are so fettered, and so much absorbed in a common struggle for bread, that few of them have an opportunity to develop the God-like attributes of the mind, though perhaps gifted with abilities which, were they not stultified or choked by the rank weeds of poverty and prejudice, would eclipse one-half the oracular pretenders of the age. Give them but *time* and *opportunity* to think, with even limited education, and neither the heat of furnaces, the clang of machinery, the stifled air of manufactories, nor the heat of midsummer's sun, would be sufficient to chain them to the contracted sphere assigned them by the aristocracy of intellect. As it is, the scientific and literary world are frequently startled by the appearance of "some bright particular star," whose master mind has burst through adverse clouds, and emerged from the midnight of obscurity, to throw additional light and knowledge upon long explored subjects.

In this country, however, the elements of self-elevation are more accessible to the masses; and, if properly applied, neither mind nor body need be fettered. The fault with us is, not that we lack the means of guarding against the pretensions of those who would despoil us of mind, as they do of labor; but that we neglect to exercise our *rights*, as men, in such a way as will make us secure in our privileges. Man, it is said, is an imitator; and we are not surprised to find those among us who would inaugurate here the same distinctive features which send one class higher and another lower, in the Old World. Once concede a superiority of intellect to those who base their pretensions upon wealth, and you admit an entering wedge which will inevitably divide society, and result in the establishment of privileged classes. This accomplished, what is to save us from the social and intellectual degradation which money and power have fastened upon mankind elsewhere.

Workingmen of America, never forget that God's ordained equality of man is recognized in the laws and institutions of *our* country; and to admit of, or submit to, a distinction, based on a difference of circumstances in life, would be rank sacrilege. To suppose that He could, in His immaculate conception and execution of creating and peopling worlds, design that a man's mind should grow with his money-bags, or expand with his broad acres, would be an infamous calumny upon Divine wisdom and justice. Were this possible, the world would never have been blessed with more than half the mechanical inventions and scientific discoveries which have marked the progress of man. Godfrey, Franklin, Fitch, and Fulton could never have conferred upon us the countless benefits which still flow from their towering genius. But, aside from the men associated with poverty and toil, who have so largely contributed to the advancement of art and science, the great majority of our orators, heroes, and statesmen came from the ranks of labor.

But, in our opinion, these pretensions to an aristocracy of intellect cannot stand the test of either observation or experience. Take an equal number of those who live upon the labor of others, and of those who labor for a living, and scrutinize their progress through life. Who will question the preponderance of all that is practical and useful in favor of the latter? It is because the act of *producing* tends to develop the powers of the mind, while the luxury of *consuming*, blended with the vice of idleness, generally renders it inert and contracted. The same may be said of the children of each. The child of wealth, though favored by the best education that money can procure, often becomes an imbecile, or a mere book-worm at most, in the absence of all opportunity to apply his mind to mechanical, agricultural, or other useful pursuits; while the child of poverty, with limited schooling, and that obtained at an early age, often outstrips the other in the race of life, for the reason that his little learning is assisted by industrial associations which daily tax his intellect as well as the body; for just as the muscles are strengthened by exercise, so the mind becomes enlarged by the variety of its application. With so many living illustrations of the truth of our position, we can but smile at the loose "mental philosophy" of the day, which would violate every natural law in the effort to build up an aristocracy of intellect. Its votaries may maintain one of wealth, because that is as often associated with ignorance as with intelligence; but you might as well attempt to monopolize the sunlight, or the air we breathe, as to confine intellect to a class. It dwells in cot and palace, and, like heaven's dew, falls upon the rich and poor alike.

THE RESPECTABILITY OF LABOR.

A GREAT deal of distinction is made between the different trades, arising from a silly prejudice which concedes more respectability to one trade than another. Labor is labor all the world over, and the only difference consists in the various modes of its application. The shoemaker plies his awl and hammer, the tailor his needle and shears, the carpenter his jack-plane, the moulder his rammer, and so on, through the whole catalogue of mechanism. Each and all give brain and muscle to these several occupations; and, for the life of us, we cannot see the claim to superiority of a single one over another. The grubbing-hoe, the hod, or the mud-spud, are equally honorable implements of industry, although coming under the class of unskilled labor; but, should all receive equal compensation, where shall the higher grade of respectability begin? If we accept the difference justly existing between a mechanical trade which takes years of apprenticeship to acquire, and that species of labor which depends more upon physical than mental capacity, we see nothing at variance with a common interest and a common destiny.

We look upon every kind of labor as respectable, because *necessary;* and no man, should he reach the most exalted position in life, could possibly lessen the dignity of himself, or compromise the sphere in which he moved, by resuming the humble occupation from which he sprung, for either pastime or convenience, so long as he faithfully discharged the duties of that position. Would Abraham Lincoln, while President, have degraded himself or his office had he "took a turn" at splitting rails, or grasped the helm of a flat-boat? Could Andrew Johnson have done the same by patching his coat, or sewing up a rip in his pantaloons? On the contrary, the one felt a glow of honest pride when living, as the other does now, while alluding to their past occupations. Then, if proud to boast, as Presidents, of the trades they followed in poverty, why should they not, with equal pride and satisfaction, split a rail or mend a coat, as Presidents?

It is evident that neither of these great men recognized a distinction between the labor of the mechanic or workman, and that of a President. In fact, while free to boast of their performance as laborers, they were by no means vainglorious while occupying the highest position in the country. It is the wide difference of compensation which creates the distinction, and not the occupation. We have often read sneering criticisms of both, whenever they made allusions to their past history; but while the occupation of either may stink in aristocratic nostrils, one had, and the other has, the moral courage to throw the mantle of respectability around the humblest calling.

DISCONTENT.

How much of happiness has been destroyed, how many fortunes have been lost, by a spirit of discontent? The restless, dissatisfied man will create countless obstacles to his progress by devoting his greatest powers of thought to chimerical schemes and impracticable theories, when, if the strength of his mind were applied to present pursuits, he might soon acquire the means and the position to free himself from incessant toil; or, at least enable him to accomplish as much by head-work as hand-work. How many have brooded over what they conceived to be a hard lot, until they became indifferent, and foolishly imagined that the door of deliverance was shut against them forever; but how little of manliness, how little of intelligence, is developed in the fickle-minded being who surrenders to such influences? Show us a man who goes to his daily labor whistling on his way, greets his shopmates with a smile, and returns to his family in the evening to meet the caresses of his loved ones in a reciprocal spirit, and we will show you a man who can and will rise above misfortune, and cast off depression, though fate itself should war against him. Mountains to others would be to him mole-hills, and while some would be creating imaginary barriers to their progress, he would pluck roses instead of thorns on the pathway of life.

This spirit of discontent, we regret to say, prevails to a great extent among workingmen. Perhaps the most prolific source of this evil can be traced to a distaste for, or prejudice against, the particular trade or calling which they follow. It has become fashionable to dwell upon the objectionable features of a business, and magnify its disadvantages to an extent that produces a self-terrifying feeling, and we gaze so long upon the dark side of our lot, that we become blind to every source of alleviation. We can see the good points in all other trades, but none in our own; yet, were we to take the same liberal view of the calling we follow as we bestow upon others, we would soon be content.

Every man should honor his own trade and feel that his interests can be promoted proportionate to a just appreciation of the dignity which belongs to it; and it rests with him to add to, or detract from, that dignity. In elevating it, he elevates himself. In fact, when he persistently disparages his own trade, it is natural to infer that he is in a measure disqualified to follow any other; for if he has no respect for the agency through which he derives support for himself and family, it is more than probable he would go on grumbling and croaking to his grave, and die a discontented man. It is natural that the fault-finding propensity which he cultivated at the calling with which he is most familiar, would obtrude upon him with a fourfold force, should he engage in another, of which he may only have a theoretical knowledge. We therefore conceive it to be the duty of every workingman to not only esteem his trade worthy of himself, but to *make* himself worthy of his trade.

We often hear workingmen complain of their occupation, and brand it as good for nothing. They will quit it—will starve—will follow it no longer, &c. Rest assured, reader, that the fault, in ninety-nine cases out of a hundred, is not with the trade, but with the man. His discontented spirit will not permit him to make a just comparison of his own condition with that of others, and his morbid feelings magnify objections, until dissatisfaction poisons the very atmosphere of his shop, and his labor becomes repugnant.

We do not know that we could present a subject to workingmen more pregnant with grave consideration; for it involves an evil which is growing upon us, and one that materially affects the happiness of every toiler. Important, therefore, as other reforms may be, we should not lose sight of this; because labor is robbed of half its burden when we can bring to our aid a contented mind, free from those envious or jealous feelings which spring from unjust comparisons. We would be the last to discourage all honorable efforts to improve the condition of workingmen; for we are always pleased when we see one of them leave the workshop for more profitable pursuits; but we fear too many need to be admonished by the old adage — "let well enough alone."

Let us stand by our trade, elevate it to the foremost position, be proud of it; by making our occupation worthy of us, we will become worthy of our occupation.

DRAWBACKS.

No enterprise was ever started, no reform was ever attempted, that failed to encounter opposition. Perhaps this is, in a measure, necessary to quicken energy and give an impetus to the work, as well as a higher appreciation of results. Every sincere reformer knows what it is to meet the prejudices of ignorance and bigotry, and to combat the adverse views — often honestly entertained — advanced by those who cannot see or think as they do. The greatest obstacle to be met with, however, in all progressive movements, is the dogmatical and uncharitable strictures and action of those who must have everything to conform to their peculiar notions to secure their co-operation. There is a class of people who move and act on the personal pronoun *I*. They must start the project, have it progress as *I* want it, finished as *I* want it, or they will give it their unqualified opposition. Their aid is measured by the eclat they hope to win; and if neither vanity nor selfishness can be gratified, they pronounce the measure a failure in advance, and at once assume an antagonistic position to verify their predictions.

These remarks, which are designed to point out the drawbacks to all reforms, apply with great force to that of the labor movement. It is unfortunate for the interests of labor that we have too many among us who seek notoriety at the expense of the cause. Ambition, jealousy, envy, often clog our onward march; and yet the labor reform, above all others, should be most free from these impediments. A feeling and interest in common affords ambition but a barren field — there is nothing upon which to base improper aspirations — no individual can be singled out for especial favors. Whatever benefits accrue are shared by all; and, for the life of us, we could never discover a single reason why there should be bickering or contention among workingmen. There are no leaders — no dictators among us; and none can occupy a position unless by the clearly expressed will of the majority. While such perform their duties faithfully, they should have their hands strengthened. If they neglect them, the *masses* have the power to remove them.

Now, with this plain, democratic system to govern us, why should we encounter such drawbacks as discord, jarring, and unjust criticism? If it is supposed that those who are forced to prominence in the labor movement sleep on a bed of roses, a greater mistake was never made. *We* can testify to the contrary by sad experience. If a target is needed for the arrows of capitalists, they never fail to select those who have been made representative men by the producing-classes; and few can know the vexations, the trials, the *persecutions* to which they are subjected. At times they are forced to assume positions and adopt measures which, for the moment, it would be imprudent to explain; and, because unexplained, they receive a fire in the rear from those who ought to be their friends while facing the foe. While doing the very best they can, they are assailed with fault-finding, their motives impugned, and sometimes even private as well as public character is assailed.

These things prove a serious drawback to the cause, because it dispirits and paralyzes the efforts of those whose zeal is equal to all opposition coming from expected enemies, but unlooked for and unmerited from men who ought to be their friends. Such as become prominent in the labor reform need the sympathy, support, and *confidence* of those whom they are striving to benefit. A careless remark, a detrimental insinuation, often made in a moment of pique, is treasured and made the most of by our opponents. This impatience — this *weakness*, if you please, on the part of workingmen — has done much to retard our progress. While our opponents prudently keep their own secrets, we emblazon ours to the world. We seldom hear of their differences, and know less of the causes — hence the public are left to infer that they derive strength from harmony and unanimity. This lesson should not be lost upon workingmen. Let our disputes be what they may, the laws of our organization are all-powerful to settle them; and we never yet could see the necessity of exposing our family quarrels to the public.

We know that frequent sources of vexation are to be found in the fact that we sometimes suffer from misplaced confidence. A defaulting treasurer, money misappropriated, desertion when struggling for our rights, or disaffection from any cause, are very apt to elicit denunciation; but it is a maxim in war never to expose a weak point; and, if we would maintain our power, *keep our troubles to ourselves.* When we do otherwise, we give vitality to opposition, and afford our enemies food for exultation. Black sheep are found in almost every flock — all reforms have stragglers who leave the ranks or faint by the wayside. There are dishonest men in all classes of society — hypocrites among the most devout congregations. Then how unreasonable to expect the labor movement to reach the acme of our hopes free from the drawbacks experienced by every other reform.

For ourselves, we do not expect it. All we ask is, the exercise of that charity and forbearance which innocence has a right to claim, until a wrong is clearly proven. When dereliction of duty is manifest, or guilt detected beyond cavil, cast the offender beyond the pale of our organizations; but because one is thus convicted of dishonesty or treachery, that is no reason why the cloud of suspicion should rest upon others. Old men will remember that the labor movement, which became so formidable in 1834, became paralyzed from the very drawbacks we have named — when such men as Luther, Farrel, Hogan, and others, finally became worn out with discord and contention, as well as the suspicion heaped upon the more active, because of the baseness of a few unprincipled men. This, with envy and jealousy combined, gave a "pull-back" to the cause, which renders our labors more arduous to-day. A confiding trust, a just appreciation, a promptness to defend our labor champions, can alone neutralize the drawbacks we have named.

THE IRON MEN OF ENGLAND.

THE spread of Christianity, the march of intelligence, and the advance of civilization, would naturally lead one to believe that the human instincts of our nature would be more prominently developed. But, in many instances, we are forced to an opposite conclusion. The horrible barbarities of war have increased fourfold; murder, assassination, and crime of every grade, are not only on the increase, but almost reduced to a science. The progress of intelligence develops new death-dealing instruments, and the inventive genius of man is taxed for the production of those of a still more fatal character; and all this, too, in a Christian, Bible-reading, missionary-sustaining age and country. Nor can the highest claims to civilization arrest the rapidly decaying sentiment of humanity which is necessary to make it work in harmony with every Christian attribute, as a great conservative element, upon which is based the happiness of man. The conviction is forced upon us that, essential as they are to man's social and eternal welfare, the distance between them is daily widening. The mind, in attaining a higher degree of discipline, seems to have robbed the heart of nearly all its charity and sympathy, and by the time we reach the greatest intellectual perfection, it may be that conscience will become seared and callous, and the breast of man closed against every ennobling impulse.

In social life, too, we find a similar contradiction. As man accumulates wealth, or prospers in his business, he is apt to become proportionately mercenary, careless of "man's obligations to man," and unscrupulous in regard to the means used to gratify his avarice. Regardless of the rights of others, he appropriates all to himself that the law, not justice, will permit; and on the principle of "your misfortune and not my fault," he demands the last drop of sweat, and the full measure of time, from those whose necessities compel them to accept his terms. This position is fully sustained by the action of the *iron* men of England, the proprietors, who inaugurated a simultaneous "lock-out" of their workmen in England and Wales, the particulars of which are already familiar to our readers. Men who give thousands to convert the heathen, command their Christian brethren to take the canopy of heaven for shelter, and the green sward for a bed, because they dare to place a price upon the labor of their hands. Helpless women and destitute children are turned upon the commons to starve and die, because their husbands and fathers are bold enough to claim the prerogatives of free agency. Yes, men who pray and who echo in sonorous tones, and parrot-like repetition, the Divine precepts of the Lord's Prayer every Sabbath, steel their hearts and close their eyes to the squalid poverty and misery in their own surroundings, and that, too, of their own creation. Let the wretched shiver and shake with cold, cry with hunger, and die with disease; what is it to their Pharisaical oppressors? Yield or die, submit or starve, become a serf instead of a man, a slave instead of a freeman. These are the terms of reconciliation that the Christianity and civilization of the *iron* men of England and Wales propose to human beings. This is a specimen of the humanity which actuates the men who would Christianize India, steal opium from China, rob the New Zealanders of their territory, and emancipate slavery in America.

But we cannot longer dwell upon this horrible picture of "man's inhumanity to man." Let us hope that the victims of this most inhuman persecution may soon hail the day of their deliverance, through the efforts of a combined labor movement throughout the world. We are not distrustful of the feeling with which workingmen are gradually being imbued through the *united* and *fraternal* agency of our organs of labor and the pleadings of our fearless champions. The revolution is gradually working, and the hour of social emancipation is not far distant; till then "bide our time," but work, work, work, for the "day of jubilee."

THE END.